Get the eBooks FREE!

(PDF, ePub, Kindle, and liveBook all included)

We believe that once you buy a book from us, you should be able to read it in any format we have available. To get electronic versions of this book at no additional cost to you, purchase and then register this book at the Manning website.

Go to https://www.manning.com/freebook and follow the instructions to complete your pBook registration.

That's it!
Thanks from Manning!

Kotlin in Action

Kotlin in Action

DMITRY JEMEROV
AND SVETLANA ISAKOVA

MANNING
SHELTER ISLAND

For online information and ordering of this and other Manning books, please visit www.manning.com. The publisher offers discounts on this book when ordered in quantity. For more information, please contact

Special Sales Department
Manning Publications Co.
20 Baldwin Road
PO Box 761
Shelter Island, NY 11964
Email: orders@manning.com

♾ Recognizing the importance of preserving what has been written, it is Manning's policy to have the books we publish printed on acid-free paper, and we exert our best efforts to that end. Recognizing also our responsibility to conserve the resources of our planet, Manning books are printed on paper that is at least 15 percent recycled and processed without the use of elemental chlorine.

Manning Publications Co.
20 Baldwin Road
PO Box 761
Shelter Island, NY 11964

Development editor: Dan Maharry
Review editor: Aleksandar Dragosavljević
Technical development editor: Brent Watson
Project editor: Kevin Sullivan
Copyeditor: Tiffany Taylor
Proofreader: Elizabeth Martin
Technical proofreader: Igor Wojda
Typesetter: Marija Tudor
Cover designer: Marija Tudor

ISBN 9781617293290
Printed in the United States of America
7 8 9 10 – CPI – 22 21 20 19 18

brief contents

contents

foreword

When I visited JetBrains for the first time in Spring 2010, I came in fairly certain that the world didn't need another general-purpose programming language. I thought that existing JVM languages were good enough, and who in their right mind creates a new language anyway? After about an hour discussing production issues in large-scale codebases I was convinced otherwise, and the first ideas that later became part of Kotlin were sketched on a whiteboard. I joined JetBrains shortly after to lead the design of the language and work on the compiler.

Today, more than six years later, we have our second release approaching. There are over 30 people on the team and thousands of active users, and we still have more exciting design ideas than I can handle easily. But don't worry, those ideas have to pass a rather thorough examination before they get into the language. We want Kotlin of the future to still fit into a single reasonably sized book.

Learning a programming language is an exciting and often very rewarding endeavor. If it's your first one, you're learning the whole new world of programming through it. If it's not, it makes you think about familiar things in new terms and thus understand them more deeply and on a higher level of abstraction. This book is primarily targeted for the latter kind of reader, those already familiar with Java.

Designing a language from scratch may be a challenging task in its own right, but making it play well with another is a different story—one with many angry ogres in it, and some gloomy dungeons too. (Ask Bjarne Stroustrup, the creator of C++, if you don't trust me on that.) Java interoperability (that is, how Java and Kotlin can mix and call each other) was one of the cornerstones of Kotlin, and this book pays a lot of attention to it. Interoperability is very important for introducing Kotlin gradually to an existing Java codebase. Even when writing a new project from scratch, one has to fit the language into the bigger picture of the platform with all of its libraries written in Java.

As I'm writing this, two new target platforms are being developed: Kotlin is now running on JavaScript VMs enabling full-stack web development, and it will soon be able to compile directly to native code and run without any VM at all, if necessary. So, while this book is JVM-oriented, much of what you learn from it can be applied to other execution environments.

The authors have been members of the Kotlin team from its early days, so they are intimately familiar with the language and its internals. Their experience in conference presentations, workshops, and courses about Kotlin has enabled them to deliver good explanations that anticipate common questions and possible pitfalls. The book explains high-level concepts behind language features and provides all the necessary details as well.

I hope you'll enjoy your time with our language and this book. As I often say in our community postings: *Have a nice Kotlin!*

ANDREY BRESLAV
LEAD DESIGNER OF KOTLIN AT JETBRAINS

preface

The idea of Kotlin was conceived at JetBrains in 2010. By that time, JetBrains was an established vendor of development tools for many languages, including Java, C#, JavaScript, Python, Ruby, and PHP. IntelliJ IDEA, the Java IDE that is our flagship product, also included plugins for Groovy and Scala.

The experience of building the tooling for such a diverse set of languages gave us a unique understanding of and perspective on the language design space as a whole. And yet the IntelliJ Platform-based IDEs, including IntelliJ IDEA, were still being developed in Java. We were somewhat envious of our colleagues on the .NET team who were developing in C#, a modern, powerful, rapidly evolving language. But we didn't see any language that we could use instead of Java.

What were our requirements for such a language? The first and most obvious was static typing. We don't know any other way to develop a multimillion-line codebase over many years without going crazy. Second, we needed full compatibility with the existing Java code. That codebase is a hugely valuable asset for JetBrains, and we couldn't afford to lose it or devalue it through difficulties with interoperability. Third, we didn't want to accept any compromises in terms of tooling quality. Developer productivity is the most important value for JetBrains as a company, and great tooling is essential to achieving that. Finally we needed a language that was easy to learn and to reason about.

When we see an unmet need for our company, we know there are other companies in similar situations, and we expect that our solution will find many users outside of JetBrains. With this in mind, we decided to embark on the project of creating a new language: Kotlin. As it happens, the project took longer than we expected, and Kotlin 1.0

came out more than five years after the first commit to the repository; but now we can be certain that the language has found its audience and is here to stay.

Kotlin is named after an island near St. Petersburg, Russia, where most of the Kotlin development team is located. In using an island name, we followed the precedent established by Java and Ceylon, but we decided to go for something closer to our homes. (In English, the name is usually pronounced "cot-lin," not "coat-lin" or "caught-lin.")

As the language was approaching release, we realized that it would be valuable to have a book about Kotlin, written by people who were involved in making design decisions for the language and who could confidently explain why things in Kotlin are the way they are. This book is a result of that effort, and we hope it will help you learn and understand the Kotlin language. Good luck, and may you always develop with pleasure!

acknowledgments

First of all, we'd like to thank Sergey Dmitriev and Max Shafirov for believing in the idea of a new language and deciding to invest JetBrains' resources. Without them, neither the language nor this book would exist.

We would especially like to acknowledge Andrey Breslav, who is the main person to blame for designing a language that's a pleasure to write about (and to code in). Andrey, despite having to lead the continuously growing Kotlin team, was able to give us a lot of helpful feedback, which we greatly appreciate. In addition, you can be assured that this book received a stamp of approval from the lead language designer, in the form of the foreword that he kindly agreed to write.

We're grateful to the team at Manning who guided us through the process of writing this book and helped make the text readable and well-structured—particularly our development editor, Dan Maharry, who bravely strove to find time to talk despite our busy schedules, as well as Michael Stephens, Helen Stergius, Kevin Sullivan, Tiffany Taylor, Elizabeth Martin, and Marija Tudor. The feedback from our technical reviewers, Brent Watson and Igor Wojda, was also invaluable, as were the comments of the reviewers who read the manuscript during the development process: Alessandro Campeis, Amit Lamba, Angelo Costa, Boris Vasile, Brendan Grainger, Calvin Fernandes, Christopher Bailey, Christopher Bortz, Conor Redmond, Dylan Scott, Filip Pravica, Jason Lee, Justin Lee, Kevin Orr, Nicolas Frankel, Paweł Gajda, Ronald Tischliar, and Tim Lavers. Thanks go also to everyone who submitted feedback during the MEAP program and in the book's forum; we've improved the text based on your comments.

We're grateful to the entire Kotlin team, who had to listen to daily reports like "One more section is finished!" throughout the time we spent writing this book. We want to thank our colleagues who helped us plan the book and gave feedback on its drafts, especially Ilya Ryzhenkov, Hadi Hariri, Michael Glukhikh, and Ilya Gorbunov. We'd also like to thank our friends who not only were supportive but also had to read the text and provide feedback (sometimes in ski resorts during vacations): Lev Sere-bryakov, Pavel Nikolaev, and Alisa Afonina.

Finally, we'd like to thank our families and cats for making this world a better place.

about this book

Kotlin in Action teaches you the Kotlin programming language and how to use it to build applications running on the Java virtual machine and Android. It starts with the basic features of the language and proceeds to cover the more distinctive aspects of Kotlin, such as its support for building high-level abstractions and domain-specific languages. The book pays a lot of attention to integrating Kotlin with existing Java projects and helping you introduce Kotlin into your current working environment.

The book covers Kotlin 1.0. Kotlin 1.1 has been in development in parallel to the writing of the book, and whenever possible, we've mentioned the changes made in 1.1. But because the new version is still a work in progress as of this writing, we haven't been able to provide complete coverage. For ongoing updates about the new features and changes, please refer to the online documentation at https://kotlinlang.org.

Who should read this book

Kotlin in Action is primarily focused on developers with some level of Java experience. Kotlin builds on many concepts and techniques from Java, and the book strives to get you up to speed quickly by using your existing knowledge. If you're only just learning Java, or if you're experienced with other programming languages such as C# or Java-Script, you may need to refer to other sources of information to understand the more intricate aspects of Kotlin's interaction with the JVM, but you'll still be able to learn Kotlin using this book. We focus on the Kotlin language as a whole and not on a specific problem domain, so the book should be equally useful for server-side developers, Android developers, and everyone else who builds projects targeting the JVM.

How this book is organized

The book is divided into two parts. Part 1 explains how to get started using Kotlin together with existing libraries and APIs:

- Chapter 1 talks about the key goals, values, and areas of application for Kotlin, and it shows you the possible ways to run Kotlin code.
- Chapter 2 explains the essential elements of any Kotlin program, including control structures and variable and function declarations.
- Chapter 3 goes into detail about how functions are declared in Kotlin and introduces the concept of extension functions and properties.
- Chapter 4 is focused on class declarations and introduces the concepts of data classes and companion objects.
- Chapter 5 introduces the use of lambdas in Kotlin and showcases a number of Kotlin standard library functions using lambdas.
- Chapter 6 describes the Kotlin type system, with a particular focus on the topics of nullability and collections.

Part 2 teaches you how to build your own APIs and abstractions in Kotlin and covers some of the language's deeper features:

- Chapter 7 talks about the principle of conventions, which assigns special meaning to methods and properties with specific names, and it introduces the concept of delegated properties.
- Chapter 8 shows how to declare higher-order functions—functions that take other functions and parameters or return them. It also introduces the concept of inline functions.
- Chapter 9 is a deep dive into the topic of generics in Kotlin, starting with the basic syntax and going into more-advanced areas such as reified type parameters and variance.
- Chapter 10 covers the use of annotations and reflection and is centered around JKid, a small, real-life JSON serialization library that makes heavy use of those concepts.
- Chapter 11 introduces the concept of domain-specific languages, describes Kotlin's tools for building them, and demonstrates many DSL examples.

There are also three appendices. Appendix A explains how to build Kotlin code with Gradle, Maven, and Ant. Appendix B focuses on writing documentation comments and generating API documentation for Kotlin modules. Appendix C is a guide for exploring the Kotlin ecosystem and finding the latest online information.

The book works best when you read it all the way through, but you're also welcome to refer to individual chapters covering specific subjects you're interested in and to follow the cross-references if you run into an unfamiliar concept.

Code conventions and downloads

The following typographical conventions are used throughout this book:

- *Italic* font is used to introduce new terms.
- `Fixed-width font` is used to denote code samples, as well as function names, classes, and other identifiers.
- Code annotations accompany many of the code listings and highlight important concepts.

Many source listings in the book show code together with its output. In those cases, we've prefixed the code lines that produce the output with >>>, and the output itself is shown as is:

```
>>> println("Hello World")
Hello World
```

Some of the examples are intended to be complete runnable programs, whereas others are snippets used to demonstrate certain concepts and may contain omissions (indicated with . . .) or syntax errors (described in the book text or in the examples themselves). The runnable examples can be downloaded as a zip file from the publisher's website at www.manning.com/books/kotlin-in-action. The examples from the book are also preloaded into the online environment at http://try.kotlinlang.org, so you can run any example with just a few clicks directly from your browser.

Author Online

Purchase of *Kotlin in Action* includes free access to a private web forum run by Manning Publications where you can make comments about the book, ask technical questions, and receive help from the authors and from other users. To access the forum and subscribe to it, point your web browser to www.manning.com/books/kotlin-in-action. This page provides information on how to get on the forum once you're registered, what kind of help is available, and the rules of conduct on the forum.

Manning's commitment to our readers is to provide a venue where a meaningful dialog between individual readers and between readers and the authors can take place. It is not a commitment to any specific amount of participation on the part of the authors, whose contributions to the AO forum remain voluntary (and unpaid). We suggest you ask the authors challenging questions, lest their interest stray!

Other online resources

Kotlin has a lively online community, so if you have questions or want to chat with fellow Kotlin users, you can use the following resources:

- *The official Kotlin forums*—https://discuss.kotlinlang.org
- *Slack chat*—http://kotlinlang.slack.com (you can get an invitation at http://kotlinslackin.herokuapp.com)
- *Kotlin tag on Stack Overflow*—http://stackoverflow.com/questions/tagged/kotlin
- *Kotlin Reddit*—www.reddit.com/r/Kotlin

about the authors

DMITRY JEMEROV has been working with JetBrains since 2003 and has participated in the development of many products, including IntelliJ IDEA, PyCharm, and WebStorm. He was one of earliest contributors to Kotlin, having created the initial version of Kotlin's JVM bytecode generator, and he has given many presentations about Kotlin at events around the world. Right now he leads the team working on the Kotlin IntelliJ IDEA plugin.

SVETLANA ISAKOVA has been part of the Kotlin team since 2011. She worked on the type-inference and overload-resolution subsystems of the compiler. Now she's a technical evangelist, speaking about Kotlin at conferences and working on the online course for Kotlin.

about the cover illustration

The figure on the cover of *Kotlin in Action* is captioned "Habit of a Russian Lady at Valday in 1764." The town of Valday is located in the Novgorod Oblast region, on the road between Moscow and St. Petersburg. The illustration is taken from Thomas Jefferys' *A Collection of the Dresses of Different Nations, Ancient and Modern,* London, published between 1757 and 1772. The title page states that these are hand-colored copperplate engravings, heightened with gum arabic. Thomas Jefferys (1719–1771) was called "Geographer to King George III." He was an English cartographer who was the leading map supplier of his day. He engraved and printed maps for government and other official bodies and produced a wide range of commercial maps and atlases, especially of North America. His work as a map maker sparked an interest in local dress customs of the lands he surveyed and mapped; they are brilliantly displayed in this four-volume collection.

Fascination with faraway lands and travel for pleasure were relatively new phenomena in the eighteenth century, and collections such as this one were popular, introducing both the tourist and the armchair traveler to the inhabitants of other countries. The diversity of the drawings in Jefferys' volumes speaks vividly of the uniqueness and individuality of the world's nations centuries ago. Dress codes have changed, and the diversity by region and country, so rich at one time, has faded away. It is now often hard to tell the inhabitant of one continent from another. Perhaps, trying to view it optimistically, we have traded a cultural and visual diversity for a more varied personal life—or a more varied and interesting intellectual and technical life.

At a time when it is hard to tell one computer book from another, Manning celebrates the inventiveness and initiative of the computer business with book covers based on the rich diversity of national costumes three centuries ago, brought back to life by Jefferys' pictures.

Part 1

Introducing Kotlin

The goal of this part of the book is to get you productive writing Kotlin code that uses existing APIs. Chapter 1 will introduce you to the general traits of Kotlin. In chapters 2-4, you'll learn how the most basic Java programming concepts—statements, functions, classes, and types—map to Kotlin code, and how Kotlin enriches them to make programming more pleasant. You'll be able to rely on your existing knowledge of Java, as well as tools such as IDE coding-assistance features and the Java-to-Kotlin converter, to get up to speed quickly. In chapter 5, you'll find out how lambdas help you effectively solve some of the most common programming tasks, such as working with collections. Finally, in chapter 6, you'll become familiar with one of the key Kotlin specialties: its support for dealing with `null` values.

Kotlin: what and why

This chapter covers
- A basic demonstration of Kotlin
- The main traits of the Kotlin language
- Possibilities for Android and server-side development
- What distinguishes Kotlin from other languages
- Writing and running code in Kotlin

What is Kotlin all about? It's a new programming language targeting the Java platform. Kotlin is concise, safe, pragmatic, and focused on interoperability with Java code. It can be used almost everywhere Java is used today: for server-side development, Android apps, and much more. Kotlin works great with all existing Java libraries and frameworks and runs with the same level of performance as Java. In this chapter, we'll explore Kotlin's main traits in detail.

1.1 A taste of Kotlin

Let's start with a small example to demonstrate what Kotlin looks like. This example defines a `Person` class, creates a collection of people, finds the oldest one, and prints the result. Even in this small piece of code, you can see many interesting features of Kotlin; we've highlighted some of them so you can easily find them later in the book. The code is explained briefly, but please don't worry if something isn't clear right away. We'll discuss everything in detail later.

If you'd like to try running this example, the easiest option is to use the online playground at http://try.kotl.in. Type in the example and click the Run button, and the code will be executed.

Listing 1.1 An early taste of Kotlin

"data" class →
Top-level function →
String template →

```
data class Person(val name: String,
                  val age: Int? = null)            ← Nullable type (Int?); the default
                                                      value for the argument

fun main(args: Array<String>) {
    val persons = listOf(Person("Alice"),
                         Person("Bob", age = 29))   ← Named argument

    val oldest = persons.maxBy { it.age ?: 0 }      ← Lambda expression;
    println("The oldest is: $oldest")                 Elvis operator
}

// The oldest is: Person(name=Bob, age=29)          ← Autogenerated toString
```

You declare a simple data class with two properties: `name` and `age`. The `age` property is `null` by default (if it isn't specified). When creating the list of people, you omit Alice's age, so the default value `null` is used. Then you use the `maxBy` function to find the oldest person in the list. The lambda expression passed to the function takes one parameter, and you use `it` as the default name of that parameter. The *Elvis operator* (`?:`) returns zero if `age` is `null`. Because Alice's age isn't specified, the Elvis operator replaces it with zero, so Bob wins the prize for being the oldest person.

Do you like what you've seen? Read on to learn more and become a Kotlin expert. We hope that soon you'll see such code in your own projects, not only in this book.

1.2 Kotlin's primary traits

You probably already have an idea what kind of language Kotlin is. Let's look at its key attributes in more detail. First, let's see what kinds of applications you can build with Kotlin.

1.2.1 Target platforms: server-side, Android, anywhere Java runs

The primary goal of Kotlin is to provide a more concise, more productive, safer alternative to Java that's suitable in all contexts where Java is used today. Java is an extremely popular language, and it's used in a broad variety of environments, from smart cards (Java Card technology) to the largest data centers run by Google, Twitter, LinkedIn, and other internet-scale companies. In most of these places, using Kotlin can help developers achieve their goals with less code and fewer annoyances along the way.

The most common areas to use Kotlin are:

- Building server-side code (typically, backends of web applications)
- Building mobile applications that run on Android devices

But Kotlin works in other contexts as well. For example, you can use the Intel Multi-OS Engine (https://software.intel.com/en-us/multi-os-engine) to run Kotlin code on iOS devices. To build desktop applications, you can use Kotlin together with TornadoFX (https://github.com/edvin/tornadofx) and JavaFX.[1]

In addition to Java, Kotlin can be compiled to JavaScript, allowing you to run Kotlin code in the browser. But as of this writing, JavaScript support is still being explored and prototyped at JetBrains, so it's out of scope for this book. Other platforms are also under consideration for future versions of the language.

As you can see, Kotlin's target is quite broad. Kotlin doesn't focus on a single problem domain or address a single type of challenge faced by software developers today. Instead, it provides across-the-board productivity improvements for all tasks that come up during the development process. It gives you an excellent level of integration with libraries that support specific domains or programming paradigms. Let's look next at the key qualities of Kotlin as a programming language.

1.2.2 *Statically typed*

Just like Java, Kotlin is a *statically typed* programming language. This means the type of every expression in a program is known at compile time, and the compiler can validate that the methods and fields you're trying to access exist on the objects you're using.

This is in contrast to *dynamically typed* programming languages, which are represented on the JVM by, among others, Groovy and JRuby. Those languages let you define variables and functions that can store or return data of any type and resolve the method and field references at runtime. This allows for shorter code and greater flexibility in creating data structures. But the downside is that problems like misspelled names can't be detected during compilation and can lead to runtime errors.

On the other hand, in contrast to Java, Kotlin doesn't require you to specify the type of every variable explicitly in your source code. In many cases, the type of a variable can automatically be determined from the context, allowing you to omit the type declaration. Here's the simplest possible example of this:

```
val x = 1
```

You're declaring a variable, and because it's initialized with an integer value, Kotlin automatically determines that its type is Int. The ability of the compiler to determine types from context is called *type inference*.

Following are some of the benefits of static typing:

- *Performance*—Calling methods is faster because there's no need to figure out at runtime which method needs to be called.
- *Reliability*—The compiler verifies the correctness of the program, so there are fewer chances for crashes at runtime.
- *Maintainability*—Working with unfamiliar code is easier because you can see what kind of objects the code is working with.

---

[1] "JavaFX: Getting Started with JavaFX," Oracle, http://mng.bz/500y.

- *Tool support*—Static typing enables reliable refactorings, precise code completion, and other IDE features.

Thanks to Kotlin's support for type inference, most of the extra verbosity associated with static typing disappears, because you don't need to declare types explicitly.

If you look at the specifics of Kotlin's type system, you'll find many familiar concepts. Classes, interfaces, and generics work in a way very similar to Java, so most of your Java knowledge should easily transfer to Kotlin. Some things are new, though.

The most important of those is Kotlin's support for *nullable types*, which lets you write more reliable programs by detecting possible `null` pointer exceptions at compile time. We'll come back to nullable types later in this chapter and discuss them in detail in chapter 6.

Another new thing in Kotlin's type system is its support for *function types*. To see what this is about, let's look at the main ideas of functional programming and see how it's supported in Kotlin.

1.2.3 *Functional and object-oriented*

As a Java developer, you're no doubt familiar with the core concepts of object-oriented programming, but functional programming may be new to you. The key concepts of functional programming are as follows:

- *First-class functions*—You work with functions (pieces of behavior) as values. You can store them in variables, pass them as parameters, or return them from other functions.
- *Immutability*—You work with immutable objects, which guarantees that their state can't change after their creation.
- *No side effects*—You use pure functions that return the same result given the same inputs and don't modify the state of other objects or interact with the outside world.

What benefits can you gain from writing code in the functional style? First, *conciseness*. Functional code can be more elegant and succinct compared to its imperative counterpart, because working with functions as values gives you much more power of abstraction, which lets you avoid duplication in your code.

Imagine that you have two similar code fragments that implement a similar task (for example, looking for a matching element in a collection) but differ in the details (how the matching element is detected). You can easily extract the common part of the logic into a function and pass the differing parts as arguments. Those arguments are themselves functions, but you can express them using a concise syntax for anonymous functions called *lambda expressions*:

```
fun findAlice() = findPerson { it.name == "Alice" }
fun findBob() = findPerson { it.name == "Bob" }
```

findPerson() contains the general logic of finding a person.

The block in curly braces identifies the specific person you need to find.

The second benefit of functional code is *safe multithreading*. One of the biggest sources of errors in multithreaded programs is modification of the same data from multiple threads without proper synchronization. If you use immutable data structures and pure functions, you can be sure that such unsafe modifications won't happen, and you don't need to come up with complicated synchronization schemes.

Finally, functional programming means *easier testing*. Functions without side effects can be tested in isolation without requiring a lot of setup code to construct the entire environment that they depend on.

Generally speaking, the functional style can be used with any programming language, including Java, and many parts of it are advocated as good programming style. But not all languages provide the syntactic and library support required to use it effortlessly; for example, this support was mostly missing from versions of Java before Java 8. Kotlin has a rich set of features to support functional programming from the get-go. These include the following:

- *Function types*, allowing functions to receive other functions as parameters or return other functions
- *Lambda expressions*, letting you pass around blocks of code with minimum boilerplate
- *Data classes*, providing a concise syntax for creating immutable value objects
- A rich set of *APIs* in the standard library for working with objects and collections in the functional style

Kotlin lets you program in the functional style but doesn't enforce it. When you need it, you can work with mutable data and write functions that have side effects without jumping through any extra hoops. And, of course, working with frameworks that are based on interfaces and class hierarchies is just as easy as with Java. When writing code in Kotlin, you can combine both the object-oriented and functional approaches and use the tools that are most appropriate for the problem you're solving.

1.2.4   Free and open source

The Kotlin language, including the compiler, libraries, and all related tooling, is entirely open source and free to use for any purpose. It's available under the Apache 2 license; development happens in the open on GitHub (http://github.com/ jetbrains/ kotlin), and community contributions are welcome. You also have a choice of three open source IDEs for developing your Kotlin applications: IntelliJ IDEA Community Edition, Android Studio, and Eclipse are fully supported. (Of course, IntelliJ IDEA Ultimate works as well.)

Now that you understand what kind of language Kotlin is, let's see how the benefits of Kotlin work in specific practical applications.

1.3   *Kotlin applications*

As we mentioned earlier, the two main areas where Kotlin can be used are server-side and Android development. Let's look at those areas in turn and see why Kotlin is a good fit for them.

1.3.1   *Kotlin on the server side*

Server-side programming is a fairly broad concept. It encompasses all of the following types of applications and much more:

- Web applications that return HTML pages to a browser
- Backends of mobile applications that expose a JSON API over HTTP
- Microservices that communicate with other microservices over an RPC protocol

Developers have been building these kinds of applications in Java for many years and have accumulated a huge stack of frameworks and technologies to help build them. Such applications usually aren't developed in isolation or started from scratch. There's almost always an existing system that is being extended, improved, or replaced, and new code has to integrate with existing parts of the system, which may have been written many years ago.

The big advantage of Kotlin in this environment is its seamless interoperability with existing Java code. Regardless of whether you're writing a new component or migrating the code of an existing service into Kotlin, Kotlin will fit right in. You won't run into problems when you need to extend Java classes in Kotlin or annotate the methods and fields of a class in a certain way. And the benefit is that the system's code will be more compact, more reliable, and easier to maintain.

At the same time, Kotlin enables a number of new techniques for developing such systems. For example, its support for the Builder pattern lets you create any object graph with concise syntax, while keeping the full set of abstraction and code-reuse tools in the language.

One of the simplest use cases for that feature is an HTML generation library, which can replace an external template language with a concise and fully type-safe solution. Here's an example:

```
fun renderPersonList(persons: Collection<Person>) =
    createHTML().table {                              ←─────┐
        for (person in persons) {                           │  Functions that map
            tr {                                       ←─────┤  to HTML tags
                td { +person.name }                    ←─────┤
                td { +person.age }                     ←─────┘
            }
        }
    }
```

Regular
Kotlin loop `──→` (points to `for (person in persons) {`)

You can easily combine functions that map to HTML tags and regular Kotlin language constructs. You no longer need to use a separate template language, with a separate syntax to learn, just to use a loop when generating a page of HTML.

Another case where you can use Kotlin's clean, concise DSLs is persistence frameworks. For example, the Exposed framework (https://github.com/jetbrains/exposed) provides an easy-to-read DSL for describing the structure of an SQL database and performing queries entirely from Kotlin code, with full type checking. Here's a small example to show you what's possible:

```
object CountryTable : IdTable() {                    Describes a table
    val name = varchar("name", 250).uniqueIndex()    in the database
    val iso = varchar("iso", 2).uniqueIndex()
}

class Country(id: EntityID) : Entity(id) {           Creates a class corresponding
    var name: String by CountryTable.name            to a database entity
    var iso: String by CountryTable.iso
}

val russia = Country.find {                           You can query this database
    CountryTable.iso.eq("ru")                         using pure Kotlin code.
}.first()

println(russia.name)
```

We'll look at these techniques in more detail later in the book, in section 7.5, and in chapter 11.

1.3.2 *Kotlin on Android*

A typical mobile application is much different from a typical enterprise application. It's much smaller, it's less dependent on integration with existing codebases, and it usually needs to be delivered quickly while ensuring reliable operation on a large variety of devices. Kotlin works just as well for projects of that kind.

Kotlin's language features, combined with a special compiler plug-in supporting the Android framework, turn Android development into a much more productive and pleasurable experience. Common development tasks, such as adding listeners to controls or binding layout elements to fields, can be accomplished with much less code, or sometimes with no code at all (the compiler will generate it for you). The Anko library (https://github.com/kotlin/anko), also built by the Kotlin team, improves your experience even further by adding Kotlin-friendly adapters around many standard Android APIs.

Here's a simple example of Anko, just to give you a taste of what Android development with Kotlin feels like. You can put this code in an `Activity`, and a simple Android application is ready!

```
                                                    When clicked, this button displays
verticalLayout {                                    the value of the text field.
    val name = editText()
Creates      button("Say Hello") {
a simple         onClick { toast("Hello, ${name.text}!") }   Concise APIs for attaching a
text field   }                                               listener and showing a toast
}
```

Another big advantage of using Kotlin is better application reliability. If you have any experience developing Android applications, you're no doubt familiar with the Unfortunately, Process Has Stopped dialog. This dialog is shown when your application throws an unhandled exception—often, a `NullPointerException`. Kotlin's type system, with its precise tracking of `null` values, makes the problem of `null` pointer exceptions much less pressing. Most of the code that would lead to a `NullPointerException` in Java fails to compile in Kotlin, ensuring that you fix the error before the application gets to your users.

At the same time, because Kotlin is fully compatible with Java 6, its use doesn't introduce any new compatibility concerns. You'll benefit from all the cool new language features of Kotlin, and your users will still be able to run your application on their devices, even if they don't run the latest version of Android.

In terms of performance, using Kotlin doesn't bring any disadvantages, either. The code generated by the Kotlin compiler is executed as efficiently as regular Java code. The runtime used by Kotlin is fairly small, so you won't experience a large increase in the size of the compiled application package. And when you use lambdas, many of the Kotlin standard library functions will inline them. Inlining lambdas ensures that no new objects will be created and the application won't suffer from extra GC pauses.

Having looked at the advantages of Kotlin compared to Java, let's now look at Kotlin's philosophy—the main characteristics that distinguish Kotlin from other modern languages targeting the JVM.

1.4   *The philosophy of Kotlin*

When we talk about Kotlin, we like to say that it's a pragmatic, concise, safe language with a focus on interoperability. What exactly do we mean by each of those words? Let's look at them in turn.

1.4.1   *Pragmatic*

Being *pragmatic* means a simple thing to us: Kotlin is a practical language designed to solve real-world problems. Its design is based on many years of industry experience creating large-scale systems, and its features are chosen to address use cases encountered by many software developers. Moreover, developers both inside JetBrains and in the community have been using early versions of Kotlin for several years, and their feedback has shaped the released version of the language. This makes us confident in saying that Kotlin can help solve problems in real projects.

Kotlin also is not a research language. We aren't trying to advance the state of the art in programming language design and explore innovative ideas in computer science. Instead, whenever possible, we're relying on features and solutions that have already appeared in other programming languages and have proven to be successful. This reduces the complexity of the language and makes it easier to learn by letting you rely on familiar concepts.

In addition, Kotlin doesn't enforce using any particular programming style or paradigm. As you begin to study the language, you can use the style and techniques that are familiar to you from your Java experience. Later, you'll gradually discover the more powerful features of Kotlin and learn to apply them in your own code, to make it more concise and idiomatic.

Another aspect of Kotlin's pragmatism is its focus on tooling. A smart development environment is just as essential for a developer's productivity as a good language; and because of that, treating IDE support as an afterthought isn't an option. In the case of Kotlin, the IntelliJ IDEA plug-in was developed in lockstep with the compiler, and language features were always designed with tooling in mind.

The IDE support also plays a major role in helping you discover the features of Kotlin. In many cases, the tools will automatically detect common code patterns that can be replaced by more concise constructs, and offer to fix the code for you. By studying the language features used by the automated fixes, you can learn to apply those features in your own code as well.

1.4.2 Concise

It's common knowledge that developers spend more time reading existing code than writing new code. Imagine you're a part of a team developing a big project, and you need to add a new feature or fix a bug. What are your first steps? You look for the exact section of code that you need to change, and only then do you implement a fix. You read a lot of code to find out what you have to do. This code might have been written recently by your colleagues, or by someone who no longer works on the project, or by you, but long ago. Only after understanding the surrounding code can you make the necessary modifications.

The simpler and more concise the code is, the faster you'll understand what's going on. Of course, good design and expressive names play a significant role here. But the choice of the language and its conciseness are also important. The language is *concise* if its syntax clearly expresses the intent of the code you read and doesn't obscure it with boilerplate required to specify how the intent is accomplished.

In Kotlin, we've tried hard to ensure that all the code you write carries meaning and isn't just there to satisfy code structure requirements. A lot of the standard Java boilerplate, such as getters, setters, and the logic for assigning constructor parameters to fields, is implicit in Kotlin and doesn't clutter your source code.

Another reason code can be unnecessarily long is having to write explicit code to perform common tasks, such as locating an element in a collection. Just like many other modern languages, Kotlin has a rich standard library that lets you replace these long, repetitive sections of code with library method calls. Kotlin's support for lambdas makes it easy to pass small blocks of code to library functions. This lets you encapsulate all the common parts in the library and keep only the unique, task-specific portion in the user code.

At the same time, Kotlin doesn't try to collapse the source code to the smallest number of characters possible. For example, even though Kotlin supports operator overloading, users can't define their own operators. Therefore, library developers can't replace the method names with cryptic punctuation sequences. Words are typically easier to read than punctuation and easier to find documentation on.

More concise code takes less time to write and, more important, less time to read. This improves your productivity and lets you get things done faster.

1.4.3   *Safe*

In general, when we speak of a programming language as *safe*, we mean its design prevents certain kinds of errors in a program. Of course, this isn't an absolute quality; no language prevents all possible errors. In addition, preventing errors usually comes at a cost. You need to give the compiler more information about the intended operation of the program, so the compiler can then verify that the information matches what the program does. Because of that, there's always a trade-off between the level of safety you get and the loss of productivity required to put in more detailed annotations.

With Kotlin, we've attempted to achieve a higher level of safety than in Java, with a smaller overall cost. Running on the JVM already provides a lot of safety guarantees: for example, memory safety, preventing buffer overflows, and other problems caused by incorrect use of dynamically allocated memory. As a statically typed language on the JVM, Kotlin also ensures the type safety of your applications. This comes at a smaller cost than with Java: you don't have to specify all the type declarations, because in many cases the compiler infers the types automatically.

Kotlin also goes beyond that, meaning more errors can be prevented by checks at compile time instead of failing at runtime. Most important, Kotlin strives to remove the `NullPointerException` from your program. Kotlin's type system tracks values that can and can't be `null` and forbids operations that can lead to a `NullPointer-Exception` at runtime. The additional cost required for this is minimal: marking a type as nullable takes only a single character, a question mark at the end:

```
val s: String? = null                    ◁──── May be null
val s2: String = ""          ◁──── May not be null
```

In addition, Kotlin provides many convenient ways to handle nullable data. This helps greatly in eliminating application crashes.

Another type of exception that Kotlin helps avoid is the `ClassCastException`. It happens when you cast an object to a type without first checking that it has the right type. In Java, developers often leave out the check, because the type name must be repeated in the check and in the following cast. In Kotlin, on the other hand, the check and the cast are combined into a single operation: once you've checked the type, you can refer to members of that type without any additional casts. Thus, there's no reason to skip the check and no chance to make an error. Here's how this works:

```
if (value is String)                              ◁──── Checks the type
    println(value.toUpperCase())         ◁─┐ Uses the method
                                           └ of the type
```

1.4.4   *Interoperable*

Regarding interoperability, your first concern probably is, "Can I use my existing libraries?" With Kotlin, the answer is, "Yes, absolutely." Regardless of the kind of APIs the library requires you to use, you can work with them from Kotlin. You can call Java methods, extend Java classes and implement interfaces, apply Java annotations to your Kotlin classes, and so on.

Unlike some other JVM languages, Kotlin goes even further with interoperability, making it effortless to call Kotlin code from Java as well. No tricks are required: Kotlin classes and methods can be called exactly like regular Java classes and methods. This gives you the ultimate flexibility in mixing Java and Kotlin code anywhere in your project. When you start adopting Kotlin in your Java project, you can run the Java-to-Kotlin converter on any single class in your codebase, and the rest of the code will continue to compile and work without any modifications. This works regardless of the role of the class you've converted.

Another area where Kotlin focuses on interoperability is its use of existing Java libraries to the largest degree possible. For example, Kotlin doesn't have its own collections library. It relies fully on Java standard library classes, extending them with additional functions for more convenient use in Kotlin. (We'll look at the mechanism for this in more detail in section 3.3.) This means you never need to wrap or convert objects when you call Java APIs from Kotlin, or vice versa. All the API richness provided by Kotlin comes at no cost at runtime.

The Kotlin tooling also provides full support for cross-language projects. It can compile an arbitrary mix of Java and Kotlin source files, regardless of how they depend on each other. The IDE features work across languages as well, allowing you to:

- Navigate freely between Java and Kotlin source files
- Debug mixed-language projects and step between code written in different languages
- Refactor your Java methods and have their use in Kotlin code correctly updated, and vice versa

Hopefully by now we've convinced you to give Kotlin a try. Now, how can you start using it? In the next section, we'll discuss the process of compiling and running Kotlin code, both from the command line and using different tools.

1.5 Using the Kotlin tools

Just like Java, Kotlin is a compiled language. This means before you can run Kotlin code, you need to compile it. Let's discuss how the compilation process works and then look at the different tools that take care of it for you. If you need more information about getting your environment set up, please refer to the "Tutorials" section of the Kotlin website (https://kotlinlang.org/docs/tutorials).

1.5.1 Compiling Kotlin code

Kotlin source code is normally stored in files with the extension .kt. The Kotlin compiler analyzes the source code and generates .class files, just like the Java compiler does. The generated .class files are then packaged and executed using the standard procedure for the type of application you're working on. In the simplest case, you can use the `kotlinc` command to compile your code from the command line and use the `java` command to execute your code:

```
kotlinc <source file or directory> -include-runtime -d <jar name>
java -jar <jar name>
```

A simplified description of the Kotlin build process is shown in figure 1.1.

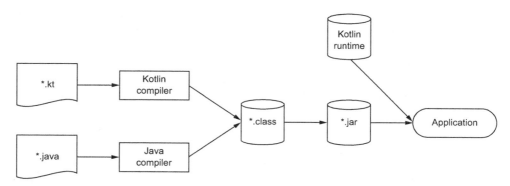

Figure 1.1   Kotlin build process

Code compiled with the Kotlin compiler depends on the *Kotlin runtime library*. It contains the definitions of Kotlin's own standard library classes and the extensions that Kotlin adds to the standard Java APIs. The runtime library needs to be distributed with your application.

In most real-life cases, you'll be using a build system such as Maven, Gradle, or Ant to compile your code. Kotlin is compatible with all those build systems, and we'll discuss the details in appendix A. All of those build systems also support mixed-language projects that combine Kotlin and Java in the same codebase. In addition, Maven and Gradle take care of including the Kotlin runtime library as a dependency of your application.

1.5.2   *Plug-in for IntelliJ IDEA and Android Studio*

The IntelliJ IDEA plug-in for Kotlin has been developed in parallel with the language, and it's the most full-featured development environment available for Kotlin. It's mature and stable, and it provides a complete set of tools for Kotlin development.

The Kotlin plug-in is included out of the box with IntelliJ IDEA 15 and later versions, so no additional setup is necessary. You can use either the free, open source IntelliJ IDEA Community Edition or IntelliJ IDEA Ultimate. Select Kotlin in the New Project dialog, and you're good to go.

If you're using Android Studio, you can install the Kotlin plug-in from the plug-in manager. In the Settings dialog, select Plugins, then click the Install JetBrains Plugin button, and select Kotlin from the list.

1.5.3   *Interactive shell*

If you want to quickly try out small fragments of Kotlin code, you can do that using the interactive shell (the so-called *REPL*). In the REPL, you can type Kotlin code line by line and immediately see the results of its execution. To start the REPL, you can either run the `kotlinc` command with no arguments or use the corresponding menu item in the IntelliJ IDEA plug-in.

1.5.4   *Eclipse plug-in*

If you're an Eclipse user, you also have the option to use Kotlin in your IDE. The Kotlin Eclipse plug-in provides essential IDE functionality such as navigation and code completion. The plug-in is available in the Eclipse Marketplace. To install it, choose the Help > Eclipse Marketplace menu item, and search for Kotlin in the list.

1.5.5   *Online playground*

The easiest way to try Kotlin doesn't require any installation or configuration. At http://try.kotl.in, you can find an online playground where you can write, compile, and run small Kotlin programs. The playground has code samples demonstrating the features of Kotlin including all examples from this book, as well as a series of exercises for learning Kotlin interactively.

1.5.6   *Java-to-Kotlin converter*

Getting up to speed with a new language is never effortless. Fortunately, we've built a nice little shortcut that lets you speed up your learning and adoption by relying on your existing knowledge of Java. This tool is the automated Java-to-Kotlin converter.

As you start learning Kotlin, the converter can help you express something when you don't remember the exact syntax. You can write the corresponding snippet in Java and then paste it into a Kotlin file, and the converter will automatically offer to translate the code into Kotlin. The result won't always be the most idiomatic, but it will be working code, and you'll be able to make progress with your task.

The converter is also great for introducing Kotlin into an existing Java project. When you need to write a new class, you can do it in Kotlin right from the beginning. But if you need to make significant changes to an existing class, you may also want to use Kotlin in the process. That's where the converter comes into play. You convert the class into Kotlin first, and then you add the changes using all the benefits of a modern language.

Using the converter in IntelliJ IDEA is extremely easy. You can either copy a Java code fragment and paste it into a Kotlin file, or invoke the Convert Java File to Kotlin File action if you need to convert an entire file. The converter is accessible in Eclipse and online as well.

1.6   *Summary*

- Kotlin is statically typed and supports type inference, allowing it to maintain correctness and performance while keeping the source code concise.

- Kotlin supports both object-oriented and functional programming styles, enabling higher-level abstractions through first-class functions and simplifying testing and multithreaded development through the support of immutable values.
- It works well for server-side applications, fully supporting all existing Java frameworks and providing new tools for common tasks such as HTML generation and persistence.
- It works for Android as well, thanks to a compact runtime, special compiler support for Android APIs, and a rich library providing Kotlin-friendly functions for common Android development tasks.
- It's free and open source, with full support for the major IDEs and build systems.
- Kotlin is pragmatic, safe, concise, and interoperable, meaning it focuses on using proven solutions for common tasks, preventing common errors such as `NullPointerExceptions`, supporting compact and easy-to-read code, and providing unrestricted integration with Java.

Kotlin basics

This chapter covers

- Declaring functions, variables, classes, enums, and properties
- Control structures in Kotlin
- Smart casts
- Throwing and handling exceptions

In this chapter, you'll learn how to declare in Kotlin the essential elements of any program: variables, functions, and classes. Along the way, you'll get acquainted with the concept of properties in Kotlin.

You'll learn how to use different control structures in Kotlin. They're mostly similar to those that are familiar to you from Java, but enhanced in important ways.

We'll introduce the concept of *smart casts*, which combine a type check and a cast into one operation. Finally, we'll talk about exception handling. By the end of this chapter, you'll be able to use the basics of the language to write working Kotlin code, even if it might not be the most idiomatic.

2.1   *Basic elements: functions and variables*

This section will introduce you to the basic elements that every Kotlin program consists of: functions and variables. You'll see how Kotlin lets you omit many type declarations and how it encourages you to use immutable, rather than mutable, data.

2.1.1   *Hello, world!*

Let's start with the classical example: a program that prints "Hello, world!". In Kotlin, it's just one function:

Listing 2.1   "Hello World!" in Kotlin

```
fun main(args: Array<String>) {
    println("Hello, world!")
}
```

What features and parts of the language syntax can you observe in this simple code snippet? Check out this list:

- The `fun` keyword is used to declare a function. Programming in Kotlin is lots of fun, indeed!
- The parameter type is written after its name. This applies to variable declarations as well, as you'll see later.
- The function can be declared at the top level of a file; you don't need to put it in a class.
- Arrays are just classes. Unlike Java, Kotlin doesn't have a special syntax for declaring array types.
- You write `println` instead of `System.out.println`. The Kotlin standard library provides many wrappers around standard Java library functions, with more concise syntax, and `println` is one of them.
- You can omit the semicolon from the end of a line, just as in many other modern languages.

So far, so good! We'll discuss some of these topics in more detail later. Now, let's explore the function declaration syntax.

2.1.2   *Functions*

You saw how to declare a function that has nothing to return. But where should you put a return type for a function that has a meaningful result? You can guess that it should go somewhere after the parameter list:

```
fun max(a: Int, b: Int): Int {
    return if (a > b) a else b
}

>>> println(max(1, 2))
2
```

The function declaration starts with the `fun` keyword, followed by the function name: `max`, in this case. It's followed by the parameter list in parentheses. The return type comes after the parameter list, separated from it by a colon.

Figure 2.1 shows you the basic structure of a function. Note that in Kotlin, `if` is an expression with a result value. It's similar to a ternary operator in Java: `(a > b) ? a : b`.

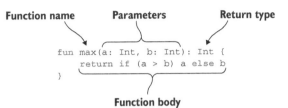

Figure 2.1 Kotlin function declaration

Statements and expressions

In Kotlin, `if` is an expression, not a statement. The difference between a statement and an expression is that an expression has a value, which can be used as part of another expression, whereas a statement is always a top-level element in its enclosing block and doesn't have its own value. In Java, all control structures are statements. In Kotlin, most control structures, except for the loops (`for`, `do`, and `do/while`) are expressions. The ability to combine control structures with other expressions lets you express many common patterns concisely, as you'll see later in the book.

On the other hand, assignments are expressions in Java and become statements in Kotlin. This helps avoid confusion between comparisons and assignments, which is a common source of mistakes.

EXPRESSION BODIES

You can simplify the previous function even further. Because its body consists of a single expression, you can use that expression as the entire body of the function, removing the curly braces and the `return` statement:

```
fun max(a: Int, b: Int): Int = if (a > b) a else b
```

If a function is written with its body in curly braces, we say that this function has a *block body*. If it returns an expression directly, it has an *expression body*.

> **INTELLIJ IDEA TIP** IntelliJ IDEA provides intention actions to convert between the two styles of functions: "Convert to expression body" and "Convert to block body."

Functions with an expression body can be found in Kotlin code quite often. This style is used not only for trivial one-line functions, but also for functions that evaluate a single, more complex expression, such as if, when, or try. You'll see such functions later in this chapter, when we talk about the when construct.

You can simplify the max function even more and omit the return type:

```
fun max(a: Int, b: Int) = if (a > b) a else b
```

Why are there functions without return-type declarations? Doesn't Kotlin, as a statically typed language, require every expression to have a type at compile time? Indeed, every variable and every expression has a type, and every function has a return type. But for expression-body functions, the compiler can analyze the expression used as the body of the function and use its type as the function return type, even when it's not spelled out explicitly. This type of analysis is usually called *type inference.*

Note that omitting the return type is allowed only for functions with an expression body. For functions with a block body that return a value, you have to specify the return type and write the return statements explicitly. That's a conscious choice. A real-world function often is long and can contain several return statements; having the return type and the return statements written explicitly helps you quickly grasp what can be returned. Let's look at the syntax for variable declarations next.

2.1.3 *Variables*

In Java, you start a variable declaration with a type. This wouldn't work for Kotlin, because it lets you omit the types from many variable declarations. Thus in Kotlin you start with a keyword, and you may (or may not) put the type after the variable name. Let's declare two variables:

```
val question =
    "The Ultimate Question of Life, the Universe, and Everything"
val answer = 42
```

This example omits the type declarations, but you can also specify the type explicitly if you want to:

```
val answer: Int = 42
```

Just as with expression-body functions, if you don't specify the type, the compiler analyzes the initializer expression and uses its type as the variable type. In this case, the initializer, 42, has Int type, so the variable will have the same type.

If you use a floating-point constant, the variable will have the type Double:

```
val yearsToCompute = 7.5e6          ◁——— 7.5 * 10⁶ = 7500000.0
```

The number types are covered in more depth in section 6.2.

If a variable doesn't have an initializer, you need to specify its type explicitly:

```
val answer: Int
answer = 42
```

The compiler can't infer the type if you give no information about the values that can be assigned to this variable.

MUTABLE AND IMMUTABLE VARIABLES

There are two keywords to declare a variable:

- `val` (from *value*)—Immutable reference. A variable declared with `val` can't be reassigned after it's initialized. It corresponds to a final variable in Java.
- `var` (from *variable*)—Mutable reference. The value of such a variable can be changed. This declaration corresponds to a regular (non-final) Java variable.

By default, you should strive to declare all variables in Kotlin with the `val` keyword. Change it to `var` only if necessary. Using immutable references, immutable objects, and functions without side effects makes your code closer to the functional style. We touched briefly on its advantages in chapter 1, and we'll return to this topic in chapter 5.

A `val` variable must be initialized exactly once during the execution of the block where it's defined. But you can initialize it with different values depending on some condition, if the compiler can ensure that only one of the initialization statements will be executed:

```
val message: String
if (canPerformOperation()) {
    message = "Success"
    // ... perform the operation
}
else {
    message = "Failed"
}
```

Note that, even though a `val` reference is itself immutable and can't be changed, the object that it points to may be mutable. For example, this code is perfectly valid:

Declares an immutable reference ┌─▷
```
val languages = arrayListOf("Java")
languages.add("Kotlin")
```
◁─── **Mutates the object pointed to by the reference**

In chapter 6, we'll discuss mutable and immutable objects in more detail.

Even though the `var` keyword allows a variable to change its value, its type is fixed. For example, this code doesn't compile:

```
var answer = 42
answer = "no answer"
```
◁─── **Error: type mismatch**

There's an error on the string literal because its type (`String`) isn't as expected (`Int`). The compiler infers the variable type only from the initializer and doesn't take subsequent assignments into account when determining the type.

If you need to store a value of a mismatching type in a variable, you must manually convert or coerce the value into the right type. We'll discuss primitive type conversions in section 6.2.3.

Now that you know how to define variables, it's time to see some new tricks for referring to values of those variables.

2.1.4 *Easier string formatting: string templates*

Let's get back to the "Hello World" example that opened this section. Here's how to do the next step of the traditional exercise and greet people by name the Kotlin way:

Listing 2.2 **Using string templates**

```
fun main(args: Array<String>) {
    val name = if (args.size > 0) args[0] else "Kotlin"
    println("Hello, $name!")
}
```

Prints "Hello, Kotlin", or "Hello, Bob" if you pass "Bob" as an argument

This example introduces a feature called *string templates*. In the code, you declare a variable name and then use it in the following string literal. Like many scripting languages, Kotlin allows you to refer to local variables in string literals by putting the $ character in front of the variable name. This is equivalent to Java's string concatenation ("Hello, " + name + "!") but is more compact and just as efficient.[1] And of course, the expressions are statically checked, and the code won't compile if you try to refer to a variable that doesn't exist.

If you need to include the $ character in a string, you escape it: `println("\$x")` prints $x and doesn't interpret x as a variable reference.

You're not restricted to simple variable names; you can use more complex expressions as well. All it takes is putting curly braces around the expression:

```
fun main(args: Array<String>) {
    if (args.size > 0) {
        println("Hello, ${args[0]}!")
    }
}
```

Uses the ${} syntax to insert the first element of the args array

You can also nest double quotes within double quotes, as long as they're within an expression:

```
fun main(args: Array<String>) {
    println("Hello, ${if (args.size > 0) args[0] else "someone"}!")
}
```

Later, in section 3.5, we'll return to strings and talk more about what you can do with them.

Now you know how to declare functions and variables. Let's go one step up in the hierarchy and look at classes. This time, you'll use the Java-to-Kotlin converter to help you get started using the new language features.

---

[1] The compiled code creates a `StringBuilder` and appends the constant parts and variable values to it.

2.2   *Classes and properties*

You probably aren't new to object-oriented programming and are familiar with the abstraction of a *class*. Kotlin's concepts in this area will be familiar to you, but you'll find that many common tasks can be accomplished with much less code. This section will introduce you to the basic syntax for declaring classes. We'll go into more detail in chapter 4.

To begin, let's look at a simple JavaBean `Person` class that so far contains only one property, name.

Listing 2.3   Simple Java class `Person`

```java
/* Java */
public class Person {
    private final String name;

    public Person(String name) {
        this.name = name;
    }

    public String getName() {
        return name;
    }
}
```

In Java, the constructor body often contains code that's entirely repetitive: it assigns the parameters to the fields with corresponding names. In Kotlin, this logic can be expressed without so much boilerplate.

In section 1.5.6, we introduced the Java-to-Kotlin converter: a tool that automatically replaces Java code with Kotlin code that does the same thing. Let's look at the converter in action and convert the `Person` class to Kotlin.

Listing 2.4   `Person` class converted to Kotlin

```kotlin
class Person(val name: String)
```

Looks good, doesn't it? If you've tried another modern JVM language, you may have seen something similar. Classes of this type (containing only data but no code) are often called *value objects*, and many languages offer a concise syntax for declaring them.

Note that the modifier `public` disappeared during the conversion from Java to Kotlin. In Kotlin, `public` is the default visibility, so you can omit it.

2.2.1   *Properties*

As you no doubt know, the idea of a class is to encapsulate data and code that works on that data into a single entity. In Java, the data is stored in fields, which are usually private. If you need to let clients of the class access that data, you provide *accessor methods*: a getter and possibly a setter. You saw an example of this in the Person class. The setter can also contain additional logic for validating the passed value, sending notifications about the change and so on.

In Java, the combination of the field and its accessors is often referred to as a *property*, and many frameworks make heavy use of that concept. In Kotlin, properties are a first-class language feature, which entirely replaces fields and accessor methods. You declare a property in a class the same way you declare a variable: with val and var keywords. A property declared as val is read-only, whereas a var property is mutable and can be changed.

Listing 2.5　Declaring a mutable property in a class

```
class Person(
    val name: String,                    Read-only property: generates
    var isMarried: Boolean               a field and a trivial getter
)                                        Writable property: a field,
                                         a getter, and a setter
```

Basically, when you declare a property, you declare the corresponding accessors (a getter for a read-only property, and both a getter and a setter for a writable one). By default, the implementation of accessors is trivial: a field is created to store the value, and the getter and setter return and update its value. But if you want to, you may declare a custom accessor that uses different logic to compute or update the property value.

The concise declaration of the Person class in listing 2.5 hides the same underlying implementation as the original Java code: it's a class with private fields that is initialized in the constructor and can be accessed through the corresponding getter. That means you can use this class from Java and from Kotlin the same way, independent of where it was declared. The use looks identical. Here's how you can use Person from Java code.

Listing 2.6　Using the Person class from Java

```
/* Java */
>>> Person person = new Person("Bob", true);
>>> System.out.println(person.getName());
Bob
>>> System.out.println(person.isMarried());
true
```

Note that this looks the same when Person is defined in Java and in Kotlin. Kotlin's name property is exposed to Java as a getter method called getName. The getter and setter naming rule has an exception: if the property name starts with is, no additional prefix for the getter is added and in the setter name, is is replaced with set. Thus, from Java, you call isMarried().

If you convert listing 2.6 to Kotlin, you get the following result.

Listing 2.7 Using the Person class from Kotlin

```
>>> val person = Person("Bob", true)
>>> println(person.name)
Bob
>>> println(person.isMarried)
true
```

Call the constructor without the "new" keyword.

You access the property directly, but the getter is invoked.

Now, instead of invoking the getter, you reference the property directly. The logic stays the same, but the code is more concise. Setters of mutable properties work the same way: while in Java, you use person.setMarried(false) to tell about a divorce; in Kotlin, you can write person.isMarried = false.

> **TIP** You can also use the Kotlin property syntax for classes defined in Java. Getters in a Java class can be accessed as val properties from Kotlin, and getter/setter pairs can be accessed as var properties. For example, if a Java class defines methods called getName and setName, you can access it as a property called name. If it defines isMarried and setMarried methods, the name of the corresponding Kotlin property will be isMarried.

In most cases, the property has a corresponding backing field that stores the property value. But if the value can be computed on the fly—for example, from other properties—you can express that using a custom getter.

2.2.2 *Custom accessors*

This section shows you how to write a custom implementation of a property accessor. Suppose you declare a rectangle that can say whether it's a square. You don't need to store that information as a separate field, because you can check whether the height is equal to the width on the go:

```
class Rectangle(val height: Int, val width: Int) {
    val isSquare: Boolean
        get() {
            return height == width
        }
}
```

Property getter declaration

The property isSquare doesn't need a field to store its value. It only has a custom getter with the implementation provided. The value is computed every time the property is accessed.

Note that you don't have to use the full syntax with curly braces; you could write get() = height == width, as well. The invocation of such a property stays the same:

```
>>> val rectangle = Rectangle(41, 43)
>>> println(rectangle.isSquare)
false
```

If you need to access this property from Java, you call the `isSquare` method as before.

You might ask whether it's better to declare a function without parameters or a property with a custom getter. Both options are similar: There is no difference in implementation or performance; they only differ in readability. Generally, if you describe the characteristic (the property) of a class, you should declare it as a property.

In chapter 4, we'll present more examples that use classes and properties, and we'll look at the syntax to explicitly declare constructors. If you're impatient in the meantime, you can always use the Java-to-Kotlin converter. Now let's examine briefly how Kotlin code is organized on disk before we move on to discuss other language features.

2.2.3   *Kotlin source code layout: directories and packages*

You know that Java organizes all classes into packages. Kotlin also has the concept of packages, similar to that in Java. Every Kotlin file can have a `package` statement at the beginning, and all declarations (classes, functions, and properties) defined in the file will be placed in that package. Declarations defined in other files can be used directly if they're in the same package; they need to be imported if they're in a different package. As in Java, import statements are placed at the beginning of the file and use the `import` keyword. Here's an example of a source file showing the syntax for the package declaration and import statement.

Listing 2.8   Putting a class and a function declaration in a package

```
package geometry.shapes                          ← Package declaration

import java.util.Random                          ← Imports the standard
                                                   Java library class
class Rectangle(val height: Int, val width: Int) {
    val isSquare: Boolean
        get() = height == width
}

fun createRandomRectangle(): Rectangle {
    val random = Random()
    return Rectangle(random.nextInt(), random.nextInt())
}
```

Kotlin doesn't make a distinction between importing classes and functions, and it allows you to import any kind of declaration using the `import` keyword. You can import the top-level function by name.

Listing 2.9   Importing the function from another package

```
package geometry.example

import geometry.shapes.createRandomRectangle     ← Imports a function
                                                   by name
fun main(args: Array<String>) {
```

```
        println(createRandomRectangle().isSquare)
}
```
◁─┐ **Prints "true"**
   │ **incredibly rarely**

You can also import all declarations defined in a particular package by putting `.*` after the package name. Note that this *star import* will make visible not only classes defined in the package, but also top-level functions and properties. In listing 2.9, writing `import geometry.shapes.*` instead of the explicit import makes the code compile correctly as well.

In Java, you put your classes into a structure of files and directories that matches the package structure. For example, if you have a package named `shapes` with several classes, you need to put every class into a separate file with a matching name and store those files in a directory also called shapes. Figure 2.2 shows how the `geometry` package and its subpackages could be organized in Java. Assume that the `createRandom-Rectangle` function is located in a separate class, `RectangleUtil`.

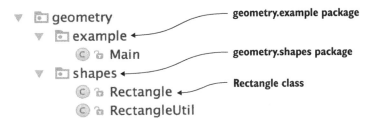

Figure 2.2   In Java, the directory hierarchy duplicates the package hierarchy.

In Kotlin, you can put multiple classes in the same file and choose any name for that file. Kotlin also doesn't impose any restrictions on the layout of source files on disk; you can use any directory structure to organize your files. For instance, you can define all the content of the package `geometry.shapes` in the file shapes.kt and place this file in the geometry folder without creating a separate shapes folder (see figure 2.3).

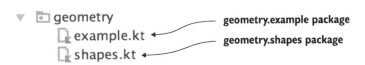

Figure 2.3   Your package hierarchy doesn't need to follow the directory hierarchy.

In most cases, however, it's still a good practice to follow Java's directory layout and to organize source files into directories according to the package structure. Sticking to that structure is especially important in projects where Kotlin is mixed with Java, because doing so lets you migrate the code gradually without introducing any surprises. But you shouldn't hesitate to pull multiple classes into the same file, especially if the classes are small (and in Kotlin, they often are).

Now you know how programs are structured. Let's move on with learning basic concepts and look at control structures in Kotlin.

2.3   *Representing and handling choices: enums and "when"*

In this section, we're going to talk about the when construct. It can be thought of as a replacement for the switch construct in Java, but it's more powerful and is used more often. Along the way, we'll give you an example of declaring enums in Kotlin and discuss the concept of *smart casts*.

2.3.1   *Declaring enum classes*

Let's start by adding some imaginary bright pictures to this serious book and looking at an enum of colors.

Listing 2.10   Declaring a simple enum class

```
enum class Color {
    RED, ORANGE, YELLOW, GREEN, BLUE, INDIGO, VIOLET
}
```

This is a rare case when a Kotlin declaration uses more keywords than the corresponding Java one: enum class versus just enum in Java. In Kotlin, enum is a so-called *soft keyword*: it has a special meaning when it comes before class, but you can use it as a regular name in other places. On the other hand, class is still a keyword, and you'll continue to declare variables named clazz or aClass.

Just as in Java, enums aren't lists of values: you can declare properties and methods on enum classes. Here's how it works.

Listing 2.11   Declaring an enum class with properties

```
enum class Color(                                    Declares properties
        val r: Int, val g: Int, val b: Int           of enum constants
) {
    RED(255, 0, 0), ORANGE(255, 165, 0),
    YELLOW(255, 255, 0), GREEN(0, 255, 0), BLUE(0, 0, 255),
    INDIGO(75, 0, 130), VIOLET(238, 130, 238);       The semicolon
                                                     here is required.
    fun rgb() = (r * 256 + g) * 256 + b              Defines a method
}                                                    on the enum class
>>> println(Color.BLUE.rgb())
255
```

Specifies property values when each constant is created

Enum constants use the same constructor and property declaration syntax as you saw earlier for regular classes. When you declare each enum constant, you need to provide the property values for that constant. Note that this example shows the only place in the Kotlin syntax where you're required to use semicolons: if you define any methods in the enum class, the semicolon separates the enum constant list from the method definitions. Now let's see some cool ways to deal with enum constants in your code.

2.3.2   *Using "when" to deal with enum classes*

Do you remember how children use mnemonic phrases to memorize the colors of the rainbow? Here's one: "Richard Of York Gave Battle In Vain!" Imagine you need a function that gives you a mnemonic for each color (and you don't want to store this information in the enum itself). In Java, you can use a `switch` statement for this. The corresponding Kotlin construct is `when`.

Like `if`, `when` is an expression that returns a value, so you can write a function with an expression body, returning the `when` expression directly. When we talked about functions at the beginning of the chapter, we promised an example of a multi-line function with an expression body. Here's such an example.

Listing 2.12   Using `when` for choosing the right enum value

```
fun getMnemonic(color: Color) =
    when (color) {                              Returns a "when"
        Color.RED -> "Richard"                  expression directly
        Color.ORANGE -> "Of"
        Color.YELLOW -> "York"           Returns the corresponding
        Color.GREEN -> "Gave"            string if the color equals
        Color.BLUE -> "Battle"           the enum constant
        Color.INDIGO -> "In"
        Color.VIOLET -> "Vain"
    }

>>> println(getMnemonic(Color.BLUE))
Battle
```

The code finds the branch corresponding to the passed `color` value. Unlike in Java, you don't need to write `break` statements in each branch (a missing `break` is often a cause for bugs in Java code). If a match is successful, only the corresponding branch is executed. You can also combine multiple values in the same branch if you separate them with commas.

Listing 2.13   Combining options in one `when` branch

```
fun getWarmth(color: Color) = when(color) {
    Color.RED, Color.ORANGE, Color.YELLOW -> "warm"
    Color.GREEN -> "neutral"
    Color.BLUE, Color.INDIGO, Color.VIOLET -> "cold"
}

>>> println(getWarmth(Color.ORANGE))
warm
```

These examples use enum constants by their full name, specifying the `Color` enum class name. You can simplify the code by importing the constant values.

Listing 2.14   Importing enum constants to access without qualifier

```
import ch02.colors.Color
import ch02.colors.Color.*

fun getWarmth(color: Color) = when(color) {
    RED, ORANGE, YELLOW -> "warm"
    GREEN -> "neutral"
    BLUE, INDIGO, VIOLET -> "cold"
}
```

Imports the Color class declared in another package

Explicitly imports enum constants to use them by names

Uses imported constants by name

2.3.3   Using "when" with arbitrary objects

The `when` construct in Kotlin is more powerful than Java's `switch`. Unlike `switch`, which requires you to use constants (enum constants, strings, or number literals) as branch conditions, when allows any objects. Let's write a function that mixes two colors if they can be mixed in this small palette. You don't have lots of options, and you can easily enumerate them all.

Listing 2.15   Using different objects in when branches

```
fun mix(c1: Color, c2: Color) =
        when (setOf(c1, c2)) {
            setOf(RED, YELLOW) -> ORANGE
            setOf(YELLOW, BLUE) -> GREEN
            setOf(BLUE, VIOLET) -> INDIGO
            else -> throw Exception("Dirty color")
        }
>>> println(mix(BLUE, YELLOW))
GREEN
```

Enumerates pairs of colors that can be mixed

An argument of the "when" expression can be any object. It's checked for equality with the branch conditions.

Executed if none of the other branches were matched

If colors c1 and c2 are RED and YELLOW (or vice versa), the result of mixing them is ORANGE, and so on. To implement this, you use set comparison. The Kotlin standard library contains a function `setOf` that creates a `Set` containing the objects specified as its arguments. A *set* is a collection for which the order of items doesn't matter; two sets are equal if they contain the same items. Thus, if the sets `setOf(c1, c2)` and `setOf(RED, YELLOW)` are equal, it means either c1 is RED and c2 is YELLOW, or vice versa. This is exactly what you want to check.

The `when` expression matches its argument against all branches in order until some branch condition is satisfied. Thus `setOf(c1, c2)` is checked for equality: first with `setOf(RED, YELLOW)` and then with other sets of colors, one after another. If none of the other branch conditions is satisfied, the `else` branch is evaluated.

Being able to use any expression as a when branch condition lets you write concise and beautiful code in many cases. In this example, the condition is an equality check; next you'll see how the condition may be any Boolean expression.

2.3.4 Using "when" without an argument

You may have noticed that listing 2.15 is somewhat inefficient. Every time you call this function, it creates several `Set` instances that are used only to check whether two given colors match the other two colors. Normally this isn't an issue, but if the function is called often, it's worth rewriting the code in a different way to avoid creating garbage. You can do it by using the `when` expression without an argument. The code is less readable, but that's the price you often have to pay to achieve better performance.

Listing 2.16 `when` without an argument

```
fun mixOptimized(c1: Color, c2: Color) =
    when {                                          ◁──── No argument
        (c1 == RED && c2 == YELLOW) ||                    for "when"
        (c1 == YELLOW && c2 == RED) ->
            ORANGE

        (c1 == YELLOW && c2 == BLUE) ||
        (c1 == BLUE && c2 == YELLOW) ->
            GREEN

        (c1 == BLUE && c2 == VIOLET) ||
        (c1 == VIOLET && c2 == BLUE) ->
            INDIGO

        else -> throw Exception("Dirty color")
    }
>>> println(mixOptimized(BLUE, YELLOW))
GREEN
```

If no argument is supplied for the `when` expression, the branch condition is any Boolean expression. The `mixOptimized` function does the same thing as `mix` did earlier. Its advantage is that it doesn't create any extra objects, but the cost is that it's harder to read.

Let's move on and look at examples of the `when` construct in which *smart casts* come into play.

2.3.5 Smart casts: combining type checks and casts

As the example for this section, you'll write a function that evaluates simple arithmetic expressions like (1 + 2) + 4. The expressions will contain only one type of operation: the sum of two numbers. Other arithmetic operations (subtraction, multiplication, division) can be implemented in a similar way, and you can do that as an exercise.

First, how do you encode the expressions? You store them in a tree-like structure, where each node is either a sum (`Sum`) or a number (`Num`). `Num` is always a leaf node, whereas a `Sum` node has two children: the arguments of the `sum` operation. The following listing shows a simple structure of classes used to encode the expressions: an interface called `Expr` and two classes, `Num` and `Sum`, that implement it. Note that the `Expr` interface doesn't declare any methods; it's used as a marker interface to provide a common type for different kinds of expressions. To mark that a class implements an interface, you use a colon (:) followed by the interface name:

Listing 2.17   Expression class hierarchy

```
interface Expr
class Num(val value: Int) : Expr
class Sum(val left: Expr, val right: Expr) : Expr
```

> **Simple value object class with one property, value, implementing the Expr interface**

> **The argument of a Sum operation can be any Expr: either Num or another Sum**

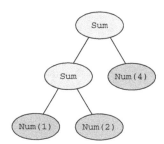

Sum stores the references to `left` and `right` arguments of type `Expr`; in this small example, they can be either `Num` or `Sum`. To store the expression (1 + 2) + 4 mentioned earlier, you create an object `Sum(Sum(Num(1), Num(2)), Num(4))`. Figure 2.4 shows its tree representation.

Now let's look at how to compute the value of an expression. Evaluating the example expression should return 7:

```
>>> println(eval(Sum(Sum(Num(1), Num(2)), Num(4))))
7
```

Figure 2.4   A representation of the expression `Sum(Sum-Num(1), Num(2)), Num(4)`

The `Expr` interface has two implementations, so you have to try two options in order to evaluate a result value for an expression:

- If an expression is a number, you return the corresponding value.
- If it's a sum, you have to evaluate the left and right expressions and return their sum.

First we'll look at this function written in the normal Java way, and then we'll refactor it to be written in a Kotlin style. In Java, you'd probably use a sequence of `if` statements to check the options, so let's use the same approach in Kotlin.

Listing 2.18   Evaluating expressions with an `if`-cascade

```
fun eval(e: Expr): Int {
    if (e is Num) {
        val n = e as Num
        return n.value
    }
    if (e is Sum) {
        return eval(e.right) + eval(e.left)
    }
    throw IllegalArgumentException("Unknown expression")
}
```

> **This explicit cast to Num is redundant.**

> **The variable e is smart-cast.**

```
>>> println(eval(Sum(Sum(Num(1), Num(2)), Num(4))))
7
```

In Kotlin, you check whether a variable is of a certain type by using an `is` check. If you've programmed in C#, this notation should be familiar. The `is` check is similar to `instanceof` in Java. But in Java, if you've checked that a variable has a certain type and needs to access members of that type, you need to add an explicit cast following the `instanceof` check. When the initial variable is used more than once, you often store the cast result in a separate variable. In Kotlin, the compiler does this job for you. If you check the variable for a certain type, you don't need to cast it afterward; you can use it as having the type you checked for. In effect, the compiler performs the cast for you, and we call it a *smart cast*.

In the `eval` function, after you check whether the variable `e` has `Num` type, the compiler interprets it as a `Num` variable. You can then access the `value` property of `Num` without an explicit cast: `e.value`. The same goes for the `right` and `left`

```
if (e is Sum) {
    return eval(e.right) + eval(e.left)
}
```

Figure 2.5   The IDE highlights smart casts with a background color.

properties of `Sum`: you write only `e.right` and `e.left` in the corresponding context. In the IDE, these smart-cast values are emphasized with a background color, so it's easy to grasp that this value was checked beforehand. See figure 2.5.

The smart cast works only if a variable couldn't have changed after the `is` check. When you're using a smart cast with a property of a class, as in this example, the property has to be a `val` and it can't have a custom accessor. Otherwise, it would not be possible to verify that every access to the property would return the same value.

An explicit cast to the specific type is expressed via the `as` keyword:

```
val n = e as Num
```

Now let's look at how to refactor the `eval` function into a more idiomatic Kotlin style.

2.3.6   *Refactoring: replacing "if" with "when"*

How does `if` in Kotlin differ from `if` in Java? You have seen the difference already. At the beginning of the chapter, you saw the `if` expression used in the context where Java would have a ternary operator: `if (a > b) a else b` works like Java's `a > b ? a : b`. In Kotlin, there is no ternary operator, because, unlike in Java, the `if` expression returns a value. That means you can rewrite the `eval` function to use the expression-body syntax, removing the `return` statement and the curly braces and using the `if` expression as the function body instead.

Listing 2.19   Using `if`-expressions that return values

```
fun eval(e: Expr): Int =
    if (e is Num) {
        e.value
    } else if (e is Sum) {
```

```
        eval(e.right) + eval(e.left)
    } else {
        throw IllegalArgumentException("Unknown expression")
    }

>>> println(eval(Sum(Num(1), Num(2))))
3
```

The curly braces are optional if there's only one expression in an if branch. If an if branch is a block, the last expression is returned as a result.

Let's polish this code even more and rewrite it using when.

Listing 2.20 Using when instead of if-cascade

```
fun eval(e: Expr): Int =
    when (e) {
        is Num ->
            e.value
        is Sum ->
            eval(e.right) + eval(e.left)
        else ->
            throw IllegalArgumentException("Unknown expression")
    }
```

Smart casts are applied here.

"when" branches that check the argument type

The when expression isn't restricted to checking values for equality, which is what you saw earlier. Here you use a different form of when branches, allowing you to check the type of the when argument value. Just as in the if example in listing 2.19, the type check applies a smart cast, so you can access members of Num and Sum without extra casts.

Compare the last two Kotlin versions of the eval function, and think about how you can apply when as a replacement for sequences of if expressions in your own code as well. When the branch logic is complicated, you can use a block expression as a branch body. Let's see how this works.

2.3.7 Blocks as branches of "if" and "when"

Both if and when can have blocks as branches. In this case, the last expression in the block is the result. If you want to add logging to the example function, you can do so in the block and return the last value as before.

Listing 2.21 Using when with compound actions in branches

```
fun evalWithLogging(e: Expr): Int =
    when (e) {
        is Num -> {
            println("num: ${e.value}")
            e.value
        }
        is Sum -> {
            val left = evalWithLogging(e.left)
```

This is the last expression in the block and is returned if e is of type Num.

```
        val right = evalWithLogging(e.right)
        println("sum: $left + $right")
        left + right
    }
    else -> throw IllegalArgumentException("Unknown expression")
}
```

> ◁── This expression is returned if e is of type Sum.

Now you can look at the logs printed by the `evalWithLogging` function and follow the order of computation:

```
>>> println(evalWithLogging(Sum(Sum(Num(1), Num(2)), Num(4))))
num: 1
num: 2
sum: 1 + 2
num: 4
sum: 3 + 4
7
```

The rule "the last expression in a block is the result" holds in all cases where a block can be used and a result is expected. As you'll see at the end of this chapter, the same rule works for the `try` body and `catch` clauses, and chapter 5 discusses its application to lambda expressions. But as we mentioned in section 2.2, this rule doesn't hold for regular functions. A function can have either an expression body that can't be a block or a block body with explicit `return` statements inside.

You've become acquainted with Kotlin ways to choose the right things among many. Now it's a good time to see how you can iterate over things.

2.4 *Iterating over things: "while" and "for" loops*

Of all the features discussed in this chapter, iteration in Kotlin is probably the most similar to Java. The `while` loop is identical to the one in Java, so it deserves only a brief mention in the beginning of this section. The `for` loop exists in only one form, which is equivalent to Java's `for-each` loop. It's written `for <item> in <elements>`, as in C#. The most common application of this loop is iterating over collections, just as in Java. We'll explore how it can cover other looping scenarios as well.

2.4.1 *The "while" loop*

Kotlin has `while` and `do-while` loops, and their syntax doesn't differ from the corresponding loops in Java:

```
while (condition) {
    /*...*/
}
```
> ◁── The body is executed while the condition is true.

```
do {
    /*...*/
} while (condition)
```
> ◁── The body is executed for the first time unconditionally. After that, it's executed while the condition is true.

Kotlin doesn't bring anything new to these simple loops, so we won't linger. Let's move on to discuss the various uses of the `for` loop.

2.4.2 *Iterating over numbers: ranges and progressions*

As we just mentioned, in Kotlin there's no regular Java `for` loop, where you initialize a variable, update its value on every step through the loop, and exit the loop when the value reaches a certain bound. To replace the most common use cases of such loops, Kotlin uses the concepts of *ranges*.

A range is essentially just an interval between two values, usually numbers: a start and an end. You write it using the `..` operator:

```
val oneToTen = 1..10
```

Note that ranges in Kotlin are *closed* or *inclusive*, meaning the second value is always a part of the range.

The most basic thing you can do with integer ranges is loop over all the values. If you can iterate over all the values in a range, such a range is called a *progression*.

Let's use integer ranges to play the Fizz-Buzz game. It's a nice way to survive a long trip in a car and remember your forgotten division skills. Players take turns counting incrementally, replacing any number divisible by three with the word *fizz* and any number divisible by five with the word *buzz*. If a number is a multiple of both three and five, you say "FizzBuzz."

The following listing prints the right answers for the numbers from 1 to 100. Note how you check the possible conditions with a `when` expression without an argument.

Listing 2.22 Using `when` to implement the Fizz-Buzz game

```
fun fizzBuzz(i: Int) = when {
    i % 15 == 0 -> "FizzBuzz "
    i % 3 == 0 -> "Fizz "
    i % 5 == 0 -> "Buzz "
    else -> "$i "
}
>>> for (i in 1..100) {
...     print(fizzBuzz(i))
... }
}
1 2 Fizz 4 Buzz Fizz 7 ...
```

- If i is divisible by 3, returns Fizz
- Else returns the number itself
- If i is divisible by 5, returns Buzz
- Iterates over the integer range 1..100
- If i is divisible by 15, returns FizzBuzz. As in Java, % is the modulus operator.

Suppose you get tired of these rules after an hour of driving and want to complicate things a bit. Let's start counting backward from 100 and include only even numbers.

Listing 2.23 Iterating over a range with a step

```
>>> for (i in 100 downTo 1 step 2) {
...     print(fizzBuzz(i))
... }
Buzz 98 Fizz 94 92 FizzBuzz 88 ...
```

Now you're iterating over a progression that has a *step*, which allows it to skip some numbers. The step can also be negative, in which case the progression goes backward rather than forward. In this example, `100 downTo 1` is a progression that goes backward (with step -1). Then `step` changes the absolute value of the step to 2 while keeping the direction (in effect, setting the step to -2).

As we mentioned earlier, the `. .` syntax always creates a range that includes the end point (the value to the right of `. .`). In many cases, it's more convenient to iterate over half-closed ranges, which don't include the specified end point. To create such a range, use the `until` function. For example, the loop `for (x in 0 until size)` is equivalent to `for (x in 0..size-1)`, but it expresses the idea somewhat more clearly. Later, in section 3.4.3, you'll learn more about the syntax for `downTo`, `step`, and `until` in these examples.

You can see how working with ranges and progressions helped you cope with the advanced rules for the FizzBuzz game. Now let's look at other examples that use the `for` loop.

2.4.3   *Iterating over maps*

We've mentioned that the most common scenario of using a `for ... in` loop is iterating over a collection. This works exactly as it does in Java, so we won't say much about it. Let's see how you can iterate over a map, instead.

As an example, we'll look at a small program that prints binary representations for characters. You'll store these binary representations in a map (just for illustrative purposes). The following code creates a map, fills it with binary representations of some letters, and then prints the map's contents.

Listing 2.24   Initializing and iterating over a map

```
val binaryReps = TreeMap<Char, String>()          ◁── Uses TreeMap so
                                                        the keys are sorted
for (c in 'A'..'F') {                            ◁──
    val binary = Integer.toBinaryString(c.toInt())     Iterates over the
    binaryReps[c] = binary          ◁── Stores the value in a   characters from A to F
}                                        map by the c key       using a range of characters

for ((letter, binary) in binaryReps) {         ◁──
    println("$letter = $binary")                   Iterates over a map,
}                                                   assigning the map key and
                                                    value to two variables
```

Converts ASCII code to binary (annotation pointing to `val binary = Integer.toBinaryString(c.toInt())`)

The `. .` syntax to create a range works not only for numbers, but also for characters. Here you use it to iterate over all characters from *A* up to and including *F*.

Listing 2.24 shows that the `for` loop allows you to unpack an element of a collection you're iterating over (in this case, a collection of key/value pairs in the map). You store the result of the unpacking in two separate variables: `letter` receives the key, and `binary` receives the value. Later, in section 7.4.1, you'll find out more about this unpacking syntax.

Another nice trick used in listing 2.24 is the shorthand syntax for getting and updating the values of a map by key. Instead of calling `get` and `put`, you can use `map[key]` to read values and `map[key]` = value to set them. The code

```
binaryReps[c] = binary
```

is equivalent to its Java version:

```
binaryReps.put(c, binary)
```

The output is similar to the following (we've arranged it in two columns instead of one):

```
A = 1000001    D = 1000100
B = 1000010    E = 1000101
C = 1000011    F = 1000110
```

You can use the same unpacking syntax to iterate over a collection while keeping track of the index of the current item. You don't need to create a separate variable to store the index and increment it by hand:

```
val list = arrayListOf("10", "11", "1001")
for ((index, element) in list.withIndex()) {     Iterates over a collection
    println("$index: $element")                   with an index
}
```

The code prints what you expect:

```
0: 10
1: 11
2: 1001
```

We'll dig into the whereabouts of `withIndex` in the next chapter.

You've seen how you can use the `in` keyword to iterate over a range or a collection. You can also use `in` to check whether a value belongs to the range or collection.

2.4.4 Using "in" to check collection and range membership

You use the `in` operator to check whether a value is in a range, or its opposite, `!in`, to check whether a value isn't in a range. Here's how you can use `in` to check whether a character belongs to a range of characters.

Listing 2.25 Checking range membership using `in`

```
fun isLetter(c: Char) = c in 'a'..'z' || c in 'A'..'Z'
fun isNotDigit(c: Char) = c !in '0'..'9'

>>> println(isLetter('q'))
true
>>> println(isNotDigit('x'))
true
```

This technique for checking whether a character is a letter looks simple. Under the hood, nothing tricky happens: you still check that the character's code is somewhere between the code of the first letter and the code of the last one. But this logic is concisely hidden in the implementation of the range classes in the standard library:

```
c in 'a'..'z'
```
← **Transforms to a <= c && c <= z**

The in and !in operators also work in when expressions.

Listing 2.26 Using in checks as when branches

You can combine multiple ranges. →
```
fun recognize(c: Char) = when (c) {
    in '0'..'9' -> "It's a digit!"
    in 'a'..'z', in 'A'..'Z' -> "It's a letter!"
    else -> "I don't know…"
}
>>> println(recognize('8'))
It's a digit!
```
← **Checks whether the value is in the range from 0 to 9**

Ranges aren't restricted to characters, either. If you have any class that supports comparing instances (by implementing the java.lang.Comparable interface), you can create ranges of objects of that type. If you have such a range, you can't enumerate all objects in the range. Think about it: can you, for example, enumerate all strings between "Java" and "Kotlin"? No, you can't. But you can still check whether another object belongs to the range, using the in operator:

```
>>> println("Kotlin" in "Java".."Scala")
true
```
← **The same as "Java" <= "Kotlin" && "Kotlin" <= "Scala"**

Note that the strings are compared alphabetically here, because that's how the String class implements the Comparable interface.

The same in check works with collections as well:

```
>>> println("Kotlin" in setOf("Java", "Scala"))
false
```
← **This set doesn't contain the string "Kotlin".**

Later, in section 7.3.2, you'll see how to use ranges and progressions with your own data types and what objects in general you can use in checks with.

There's one more group of Java statements we want to look at in this chapter: statements for dealing with exceptions.

2.5 *Exceptions in Kotlin*

Exception handling in Kotlin is similar to the way it's done in Java and many other languages. A function can complete in a normal way or throw an exception if an error occurs. The function caller can catch this exception and process it; if it doesn't, the exception is rethrown further up the stack.

The basic form for exception-handling statements in Kotlin is similar to Java's. You throw an exception in a non-surprising manner:

```
if (percentage !in 0..100) {
    throw IllegalArgumentException(
        "A percentage value must be between 0 and 100: $percentage")
}
```

As with all other classes, you don't have to use the new keyword to create an instance of the exception.

Unlike in Java, in Kotlin the throw construct is an expression and can be used as a part of other expressions:

```
val percentage =
    if (number in 0..100)
        number
    else
        throw IllegalArgumentException(                    ◁──  "throw" is an
            "A percentage value must be between 0 and 100: $number")   expression.
```

In this example, if the condition is satisfied, the program behaves correctly, and the percentage variable is initialized with number. Otherwise, an exception is thrown, and the variable isn't initialized. We'll discuss the technical details of throw as a part of other expressions, in section 6.2.6.

2.5.1 *"try", "catch", and "finally"*

Just as in Java, you use the try construct with catch and finally clauses to handle exceptions. You can see it in the following listing, which reads a line from the given file, tries to parse it as a number, and returns either the number or null if the line isn't a valid number.

> **Listing 2.27   Using try as in Java**

```
fun readNumber(reader: BufferedReader): Int? {       ◁──  You don't have to explicitly
    try {                                                  specify exceptions that can be
        val line = reader.readLine()                       thrown from this function.
        return Integer.parseInt(line)
    }
    catch (e: NumberFormatException) {               ◁──  The exception type
        return null                                        is on the right.
    }
    finally {                                        ◁──  "finally" works just
        reader.close()                                     as it does in Java.
    }
}

>>> val reader = BufferedReader(StringReader("239"))
>>> println(readNumber(reader))
239
```

The biggest difference from Java is that the `throws` clause isn't present in the code: if you wrote this function in Java, you'd explicitly write `throws IOException` after the function declaration. You'd need to do this because `IOException` is a *checked exception*. In Java, it's an exception that needs to be handled explicitly. You have to declare all checked exceptions that your function can throw, and if you call another function, you need to handle its checked exceptions or declare that your function can throw them, too.

Just like many other modern JVM languages, Kotlin doesn't differentiate between checked and unchecked exceptions. You don't specify the exceptions thrown by a function, and you may or may not handle any exceptions. This design decision is based on the practice of using checked exceptions in Java. Experience has shown that the Java rules often require a lot of meaningless code to rethrow or ignore exceptions, and the rules don't consistently protect you from the errors that can happen.

For example, in listing 2.27, `NumberFormatException` isn't a checked exception. Therefore, the Java compiler doesn't force you to catch it, and you can easily see the exception happen at runtime. This is unfortunate, because invalid input data is a common situation and should be handled gracefully. At the same time, the `Buffered-Reader.close` method can throw an `IOException`, which is a checked exception and needs to be handled. Most programs can't take any meaningful action if closing a stream fails, so the code required to catch the exception from the `close` method is boilerplate.

What about Java 7's `try-with-resources`? Kotlin doesn't have any special syntax for this; it's implemented as a library function. In section 8.2.5, you'll see how this is possible.

2.5.2 *"try" as an expression*

To see another significant difference between Java and Kotlin, let's modify the example a little. Let's remove the `finally` section (because you've already seen how this works) and add some code to print the number you read from the file.

Listing 2.28 Using `try` as an expression

```
fun readNumber(reader: BufferedReader) {
    val number = try {
        Integer.parseInt(reader.readLine())          ← Becomes the value of
    } catch (e: NumberFormatException) {               the "try" expression
        return
    }

    println(number)
}

>>> val reader = BufferedReader(StringReader("not a number"))     Nothing
>>> readNumber(reader)                                          ← is printed.
```

The `try` keyword in Kotlin, just like `if` and `when`, introduces an expression, and you can assign its value to a variable. Unlike with `if`, you always need to enclose the statement body in curly braces. Just as in other statements, if the body contains multiple expressions, the value of the `try` expression as a whole is the value of the last expression.

This example puts a `return` statement in the `catch` block, so the execution of the function doesn't continue after the `catch` block. If you want to continue execution, the `catch` clause also needs to have a value, which will be the value of the last expression in it. Here's how this works.

Listing 2.29   Returning a value in `catch`

```
fun readNumber(reader: BufferedReader) {
    val number = try {
        Integer.parseInt(reader.readLine())        This value is used when
    } catch (e: NumberFormatException) {           no exception happens.
        null
    }                                              The null value is used
                                                   in case of an exception.
    println(number)
}                                                  An exception is
>>> val reader = BufferedReader(StringReader("not a number"))   thrown, so the function
>>> readNumber(reader)                                          prints "null".
null
```

If the execution of a `try` code block behaves normally, the last expression in the block is the result. If an exception is caught, the last expression in a corresponding `catch` block is the result. In listing 2.29, the result value is `null` if a `NumberFormat-Exception` is caught.

At this point, if you're impatient, you can start writing programs in Kotlin in a way that's similar to how you code in Java. As you read this book, you'll continue to learn how to change your habitual ways of thinking and use the full power of the new language.

2.6   *Summary*

- The `fun` keyword is used to declare a function. The `val` and `var` keywords declare read-only and mutable variables, respectively.
- String templates help you avoid noisy string concatenation. Prefix a variable name with `$` or surround an expression with `${ }` to have its value injected into the string.
- Value-object classes are expressed in a concise way in Kotlin.
- The familiar `if` is now an expression with a return value.
- The `when` expression is analogous to `switch` in Java but is more powerful.
- You don't have to cast a variable explicitly after checking that it has a certain type: the compiler casts it for you automatically using a smart cast.

- The `for`, `while`, and `do-while` loops are similar to their counterparts in Java, but the `for` loop is now more convenient, especially when you need to iterate over a map or a collection with an index.
- The concise syntax `1..5` creates a range. Ranges and progressions allow Kotlin to use a uniform syntax and set of abstractions in `for` loops and also work with the `in` and `!in` operators that check whether a value belongs to a range.
- Exception handling in Kotlin is very similar to that in Java, except that Kotlin doesn't require you to declare the exceptions that can be thrown by a function.

Defining and calling functions

This chapter covers

- Functions for working with collections, strings, and regular expressions
- Using named arguments, default parameter values, and the infix call syntax
- Adapting Java libraries to Kotlin through extension functions and properties
- Structuring code with top-level and local functions and properties

By now, you should be fairly comfortable with using Kotlin the same way you use Java. You've seen how the concepts familiar to you from Java translate to Kotlin, and how Kotlin often makes them more concise and readable.

In this chapter, you'll see how Kotlin improves on one of the key elements of every program: declaring and calling functions. We'll also look into the possibilities for adapting Java libraries to the Kotlin style through the use of extension functions, allowing you to gain the full benefits of Kotlin in mixed-language projects.

To make our discussion more useful and less abstract, we'll focus on Kotlin collections, strings, and regular expressions as our problem domain. As an introduction, let's look at how to create collections in Kotlin.

3.1 *Creating collections in Kotlin*

Before you can do interesting things with collections, you need to learn how to create them. In section 2.3.3, you bumped into the way to create a new set: the `setOf` function. You created a set of colors then, but for now, let's keep it simple and work with numbers:

```
val set = hashSetOf(1, 7, 53)
```

You create a list or a map in a similar way:

```
val list = arrayListOf(1, 7, 53)
val map = hashMapOf(1 to "one", 7 to "seven", 53 to "fifty-three")
```

Note that `to` isn't a special construct, but a normal function. We'll return to it later in the chapter.

Can you guess the classes of objects that are created here? Run the following example to see this for yourself:

```
>>> println(set.javaClass)
class java.util.HashSet

>>> println(list.javaClass)
class java.util.ArrayList

>>> println(map.javaClass)
class java.util.HashMap
```

⊲┐ **javaClass is Kotlin's equivalent of Java's getClass().**

As you can see, Kotlin uses the standard Java collection classes. This is good news for Java developers: Kotlin doesn't have its own set of collection classes. All of your existing knowledge about Java collections still applies here.

Why are there no Kotlin collections? Because using the standard Java collections makes it much easier to interact with Java code. You don't need to convert collections one way or the other when you call Java functions from Kotlin or vice versa.

Even though Kotlin's collections are exactly the same classes as Java collections, you can do much more with them in Kotlin. For example, you can get the last element in a list or find a maximum in a collection of numbers:

```
>>> val strings = listOf("first", "second", "fourteenth")

>>> println(strings.last())
fourteenth

>>> val numbers = setOf(1, 14, 2)

>>> println(numbers.max())
14
```

In this chapter, we'll explore in detail how this works and where all the new methods on the Java classes come from.

In future chapters, when we start talking about lambdas, you'll see much more that you can do with collections, but we'll keep using the same standard Java collection classes. And in section 6.3, you'll learn how the Java collection classes are represented in the Kotlin type system.

Before discussing how the magic functions `last` and `max` work on Java collections, let's learn some new concepts for declaring a function.

3.2 *Making functions easier to call*

Now that you know how to create a collection of elements, let's do something straight-forward: print its contents. Don't worry if this seems overly simple; along the way, you'll meet a bunch of important concepts.

Java collections have a default `toString` implementation, but the formatting of the output is fixed and not always what you need:

```
>>> val list = listOf(1, 2, 3)
>>> println(list)                    ◁——— Invokes toString()
[1, 2, 3]
```

Imagine that you need the elements to be separated by semicolons and surrounded by parentheses, instead of the brackets used by the default implementation: `(1; 2; 3)`. To solve this, Java projects use third-party libraries such as Guava and Apache Commons, or reimplement the logic inside the project. In Kotlin, a function to handle this is part of the standard library.

In this section, you'll implement this function yourself. You'll begin with a straight-forward implementation that doesn't use Kotlin's facilities for simplifying function declarations, and then you'll rewrite it in a more idiomatic style.

The `joinToString` function shown next appends the elements of the collection to a `StringBuilder`, with a separator between them, a prefix at the beginning, and a postfix at the end.

> **Listing 3.1 Initial implementation of `joinToString()`**

```
fun <T> joinToString(
        collection: Collection<T>,
        separator: String,
        prefix: String,
        postfix: String
): String {

    val result = StringBuilder(prefix)

    for ((index, element) in collection.withIndex()) {
        if (index > 0) result.append(separator)       ◁—┐ Don't append a separator
        result.append(element)                           │ before the first element.
    }

    result.append(postfix)
    return result.toString()
}
```

The function is generic: it works on collections that contain elements of any type. The syntax for generics is similar to Java. (A more detailed discussion of generics will be the subject of chapter 9.)

Let's verify that the function works as intended:

```
>>> val list = listOf(1, 2, 3)
>>> println(joinToString(list, "; ", "(", ")"))
(1; 2; 3)
```

The implementation is fine, and you'll mostly leave it as is. What we'll focus on is the declaration: how can you change it to make calls of this function less verbose? Maybe you could avoid having to pass four arguments every time you call the function. Let's see what you can do.

3.2.1　*Named arguments*

The first problem we'll address concerns the readability of function calls. For example, look at the following call of `joinToString`:

```
joinToString(collection, " ", " ", ".")
```

Can you tell what parameters all these `Strings` correspond to? Are the elements separated by the whitespace or the dot? These questions are hard to answer without looking at the signature of the function. Maybe you remember it, or maybe your IDE can help you, but it's not obvious from the calling code.

This problem is especially common with Boolean flags. To solve it, some Java coding styles recommend creating enum types instead of using Booleans. Others even require you to specify the parameter names explicitly in a comment, as in the following example:

```
/* Java */
joinToString(collection, /* separator */ " ",  /* prefix */ " ",
    /* postfix */ ".");
```

With Kotlin, you can do better:

```
joinToString(collection, separator = " ", prefix = " ", postfix = ".")
```

When calling a function written in Kotlin, you can specify the names of some arguments that you're passing to the function. If you specify the name of an argument in a call, you should also specify the names for all the arguments after that, to avoid confusion.

> **TIP** IntelliJ IDEA can keep explicitly written argument names up to date if you rename the parameter of the function being called. Just ensure that you use the Rename or Change Signature action instead of editing the parameter names by hand.

> **WARNING** Unfortunately, you can't use named arguments when calling methods written in Java, including methods from the JDK and the Android

framework. Storing parameter names in .class files is supported as an optional feature only starting with Java 8, and Kotlin maintains compatibility with Java 6. As a result, the compiler can't recognize the parameter names used in your call and match them against the method definition.

Named arguments work especially well with default parameter values, which we'll look at next.

3.2.2   Default parameter values

Another common Java problem is the overabundance of overloaded methods in some classes. Just look at `java.lang.Thread` and its eight constructors (http://mng.bz/ 4KZC)! The overloads can be provided for the sake of backward compatibility, for convenience of API users, or for other reasons, but the end result is the same: duplication. The parameter names and types are repeated over and over, and if you're being a good citizen, you also have to repeat most of the documentation in every overload. At the same time, if you call an overload that omits some parameters, it's not always clear which values are used for them.

In Kotlin, you can often avoid creating overloads because you can specify default values for parameters in a function declaration. Let's use that to improve the `joinTo-String` function. For most cases, the strings can be separated by commas without any prefix or postfix. So, let's make these values the defaults.

> **Listing 3.2   Declaring `joinToString()` with default parameter values**

```
fun <T> joinToString(
        collection: Collection<T>,
        separator: String = ", ",        ┐
        prefix: String = "",             │  Parameters with
        postfix: String = ""             │  default values
) : String                               ┘
```

Now you can either invoke the function with all the arguments or omit some of them:

```
>>> joinToString(list, ", ", "", "")
1, 2, 3
>>> joinToString(list)
1, 2, 3
>>> joinToString(list, "; ")
1; 2; 3
```

When using the regular call syntax, you have to specify the arguments in the same order as in the function declaration, and you can omit only trailing arguments. If you use named arguments, you can omit some arguments from the middle of the list and specify only the ones you need, in any order you want:

```
>>> joinToString(list, suffix = ";", prefix = "# ")
# 1, 2, 3;
```

Note that the default values of the parameters are encoded in the function being called, not at the call site. If you change the default value and recompile the class containing the function, the callers that haven't specified a value for the parameter will start using the new default value.

Default values and Java

Given that Java doesn't have the concept of default parameter values, you have to specify all the parameter values explicitly when you call a Kotlin function with default parameter values. If you frequently need to call a function from Java and want to make it easier to use for Java callers, you can annotate it with `@Jvm-Overloads`. This instructs the compiler to generate Java overloaded methods, omitting each of the parameters one by one, starting from the last one.

For example, if you annotate `joinToString` with `@JvmOverloads`, the following overloads are generated:

```
/* Java */
String joinToString(Collection<T> collection, String separator,
    String prefix, String postfix);

String joinToString(Collection<T> collection, String separator,
    String prefix);

String joinToString(Collection<T> collection, String separator);

String joinToString(Collection<T> collection);
```

Each overload uses the default values for the parameters that have been omitted from the signature.

So far, you've been working on your utility function without paying much attention to the surrounding context. Surely it must have been a method of some class that wasn't shown in the example listings, right? In fact, Kotlin makes this unnecessary.

3.2.3 *Getting rid of static utility classes: top-level functions and properties*

We all know that Java, as an object-oriented language, requires all code to be written as methods of classes. Usually, this works out nicely; but in reality, almost every large project ends up with a lot of code that doesn't clearly belong to any single class. Sometimes an operation works with objects of two different classes that play an equally important role for it. Sometimes there is one primary object, but you don't want to bloat its API by adding the operation as an instance method.

As a result, you end up with classes that don't contain any state or any instance methods and that act as containers for a bunch of static methods. A perfect example is the `Collections` class in the JDK. To find other examples in your own code, look for classes that have `Util` as part of the name.

In Kotlin, you don't need to create all those meaningless classes. Instead, you can place functions directly at the top level of a source file, outside of any class. Such functions are still members of the package declared at the top of the file, and you still need to import them if you want to call them from other packages, but the unnecessary extra level of nesting no longer exists.

Let's put the `joinToString` function into the `strings` package directly. Create a file called join.kt with the following contents.

Listing 3.3   Declaring `joinToString()` as a top-level function

```
package strings

fun joinToString(...): String { ... }
```

How does this run? You know that, when you compile the file, some classes will be produced, because the JVM can only execute code in classes. When you work only with Kotlin, that's all you need to know. But if you need to call such a function from Java, you have to understand how it will be compiled. To make this clear, let's look at the Java code that would compile to the same class:

```
/* Java */
package strings;

public class JoinKt {                              Corresponds to join.kt,
    public static String joinToString(...) { ... } the filename of listing 3.3
}
```

You can see that the name of the class generated by the Kotlin compiler corresponds to the name of the file containing the function. All top-level functions in the file are compiled to static methods of that class. Therefore, calling this function from Java is as easy as calling any other static method:

```
/* Java */
import strings.JoinKt;

...

JoinKt.joinToString(list, ", ", "", "");
```

Changing the file class name

To change the name of the generated class that contains Kotlin top-level functions, you add a @JvmName annotation to the file. Place it at the beginning of the file, before the package name:

```
@file:JvmName("StringFunctions")      Annotation to specify
                                      the class name
package strings                       The package statement
                                      follows the file annotations.
fun joinToString(...): String { ... }
```

Now the function can be called as follows:

```
/* Java */
import strings.StringFunctions;
StringFunctions.joinToString(list, ", ", "", "");
```

A detailed discussion of the annotation syntax comes later, in chapter 10.

TOP-LEVEL PROPERTIES

Just like functions, properties can be placed at the top level of a file. Storing individual pieces of data outside of a class isn't needed as often but is still useful.

For example, you can use a var property to count the number of times some operation has been performed:

```
var opCount = 0                              Declares a
                                             top-level property
fun performOperation() {
    opCount++                                Changes the value
    // ...                                   of the property
}
                                                          Reads the value
fun reportOperationCount() {                              of the property
    println("Operation performed $opCount times")
}
```

The value of such a property will be stored in a static field.

Top-level properties also allow you to define constants in your code:

```
val UNIX_LINE_SEPARATOR = "\n"
```

By default, top-level properties, just like any other properties, are exposed to Java code as accessor methods (a getter for a val property and a getter/setter pair for a var property). If you want to expose a constant to Java code as a public static final field, to make its use more natural, you can mark it with the const modifier (this is allowed for properties of primitive types, as well as String):

```
const val UNIX_LINE_SEPARATOR = "\n"
```

This gets you the equivalent of the following Java code:

```
/* Java */
public static final String  UNIX_LINE_SEPARATOR = "\n";
```

You've improved the initial joinToString utility function quite a lot. Now let's look at how to make it even handier.

3.3 Adding methods to other people's classes: extension functions and properties

One of the main themes of Kotlin is smooth integration with existing code. Even pure Kotlin projects are built on top of Java libraries such as the JDK, the Android framework, and other third-party frameworks. And when you integrate Kotlin into a Java project, you're also dealing with the existing code that hasn't been or won't be converted to Kotlin. Wouldn't it be nice to be able to use all the niceties of Kotlin when working with those APIs, without having to rewrite them? That's what extension functions allow you to do.

Conceptually, an *extension function* is a simple thing: it's a function that can be called as a member of a class but is defined outside of it. To demonstrate that, let's add a method for computing the last character of a string:

```
package strings

fun String.lastChar(): Char = this.get(this.length - 1)
```

All you need to do is put the name of the class or interface that you're extending before the name of the function you're adding. This class name is called the *receiver type*; the value on which you're calling the extension function is called the *receiver object*. This is illustrated in figure 3.1.

Figure 3.1 The receiver type is the type on which the extension is defined, and the receiver object is the instance of that type.

You can call the function using the same syntax you use for ordinary class members:

```
>>> println("Kotlin".lastChar())
n
```

In this example, `String` is the receiver type, and `"Kotlin"` is the receiver object.

In a sense, you've added your own method to the `String` class. Even though `String` isn't part of your code, and you may not even have the source code to that class, you can still extend it with the methods you need in your project. It doesn't even matter whether `String` is written in Java, Kotlin, or some other JVM language, such as Groovy. As long as it's compiled to a Java class, you can add your own extensions to that class.

In the body of an extension function, you use `this` as you'd use it in a method. And, as in a regular method, you can omit it:

```
package strings

fun String.lastChar(): Char = get(length - 1)
```
⟵ **Receiver object members can be accessed without "this".**

In the extension function, you can directly access the methods and properties of the class you're extending, as in methods defined in the class itself. Note that extension functions don't allow you to break encapsulation. Unlike methods defined in the class, extension functions don't have access to private or protected members of the class.

Later we'll use the term *method* for both members of the class and extensions functions. For instance, we can say that in the body of the extension function you can call any method on the receiver, meaning you can call both members and extension functions. On the call site, extension functions are indistinguishable from members, and often it doesn't matter whether the particular method is a member or an extension.

3.3.1　*Imports and extension functions*

When you define an extension function, it doesn't automatically become available across your entire project. Instead, it needs to be imported, just like any other class or function. This helps avoid accidental name conflicts. Kotlin allows you to import individual functions using the same syntax you use for classes:

```
import strings.lastChar

val c = "Kotlin".lastChar()
```

Of course, * imports work as well:

```
import strings.*

val c = "Kotlin".lastChar()
```

You can change the name of the class or function you're importing using the as keyword:

```
import strings.lastChar as last

val c = "Kotlin".last()
```

Changing a name on import is useful when you have several functions with the same name in different packages and you want to use them in the same file. For regular classes or functions, you have another choice in this situation: You can use a fully qualified name to refer to the class or function. For extension functions, the syntax requires you to use the short name, so the as keyword in an import statement is the only way to resolve the conflict.

3.3.2　*Calling extension functions from Java*

Under the hood, an extension function is a static method that accepts the receiver object as its first argument. Calling it doesn't involve creating adapter objects or any other runtime overhead.

That makes using extension functions from Java pretty easy: you call the static method and pass the receiver object instance. Just as with other top-level functions, the name of the Java class containing the method is determined from the name of the file where the function is declared. Let's say it was declared in a StringUtil.kt file:

```
/* Java */
char c = StringUtilKt.lastChar("Java");
```

This extension function is declared as a top-level function, so it's compiled to a static method. You can import the `lastChar` method statically from Java, simplifying the use to just `lastChar("Java")`. This code is somewhat less readable than the Kotlin version, but it's idiomatic from the Java point of view.

3.3.3 *Utility functions as extensions*

Now you can write the final version of the `joinToString` function. This is almost exactly what you'll find in the Kotlin standard library.

> **Listing 3.4   Declaring `joinToString()` as an extension**

```
fun <T> Collection<T>.joinToString(              ◁─────┐ Declares an extension
        separator: String = ", ",                        │ function on Collection<T>
        prefix: String = "",        ┆ Assigns default values
        postfix: String = ""        ┆ for parameters
): String {
    val result = StringBuilder(prefix)

    for ((index, element) in this.withIndex())   ◁─────┐ "this" refers to the receiver
        if (index > 0) result.append(separator)          │ object: a collection of T.
        result.append(element)
    }

    result.append(postfix)
    return result.toString()
}

>>> val list = listOf(1, 2, 3)
>>> println(list.joinToString(separator = "; ",
...        prefix = "(", postfix = ")"))
(1; 2; 3)
```

You make it an extension to a collection of elements, and you provide default values for all the arguments. Now you can invoke `joinToString` like a member of a class:

```
>>> val list = arrayListOf(1, 2, 3)
>>> println(list.joinToString(" "))
1 2 3
```

Because extension functions are effectively syntactic sugar over static method calls, you can use a more specific type as a receiver type, not only a class. Let's say you want to have a `join` function that can be invoked only on collections of strings.

```
fun Collection<String>.join(
        separator: String = ", ",
        prefix: String = "",
        postfix: String = ""
) = joinToString(separator, prefix, postfix)

>>> println(listOf("one", "two", "eight").join(" "))
one two eight
```

Calling this function with a list of objects of another type won't work:

```
>>> listOf(1, 2, 8).join()
Error: Type mismatch: inferred type is List<Int> but Collection<String>
was expected.
```

The static nature of extensions also means that extension functions can't be overridden in subclasses. Let's look at an example.

3.3.4 No overriding for extension functions

Method overriding in Kotlin works as usual for member functions, but you can't override an extension function. Let's say you have two classes, `View` and its subclass `Button`, and the `Button` class overrides the `click` function from the superclass.

Listing 3.5 Overriding a member function

```
open class View {
    open fun click() = println("View clicked")
}

class Button: View() {                                    Button extends
    override fun click() = println("Button clicked")      View.
}
```

If you declare a variable of type `View`, you can store a value of type `Button` in that variable, because `Button` is a subtype of `View`. If you call a regular method, such as `click`, on this variable, and that method is overridden in the `Button` class, the overridden implementation from the `Button` class will be used:

```
>>> val view: View = Button()
>>> view.click()                    Determines the method to call based
Button clicked                      on the actual value of "view"
```

But it doesn't work that way for extensions, as shown in figure 3.2.

Extension functions aren't a part of the class; they're declared externally to it. Even though you can define extension functions with the same name and parameter types for a base class and its subclass, the function that's called depends on the declared static type of the variable, not on the runtime type of the value stored in that variable.

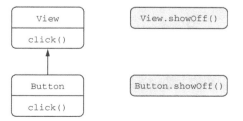

Figure 3.2 Extension functions are declared outside of the class.

The following example shows two showOff extension functions declared on the View and Button classes.

Listing 3.6   No overriding for extension functions

```
fun View.showOff() = println("I'm a view!")
fun Button.showOff() = println("I'm a button!")

>>> val view: View = Button()                          The extension function
>>> view.showOff()                          ⟵——|  is resolved statically.
I'm a view!
```

When you call showOff on a variable of type View, the corresponding extension is called, even though the actual type of the value is Button.

If you recall that an extension function is compiled to a static function in Java with the receiver as the first argument, this behavior should be clear to you, because Java chooses the function the same way:

```
/* Java */
>>> View view = new Button();                          showOff functions are declared
>>> ExtensionsKt.showOff(view);             ⟵——|  in the extensions.kt file.
I'm a view!
```

As you can see, overriding doesn't apply to extension functions: Kotlin resolves them statically.

> **NOTE**   If the class has a member function with the same signature as an extension function, the member function always takes precedence. You should keep this in mind when extending the API of classes: if you add a member function with the same signature as an extension function that a client of your class has defined, and they then recompile their code, it will change its meaning and start referring to the new member function.

We've discussed how to provide additional methods for external classes. Now let's see how to do the same with properties.

3.3.5   Extension properties

Extension properties provide a way to extend classes with APIs that can be accessed using the property syntax, rather than the function syntax. Even though they're called *properties*, they can't have any state, because there's no proper place to store it: it's not possible to add extra fields to existing instances of Java objects. But the shorter syntax is still sometimes handy.

In the previous section, you defined a function lastChar. Now let's convert it into a property.

Listing 3.7   Declaring an extension property

```
val String.lastChar: Char
    get() = get(length - 1)
```

You can see that, just as with functions, an extension property looks like a regular property with a receiver type added. The getter must always be defined, because there's no backing field and therefore no default getter implementation. Initializers aren't allowed for the same reason: there's nowhere to store the value specified as the initializer.

If you define the same property on a `StringBuilder`, you can make it a `var`, because the contents of a `StringBuilder` can be modified.

Listing 3.8   Declaring a mutable extension property

```
var StringBuilder.lastChar: Char
    get() = get(length - 1)                                  ◁──── Property getter
    set(value: Char) {
        this.setCharAt(length - 1, value)                    ◁──── Property setter
    }
```

You access extension properties exactly like member properties:

```
>>> println("Kotlin".lastChar)
n
>>> val sb = StringBuilder("Kotlin?")
>>> sb.lastChar = '!'
>>> println(sb)
Kotlin!
```

Note that when you need to access an extension property from Java, you should invoke its getter explicitly: `StringUtilKt.getLastChar("Java")`.

We've discussed the concept of extensions in general. Now let's return to the topic of collections and look at a few more library functions that help you handle them, as well as language features that come up in those functions.

3.4   Working with collections: varargs, infix calls, and library support

This section shows some of the functions from the Kotlin standard library for working with collections. Along the way, it describes a few related language features:

- The `vararg` keyword, which allows you to declare a function taking an arbitrary number of arguments
- An *infix* notation that lets you call some one-argument functions without ceremony
- *Destructuring declarations* that allow you to unpack a single composite value into multiple variables

3.4.1   Extending the Java Collections API

We started this chapter with the idea that collections in Kotlin are the same classes as in Java, but with an extended API. You saw examples of getting the last element in a list and finding the maximum in a collection of numbers:

```
>>> val strings: List<String> = listOf("first", "second", "fourteenth")
>>> strings.last()
fourteenth

>>> val numbers: Collection<Int> = setOf(1, 14, 2)
>>> numbers.max()
14
```

We were interested in how it works: why it's possible to do so many things with collections in Kotlin even though they're instances of the Java library classes. Now the answer should be clear: the last and max functions are declared as extension functions!

The last function is no more complex than lastChar for String, discussed in the previous section: it's an extension on the List class. For max, we show a simplified declaration (the real library function works not only for Int numbers, but for any comparable elements):

```
fun <T> List<T>.last(): T { /* returns the last element */ }
fun Collection<Int>.max(): Int { /* finding a maximum in a collection */ }
```

Many extension functions are declared in the Kotlin standard library, and we won't list all of them here. You may wonder about the best way to learn everything in the Kotlin standard library. You don't have to—any time you need to do something with a collection or any other object, the code completion in the IDE will show you all the possible functions available for that type of object. The list includes both regular methods and extension functions; you can choose the function you need. In addition to that, the standard library reference lists all the methods available for each library class—members as well as extensions.

At the beginning of the chapter, you also saw the functions for creating collections. A common trait of those functions is that they can be called with an arbitrary number of arguments. In the following section, you'll see the syntax for declaring such functions.

3.4.2 *Varargs: functions that accept an arbitrary number of arguments*

When you call a function to create a list, you can pass any number of arguments to it:

```
val list = listOf(2, 3, 5, 7, 11)
```

If you look up how this function is declared in the library, you'll find the following:

```
fun listOf<T>(vararg values: T): List<T> { ... }
```

You're probably familiar with Java's varargs: a feature that allows you to pass an arbitrary number of values to a method by packing them in an array. Kotlin's varargs are similar to those in Java, but the syntax is slightly different: instead of three dots after the type, Kotlin uses the vararg modifier on the parameter.

One other difference between Kotlin and Java is the syntax of calling the function when the arguments you need to pass are already packed in an array. In Java, you pass the array as is, whereas Kotlin requires you to explicitly unpack the array, so that every array element becomes a separate argument to the function being called. Technically, this feature is called using a *spread operator*, but in practice it's as simple as putting the `*` character before the corresponding argument:

```
fun main(args: Array<String>) {
    val list = listOf("args: ", *args)      ◁──┐ Spread operator unpacks
    println(list)                              │ the array contents
}
```

This example shows that the spread operator lets you combine the values from an array and some fixed values in a single call. This isn't supported in Java.

Now let's move on to maps. We'll briefly discuss another way to improve the readability of Kotlin function invocations: the *infix call*.

3.4.3 Working with pairs: infix calls and destructuring declarations

To create maps, you use the `mapOf` function:

```
val map = mapOf(1 to "one", 7 to "seven", 53 to "fifty-three")
```

This is a good time to provide another explanation we promised you at the beginning of the chapter. The word `to` in this line of code isn't a built-in construct, but rather a method invocation of a special kind, called an *infix call*.

In an infix call, the method name is placed immediately between the target object name and the parameter, with no extra separators. The following two calls are equivalent:

```
1.to("one")      ◁──┐ Calls the "to" function the regular way
1 to "one"          ◁──┐ Calls the "to" function using an infix notation
```

Infix calls can be used with regular methods and extension functions that have one required parameter. To allow a function to be called using the infix notation, you need to mark it with the `infix` modifier. Here's a simplified version of the declaration of the `to` function:

```
infix fun Any.to(other: Any) = Pair(this, other)
```

The `to` function returns an instance of `Pair`, which is a Kotlin standard library class that, unsurprisingly, represents a pair of elements. The actual declarations of `Pair` and `to` use generics, but we're omitting them here to keep things simple.

Note that you can initialize two variables with the contents of a `Pair` directly:

```
val (number, name) = 1 to "one"
```

This feature is called a *destructuring declaration*. Figure 3.3 illustrates how it works with pairs.

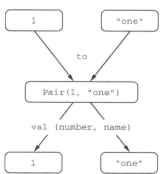

Figure 3.3   You create a pair using the `to` function and unpack it with a destructuring declaration.

The destructuring declaration feature isn't limited to pairs. For example, you can also initialize two variables, `key` and `value`, with the contents of a map entry.

This also works with loops, as you've seen in the implementation of `joinTo-String`, which uses the `withIndex` function:

```
for ((index, element) in collection.withIndex()) {
    println("$index: $element")
}
```

Section 7.4 will describe the general rules for destructuring an expression and using it to initialize several variables.

The `to` function is an extension function. You can create a pair of any elements, which means it's an extension to a generic receiver: you can write `1 to "one"`, `"one"` to `1`, `list to list.size()`, and so on. Let's look at the declaration of the `mapOf` function:

```
fun <K, V> mapOf(vararg values: Pair<K, V>): Map<K, V>
```

Like `listOf`, `mapOf` accepts a variable number of arguments, but this time they should be pairs of keys and values.

Even though the creation of a new map may look like a special construct in Kotlin, it's a regular function with a concise syntax. Next, let's discuss how extensions simplify dealing with strings and regular expressions.

3.5   *Working with strings and regular expressions*

Kotlin strings are exactly the same things as Java strings. You can pass a string created in Kotlin code to any Java method, and you can use any Kotlin standard library methods on strings that you receive from Java code. No conversion is involved, and no additional wrapper objects are created.

Kotlin makes working with standard Java strings more enjoyable by providing a bunch of useful extension functions. Also, it hides some confusing methods, adding extensions that are clearer. As our first example of the API differences, let's look at how Kotlin handles splitting strings.

3.5.1   *Splitting strings*

You're probably familiar with the `split` method on `String`. Everyone uses it, but sometimes people complain about it on Stack Overflow (http://stackoverflow.com): "The `split` method in Java doesn't work with a dot." It's a common trap to write `"12.345-6.A".split(".")` and to expect an array `[12, 345-6, A]` as a result. But Java's `split` method returns an empty array! That happens because it takes a regular expression as a parameter, and it splits a string into several strings according to the expression. Here, the dot (`.`) is a regular expression that denotes any character.

Kotlin hides the confusing method and provides as replacements several overloaded extensions named `split` that have different arguments. The one that takes a regular expression requires a value of `Regex` type, not `String`. This ensures that it's always clear whether a string passed to a method is interpreted as plain text or a regular expression.

Here's how you'd split the string with either a dot or a dash:

```
>>> println("12.345-6.A".split("\\.|-".toRegex()))
[12, 345, 6, A]
```
← Creates a regular expression explicitly

Kotlin uses exactly the same regular expression syntax as in Java. The pattern here matches a dot (we escaped it to indicate that we mean a literal character, not a wildcard) or a dash. The APIs for working with regular expressions are also similar to the standard Java library APIs, but they're more idiomatic. For instance, in Kotlin you use an extension function toRegex to convert a string into a regular expression.

But for such a simple case, you don't need to use regular expressions. The other overload of the split extension function in Kotlin takes an arbitrary number of delimiters as plain-text strings:

```
>>> println("12.345-6.A".split(".", "-"))
[12, 345, 6, A]
```
← Specifies several delimiters

Note that you can specify character arguments instead and write "12.345-6.A" .split('.', '-'), which will lead to the same result. This method replaces the similar Java method that can take only one character as a delimiter.

3.5.2 *Regular expressions and triple-quoted strings*

Let's look at another example with two different implementations: the first one will use extensions on String, and the second will work with regular expressions. Your task will be to parse a file's full path name into its components: a directory, a filename, and an extension. The Kotlin standard library contains functions to get the substring

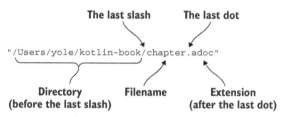

Figure 3.4 Splitting a path into a directory, a filename, and a file extension by using the substring-BeforeLast and substringAfterLast functions

before (or after) the first (or the last) occurrence of the given delimiter. Here's how you can use them to solve this task (also see figure 3.4).

Listing 3.9 Using String extensions for parsing paths

```
fun parsePath(path: String) {
    val directory = path.substringBeforeLast("/")
    val fullName = path.substringAfterLast("/")

    val fileName = fullName.substringBeforeLast(".")
    val extension = fullName.substringAfterLast(".")

    println("Dir: $directory, name: $fileName, ext: $extension")
```

```
}
>>> parsePath("/Users/yole/kotlin-book/chapter.adoc")
Dir: /Users/yole/kotlin-book, name: chapter, ext: adoc
```

The substring before the last slash symbol of the file `path` is the path to an enclosing directory, the substring after the last dot is a file extension, and the filename goes between them.

Kotlin makes it easier to parse strings without resorting to regular expressions, which are powerful but also sometimes hard to understand after they've been written. If you do want to use regular expressions, the Kotlin standard library can help. Here's how the same task can be done using regular expressions:

> **Listing 3.10 Using regular expressions for parsing paths**

```
fun parsePath(path: String) {
    val regex = """(.+)/(.+)\.(.+)""".toRegex()
    val matchResult = regex.matchEntire(path)
    if (matchResult != null) {
        val (directory, filename, extension) = matchResult.destructured
        println("Dir: $directory, name: $filename, ext: $extension")
    }
}
```

In this example, the regular expression is written in a *triple-quoted string*. In such a string, you don't need to escape any characters, including the backslash, so you can encode the dot symbol with `\.` rather than `\\.` as you'd write in an ordinary string literal (see figure 3.5). This regular expression divides a path into three groups separated by a slash and a dot. The pattern `.` matches any character from the beginning, so the first group `(.+)` contains the substring before the last slash. This substring includes all the previous slashes,

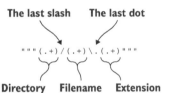

Figure 3.5 The regular expression for splitting a path into a directory, a filename, and a file extension

because they match the pattern "any character". Similarly, the second group contains the substring before the last dot, and the third group contains the remaining part.

Now let's discuss the implementation of the `parsePath` function from the previous example. You create a regular expression and match it against an input path. If the match is successful (the result isn't `null`), you assign the value of its `destructured` property to the corresponding variables. This is the same syntax used when you initialized two variables with a `Pair`; section 7.4 will cover the details.

3.5.3 *Multiline triple-quoted strings*

The purpose of triple-quoted strings is not only to avoid escaping characters. Such a string literal can contain any characters, including line breaks. That gives you an easy way to embed in your programs text containing line breaks. As an example, let's draw some ASCII art:

```
val kotlinLogo = """| //
                   .|//
                   .|/ \"""
>>> println(kotlinLogo.trimMargin("."))
| //
|//
|/ \
```

The multiline string contains all the characters between the triple quotes, including indents used to format the code. If you want a better representation of such a string, you can trim the indentation (in other words, the left margin). To do that, you add a prefix to the string content, marking the end of the margin, and then call `trim-Margin` to delete the prefix and the preceding whitespace in each line. This example uses the dot as such a prefix.

A triple-quoted string can contain line breaks, but you can't use special characters like \n. On the other hand, you don't have to escape \, so the Windows-style path `"C:\\Users\\yole\\kotlin-book"` can be written as `"""C:\Users\yole\ kotlin-book"""`.

You can also use string templates in multiline strings. Because multiline strings don't support escape sequences, you have to use an embedded expression if you need to use a literal dollar sign in the contents of your string. It looks like this: `val price = """${'$'}99.9"""`.

One of the areas where multiline strings can be useful in your programs (besides games that use ASCII art) is tests. In tests, it's fairly common to execute an operation that produces multiline text (for example, a web page fragment) and to compare the result with the expected output. Multiline strings give you a perfect solution for including the expected output as part of your test. No need for clumsy escaping or loading the text from external files—just put in some quotation marks and place the expected HTML or other output between them. And for better formatting, use the aforementioned `trimMargin` function, which is another example of an extension function.

> **NOTE** You can now see that extension functions are a powerful way to extend the APIs of existing libraries and to adapt them to the idioms of your new language—something called the Pimp My Library pattern.[1] And indeed, a large portion of the Kotlin standard library is made up of extension functions for standard Java classes. The Anko library (https://github.com/kotlin/anko), also built by JetBrains, provides extension functions that make the Android API more Kotlin-friendly. You can also find many community-developed libraries that provide Kotlin-friendly wrappers around major third-party libraries such as Spring.

Now that you can see how Kotlin gives you better APIs for the libraries you use, let's turn our attention back to your code. You'll see some new uses for extension functions, and we'll also discuss a new concept: *local functions*.

---

[1] Martin Odersky, "Pimp My Library," *Artima Developer*, October 9, 2006, http://mng.bz/86Qh.

3.6   *Making your code tidy: local functions and extensions*

Many developers believe that one of the most important qualities of good code is the lack of duplication. There's even a special name for this principle: Don't Repeat Yourself (DRY). But when you write in Java, following this principle isn't always trivial. In many cases, it's possible to use the Extract Method refactoring feature of your IDE to break longer methods into smaller chunks, and then to reuse those chunks. But this can make code more difficult to understand, because you end up with a class with many small methods and no clear relationship between them. You can go even further and group the extracted methods into an inner class, which lets you maintain the structure, but this approach requires a significant amount of boilerplate.

Kotlin gives you a cleaner solution: you can nest the functions you've extracted in the containing function. This way, you have the structure you need without any extra syntactic overhead.

Let's see how to use local functions to fix a fairly common case of code duplication. In the following listing, a function saves a user to a database, and you need to make sure the user object contains valid data.

> **Listing 3.11   A function with repetitive code**

```
class User(val id: Int, val name: String, val address: String)

fun saveUser(user: User) {
    if (user.name.isEmpty()) {
        throw IllegalArgumentException(
            "Can't save user ${user.id}: empty Name")
    }

    if (user.address.isEmpty()) {
        throw IllegalArgumentException(
            "Can't save user ${user.id}: empty Address")
    }

    // Save user to the database
}

>>> saveUser(User(1, "", ""))
java.lang.IllegalArgumentException: Can't save user 1: empty Name
```

Field validation is duplicated.

The amount of duplicated code here is fairly small, and you probably won't want to have a full-blown method in your class that handles one special case of validating a user. But if you put the validation code into a local function, you can get rid of the duplication and still maintain a clear code structure. Here's how it works.

> **Listing 3.12   Extracting a local function to avoid repetition**

```
class User(val id: Int, val name: String, val address: String)

fun saveUser(user: User) {
```

```
fun validate(user: User,                          ◁──┐ Declares a local function
         value: String,                               │ to validate any field
         fieldName: String) {
    if (value.isEmpty()) {
        throw IllegalArgumentException(
            "Can't save user ${user.id}: empty $fieldName")
    }
}

validate(user, user.name, "Name")                  │ Calls the local function to
validate(user, user.address, "Address")            │ validate the specific fields

// Save user to the database
}
```

This looks better. The validation logic isn't duplicated, and you can easily add more
validations if you need to add other fields to User as the project evolves. But having to
pass the User object to the validation function is somewhat ugly. The good news is
that it's entirely unnecessary, because local functions have access to all parameters and
variables of the enclosing function. Let's take advantage of that and get rid of the
extra User parameter.

Listing 3.13   Accessing outer function parameters in a local function

```
class User(val id: Int, val name: String, val address: String)

fun saveUser(user: User) {
    fun validate(value: String, fieldName: String) {    ◁──┐ Now you don't duplicate
        if (value.isEmpty()) {                               │ the user parameter of the
            throw IllegalArgumentException(                  │ saveUser function.
                "Can't save user ${user.id}: " +    ◁──┐
                    "empty $fieldName")                  │ You can access parameters of
        }                                                │ the outer function directly.
    }

    validate(user.name, "Name")
    validate(user.address, "Address")

    // Save user to the database
}
```

To improve this example even further, you can move the validation logic into an
extension function of the User class.

Listing 3.14   Extracting the logic into an extension function

```
class User(val id: Int, val name: String, val address: String)

fun User.validateBeforeSave() {
    fun validate(value: String, fieldName: String) {
        if (value.isEmpty()) {
            throw IllegalArgumentException(
                "Can't save user $id: empty $fieldName")    ◁──┐ You can access properties
        }                                                        │ of User directly.
    }
}
```

```
        validate(name, "Name")
        validate(address, "Address")
    }

    fun saveUser(user: User) {
        user.validateBeforeSave()                    ◁─────┐  Calls the extension
                                                          │  function
        // Save user to the database
    }
```

Extracting a piece of code into an extension function turns out to be surprisingly useful. Even though User is a part of your codebase and not a library class, you don't want to put this logic into a method of User, because it's not relevant to any other places where User is used. If you follow this approach the API of the class contains only the essential methods used everywhere, so the class remains small and easy to wrap your head around. On the other hand, functions that primarily deal with a single object and don't need access to its private data can access its members without extra qualification, as in listing 3.14.

Extension functions can also be declared as local functions, so you could go even further and put User.validateBeforeSave as a local function in saveUser. But deeply nested local functions are usually fairly hard to read; so, as a general rule, we don't recommend using more than one level of nesting.

Having looked at all the cool things you can do with functions, in the next chapter we'll look at what you can do with classes.

3.7   *Summary*

- Kotlin doesn't define its own collection classes and instead enhances the Java collection classes with a richer API.
- Defining default values for function parameters greatly reduces the need to define overloaded functions, and the named-argument syntax makes calls to functions with many parameters much more readable.
- Functions and properties can be declared directly in a file, not just as members of a class, allowing for a more flexible code structure.
- Extension functions and properties let you extend the API of any class, including classes defined in external libraries, without modifying its source code and with no runtime overhead.
- Infix calls provide a clean syntax for calling operator-like methods with a single argument.
- Kotlin provides a large number of convenient string-handling functions for both regular expressions and plain strings.
- Triple-quoted strings provide a clean way to write expressions that would require a lot of noisy escaping and string concatenation in Java.
- Local functions help you structure your code more cleanly and eliminate duplication.

Classes, objects, and interfaces

This chapter gives you a deeper understanding of working with classes in Kotlin. In chapter 2, you saw the basic syntax for declaring a class. You know how to declare methods and properties, use simple primary constructors (aren't they nice?), and work with enums. But there's more to see.

Kotlin's classes and interfaces differ a bit from their Java counterparts: for example, interfaces can contain property declarations. Unlike in Java, Kotlin's declarations are `final` and `public` by default. In addition, nested classes aren't inner by default: they don't contain an implicit reference to their outer class.

For constructors, the short primary constructor syntax works great for the majority of cases, but there's also the full syntax that lets you declare constructors with nontrivial initialization logic. The same works for properties: the concise syntax is nice, but you can easily define your own implementations of accessors.

The Kotlin compiler can generate useful methods to avoid verbosity. Declaring a class as a data class instructs the compiler to generate several standard methods for this class. You can also avoid writing delegating methods by hand, because the delegation pattern is supported natively in Kotlin.

This chapter also describes a new object keyword that declares a class and also creates an instance of the class. The keyword is used to express singleton objects, companion objects, and object expressions (analogous to Java anonymous classes). Let's start by talking about classes and interfaces and the subtleties of defining class hierarchies in Kotlin.

4.1   Defining class hierarchies

This section discusses defining class hierarchies in Kotlin as compared to Java. We'll look at Kotlin's visibility and access modifiers, which are similar to Java's but with some different defaults. You'll also learn about the new sealed modifier, which restricts the possible subclasses of a class.

4.1.1   Interfaces in Kotlin

We'll begin with a look at defining and implementing interfaces. Kotlin interfaces are similar to those of Java 8: they can contain definitions of abstract methods as well as implementations of non-abstract methods (similar to the Java 8 default methods), but they can't contain any state.

To declare an interface in Kotlin, use the interface keyword instead of class.

Listing 4.1   Declaring a simple interface

```
interface Clickable {
    fun click()
}
```

This declares an interface with a single abstract method named click. All non-abstract classes implementing the interface need to provide an implementation of this method. Here's how you implement the interface.

Listing 4.2   Implementing a simple interface

```
class Button : Clickable {
    override fun click() = println("I was clicked")
}
```

```
>>> Button().click()
I was clicked
```

Kotlin uses the colon after the class name to replace both the extends and implements keywords used in Java. As in Java, a class can implement as many interfaces as it wants, but it can extend only one class.

The `override` modifier, similar to the `@Override` annotation in Java, is used to mark methods and properties that override those from the superclass or interface. Unlike Java, *using the `override` modifier is mandatory* in Kotlin. This saves you from accidentally overriding a method if it's added after you wrote your implementation; your code won't compile unless you explicitly mark the method as `override` or rename it.

An interface method can have a default implementation. Unlike Java 8, which requires you to mark such implementations with the `default` keyword, Kotlin has no special annotation for such methods: you just provide a method body. Let's change the `Clickable` interface by adding a method with a default implementation.

Listing 4.3 Defining a method with a body in an interface

```
interface Clickable {
    fun click()
    fun showOff() = println("I'm clickable!")
}
```

Regular method declaration →

← Method with a default implementation

If you implement this interface, you need to provide an implementation for `click`. You can redefine the behavior of the `showOff` method, or you can omit it if you're fine with the default behavior.

Let's suppose now that another interface also defines a `showOff` method and has the following implementation for it.

Listing 4.4 Defining another interface implementing the same method

```
interface Focusable {
    fun setFocus(b: Boolean) =
        println("I ${if (b) "got" else "lost"} focus.")

    fun showOff() = println("I'm focusable!")
}
```

What happens if you need to implement both interfaces in your class? Each of them contains a `showOff` method with a default implementation; which implementation wins? Neither one wins. Instead, you get the following compiler error if you don't implement `showOff` explicitly:

```
The class 'Button' must
override public open fun showOff() because it inherits
many implementations of it.
```

The Kotlin compiler forces you to provide your own implementation.

Listing 4.5 Invoking an inherited interface method implementation

```
class Button : Clickable, Focusable {
    override fun click() = println("I was clicked")
```

```
override fun showOff() {
    super<Clickable>.showOff()
    super<Focusable>.showOff()
}
}
```

← **You must provide an explicit implementation if more than one implementation for the same member is inherited.**

"super" qualified by the supertype name in angle brackets specifies the parent whose method you want to call.

The Button class now implements two interfaces. You implement showOff() by calling both implementations that you inherited from supertypes. To invoke an inherited implementation, you use the same keyword as in Java: super. But the syntax for selecting a specific implementation is different. Whereas in Java you can put the base type name before the super keyword, as in Clickable.super.showOff(), in Kotlin you put the base type name in angle brackets: super<Clickable>.showOff().

If you only need to invoke one inherited implementation, you can write this:

```
override fun showOff() = super<Clickable>.showOff()
```

You can create an instance of this class and verify that all the inherited methods can be called.

```
fun main(args: Array<String>) {
    val button = Button()
    button.showOff()
    button.setFocus(true)
    button.click()
}
```

I got focus. →

→ **I'm clickable!**
I'm focusable!

← **I was clicked.**

The implementation of setFocus is declared in the Focusable interface and is automatically inherited in the Button class.

> **Implementing interfaces with method bodies in Java**
>
> Kotlin 1.0 has been designed to target Java 6, which doesn't support default methods in interfaces. Therefore, it compiles each interface with default methods to a combination of a regular interface and a class containing the method bodies as static methods. The interface contains only declarations, and the class contains all the implementations as static methods. Therefore, if you need to implement such an interface in a Java class, you have to define your own implementations of all methods, including those that have method bodies in Kotlin.

Now that you've seen how Kotlin allows you to implement methods defined in interfaces, let's look at the second half of that story: overriding members defined in base classes.

4.1.2   Open, final, and abstract modifiers: final by default

As you know, Java allows you to create subclasses of any class, and to override any method, unless it has been explicitly marked with the final keyword. This is often convenient, but it's also problematic.

The so-called *fragile base class* problem occurs when modifications of a base class can cause incorrect behavior of subclasses because the changed code of the base class no longer matches the assumptions in its subclasses. If the class doesn't provide exact rules for how it should be subclassed (which methods are supposed to be overridden and how), the clients are at risk of overriding the methods in a way the author of the base class didn't expect. Because it's impossible to analyze all the subclasses, the base class is "fragile" in the sense that any change in it may lead to unexpected changes of behavior in subclasses.

To protect against this problem, *Effective Java* by Joshua Bloch (Addison-Wesley, 2008), one of the best-known books on good Java programming style, recommends that you "design and document for inheritance or else prohibit it." This means all classes and methods that aren't specifically intended to be overridden in subclasses ought to be explicitly marked as `final`.

Kotlin follows the same philosophy. Whereas Java's classes and methods are open by default, Kotlin's are `final` by default.

If you want to allow the creation of subclasses of a class, you need to mark the class with the `open` modifier. In addition, you need to add the `open` modifier to every property or method that can be overridden.

Listing 4.6   Declaring an open class with an open method

```
open class RichButton : Clickable {          This class is open: others
                                             can inherit from it.

    fun disable() {}          This function is final: you can't
                              override it in a subclass.

    open fun animate() {}                    This function is open: you may
                                             override it in a subclass.

    override fun click() {}          This function overrides an open
}                                    function and is open as well.
```

Note that if you override a member of a base class or interface, the overriding member will also be `open` by default. If you want to change this and forbid the subclasses of your class from overriding your implementation, you can explicitly mark the overriding member as `final`.

Listing 4.7   Forbidding an override

```
open class RichButton : Clickable {
    final override fun click() {}          "final" isn't redundant here
}                                          because "override" without
                                           "final" implies being open.
```

Open classes and smart casts

One significant benefit of classes that are `final` by default is that they enable smart casts in a larger variety of scenarios. As we mentioned in section 2.3.5, smart casts work only for variables that couldn't have changed after the type check. For a class, this means smart casts can only be used with a class property that is a `val` and that doesn't have a custom accessor. This requirement means the property has to be `final`, because otherwise a subclass could override the property and define a custom accessor, breaking the key requirement of smart casts. Because properties are `final` by default, you can use smart casts with most properties without thinking about it explicitly, which improves the expressiveness of your code.

In Kotlin, as in Java, you may declare a class `abstract`, and such classes can't be instantiated. An abstract class usually contains abstract members that don't have implementations and must be overridden in subclasses. Abstract members are always open, so you don't need to use an explicit `open` modifier. Here's an example.

Listing 4.8 Declaring an abstract class

```
abstract class Animated {                  This class is abstract: you
                                           can't create an instance of it.
    abstract fun animate()

    open fun stopAnimating() {
    }                                      Non-abstract functions in abstract
                                           classes aren't open by default but
    fun animateTwice() {                   can be marked as open.
    }
}
```

This function is abstract: it doesn't have an implementation and must be overridden in subclasses.

Table 4.1 lists the access modifiers in Kotlin. The comments in the table are applicable to modifiers in classes; in interfaces, you don't use `final`, `open`, or `abstract`. A member in an interface is always open; you can't declare it as `final`. It's abstract if it has no body, but the keyword isn't required.

Table 4.1 The meaning of access modifiers in a class

Modifier	Corresponding member	Comments
final	Can't be overridden	Used by default for class members
open	Can be overridden	Should be specified explicitly
abstract	Must be overridden	Can be used only in abstract classes; abstract members can't have an implementation
override	Overrides a member in a superclass or interface	Overridden member is open by default, if not marked `final`

Having discussed the modifiers that control inheritance, let's now move on to another type of modifiers: visibility modifiers.

4.1.3 *Visibility modifiers: public by default*

Visibility modifiers help to control access to declarations in your code base. By restricting the visibility of a class's implementation details, you ensure that you can change them without the risk of breaking code that depends on the class.

Basically, visibility modifiers in Kotlin are similar to those in Java. You have the same `public`, `protected`, and `private` modifiers. But the default visibility is different: if you omit a modifier, the declaration becomes `public`.

The default visibility in Java, package-private, isn't present in Kotlin. Kotlin uses packages only as a way of organizing code in namespaces; it doesn't use them for visibility control.

As an alternative, Kotlin offers a new visibility modifier, `internal`, which means "visible inside a module." A *module* is a set of Kotlin files compiled together. It may be an IntelliJ IDEA module, an Eclipse project, a Maven or Gradle project, or a set of files compiled with an invocation of the Ant task.

The advantage of `internal` visibility is that it provides real encapsulation for the implementation details of your module. With Java, the encapsulation can be easily broken, because external code can define classes in the same packages used by your code and thus get access to your package-private declarations.

Another difference is that Kotlin allows the use of `private` visibility for top-level declarations, including classes, functions, and properties. Such declarations are visible only in the file where they are declared. This is another useful way to hide the implementation details of a subsystem. Table 4.2 summarizes all the visibility modifiers.

Table 4.2 Kotlin visibility modifiers

Modifier	Class member	Top-level declaration
`public` (default)	Visible everywhere	Visible everywhere
`internal`	Visible in a module	Visible in a module
`protected`	Visible in subclasses	—
`private`	Visible in a class	Visible in a file

Let's look at an example. Every line in the `giveSpeech` function tries to violate the visibility rules. It compiles with an error.

```
internal open class TalkativeButton : Focusable {
    private fun yell() = println("Hey!")
    protected fun whisper() = println("Let's talk!")
}

fun TalkativeButton.giveSpeech() {
```

Error: "public" member exposes its "internal" receiver type TalkativeButton

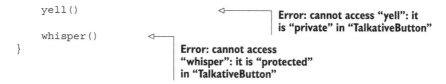

```
    yell()
    whisper()
}
```

Error: cannot access "yell": it is "private" in "TalkativeButton"

Error: cannot access "whisper": it is "protected" in "TalkativeButton"

Kotlin forbids you to reference the less-visible type `TalkativeButton` (`internal`, in this case) from the `public` function `giveSpeech`. This is a case of a general rule that requires all types used in the list of base types and type parameters of a class, or the signature of a method, to be as visible as the class or method itself. This rule ensures that you always have access to all types you might need to invoke the function or extend a class. To solve the problem, you can either make the function `internal` or make the class `public`.

Note the difference in behavior for the `protected` modifier in Java and in Kotlin. In Java, you can access a `protected` member from the same package, but Kotlin doesn't allow that. In Kotlin, visibility rules are simple, and a `protected` member is *only* visible in the class and its subclasses. Also note that extension functions of a class don't get access to its `private` or `protected` members.

Kotlin's visibility modifiers and Java

`public`, `protected`, and `private` modifiers in Kotlin are preserved when compiling to Java bytecode. You use such Kotlin declarations from Java code as if they were declared with the same visibility in Java. The only exception is a `private` class: it's compiled to a package-private declaration under the hood (you can't make a class `private` in Java).

But, you may ask, what happens with the `internal` modifier? There's no direct analogue in Java. Package-private visibility is a totally different thing: a module usually consists of several packages, and different modules may contain declarations from the same package. Thus an `internal` modifier becomes `public` in the bytecode.

This correspondence between Kotlin declarations and their Java analogues (or their bytecode representation) explains why sometimes you can access something from Java code that you can't access from Kotlin. For instance, you can access an `internal` class or a top-level declaration from Java code in another module, or a `protected` member from Java code in the same package (similar to how you do that in Java).

But note that the names of `internal` members of a class are mangled. Technically, `internal` members can be used from Java, but they look ugly in the Java code. That helps avoid unexpected clashes in overrides when you extend a class from another module, and it prevents you from accidentally using `internal` classes.

One more difference in visibility rules between Kotlin and Java is that an outer class doesn't see `private` members of its inner (or nested) classes in Kotlin. Let's discuss inner and nested classes in Kotlin next and look at an example.

4.1.4   *Inner and nested classes: nested by default*

As in Java, in Kotlin you can declare a class in another class. Doing so can be useful for encapsulating a helper class or placing the code closer to where it's used. The difference is that Kotlin nested classes don't have access to the outer class instance, unless you specifically request that. Let's look at an example showing why this is important.

Imagine you want to define a `View` element, the state of which can be serialized. It may not be easy to serialize a view, but you can copy all the necessary data to another helper class. You declare the `State` interface that implements `Serializable`. The `View` interface declares `getCurrentState` and `restoreState` methods that can be used to save the state of a view.

> **Listing 4.9   Declaring a view with serializable state**

```
interface State: Serializable

interface View {
    fun getCurrentState(): State
    fun restoreState(state: State) {}
}
```

It's handy to define a class that saves a button state in the `Button` class. Let's see how it can be done in Java (the similar Kotlin code will be shown in a moment).

> **Listing 4.10   Implementing `View` in Java with an inner class**

```
/* Java */
public class Button implements View {
    @Override
    public State getCurrentState() {
        return new ButtonState();
    }

    @Override
    public void restoreState(State state) { /*...*/ }

    public class ButtonState implements State { /*...*/ }
}
```

You define the `ButtonState` class that implements the `State` interface and holds specific information for `Button`. In the `getCurrentState` method, you create a new instance of this class. In a real case, you'd initialize `ButtonState` with all necessary data.

What's wrong with this code? Why do you get a `java.io.NotSerializable-Exception: Button` exception if you try to serialize the state of the declared button? That may look strange at first: the variable you serialize is `state` of the `ButtonState` type, not the `Button` type.

Everything becomes clear when you recall that in Java, when you declare a class in another class, it becomes an inner class by default. The `ButtonState` class in the example implicitly stores a reference to its outer `Button` class. That explains why

ButtonState can't be serialized: Button isn't serializable, and the reference to it breaks the serialization of ButtonState.

To fix this problem, you need to declare the ButtonState class as static. Declaring a nested class as static removes the implicit reference from that class to its enclosing class.

In Kotlin, the default behavior of inner classes is the opposite of what we've just described, as shown next.

Listing 4.11   Implementing View in Kotlin with a nested class

```
class Button : View {
    override fun getCurrentState(): State = ButtonState()

    override fun restoreState(state: State) { /*...*/ }          ┐ This class is an analogue of
                                                                  ┘ a static nested class in Java.
    class ButtonState : State { /*...*/ }       ◄─┘
}
```

A nested class in Kotlin with no explicit modifiers is the same as a static nested class in Java. To turn it into an inner class so that it contains a reference to an outer class, you use the inner modifier. Table 4.3 describes the differences in this behavior between Java and Kotlin; and the difference between nested and inner classes is illustrated in figure 4.1.

Table 4.3   Correspondence between nested and inner classes in Java and Kotlin

Class A declared within another class B	In Java	In Kotlin
Nested class (doesn't store a reference to an outer class)	static class A	class A
Inner class (stores a reference to an outer class)	class A	inner class A

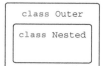
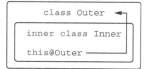

Figure 4.1   Nested classes don't reference their outer class, whereas inner classes do.

The syntax to reference an instance of an outer class in Kotlin also differs from Java. You write this@Outer to access the Outer class from the Inner class:

```
class Outer {
    inner class Inner {
        fun getOuterReference(): Outer = this@Outer
    }
}
```

You've learned the difference between inner and nested classes in Java and in Kotlin. Now let's discuss another use case when nested classes may be useful in Kotlin: creating a hierarchy containing a limited number of classes.

4.1.5 *Sealed classes: defining restricted class hierarchies*

Recall the expression hierarchy example from section 2.3.5. The superclass `Expr` has two subclasses: `Num`, which represents a number; and `Sum`, which represents a sum of two expressions. It's convenient to handle all the possible subclasses in a `when` expression. But you have to provide the `else` branch to specify what should happen if none of the other branches match:

Listing 4.12 Expressions as interface implementations

```
interface Expr
class Num(val value: Int) : Expr
class Sum(val left: Expr, val right: Expr) : Expr

fun eval(e: Expr): Int =
    when (e) {
        is Num -> e.value
        is Sum -> eval(e.right) + eval(e.left)
        else ->                                              You have to check
            throw IllegalArgumentException("Unknown expression")   the "else" branch.
    }
```

When you evaluate an expression using the `when` construct, the Kotlin compiler forces you to check for the default option. In this example, you can't return something meaningful, so you throw an exception.

Always having to add a default branch isn't convenient. What's more, if you add a new subclass, the compiler won't detect that something has changed. If you forget to add a new branch, the default one will be chosen, which can lead to subtle bugs.

Kotlin provides a solution to this problem: `sealed` classes. You mark a superclass with the `sealed` modifier, and that restricts the possibility of creating subclasses. All the direct subclasses must be nested in the superclass:

Listing 4.13 Expressions as sealed classes

```
sealed class Expr {                                     Mark a base class as sealed ...
    class Num(val value: Int) : Expr()
    class Sum(val left: Expr, val right: Expr) : Expr()    ... and list all the
}                                                          possible subclasses
                                                           as nested classes.
fun eval(e: Expr): Int =
    when (e) {                                          The "when" expression
        is Expr.Num -> e.value                          covers all possible cases, so
        is Expr.Sum -> eval(e.right) + eval(e.left)     no "else" branch is needed.
    }
```

If you handle all subclasses of a sealed class in a when expression, you don't need to provide the default branch. Note that the sealed modifier implies that the class is open; you don't need an explicit open modifier. The behavior of sealed classes is illustrated in figure 4.2.

Figure 4.2   Sealed classes can't have inheritors defined outside of the class.

When you use when with sealed classes and add a new subclass, the when expression returning a value fails to compile, which points you to the code that must be changed.

Under the hood, the Expr class has a private constructor, which can be called only inside the class. You can't declare a sealed interface. Why? If you could, the Kotlin compiler wouldn't be able to guarantee that someone couldn't implement this interface in the Java code.

> **NOTE**   In Kotlin 1.0, the sealed functionality is rather restricted. For instance, all the subclasses must be nested, and a subclass can't be made a data class (data classes are covered later in this chapter). Kotlin 1.1 relaxes the restrictions and lets you define subclasses of sealed classes anywhere in the same file.

As you'll recall, in Kotlin, you use a colon both to extend a class and to implement an interface. Let's take a closer look at a subclass declaration:

```
class Num(val value: Int) : Expr()
```

This simple example should be clear, except for the meaning of the parentheses after the class name in Expr(). We'll talk about them in the next section, which covers initializing classes in Kotlin.

4.2   *Declaring a class with nontrivial constructors or properties*

In Java, as you know, a class can declare one or more constructors. Kotlin is similar, with one additional change: it makes a distinction between a *primary* constructor (which is usually the main, concise way to initialize a class and is declared outside of the class body) and a *secondary* constructor (which is declared in the class body). It also allows you to put additional initialization logic in *initializer blocks*. First we'll look at the syntax of declaring the primary constructor and initializer blocks, and then we'll explain how to declare several constructors. After that, we'll talk more about properties.

4.2.1 Initializing classes: primary constructor and initializer blocks

In chapter 2, you saw how to declare a simple class:

```
class User(val nickname: String)
```

Normally, all the declarations in a class go inside curly braces. You may wonder why this class has no curly braces and instead has only a declaration in parentheses. This block of code surrounded by parentheses is called a *primary constructor.* It serves two purposes: specifying constructor parameters and defining properties that are initialized by those parameters. Let's unpack what happens here and look at the most explicit code you can write that does the same thing:

```
class User constructor(_nickname: String) {      ◄──┐ Primary constructor
    val nickname: String                            │ with one parameter

    init {                ◄─── Initializer block
        nickname = _nickname
    }
}
```

In this example, you see two new Kotlin keywords: `constructor` and `init`. The `constructor` keyword begins the declaration of a primary or secondary constructor. The `init` keyword introduces an *initializer block.* Such blocks contain initialization code that's executed when the class is created, and are intended to be used together with primary constructors. Because the primary constructor has a constrained syntax, it can't contain the initialization code; that's why you have initializer blocks. If you want to, you can declare several initializer blocks in one class.

The underscore in the constructor parameter `_nickname` serves to distinguish the name of the property from the name of the constructor parameter. An alternative possibility is to use the same name and write `this` to remove the ambiguity, as is commonly done in Java: `this.nickname = nickname`.

In this example, you don't need to place the initialization code in the initializer block, because it can be combined with the declaration of the `nickname` property. You can also omit the `constructor` keyword if there are no annotations or visibility modifiers on the primary constructor. If you apply those changes, you get the following:

```
class User(_nickname: String) {      ◄──┐ Primary constructor
    val nickname = _nickname             │ with one parameter
}                                    ◄──┐ The property is initialized
                                        │ with the parameter.
```

This is another way to declare the same class. Note how you can refer to primary constructor parameters in property initializers and in initializer blocks.

The two previous examples declared the property by using the `val` keyword in the body of the class. If the property is initialized with the corresponding constructor parameter, the code can be simplified by adding the `val` keyword before the parameter. This replaces the property definition in the class:

```
class User(val nickname: String)
```
⟵─┐ **"val" means the corresponding property is generated for the constructor parameter.**

All the declarations of the `User` class are equivalent, but the last one uses the most concise syntax.

You can declare default values for constructor parameters just as you can for function parameters:

```
class User(val nickname: String,
           val isSubscribed: Boolean = true)
```
⟵─┘ **Provides a default value for the constructor parameter**

To create an instance of a class, you call the constructor directly, without the `new` keyword:

```
>>> val alice = User("Alice")
>>> println(alice.isSubscribed)
true
>>> val bob = User("Bob", false)
>>> println(bob.isSubscribed)
false
>>> val carol = User("Carol", isSubscribed = false)
>>> println(carol.isSubscribed)
false
```
⟵─┐ **Uses the default value "true" for the isSubscribed parameter**

⟵─┐ **You can specify all parameters according to declaration order.**

⟵─┐ **You can explicitly specify names for some constructor arguments.**

It seems that Alice subscribed to the mailing list by default, whereas Bob read the terms and conditions carefully and deselected the default option.

> **NOTE** If all the constructor parameters have default values, the compiler generates an additional constructor without parameters that uses all the default values. That makes it easier to use Kotlin with libraries that instantiate classes via parameterless constructors.

If your class has a superclass, the primary constructor also needs to initialize the superclass. You can do so by providing the superclass constructor parameters after the superclass reference in the base class list:

```
open class User(val nickname: String) { ... }

class TwitterUser(nickname: String) : User(nickname) { ... }
```

If you don't declare any constructors for a class, a default constructor that does nothing will be generated for you:

⟵─┐ **The default constructor without arguments is generated.**

```
open class Button
```

If you inherit the `Button` class and don't provide any constructors, you have to explicitly invoke the constructor of the superclass even if it doesn't have any parameters:

```
class RadioButton: Button()
```

That's why you need empty parentheses after the name of the superclass. Note the difference with interfaces: interfaces don't have constructors, so if you implement an interface, you never put parentheses after its name in the supertype list.

   If you want to ensure that your class can't be instantiated by other code, you have to make the constructor `private`. Here's how you make the primary constructor private:

```
class Secretive private constructor() {}
```
                                            ← ⌐ **This class has a**
                                                private constructor.

Because the `Secretive` class has only a `private` constructor, the code outside of the class can't instantiate it. Later in this chapter, we'll talk about companion objects, which may be a good place to call such constructors.

Alternatives to private constructors

In Java, you can use a `private` constructor that prohibits class instantiation to express a more general idea: that the class is a container of static utility members or is a singleton. Kotlin has built-in language features for these purposes. You use top-level functions (which you saw in section 3.2.3) as static utilities. To express singletons, you use object declarations, as you'll see in section 4.4.1.

In most real use cases, the constructor of a class is straightforward: it contains no parameters or assigns the parameters to the corresponding properties. That's why Kotlin has concise syntax for primary constructors: it works great for the majority of cases. But life isn't always that easy, so Kotlin allows you to define as many constructors as your class needs. Let's see how this works.

4.2.2 Secondary constructors: initializing the superclass in different ways

Generally speaking, classes with multiple constructors are much less common in Kotlin code than in Java. The majority of situations where you'd need overloaded constructors in Java are covered by Kotlin's support for default parameter values and named argument syntax.

> **TIP** Don't declare multiple secondary constructors to overload and provide default values for arguments. Instead, specify default values directly.

But there are still situations when multiple constructors are required. The most common one comes up when you need to extend a framework class that provides multiple constructors that initialize the class in different ways. Imagine a `View` class that's declared in Java and that has two constructors (you may recognize the definition if you're an Android developer). A similar declaration in Kotlin is as follows:

```
open class View {
    constructor(ctx: Context) {
        // some code
    }
    constructor(ctx: Context, attr: AttributeSet) {
        // some code
    }
}
```

◁─┐
Secondary
constructors
◁─┘

This class doesn't declare a primary constructor (as you can tell because there are no parentheses after the class name in the class header), but it declares two secondary constructors. A secondary constructor is introduced using the `constructor` keyword. You can declare as many secondary constructors as you need.

If you want to extend this class, you can declare the same constructors:

```
class MyButton : View {
    constructor(ctx: Context)
        : super(ctx) {
        // ...
    }
    constructor(ctx: Context, attr: AttributeSet)
        : super(ctx, attr) {
        // ...
    }
}
```

◁─┐
Calling superclass
constructors
◁─┘

Here you define two constructors, each of which calls the corresponding constructor of the superclass using the `super()` keyword. This is illustrated in figure 4.3; an arrow shows which constructor is delegated to.

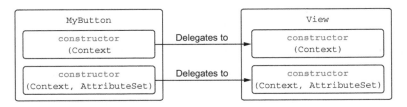

Figure 4.3   Using different superclass constructors

Just as in Java, you also have an option to call another constructor of your own class from a constructor, using the `this()` keyword. Here's how this works:

```
class MyButton : View {
    constructor(ctx: Context): this(ctx, MY_STYLE) {
        // ...
    }
}
```

◁─┐
Delegates to another
constructor of the class

```
    constructor(ctx: Context, attr: AttributeSet): super(ctx, attr) {
        // ...
    }
}
```

You change the `MyButton` class so that one of the constructors delegates to the other constructor of the same class (using `this`), passing the default value for the parameter, as shown in figure 4.4. The second constructor continues to call `super()`.

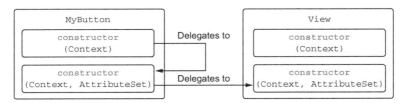

Figure 4.4   Delegating to a constructor of the same class

If the class has no primary constructor, then each secondary constructor has to initialize the base class or delegate to another constructor that does so. Thinking in terms of the previous figures, each secondary constructor must have an outgoing arrow starting a path that ends at any constructor of the base class.

Java interoperability is the main use case when you need to use secondary constructors. But there's another possible case: when you have multiple ways to create instances of your class, with different parameter lists. We'll discuss an example in section 4.4.2.

We've discussed how to define nontrivial constructors. Now let's turn our attention to nontrivial properties.

4.2.3   *Implementing properties declared in interfaces*

In Kotlin, an interface can contain abstract property declarations. Here's an example of an interface definition with such a declaration:

```
interface User {
    val nickname: String
}
```

This means classes implementing the `User` interface need to provide a way to obtain the value of `nickname`. The interface doesn't specify whether the value should be stored in a backing field or obtained through a getter. Therefore, the interface itself doesn't contain any state, and only classes implementing the interface may store the value if they need to.

Let's look at a few possible implementations for the interface: `PrivateUser`, who fills in only their nickname; `SubscribingUser`, who apparently was forced to provide an email to register; and `FacebookUser`, who rashly shared their Facebook account ID. All of these classes implement the abstract property in the interface in different ways.

Listing 4.14   Implementing an interface property

```
class PrivateUser(override val nickname: String) : User        ◁──┐ Primary constructor
class SubscribingUser(val email: String) : User {                 │ property
    override val nickname: String
        get() = email.substringBefore('@') )      ◁──┐ Custom
}                                                     │ getter
class FacebookUser(val accountId: Int) : User {
    override val nickname = getFacebookName(accountId)    ◁──┐ Property
}                                                             │ initializer
>>> println(PrivateUser("test@kotlinlang.org").nickname)
test@kotlinlang.org
>>> println(SubscribingUser("test@kotlinlang.org").nickname)
test
```

For `PrivateUser`, you use the concise syntax to declare a property directly in the primary constructor. This property implements the abstract property from `User`, so you mark it as `override`.

For `SubscribingUser`, the `nickname` property is implemented through a custom getter. This property doesn't have a backing field to store its value; it has only a getter that calculates a nickname from the email on every invocation.

For `FacebookUser`, you assign the value to the `nickname` property in its initializer. You use a `getFacebookName` function that's supposed to return the name of a Facebook user given their account ID. (Assume that it's defined somewhere else.) This function is costly: it needs to establish a connection with Facebook to get the desired data. That's why you decide to invoke it once during the initialization phase.

Pay attention to the different implementations of `nickname` in `SubscribingUser` and `FacebookUser`. Although they look similar, the first property has a custom getter that calculates `substringBefore` on every access, whereas the property in `Facebook-User` has a backing field that stores the data computed during the class initialization.

In addition to abstract property declarations, an interface can contain properties with getters and setters, as long as they don't reference a backing field. (A backing field would require storing state in an interface, which isn't allowed.) Let's look at an example:

```
interface User {
    val email: String
    val nickname: String                              Property doesn't have a
        get() = email.substringBefore('@')    ◁──┘ backing field: the result value
}                                                 is computed on each access.
```

This interface contains the abstract property `email`, as well as the `nickname` property with a custom getter. The first property must be overridden in subclasses, whereas the second one can be inherited.

Unlike properties implemented in interfaces, properties implemented in classes have full access to backing fields. Let's see how you can refer to them from accessors.

4.2.4   *Accessing a backing field from a getter or setter*

You've seen a few examples of two kinds of properties: properties that store values and properties with custom accessors that calculate values on every access. Now let's see how you can combine the two and implement a property that stores a value and provides additional logic that's executed when the value is accessed or modified. To support that, you need to be able to access the property's backing field from its accessors.

Let's say you want to log any change of data stored in a property. You declare a mutable property and execute additional code on each setter access.

> **Listing 4.15   Accessing the backing field in a setter**

```
class User(val name: String) {
    var address: String = "unspecified"
        set(value: String) {
            println("""
                Address was changed for $name:
                "$field" -> "$value".""".trimIndent())
            field = value
        }
}

>>> val user = User("Alice")
>>> user.address = "Elsenheimerstrasse 47, 80687 Muenchen"
Address was changed for Alice:
"unspecified" -> "Elsenheimerstrasse 47, 80687 Muenchen".
```

Reads the backing field value

Updates the backing field value

You change a property value as usual by saying `user.address = "new value"`, which invokes a setter under the hood. In this example, the setter is redefined, so the additional logging code is executed (for simplicity, in this case you print it out).

In the body of the setter, you use the special identifier `field` to access the value of the backing field. In a getter, you can only read the value; and in a setter, you can both read and modify it.

Note that you can redefine only one of the accessors for a mutable property. The getter in listing 4.15 is trivial and only returns the field value, so you don't need to redefine it.

You may wonder what the difference is between making a property that has a backing field and one that doesn't. The way you access the property doesn't depend on whether it has a backing field. The compiler will generate the backing field for the property if you either reference it explicitly or use the default accessor implementation. If you provide custom accessor implementations that don't use `field` (for the getter if the property is a `val` and for both accessors if it's a mutable property), the backing field won't be present.

Sometimes you don't need to change the default implementation of an accessor, but you need to change its visibility. Let's see how you can do this.

4.2.5   *Changing accessor visibility*

The accessor's visibility by default is the same as the property's. But you can change this if you need to, by putting a visibility modifier before the get or set keyword. To see how you can use it, let's look at an example.

Listing 4.16   Declaring a property with a private setter

```
class LengthCounter {
    var counter: Int = 0
        private set                    ◁──────────    You can't change this property
                                                      outside of the class.
    fun addWord(word: String) {
        counter += word.length
    }
}
```

This class calculates the total length of the words added to it. The property holding the total length is public, because it's part of the API the class provides to its clients. But you need to make sure it's only modified in the class, because otherwise external code could change it and store an incorrect value. Therefore, you let the compiler generate a getter with the default visibility, and you change the visibility of the setter to private.

Here's how you can use this class:

```
>>> val lengthCounter = LengthCounter()
>>> lengthCounter.addWord("Hi!")
>>> println(lengthCounter.counter)
3
```

You create an instance of LengthCounter, and then you add a word "Hi!" of length 3. Now the counter property stores 3.

More about properties later

Later in the book, we'll continue our discussion of properties. Here are some references:

- The lateinit modifier on a non-null property specifies that this property is initialized later, after the constructor is called, which is a common case for some frameworks. This feature will be covered in chapter 6.
- Lazy initialized properties, as part of the more general *delegated properties* feature, will be covered in chapter 7.
  For compatibility with Java frameworks, you can use annotations that emulate Java features in Kotlin. For instance, the @JvmField annotation on a property exposes a public field without accessors. You'll learn more about annotations in chapter 10.
- The const modifier makes working with annotations more convenient and lets you use a property of a primitive type or String as an annotation argument. Chapter 10 provides details.

That concludes our discussion of writing nontrivial constructors and properties in Kotlin. Next, you'll see how to make value-object classes even friendlier, using the concept of data classes.

4.3 Compiler-generated methods: data classes and class delegation

The Java platform defines a number of methods that needs to be present in many classes and are usually implemented in a mechanical way, such as equals, hashCode, and toString. Fortunately, Java IDEs can automate the generation of these methods, so you usually don't need to write them by hand. But in this case, your codebase contains the boilerplate code. The Kotlin compiler takes a step forward: it can perform the mechanical code generation behind the scenes, without cluttering your source code files with the results.

You already saw how this works for trivial class constructor and property accessors. Let's look at more examples of cases where the Kotlin compiler generates typical methods that are useful for simple data classes and greatly simplifies the class-delegation pattern.

4.3.1 Universal object methods

As is the case in Java, all Kotlin classes have several methods you may want to override: toString, equals, and hashCode. Let's look at what these methods are and how Kotlin can help you generate their implementations automatically. As a starting point, you'll use a simple Client class that stores a client's name and postal code.

Listing 4.17 Initial declaration of the Client class

```
class Client(val name: String, val postalCode: Int)
```

Let's see how class instances are represented as strings.

STRING REPRESENTATION: TOSTRING()

All classes in Kotlin, just as in Java, provide a way to get a string representation of the class's objects. This is primarily used for debugging and logging, although you can use this functionality in other contexts as well. By default, the string representation of an object looks like Client@5e9f23b4, which isn't very useful. To change this, you need to override the toString method.

Listing 4.18 Implementing toString() for Client

```
class Client(val name: String, val postalCode: Int) {
    override fun toString() = "Client(name=$name, postalCode=$postalCode)"
}
```

Now the representation of a client looks like this:

```
>>> val client1 = Client("Alice", 342562)
>>> println(client1)
Client(name=Alice, postalCode=342562)
```

Much more informative, isn't it?

OBJECT EQUALITY: EQUALS()

All the computations with the Client class take place outside of it. This class just stores the data; it's meant to be plain and transparent. Nevertheless, you may have some requirements for the behavior of such a class. For example, suppose you want the objects to be considered equal if they contain the same data:

```
>>> val client1 = Client("Alice", 342562)
>>> val client2 = Client("Alice", 342562)
>>> println(client1 == client2)
false
```

In Kotlin, == checks whether the objects are equal, not the references. It is compiled to a call of "equals".

You see that the objects aren't equal. That means you must override equals for the Client class.

== for equality

In Java, you can use the == operator to compare primitive and reference types. If applied to primitive types, Java's == compares values, whereas == on reference types compares references. Thus, in Java, there's the well-known practice of always calling equals, and there's the well-known problem of forgetting to do so.

In Kotlin, the == operator is the default way to compare two objects: it compares their values by calling equals under the hood. Thus, if equals is overridden in your class, you can safely compare its instances using ==. For reference comparison, you can use the === operator, which works exactly the same as == in Java by comparing the object references.

Let's look at the changed Client class.

Listing 4.19   Implementing equals() for Client

Checks whether "other" is a Client

Checks whether the corresponding properties are equal

```
class Client(val name: String, val postalCode: Int) {
    override fun equals(other: Any?): Boolean {
        if (other == null || other !is Client)
            return false
        return name == other.name &&
            postalCode == other.postalCode
    }
    override fun toString() = "Client(name=$name, postalCode=$postalCode)"
}
```

"Any" is the analogue of java.lang.Object: a superclass of all classes in Kotlin. The nullable type "Any?" means "other" can be null.

Just to remind you, the is check in Kotlin is the analogue of instanceof in Java. It checks whether a value has the specified type. Like the !in operator, which is a negation for the in check (we discussed both in section 2.4.4), the !is operator denotes the negation of the is check. Such operators make your code easier to read. In chapter 6, we'll discuss nullable types in detail and why the condition other == null || other !is Client can be simplified to other !is Client.

Because in Kotlin the override modifier is mandatory, you're protected from accidentally writing fun equals(other: Client), which would add a new method instead of overriding equals. After you override equals, you may expect that clients with the same property values are equal. Indeed, the equality check client1 == client2 in the previous example returns true now. But if you want to do more complicated things with clients, it doesn't work. The usual interview question is, "What's broken, and what's the problem?" You may say that the problem is that hashCode is missing. That is in fact the case, and we'll now discuss why this is important.

HASH CONTAINERS: HASHCODE()

The hashCode method should be always overridden together with equals. This section explains why.

Let's create a set with one element: a client named Alice. Then you create a new Client instance containing the same data and check whether it's contained in the set. You'd expect the check to return true, because the two instances are equal, but in fact it returns false:

```
>>> val processed = hashSetOf(Client("Alice", 342562))
>>> println(processed.contains(Client("Alice", 342562)))
false
```

The reason is that the Client class is missing the hashCode method. Therefore, it violates the general hashCode contract: if two objects are equal, they must have the same hash code. The processed set is a HashSet. Values in a HashSet are compared in an optimized way: at first their hash codes are compared, and then, only if they're equal, the actual values are compared. The hash codes are different for two different instances of the Client class in the previous example, so the set decides that it doesn't contain the second object, even though equals would return true. Therefore, if the rule isn't followed, the HashSet can't work correctly with such objects.

To fix that, you can add the implementation of hashCode to the class.

> **Listing 4.20 Implementing** hashCode() **for** Client

```
class Client(val name: String, val postalCode: Int) {
    ...
    override fun hashCode(): Int = name.hashCode() * 31 + postalCode
}
```

Now you have a class that works as expected in all scenarios—but notice how much code you've had to write. Fortunately, the Kotlin compiler can help you by generating all of those methods automatically. Let's see how you can ask it to do that.

4.3.2 *Data classes: autogenerated implementations of universal methods*

If you want your class to be a convenient holder for your data, you need to override these methods: toString, equals, and hashCode. Usually, the implementations of those methods are straightforward, and IDEs like IntelliJ IDEA can help you generate them automatically and verify that they're implemented correctly and consistently.

The good news is, you don't have to generate all of these methods in Kotlin. If you add the modifier data to your class, the necessary methods are automatically generated for you.

Listing 4.21 Client as a data class

```
data class Client(val name: String, val postalCode: Int)
```

Easy, right? Now you have a class that overrides all the standard Java methods:

- equals for comparing instances
- hashCode for using them as keys in hash-based containers such as HashMap
- toString for generating string representations showing all the fields in declaration order

The equals and hashCode methods take into account all the properties declared in the primary constructor. The generated equals method checks that the values of all the properties are equal. The hashCode method returns a value that depends on the hash codes of all the properties. Note that properties that aren't declared in the primary constructor don't take part in the equality checks and hash code calculation.

This isn't a complete list of useful methods generated for data classes. The next section reveals one more, and section 7.4 fills in the rest.

DATA CLASSES AND IMMUTABILITY: THE COPY() METHOD

Note that even though the properties of a data class aren't required to be val—you can use var as well— it's strongly recommended that you use only read-only properties, making the instances of the data class *immutable*. This is required if you want to use such instances as keys in a HashMap or a similar container, because otherwise the container could get into an invalid state if the object used as a key was modified after it was added to the container. Immutable objects are also much easier to reason about, especially in multithreaded code: once an object has been created, it remains in its original state, and you don't need to worry about other threads modifying the object while your code is working with it.

To make it even easier to use data classes as immutable objects, the Kotlin compiler generates one more method for them: a method that allows you to *copy* the instances of your classes, changing the values of some properties. Creating a copy is usually a good alternative to modifying the instance in place: the copy has a separate lifecycle and can't affect the places in the code that refer to the original instance. Here's what the copy method would look like if you implemented it manually:

```
class Client(val name: String, val postalCode: Int) {
    ...
    fun copy(name: String = this.name,
            postalCode: Int = this.postalCode) =
        Client(name, postalCode)
}
```

And here's how the `copy` method can be used:

```
>>> val bob = Client("Bob", 973293)
>>> println(bob.copy(postalCode = 382555))
Client(name=Bob, postalCode=382555)
```

You've seen how the `data` modifier makes value-object classes more convenient to use. Now let's talk about the other Kotlin feature that lets you avoid IDE-generated boilerplate code: class delegation.

4.3.3 *Class delegation: using the "by" keyword*

A common problem in the design of large object-oriented systems is fragility caused by implementation inheritance. When you extend a class and override some of its methods, your code becomes dependent on the implementation details of the class you're extending. When the system evolves and the implementation of the base class changes or new methods are added to it, the assumptions about its behavior that you've made in your class can become invalid, so your code may end up not behaving correctly.

The design of Kotlin recognizes this problem and treats classes as `final` by default. This ensures that only those classes that are designed for extensibility can be inherited from. When working on such a class, you see that it's open, and you can keep in mind that modifications need to be compatible with derived classes.

But often you need to add behavior to another class, even if it wasn't designed to be extended. A commonly used way to implement this is known as the *Decorator* pattern. The essence of the pattern is that a new class is created, implementing the same interface as the original class and storing the instance of the original class as a field. Methods in which the behavior of the original class doesn't need to be modified are forwarded to the original class instance.

One downside of this approach is that it requires a fairly large amount of boilerplate code (so much that IDEs like IntelliJ IDEA have dedicated features to generate that code for you). For example, this is how much code you need for a decorator that implements an interface as simple as `Collection`, even when you don't modify any behavior:

```
class DelegatingCollection<T> : Collection<T> {
    private val innerList = arrayListOf<T>()

    override val size: Int get() = innerList.size
    override fun isEmpty(): Boolean = innerList.isEmpty()
    override fun contains(element: T): Boolean = innerList.contains(element)
    override fun iterator(): Iterator<T> = innerList.iterator()
    override fun containsAll(elements: Collection<T>): Boolean =
            innerList.containsAll(elements)
}
```

The good news is that Kotlin includes first-class support for delegation as a language feature. Whenever you're implementing an interface, you can say that you're *delegating* the implementation of the interface to another object, using the by keyword. Here's how you can use this approach to rewrite the previous example:

```
class DelegatingCollection<T>(
        innerList: Collection<T> = ArrayList<T>()
) : Collection<T> by innerList {}
```

All the method implementations in the class are gone. The compiler will generate them, and the implementation is similar to that in the DelegatingCollection example. Because there's little interesting content in the code, there's no point in writing it manually when the compiler can do the same job for you automatically.

Now, when you need to change the behavior of some methods, you can override them, and your code will be called instead of the generated methods. You can leave out methods for which you're satisfied with the default implementation of delegating to the underlying instance.

Let's see how you can use this technique to implement a collection that counts the number of attempts to add an element to it. For example, if you're performing some kind of deduplication, you can use such a collection to measure how efficient the process is, by comparing the number of attempts to add an element with the resulting size of the collection.

Listing 4.22   Using class delegation

```
class CountingSet<T>(
        val innerSet: MutableCollection<T> = HashSet<T>()
) : MutableCollection<T> by innerSet {        ←┐  Delegates the MutableCollection
                                               │  implementation to innerSet
    var objectsAdded = 0

    override fun add(element: T): Boolean {   ←┐
        objectsAdded++                         │
        return innerSet.add(element)           │  Does not delegate; provides a
    }                                          │  different implementation
                                               │
    override fun addAll(c: Collection<T>): Boolean {  ←┘
        objectsAdded += c.size
        return innerSet.addAll(c)
    }
}

>>> val cset = CountingSet<Int>()
>>> cset.addAll(listOf(1, 1, 2))
>>> println("${cset.objectsAdded} objects were added, ${cset.size} remain")
3 objects were added, 2 remain
```

As you see, you override the add and addAll methods to increment the count, and you delegate the rest of the implementation of the MutableCollection interface to the container you're wrapping.

The important part is that you aren't introducing any dependency on how the underlying collection is implemented. For example, you don't care whether that collection implements addAll by calling add in a loop, or if it uses a different implementation optimized for a particular case. You have full control over what happens when the client code calls your class, and you rely only on the documented API of the underlying collection to implement your operations, so you can rely on it continuing to work.

We've finished our discussion of how the Kotlin compiler can generate useful methods for classes. Let's proceed to the final big part of Kotlin's class story: the object keyword and the different situations in which it comes into play.

4.4 The "object" keyword: declaring a class and creating an instance, combined

The object keyword comes up in Kotlin in a number of cases, but they all share the same core idea: the keyword defines a class and creates an instance (in other words, an object) of that class at the same time. Let's look at the different situations when it's used:

- *Object declaration* is a way to define a singleton.
- *Companion objects* can contain factory methods and other methods that are related to this class but don't require a class instance to be called. Their members can be accessed via class name.
- *Object expression* is used instead of Java's anonymous inner class.

Now we'll discuss these Kotlin features in detail.

4.4.1 Object declarations: singletons made easy

A fairly common occurrence in the design of object-oriented systems is a class for which you need only one instance. In Java, this is usually implemented using the Singleton pattern: you define a class with a private constructor and a static field holding the only existing instance of the class.

Kotlin provides first-class language support for this using the *object declaration* feature. The object declaration combines a *class declaration* and a declaration of a *single instance* of that class.

For example, you can use an object declaration to represent the payroll of an organization. You probably don't have multiple payrolls, so using an object for this sounds reasonable:

```
object Payroll {
    val allEmployees = arrayListOf<Person>()

    fun calculateSalary() {
        for (person in allEmployees) {
            ...
        }
    }
}
```

Object declarations are introduced with the object keyword. An object declaration effectively defines a class and a variable of that class in a single statement.

Just like a class, an object declaration can contain declarations of properties, methods, initializer blocks, and so on. The only things that aren't allowed are constructors (either primary or secondary). Unlike instances of regular classes, object declarations are created immediately at the point of definition, not through constructor calls from other places in the code. Therefore, defining a constructor for an object declaration doesn't make sense.

And just like a variable, an object declaration lets you call methods and access properties by using the object name to the left of the . character:

```
Payroll.allEmployees.add(Person(...))

Payroll.calculateSalary()
```

Object declarations can also inherit from classes and interfaces. This is often useful when the framework you're using requires you to implement an interface, but your implementation doesn't contain any state. For example, let's take the java .util.Comparator interface. A Comparator implementation receives two objects and returns an integer indicating which of the objects is greater. Comparators almost never store any data, so you usually need just a single Comparator instance for a particular way of comparing objects. That's a perfect use case for an object declaration.

As a specific example, let's implement a comparator that compares file paths case-insensitively.

Listing 4.23 Implementing Comparator with an object

```
object CaseInsensitiveFileComparator : Comparator<File> {
    override fun compare(file1: File, file2: File): Int {
        return file1.path.compareTo(file2.path,
            ignoreCase = true)
    }
}

>>> println(CaseInsensitiveFileComparator.compare(
...     File("/User"), File("/user")))
0
```

You use singleton objects in any context where an ordinary object (an instance of a class) can be used. For example, you can pass this object as an argument to a function that takes a Comparator:

```
>>> val files = listOf(File("/Z"), File("/a"))
>>> println(files.sortedWith(CaseInsensitiveFileComparator))
[/a, /Z]
```

Here you're using the sortedWith function, which returns a list sorted according to the specified comparator.

Singletons and dependency injection

Just like the Singleton pattern, object declarations aren't always ideal for use in large software systems. They're great for small pieces of code that have few or no dependencies, but not for large components that interact with many other parts of the system. The main reason is that you don't have any control over the instantiation of objects, and you can't specify parameters for the constructors.

This means you can't replace the implementations of the object itself, or other classes the object depends on, in unit tests or in different configurations of the software system. If you need that ability, you should use regular Kotlin classes together with a dependency injection framework (such as Guice, https://github.com/google/guice), just as in Java.

You can also declare objects in a class. Such objects also have just a single instance; they don't have a separate instance per instance of the containing class. For example, it's logical to place a comparator comparing objects of a particular class inside that class.

Listing 4.24 Implementing `Comparator` with a nested object

```
data class Person(val name: String) {
    object NameComparator : Comparator<Person> {
        override fun compare(p1: Person, p2: Person): Int =
            p1.name.compareTo(p2.name)
    }
}

>>> val persons = listOf(Person("Bob"), Person("Alice"))
>>> println(persons.sortedWith(Person.NameComparator))
[Person(name=Alice), Person(name=Bob)]
```

Using Kotlin objects from Java

An object declaration in Kotlin is compiled as a class with a static field holding its single instance, which is always named `INSTANCE`. If you implemented the Singleton pattern in Java, you'd probably do the same thing by hand. Thus, to use a Kotlin object from the Java code, you access the static `INSTANCE` field:

```
/* Java */
CaseInsensitiveFileComparator.INSTANCE.compare(file1, file2);
```

In this example, the `INSTANCE` field has the type `CaseInsensitiveFile-Comparator`.

Now let's look at a special case of objects nested inside a class: *companion objects*.

4.4.2 *Companion objects: a place for factory methods and static members*

Classes in Kotlin can't have static members; Java's `static` keyword isn't part of the Kotlin language. As a replacement, Kotlin relies on package-level functions (which can replace Java's static methods in many situations) and object declarations (which replace Java static methods in other cases, as well as static fields). In most cases, it's recommended that you use top-level functions. But top-level functions can't access `private` members of a class, as illustrated by figure 4.5. Thus, if you need to write a function that can be called without having a class instance but needs access to the internals of a class, you can write it as a member of an object declaration inside that class. An example of such a function would be a factory method.

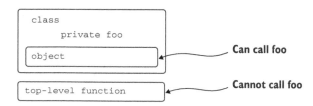

Figure 4.5   Private members can't be used in top-level functions outside of the class.

One of the objects defined in a class can be marked with a special keyword: `compan-ion`. If you do that, you gain the ability to access the methods and properties of that object directly through the name of the containing class, without specifying the name of the object explicitly. The resulting syntax looks exactly like static method invocation in Java. Here's a basic example showing the syntax:

```
class A {
    companion object {
        fun bar() {
            println("Companion object called")
        }
    }
}

>>> A.bar()
Companion object called
```

Remember when we promised you a good place to call a `private` constructor? That's the companion object. The companion object has access to all `private` members of the class, including the `private` constructor, and it's an ideal candidate to implement the Factory pattern.

Let's look at an example of declaring two constructors and then change it to use factory methods declared in the companion object. We'll build on listing 4.14, with `FacebookUser` and `SubscribingUser`. Previously, these entities were different classes implementing the common interface `User`. Now you decide to manage with only one class, but to provide different means of creating it.

Listing 4.25   Defining a class with multiple secondary constructors

```
class User {
    val nickname: String

    constructor(email: String) {                        ◁─┐
        nickname = email.substringBefore('@')             │
    }                                                     ├─  Secondary constructors
                                                          │
    constructor(facebookAccountId: Int) {               ◁─┘
        nickname = getFacebookName(facebookAccountId)
    }
}
```

An alternative approach to express the same logic, which may be beneficial for many reasons, is to use factory methods to create instances of the class. The `User` instance is created through factory methods, not via multiple constructors.

Listing 4.26   Replacing secondary constructors with factory methods

```
                                                   ┌── Marks the primary
                                                   │   constructor as private
class User private constructor(val nickname: String) {  ◁─┘
                  ⊳  companion object {
Declares the ──┐      fun newSubscribingUser(email: String) =    ◁─┐ Declaring a named
companion      │          User(email.substringBefore('@'))         │ companion object
object  ───────┘
                      fun newFacebookUser(accountId: Int) =    ◁─  Factory method creating a new
                          User(getFacebookName(accountId))         user by Facebook account ID
                  }
}
```

You can invoke the methods of `companion object` via the class name:

```
>>> val subscribingUser = User.newSubscribingUser("bob@gmail.com")
>>> val facebookUser = User.newFacebookUser(4)
>>> println(subscribingUser.nickname)
bob
```

Factory methods are very useful. They can be named according to their purpose, as shown in the example. In addition, a factory method can return subclasses of the class where the method is declared, as in the example when `SubscribingUser` and `FacebookUser` are classes. You can also avoid creating new objects when it's not necessary. For example, you can ensure that every email corresponds to a unique `User` instance and return an existing instance instead of a new one when the factory method is called with an email that's already in the cache. But if you need to extend such classes, using several constructors may be a better solution, because companion object members can't be overridden in subclasses.

4.4.3 *Companion objects as regular objects*

A companion object is a regular object that is declared in a class. It can be named, implement an interface, or have extension functions or properties. In this section, we'll look at an example.

Suppose you're working on a web service for a company's payroll, and you need to serialize and deserialize objects as JSON. You can place the serialization logic in a companion object.

Listing 4.27   Declaring a named companion object

```
class Person(val name: String) {
    companion object Loader {
        fun fromJSON(jsonText: String): Person = ...
    }
}

>>> person = Person.Loader.fromJSON("{name: 'Dmitry'}")  ◁─┐
>>> person.name                                            │  You can use both ways
Dmitry                                                     │  to call fromJSON.
>>> person2 = Person.fromJSON("{name: 'Brent'}")        ◁──┘
>>> person2.name
Brent
```

In most cases, you refer to the companion object through the name of its containing class, so you don't need to worry about its name. But you can specify it if needed, as in listing 4.27: `companion object Loader`. If you omit the name of the companion object, the default name assigned to it is `Companion`. You'll see some examples using this name later, when we talk about companion-object extensions.

IMPLEMENTING INTERFACES IN COMPANION OBJECTS

Just like any other object declaration, a companion object can implement interfaces. As you'll see in a moment, you can use the name of the containing class directly as an instance of an object implementing the interface.

Suppose you have many kinds of objects in your system, including `Person`. You want to provide a common way to create objects of all types. Let's say you have an interface `JSONFactory` for objects that can be deserialized from JSON, and all objects in your system should be created through this factory. You can provide an implementation of that interface for your `Person` class.

Listing 4.28   Implementing an interface in a companion object

```
interface JSONFactory<T> {
    fun fromJSON(jsonText: String): T
}

class Person(val name: String) {
    companion object : JSONFactory<Person> {
```

```
        override fun fromJSON(jsonText: String): Person = ...
    }
}
```
Companion object
implementing
an interface

Then, if you have a function that uses an abstract factory to load entities, you can pass the `Person` object to it.

```
fun loadFromJSON<T>(factory: JSONFactory<T>): T {
    ...
}

loadFromJSON(Person)
```
Passes the companion-object
instance to the function

Note that the name of the `Person` class is used as an instance of `JSONFactory`.

Kotlin companion objects and static members

The companion object for a class is compiled similarly to a regular object: a static field in a class refers to its instance. If the companion object isn't named, it can be accessed through the `Companion` reference from the Java code:

```
/* Java */
Person.Companion.fromJSON("...");
```

If a companion object has a name, you use this name instead of `Companion`.

But you may need to work with Java code that requires a member of your class to be static. You can achieve this with the `@JvmStatic` annotation on the corresponding member. If you want to declare a `static` field, use the `@JvmField` annotation on a top-level property or a property declared in an `object`. These features exist specifically for interoperability purposes and are not, strictly speaking, part of the core language. We'll cover annotations in detail in chapter 10.

Note that Kotlin can access static methods and fields declared in Java classes, using the same syntax as Java.

COMPANION-OBJECT EXTENSIONS

As you saw in section 3.3, extension functions allow you to define methods that can be called on instances of a class defined elsewhere in the codebase. But what if you need to define functions that can be called on the class itself, like companion-object methods or Java static methods? If the class has a companion object, you can do so by defining extension functions on it. More specifically, if class C has a companion object, and you define an extension function `func` on `C.Companion`, you can call it as `C.func()`.

For example, imagine that you want to have a cleaner separation of concerns for your `Person` class. The class itself will be part of the core business-logic module, but you don't want to couple that module to any specific data format. Because of that, the deserialization function needs to be defined in the module responsible for client/server communication. You can accomplish this using extension functions. Note how you use the default name (Companion) to refer to the companion object that was declared without an explicit name:

Listing 4.29   Defining an extension function for a companion object

```
// business logic module
class Person(val firstName: String, val lastName: String) {
    companion object {                                      ◁──┐  Declares an empty
    }                                                          │  companion object
}

// client/server communication module
fun Person.Companion.fromJSON(json: String): Person {   ◁──┐  Declares an
    ...                                                     │  extension function
}

val p = Person.fromJSON(json)
```

You call fromJSON as if it was defined as a method of the companion object, but it's actually defined outside of it as an extension function. As always with extension functions, it looks like a member, but it's not. But note that you have to declare a companion object in your class, even an empty one, in order to be able to define extensions to it.

You've seen how useful companion objects can be. Now let's move to the next feature in Kotlin that's expressed with the same object keyword: object expressions.

4.4.4   *Object expressions: anonymous inner classes rephrased*

The object keyword can be used not only for declaring named singleton-like objects, but also for declaring *anonymous objects*. Anonymous objects replace Java's use of anonymous inner classes. For example, let's see how you can convert a typical use of a Java anonymous inner class—an event listener—into Kotlin:

Listing 4.30   Implementing an event listener with an anonymous object

```
window.addMouseListener(
    object : MouseAdapter() {                              ◁──┐  Declares an anonymous
        override fun mouseClicked(e: MouseEvent) {            │  object extending
            // ...                                             │  MouseAdapter
        }

        override fun mouseEntered(e: MouseEvent) {
            // ...
        }
    }
)
```

Overrides
MouseAdapter
methods

The syntax is the same as with object declarations, except that you omit the name of the object. The object expression declares a class and creates an instance of that class, but it doesn't assign a name to the class or the instance. Typically, neither is necessary, because you'll use the object as a parameter in a function call. If you do need to assign a name to the object, you can store it in a variable:

```
val listener = object : MouseAdapter() {
    override fun mouseClicked(e: MouseEvent) { ... }
    override fun mouseEntered(e: MouseEvent) { ... }
}
```

Unlike a Java anonymous inner class, which can only extend one class or implement one interface, a Kotlin anonymous object can implement multiple interfaces or no interfaces.

> **NOTE** Unlike object declarations, anonymous objects aren't singletons. Every time an object expression is executed, a new instance of the object is created.

Just as with Java's anonymous classes, code in an object expression can access the variables in the function where it was created. But unlike in Java, this isn't restricted to `final` variables; you can also modify the values of variables from within an object expression. For example, let's see how you can use the listener to count the number of clicks in a window.

Listing 4.31 Accessing local variables from an anonymous object

```
fun countClicks(window: Window) {
    var clickCount = 0                                    ◁──────  Declares a
                                                                   local variable
    window.addMouseListener(object : MouseAdapter() {
        override fun mouseClicked(e: MouseEvent) {
            clickCount++                              ◁──────  Updates the value
        }                                                      of the variable
    })
    // ...
}
```

> **NOTE** Object expressions are mostly useful when you need to override multiple methods in your anonymous object. If you only need to implement a single-method interface (such as `Runnable`), you can rely on Kotlin's support for SAM conversion (converting a function literal to an implementation of an interface with a single abstract method) and write your implementation as a function literal (lambda). We'll discuss lambdas and SAM conversion in much more detail in chapter 5.

We've finished our discussion of classes, interfaces, and objects. In the next chapter, we'll move on to one of the most interesting areas of Kotlin: lambdas and functional programming.

4.5 *Summary*

- Interfaces in Kotlin are similar to Java's but can contain default implementations (which Java supports only since version 8) and properties.
- All declarations are `final` and `public` by default.
- To make a declaration non-`final`, mark it as `open`.

- `internal` declarations are visible in the same module.
- Nested classes aren't inner by default. Use the keyword `inner` to store a reference to the outer class.
- A `sealed` class can only have subclasses nested in its declaration (Kotlin 1.1 will allow placing them anywhere in the same file).
- Initializer blocks and secondary constructors provide flexibility for initializing class instances.
- You use the `field` identifier to reference a property backing field from the accessor body.
- Data classes provide compiler-generated `equals`, `hashCode`, `toString`, `copy`, and other methods.
- Class delegation helps to avoid many similar delegating methods in your code.
- Object declaration is Kotlin's way to define a singleton class.
- Companion objects (along with package-level functions and properties) replace Java's static method and field definitions.
- Companion objects, like other objects, can implement interfaces, as well as have extension functions and properties.
- Object expressions are Kotlin's replacement for Java's anonymous inner classes, with added power such as the ability to implement multiple interfaces and to modify the variables defined in the scope where the object is created.

Programming with lambdas

This chapter covers

- Lambda expressions and member references
- Working with collections in a functional style
- Sequences: performing collection operations lazily
- Using Java functional interfaces in Kotlin
- Using lambdas with receivers

Lambda expressions, or simply *lambdas*, are essentially small chunks of code that can be passed to other functions. With lambdas, you can easily extract common code structures into library functions, and the Kotlin standard library makes heavy use of them. One of the most common uses for lambdas is working with collections, and in this chapter you'll see many examples of replacing common collection access patterns with lambdas passed to standard library functions. You'll also see how lambdas can be used with Java libraries—even those that weren't originally designed with lambdas in mind. Finally, we'll look at lambdas with receivers—a special kind of lambdas where the body is executed in a different context than the surrounding code.

5.1   *Lambda expressions and member references*

The introduction of lambdas to Java 8 was one of the longest-awaited changes in the evolution of the language. Why was it such a big deal? In this section, you'll find out why lambdas are so useful and what the syntax of lambda expressions in Kotlin looks like.

5.1.1   *Introduction to lambdas: blocks of code as function parameters*

Passing and storing pieces of behavior in your code is a frequent task. For example, you often need to express ideas like "When an event happens, run this handler" or "Apply this operation to all elements in a data structure." In older versions of Java, you could accomplish this through anonymous inner classes. This technique works but requires verbose syntax.

Functional programming offers you another approach to solve this problem: the ability to treat functions as values. Instead of declaring a class and passing an instance of that class to a function, you can pass a function directly. With lambda expressions, the code is even more concise. You don't need to declare a function: instead, you can, effectively, pass a block of code directly as a function parameter.

Let's look at an example. Imagine that you need to define a behavior for clicking a button. You add a listener responsible for handling the click. This listener implements the corresponding `OnClickListener` interface with one method, `onClick`.

Listing 5.1   Implementing a listener with an anonymous inner class

```
/* Java */
button.setOnClickListener(new OnClickListener() {
    @Override
    public void onClick(View view) {
        /* actions on click */
    }
});
```

The verbosity required to declare an anonymous inner class becomes irritating when repeated many times. The notation to express just the behavior—what should be done on clicking—helps eliminate redundant code. In Kotlin, as in Java 8, you can use a lambda.

Listing 5.2   Implementing a listener with a lambda

```
button.setOnClickListener { /* actions on click */ }
```

This Kotlin code does the same thing as an anonymous class in Java but is more concise and readable. We'll discuss the details of this example later in this section.

You saw how a lambda can be used as an alternative to an anonymous object with only one method. Let's now continue with another classical use of lambda expressions: working with collections.

5.1.2 Lambdas and collections

One of the main tenets of good programming style is to avoid any duplication in your code. Most of the tasks we perform with collections follow a few common patterns, so the code that implements them should live in a library. But without lambdas, it's difficult to provide a good, convenient library for working with collections. Thus if you wrote your code in Java (prior to Java 8), you most likely have a habit of implementing everything on your own. This habit must be changed with Kotlin!

Let's look at an example. You'll use the `Person` class that contains information about a person's name and age.

```
data class Person(val name: String, val age: Int)
```

Suppose you have a list of people, and you need to find the oldest of them. If you had no experience with lambdas, you might rush to implement the search manually. You'd introduce two intermediate variables—one to hold the maximum age and another to store the first found person of this age—and then iterate over the list, updating these variables.

Listing 5.3 Searching through a collection manually

```
fun findTheOldest(people: List<Person>) {
    var maxAge = 0                              Stores the maximum age          Stores a person of the maximum age
    var theOldest: Person? = null
    for (person in people) {
        if (person.age > maxAge) {              If the next person is older than the current oldest person, changes the maximum
            maxAge = person.age
            theOldest = person
        }
    }
    println(theOldest)
}
>>> val people = listOf(Person("Alice", 29), Person("Bob", 31))
>>> findTheOldest(people)
Person(name=Bob, age=31)
```

With enough experience, you can bang out such loops pretty quickly. But there's quite a lot of code here, and it's easy to make mistakes. For example, you might get the comparison wrong and find the minimum element instead of the maximum.

In Kotlin, there's a better way. You can use a library function, as shown next.

Listing 5.4 Searching through a collection using a lambda

```
>>> val people = listOf(Person("Alice", 29), Person("Bob", 31))
>>> println(people.maxBy { it.age })          Finds the maximum by comparing the ages
Person(name=Bob, age=31)
```

The `maxBy` function can be called on any collection and takes one argument: the function that specifies what values should be compared to find the maximum element. The code in curly braces { it.age } is a lambda implementing that logic. It receives a collection element as an argument (referred to using it) and returns a value to compare. In this example, the collection element is a Person object, and the value to compare is its age, stored in the age property.

If a lambda just delegates to a function or property, it can be replaced by a member reference.

Listing 5.5   Searching using a member reference

```
people.maxBy(Person::age)
```

This code means the same thing as listing 5.5. Section 5.1.5 will cover the details.

Most of the things we typically do with collections in Java (prior to Java 8) can be better expressed with library functions taking lambdas or member references. The resulting code is much shorter and easier to understand. To help you start getting used to it, let's look at the syntax for lambda expressions.

5.1.3   *Syntax for lambda expressions*

As we've mentioned, a lambda encodes a small piece of behavior that you can pass around as a value. It can be declared independently and stored in a variable. But more frequently, it's declared directly when passed to a function. Figure 5.1 shows the syntax for declaring lambda expressions.

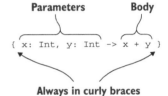

Figure 5.1   Lambda expression syntax

A lambda expression in Kotlin is always surrounded by curly braces. Note that there are no parentheses around the arguments. The arrow separates the argument list from the body of the lambda.

You can store a lambda expression in a variable and then treat this variable like a normal function (call it with the corresponding arguments):

```
>>> val sum = { x: Int, y: Int -> x + y }
>>> println(sum(1, 2))           ◁──┐ Calls the lambda
3                                    │ stored in a variable
```

If you want to, you can call the lambda expression directly:

```
>>> { println(42) }()
42
```

But such syntax isn't readable and doesn't make much sense (it's equivalent to executing the lambda body directly). If you need to enclose a piece of code in a block, you can use the library function run that executes the lambda passed to it:

```
>>> run { println(42) }          ◁──┐ Runs the code
42                                   │ in the lambda
```

In section 8.2, you'll learn why such invocations have no runtime overhead and are as efficient as built-in language constructs. Let's return to listing 5.4, which finds the oldest person in a list:

```
>>> val people = listOf(Person("Alice", 29), Person("Bob", 31))
>>> println(people.maxBy { it.age })
Person(name=Bob, age=31)
```

If you rewrite this example without using any syntax shortcuts, you get the following:

```
people.maxBy({ p: Person -> p.age })
```

It should be clear what happens here: the piece of code in curly braces is a lambda expression, and you pass it as an argument to the function. The lambda expression takes one argument of type `Person` and returns its age.

But this code is verbose. First, there's too much punctuation, which hurts readability. Second, the type can be inferred from the context and therefore omitted. Last, you don't need to assign a name to the lambda argument in this case.

Let's make these improvements, starting with braces. In Kotlin, a syntactic convention lets you move a lambda expression out of parentheses if it's the last argument in a function call. In this example, the lambda is the only argument, so it can be placed after the parentheses:

```
people.maxBy() { p: Person -> p.age }
```

When the lambda is the only argument to a function, you can also remove the empty parentheses from the call:

```
people.maxBy { p: Person -> p.age }
```

All three syntactic forms mean the same thing, but the last one is the easiest to read. If a lambda is the only argument, you'll definitely want to write it without the parentheses. When you have several arguments, you can emphasize that the lambda is an argument by leaving it inside the parentheses, or you can put it outside of them—both options are valid. If you want to pass two or more lambdas, you can't move more than one out, so it's usually better to pass them using the regular syntax.

To see what these options look like with a more complex call, let's go back to the `joinToString` function that you used extensively in chapter 3. It's also defined in the Kotlin standard library, with the difference that the standard library version takes a function as an additional parameter. This function can be used to convert an element to a string differently than the `toString` function. Here's how you can use it to print names only.

> **Listing 5.6 Passing a lambda as a named argument**

```
>>> val people = listOf(Person("Alice", 29), Person("Bob", 31))
>>> val names = people.joinToString(separator = " ",
...                       transform = { p: Person -> p.name })
>>> println(names)
Alice Bob
```

And here's how you can rewrite that call with the lambda outside the parentheses.

Listing 5.7   Passing a lambda outside of parentheses

```
people.joinToString(" ") { p: Person -> p.name }
```

Listing 5.7 uses a named argument to pass the lambda, making it clear what the lambda is used for. Listing 5.8 is more concise, but it doesn't express explicitly what the lambda is used for, so it may be harder to understand for people not familiar with the function being called.

> **INTELLIJ IDEA TIP**   To convert one syntactic form to the other, you can use the actions: "Move lambda expression out of parentheses" and "Move lambda expression into parentheses."

Let's move on with simplifying the syntax and get rid of the parameter type.

Listing 5.8   Omitting lambda parameter type

```
people.maxBy { p: Person -> p.age }        Parameter type
people.maxBy { p -> p.age }     Parameter type    explicitly written
                                inferred
```

As with local variables, if the type of a lambda parameter can be inferred, you don't need to specify it explicitly. With the `maxBy` function, the parameter type is always the same as the collection element type. The compiler knows you're calling `maxBy` on a collection of `Person` objects, so it can understand that the lambda parameter will also be of type `Person`.

There are cases when the compiler can't infer the lambda parameter type, but we won't discuss them here. The simple rule you can follow is to always start without the types; if the compiler complains, specify them.

You can specify only some of the argument types while leaving others with just names. Doing so may be convenient if the compiler can't infer one of the types or if an explicit type improves readability.

The last simplification you can make in this example is to replace a parameter with the default parameter name: `it`. This name is generated if the context expects a lambda with only one argument, and its type can be inferred.

Listing 5.9   Using the default parameter name

```
people.maxBy { it.age }        "it" is an autogenerated
                               parameter name.
```

This default name is generated only if you don't specify the argument name explicitly.

> **NOTE**   The `it` convention is great for shortening your code, but you shouldn't abuse it. In particular, in the case of nested lambdas, it's better to declare the

parameter of each lambda explicitly; otherwise it's difficult to understand which value the `it` refers to. It's useful also to declare parameters explicitly if the meaning or the type of the parameter isn't clear from the context.

If you store a lambda in a variable, there's no context from which to infer the parameter types, so you have to specify them explicitly:

```
>>> val getAge = { p: Person -> p.age }
>>> people.maxBy(getAge)
```

So far, you've only seen examples with lambdas that consist of one expression or statement. But lambdas aren't constrained to such a small size and can contain multiple statements. In this case, the last expression is the result:

```
>>> val sum = { x: Int, y: Int ->
...     println("Computing the sum of $x and $y...")
...     x + y
... }
>>> println(sum(1, 2))
Computing the sum of 1 and 2...
3
```

Next, let's talk about a concept that often goes side-by-side with lambda expressions: capturing variables from the context.

5.1.4 Accessing variables in scope

You know that when you declare an anonymous inner class in a function, you can refer to parameters and local variables of that function from inside the class. With lambdas, you can do exactly the same thing. If you use a lambda in a function, you can access the parameters of that function as well as the local variables declared before the lambda.

To demonstrate this, let's use the `forEach` standard library function. It's one of the most basic collection-manipulation functions; all it does is call the given lambda on every element in the collection. The `forEach` function is somewhat more concise than a regular `for` loop, but it doesn't have many other advantages, so you needn't rush to convert all your loops to lambdas.

The following listing takes a list of messages and prints each message with the same prefix.

Listing 5.10 Using function parameters in a lambda

```
fun printMessagesWithPrefix(messages: Collection<String>, prefix: String) {
    messages.forEach {                              ◁──── Takes as an argument a
        println("$prefix $it")                             lambda specifying what to
    }                                                      do with each element
}
```

Accesses the "prefix" parameter in the lambda

```
>>> val errors = listOf("403 Forbidden", "404 Not Found")
>>> printMessagesWithPrefix(errors, "Error:")
Error: 403 Forbidden
Error: 404 Not Found
```

One important difference between Kotlin and Java is that in Kotlin, you aren't restricted to accessing final variables. You can also modify variables from within a lambda. The next listing counts the number of client and server errors in the given set of response status codes.

Listing 5.11   Changing local variables from a lambda

```
fun printProblemCounts(responses: Collection<String>) {
    var clientErrors = 0
    var serverErrors = 0
    responses.forEach {
        if (it.startsWith("4")) {
            clientErrors++
        } else if (it.startsWith("5")) {
            serverErrors++
        }
    }
    println("$clientErrors client errors, $serverErrors server errors")
}

>>> val responses = listOf("200 OK", "418 I'm a teapot",
...                        "500 Internal Server Error")
>>> printProblemCounts(responses)
1 client errors, 1 server errors
```

Declares variables that will be accessed from the lambda

Modifies variables in the lambda

Kotlin, unlike Java, allows you to access non-final variables and even modify them in a lambda. External variables accessed from a lambda, such as `prefix`, `clientErrors`, and `serverErrors` in these examples, are said to be *captured* by the lambda.

Note that, by default, the lifetime of a local variable is constrained by the function in which the variable is declared. But if it's captured by the lambda, the code that uses this variable can be stored and executed later. You may ask how this works. When you capture a final variable, its value is stored together with the lambda code that uses it. For non-final variables, the value is enclosed in a special wrapper that lets you change it, and the reference to the wrapper is stored together with the lambda.

Capturing a mutable variable: implementation details

Java allows you to capture only final variables. When you want to capture a mutable variable, you can use one of the following tricks: either declare an array of one element in which to store the mutable value, or create an instance of a wrapper class that stores the reference that can be changed. If you used this technique explicitly in Kotlin, the code would be as follows:

```
class Ref<T>(var value: T)
>>> val counter = Ref(0)
>>> val inc = { counter.value++ }
```

Class used to simulate capturing a mutable variable

Formally, an immutable variable is captured; but the actual value is stored in a field and can be changed.

In real code, you don't need to create such wrappers. Instead, you can mutate the variable directly:

```
var counter = 0
val inc = { counter++ }
```

How does it work? The first example shows how the second example works under the hood. Any time you capture a final variable (val), its value is copied, as in Java. When you capture a mutable variable (var), its value is stored as an instance of a Ref class. The Ref variable is final and can be easily captured, whereas the actual value is stored in a field and can be changed from the lambda.

An important caveat is that, if a lambda is used as an event handler or is otherwise executed asynchronously, the modifications to local variables will occur only when the lambda is executed. For example, the following code isn't a correct way to count button clicks:

```
fun tryToCountButtonClicks(button: Button): Int {
    var clicks = 0
    button.onClick { clicks++ }
    return clicks
}
```

This function will always return 0. Even though the onClick handler will modify the value of clicks, you won't be able to observe the modification, because the onClick handler will be called after the function returns. A correct implementation of the function would need to store the click count not in a local variable, but in a location that remains accessible outside of the function—for example, in a property of a class.

We've discussed the syntax for declaring lambdas and how variables are captured in lambdas. Now let's talk about member references, a feature that lets you easily pass references to existing functions.

5.1.5   *Member references*

You've seen how lambdas allow you to pass a block of code as a parameter to a function. But what if the code that you need to pass as a parameter is already defined as a function? Of course, you can pass a lambda that calls that function, but doing so is somewhat redundant. Can you pass the function directly?

In Kotlin, just like in Java 8, you can do so if you convert the function to a value. You use the :: operator for that:

```
val getAge = Person::age
```

This expression is called *member reference*, and it provides a short syntax for creating a function value that calls exactly one method or accesses a property. A double colon separates the name of a class from the name of the member you need to reference (a method or property), as shown in figure 5.2.

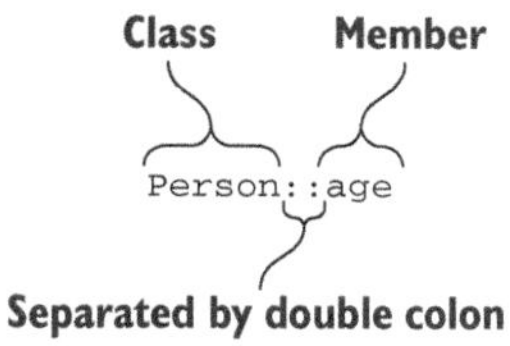

This is a more concise expression of a lambda that does the same thing:

```
val getAge = { person: Person -> person.age }
```

Note that, regardless of whether you're referencing a function or a property, you shouldn't put parentheses after its name in a member reference.

A member reference has the same type as a lambda that calls that function, so you can use the two interchangeably:

```
people.maxBy(Person::age)
```

You can have a reference to a function that's declared at the top level (and isn't a member of a class), as well:

```
fun salute() = println("Salute!")
>>> run(::salute)
Salute!
```

Reference to the top-level function

Figure 5.2 Member reference syntax

In this case, you omit the class name and start with `::`. The member reference `::salute` is passed as an argument to the library function `run`, which calls the corresponding function.

It's convenient to provide a member reference instead of a lambda that delegates to a function taking several parameters:

```
val action = { person: Person, message: String ->
    sendEmail(person, message)
}
val nextAction = ::sendEmail
```

This lambda delegates to a sendEmail function.

You can use a member reference instead.

You can store or postpone the action of creating an instance of a class using a *constructor reference*. The constructor reference is formed by specifying the class name after the double colons:

```
data class Person(val name: String, val age: Int)

>>> val createPerson = ::Person
>>> val p = createPerson("Alice", 29)
>>> println(p)
Person(name=Alice, age=29)
```

An action of creating an instance of "Person" is saved as a value.

Note that you can also reference extension functions the same way:

```
fun Person.isAdult() = age >= 21
val predicate = Person::isAdult
```

Although `isAdult` isn't a member of the `Person` class, you can access it via reference, just as you can access it as a member on an instance: `person.isAdult()`.

Bound references

In Kotlin 1.0, when you take a reference to a method or property of a class, you always need to provide an instance of that class when you call the reference. Support for bound member references, which allow you to use the member-reference syntax to capture a reference to the method on a specific object instance, is planned for Kotlin 1.1:

```
>>> val p = Person("Dmitry", 34)
>>> val personsAgeFunction = Person::age
>>> println(personsAgeFunction(p))
34
>>> val dmitrysAgeFunction = p::age          A bound member reference
>>> println(dmitrysAgeFunction())       ⟵   that you can use in Kotlin 1.1
34
```

Note that `personsAgeFunction` is a one-argument function (it returns the age of a given person), whereas `dmitrysAgeFunction` is a zero-argument function (it returns the age of a specific person). Before Kotlin 1.1, you needed to write the lambda { p.age } explicitly instead of using the bound member reference `p::age`.

In the following section, we'll look at many library functions that work great with lambda expressions, as well as member references.

5.2   *Functional APIs for collections*

Functional style provides many benefits when it comes to manipulating collections. You can use library functions for the majority of tasks and simplify your code. In this section, we'll discuss some of the functions in the Kotlin standard library for working with collections. We'll start with staples like `filter` and `map` and the concepts behind them. We'll also cover other useful functions and give you tips about how not to overuse them and how to write clear and comprehensible code.

Note that none of these functions were invented by the designers of Kotlin. These or similar functions are available for all languages that support lambdas, including C#, Groovy, and Scala. If you're already familiar with these concepts, you can quickly look through the following examples and skip the explanations.

5.2.1   *Essentials: filter and map*

The `filter` and `map` functions form the basis for manipulating collections. Many collection operations can be expressed with their help.

For each function, we'll provide one example with numbers and one using the familiar `Person` class:

```
data class Person(val name: String, val age: Int)
```

The `filter` function goes through a collection and selects the elements for which the given lambda returns `true`:

```
>>> val list = listOf(1, 2, 3, 4)
>>> println(list.filter { it % 2 == 0 })
[2, 4]
```

◁─── **Only even numbers remain.**

The result is a new collection that contains only the elements from the input collection that satisfy the predicate, as illustrated in figure 5.3.

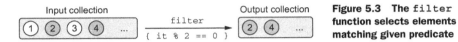

Figure 5.3   The `filter` function selects elements matching given predicate

If you want to keep only people older than 30, you can use `filter`:

```
>>> val people = listOf(Person("Alice", 29), Person("Bob", 31))
>>> println(people.filter { it.age > 30 })
[Person(name=Bob, age=31)]
```

The `filter` function can remove unwanted elements from a collection, but it doesn't change the elements. Transforming elements is where `map` comes into play.

The `map` function applies the given function to each element in the collection and collects the results into a new collection. You can transform a list of numbers into a list of their squares, for example:

```
>>> val list = listOf(1, 2, 3, 4)
>>> println(list.map { it * it })
[1, 4, 9, 16]
```

The result is a new collection that contains the same number of elements, but each element is transformed according to the given predicate (see figure 5.4).

Figure 5.4   The `map` function applies a lambda to all elements in a collection.

If you want to print just a list of names, not a list of people, you can transform the list using `map`:

```
>>> val people = listOf(Person("Alice", 29), Person("Bob", 31))
>>> println(people.map { it.name })
[Alice, Bob]
```

Note that this example can be nicely rewritten using member references:

```
people.map(Person::name)
```

You can easily chain several calls like that. For example, let's print the names of people older than 30:

```
>>> people.filter { it.age > 30 }.map(Person::name)
[Bob]
```

Now, let's say you need the names of the oldest people in the group. You can find the maximum age of the people in the group and return everyone who is that age. It's easy to write such code using lambdas:

```
people.filter { it.age == people.maxBy(Person::age).age }
```

But note that this code repeats the process of finding the maximum age for every person, so if there are 100 people in the collection, the search for the maximum age will be performed 100 times!

The following solution improves on that and calculates the maximum age only once:

```
val maxAge = people.maxBy(Person::age).age
people.filter { it.age == maxAge }
```

Don't repeat a calculation if you don't need to! Simple-looking code using lambda expressions can sometimes obscure the complexity of the underlying operations. Always keep in mind what is happening in the code you write.

You can also apply the filter and transformation functions to maps:

```
>>> val numbers = mapOf(0 to "zero", 1 to "one")
>>> println(numbers.mapValues { it.value.toUpperCase() })
{0=ZERO, 1=ONE}
```

There are separate functions to handle keys and values. filterKeys and mapKeys filter and transform the keys of a map, respectively, where as filterValues and mapValues filter and transform the corresponding values.

5.2.2 *"all", "any", "count", and "find": applying a predicate to a collection*

Another common task is checking whether all elements in a collection match a certain condition (or, as a variation, whether any elements match). In Kotlin, this is expressed through the all and any functions. The count function checks how many elements satisfy the predicate, and the find function returns the first matching element.

To demonstrate those functions, let's define the predicate canBeInClub27 to check whether a person is 27 or younger:

```
val canBeInClub27 = { p: Person -> p.age <= 27 }
```

If you're interested in whether all the elements satisfy this predicate, you use the all function:

```
>>> val people = listOf(Person("Alice", 27), Person("Bob", 31))
>>> println(people.all(canBeInClub27))
false
```

If you need to check whether there's at least one matching element, use any:

```
>>> println(people.any(canBeInClub27))
true
```

Note that !all ("not all") with a condition can be replaced with any with a negation of that condition, and vice versa. To make your code easier to understand, you should choose a function that doesn't require you to put a negation sign before it:

```
>>> val list = listOf(1, 2, 3)
>>> println(!list.all { it == 3 })
true
>>> println(list.any { it != 3 })
true
```

The negation ! isn't noticeable, so it's better to use "any" in this case.

The condition in the argument has changed to its opposite.

The first check ensures that not all elements are equal to 3. That's the same as having at least one non-3, which is what you check using any on the second line.

If you want to know how many elements satisfy this predicate, use count:

```
>>> val people = listOf(Person("Alice", 27), Person("Bob", 31))
>>> println(people.count(canBeInClub27))
1
```

> ## Using the right function for the job: "count" vs. "size"
> It's easy to forget about count and implement it by filtering the collection and getting its size:
>
> ```
> >>> println(people.filter(canBeInClub27).size)
> 1
> ```
>
> But in this case, an intermediate collection is created to store all the elements that satisfy the predicate. On the other hand, the count method tracks only the number of matching elements, not the elements themselves, and is therefore more efficient.
>
> As a general rule, try to find the most appropriate operation that suits your needs.

To find an element that satisfies the predicate, use the find function:

```
>>> val people = listOf(Person("Alice", 27), Person("Bob", 31))
>>> println(people.find(canBeInClub27))
Person(name=Alice, age=27)
```

This returns the first matching element if there are many or null if nothing satisfies the predicate. A synonym of find is firstOrNull, which you can use if it expresses the idea more clearly for you.

5.2.3 *groupBy: converting a list to a map of groups*

Imagine that you need to divide all elements into different groups according to some quality. For example, you want to group people of the same age. It's convenient to pass this quality directly as a parameter. The `groupBy` function can do this for you:

```
>>> val people = listOf(Person("Alice", 31),
...         Person("Bob", 29), Person("Carol", 31))
>>> println(people.groupBy { it.age })
```

The result of this operation is a map from the key by which the elements are grouped (age, in this case) to the groups of elements (persons); see figure 5.5.

Figure 5.5 The result of applying the `groupBy` function

For this example, the output is as follows:

```
{29=[Person(name=Bob, age=29)],
 31=[Person(name=Alice, age=31), Person(name=Carol, age=31)]}
```

Each group is stored in a list, so the result type is `Map<Int, List<Person>>`. You can do further modifications with this map, using functions such as `mapKeys` and `mapValues`.

As another example, let's see how to group strings by their first character using member references:

```
>>> val list = listOf("a", "ab", "b")
>>> println(list.groupBy(String::first))
{a=[a, ab], b=[b]}
```

Note that `first` here isn't a member of the `String` class, it's an extension. Nevertheless, you can access it as a member reference.

5.2.4 *flatMap and flatten: processing elements in nested collections*

Now let's put aside our discussion of people and switch to books. Suppose you have a storage of books, represented by the class `Book`:

```
class Book(val title: String, val authors: List<String>)
```

Each book was written by one or more authors. You can compute the set of all the authors in your library:

```
books.flatMap { it.authors }.toSet()
```
← **Set of all authors who wrote books in the "books" collection**

The `flatMap` function does two things: At first it transforms (or *maps*) each element to a collection according to the function given as an argument, and then it combines (or *flattens*) several lists into one. An example with strings illustrates this concept well (see figure 5.6):

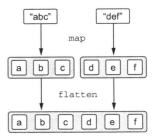

```
>>> val strings = listOf("abc", "def")
>>> println(strings.flatMap { it.toList() })
[a, b, c, d, e, f]
```

Figure 5.6 The result of applying the `flatMap` function

The `toList` function on a string converts it into a list of characters. If you used the `map` function together with `toList`, you'd get a list of lists of characters, as shown in the second row in the figure. The `flatMap` function does the following step as well, and returns one list consisting of all the elements.

Let's return to the authors:

```
>>> val books = listOf(Book("Thursday Next", listOf("Jasper Fforde")),
...                    Book("Mort", listOf("Terry Pratchett")),
...                    Book("Good Omens", listOf("Terry Pratchett",
...                                              "Neil Gaiman")))
>>> println(books.flatMap { it.authors }.toSet())
[Jasper Fforde, Terry Pratchett, Neil Gaiman]
```

Each book can be written by multiple authors, and the `book.authors` property stores the collection of authors. The `flatMap` function combines the authors of all the books in a single, flat list. The `toSet` call removes duplicates from the resulting collection—so, in this example, Terry Pratchett is listed only once in the output.

You may think of `flatMap` when you're stuck with a collection of collections of elements that have to be combined into one. Note that if you don't need to transform anything and just need to flatten such a collection, you can use the `flatten` function: `listOfLists.flatten()`.

We've highlighted a few of the collection operation functions in the Kotlin standard library, but there are many more. We won't cover them all, for reasons of space, and also because showing a long list of functions is boring. Our general advice when you write code that works with collections is to think of how the operation could be expressed as a general transformation, and to look for a library function that performs such a transformation. It's likely that you'll be able to find one and use it to solve your problem more quickly than with a manual implementation.

Now let's take a closer look at the performance of code that chains collection operations. In the next section, you'll see the different ways in which such operations can be executed.

5.3   *Lazy collection operations: sequences*

In the previous section, you saw several examples of chained collection functions, such as `map` and `filter`. These functions create intermediate collections *eagerly,* meaning the intermediate result of each step is stored in a temporary list. *Sequences* give you an alternative way to perform such computations that avoids the creation of intermediate temporary objects.

Here's an example:

```
people.map(Person::name).filter { it.startsWith("A") }
```

The Kotlin standard library reference says that both `filter` and `map` return a list. That means this chain of calls will create two lists: one to hold the results of the `filter` function and another for the results of `map`. This isn't a problem when the source list contains two elements, but it becomes much less efficient if you have a million.

To make this more efficient, you can convert the operation so it uses *sequences* instead of using collections directly:

```
people.asSequence()                          ←——— Converts the initial
    .map(Person::name)                             collection to Sequence
    .filter { it.startsWith("A") }    ←——— Sequences support the
    .toList()                              same API as collections.
                        ←——— Converts the resulting
                              Sequence back into a list
```

The result of applying this operation is the same as in the previous example: a list of people's names that start with the letter *A*. But in the second example, no intermediate collections to store the elements are created, so performance for a large number of elements will be noticeably better.

The entry point for lazy collection operations in Kotlin is the `Sequence` interface. The interface represents just that: a sequence of elements that can be enumerated one by one. `Sequence` provides only one method, `iterator`, that you can use to obtain the values from the sequence.

The strength of the `Sequence` interface is in the way operations on it are implemented. The elements in a sequence are evaluated lazily. Therefore, you can use sequences to efficiently perform chains of operations on elements of a collection without creating collections to hold intermediate results of the processing.

You can convert any collection to a sequence by calling the extension function `asSequence`. You call `toList` for backward conversion.

Why do you need to convert the sequence back to a collection? Wouldn't it be more convenient to use sequences instead of collections, if they're so much better? The answer is: sometimes. If you only need to iterate over the elements in a sequence, you can use the sequence directly. If you need to use other API methods, such as accessing the elements by index, then you need to convert the sequence to a list.

> **NOTE** As a rule, use a sequence whenever you have a chain of operations on a *large* collection. In section 8.2, we'll discuss why eager operations on regular collections are efficient in Kotlin, in spite of creating intermediate collections. But if the collection contains a large number of elements, the intermediate rearranging of elements costs a lot, so lazy evaluation is preferable.

Because operations on a sequence are lazy, in order to perform them, you need to iterate over the sequence's elements directly or by converting it to a collection. The next section explains that.

5.3.1 *Executing sequence operations: intermediate and terminal operations*

Operations on a sequence are divided into two categories: intermediate and terminal. An *intermediate operation* returns another sequence, which knows how to transform the elements of the original sequence. A *terminal operation* returns a result, which may be a collection, an element, a number, or any other object that's somehow obtained by the sequence of transformations of the initial collection (see figure 5.7).

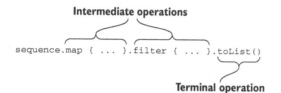

Figure 5.7 Intermediate and terminal operations on sequences

Intermediate operations are always lazy. Look at this example, where the terminal operation is missing:

```
>>> listOf(1, 2, 3, 4).asSequence()
...         .map { print("map($it) "); it * it }
...         .filter { print("filter($it) "); it % 2 == 0 }
```

Executing this code snippet prints nothing to the console. That means the map and filter transformations are postponed and will be applied only when the result is obtained (that is, when the terminal operation is called):

```
>>> listOf(1, 2, 3, 4).asSequence()
...         .map { print("map($it) "); it * it }
...         .filter { print("filter($it) "); it % 2 == 0 }
...         .toList()
map(1) filter(1) map(2) filter(4) map(3) filter(9) map(4) filter(16)
```

The terminal operation causes all the postponed computations to be performed.

One more important thing to notice in this example is the order in which the computations are performed. The naive approach would be to call the map function on each element first and then call the filter function on each element of the resulting sequence. That's how map and filter work on collections, but not on sequences. For sequences, all operations are applied to each element sequentially: the first element is processed (mapped, then filtered), then the second element is processed, and so on.

This approach means some elements aren't transformed at all if the result is obtained before they are reached. Let's look at an example with map and find operations. First you map a number to its square, and then you find the first item that's greater than 3:

```
>>> println(listOf(1, 2, 3, 4).asSequence()
                    .map { it * it }.find { it > 3 })
4
```

If the same operations are applied to a collection instead of a sequence, then the result of map is evaluated first, transforming all elements in the initial collection. In the second step, an element satisfying the predicate is found in the intermediate collection. With sequences, the lazy approach means you can skip processing some of the elements. Figure 5.8 illustrates the difference between evaluating this code in an eager (using collections) and lazy (using sequences) manner.

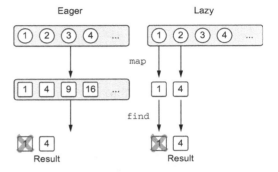

Figure 5.8 **Eager evaluation runs each operation on the entire collection; lazy evaluation processes elements one by one.**

In the first case, when you work with collections, the list is transformed into another list, so the map transformation is applied to each element, including 3 and 4. Afterward, the first element satisfying the predicate is found: the square of 2.

In the second case, the find call begins processing the elements one by one. You take a number from the original sequence, transform it with map, and then check whether it matches the predicate passed to find. When you reach 2, you see that its square is greater than 3 and return it as the result of the find operation. You don't need to look at 3 and 4, because the result was found before you reached them.

The order of the operations you perform on a collection can affect performance as well. Imagine that you have a collection of people, and you want to print their names if they're shorter than a certain limit. You need to do two things: map each person to their name, and then filter out those names that aren't short enough. You can apply map and filter operations in any order in this case. Both approaches give the same result, but they differ in the total number of transformations that should be performed (see figure 5.9).

```
>>> val people = listOf(Person("Alice", 29), Person("Bob", 31),
...          Person("Charles", 31), Person("Dan", 21))
>>> println(people.asSequence().map(Person::name)          ← "map" goes first,
...          .filter { it.length < 4 }.toList())             then "filter".
[Bob, Dan]
>>> println(people.asSequence().filter { it.name.length < 4 }
...          .map(Person::name).toList())                   ← "map" goes
[Bob, Dan]                                                    after "filter".
```

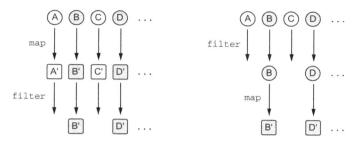

Figure 5.9   Applying `filter` **first helps to reduce the total number of transformations.**

If `map` goes first, each element is transformed. If you apply `filter` first, inappropriate elements are filtered out as soon as possible and aren't transformed.

> **Streams vs. sequences**
>
> If you're familiar with Java 8 streams, you'll see that sequences are exactly the same concept. Kotlin provides its own version of the same concept because Java 8 streams aren't available on platforms built on older versions of Java, such as Android. If you're targeting Java 8, streams give you one big feature that isn't currently implemented for Kotlin collections and sequences: the ability to run a stream operation (such as `map` or `filter`) on multiple CPUs in parallel. You can choose between streams and sequences based on the Java versions you target and your specific requirements.

5.3.2   Creating sequences

The previous examples used the same method to create a sequence: you called `asSequence()` on a collection. Another possibility is to use the `generateSequence` function. This function calculates the next element in a sequence given the previous one. For example, here's how you can use `generateSequence` to calculate the sum of all natural numbers up to 100.

Listing 5.12   Generating and using a sequence of natural numbers

```
>>> val naturalNumbers = generateSequence(0) { it + 1 }
>>> val numbersTo100 = naturalNumbers.takeWhile { it <= 100 }
>>> println(numbersTo100.sum())
5050
```
⟵ **All the delayed operations are performed when the result "sum" is obtained.**

Note that `naturalNumbers` and `numbersTo100` in this example are both sequences with postponed computation. The actual numbers in those sequences won't be evaluated until you call the terminal operation (`sum` in this case).

Another common use case is a sequence of parents. If an element has parents of its own type (such as a human being or a Java file), you may be interested in qualities of the sequence of all of its ancestors. In the following example, you inquire whether the file is located in a hidden directory by generating a sequence of its parent directories and checking this attribute on each of the directories.

> **Listing 5.13 Generating and using a sequence of parent directories**

```
fun File.isInsideHiddenDirectory() =
        generateSequence(this) { it.parentFile }.any { it.isHidden }

>>> val file = File("/Users/svtk/.HiddenDir/a.txt")
>>> println(file.isInsideHiddenDirectory())
true
```

Once again, you generate a sequence by providing the first element and a way to get each subsequent element. By replacing `any` with `find`, you'll get the desired directory. Note that using sequences allows you to stop traversing the parents as soon as you find the required directory.

We've thoroughly discussed a frequently used application of lambda expressions: using them to simplify manipulating collections. Now let's continue with another important topic: using lambdas with an existing Java API.

5.4 *Using Java functional interfaces*

Using lambdas with Kotlin libraries is nice, but the majority of APIs that you work with are probably written in Java, not Kotlin. The good news is that Kotlin lambdas are fully interoperable with Java APIs; in this section, you'll see exactly how this works.

At the beginning of the chapter, you saw an example of passing a lambda to a Java method:

```
button.setOnClickListener { /* actions on click */ }
```

Passes the lambda as an argument

The `Button` class sets a new listener to a button via an `setOnClickListener` method that takes an argument of type `OnClickListener`:

```
/* Java */
public class Button {
    public void setOnClickListener(OnClickListener l) { ... }
}
```

The `OnClickListener` interface declares one method, `onClick`:

```
/* Java */
public interface OnClickListener {
    void onClick(View v);
}
```

In Java (prior to Java 8), you have to create a new instance of an anonymous class to pass it as an argument to the `setOnClickListener` method:

```
button.setOnClickListener(new OnClickListener() {
    @Override
    public void onClick(View v) {
```

```
        . . .
    }
}
```

In Kotlin, you can pass a lambda instead:

```
button.setOnClickListener { view -> ... }
```

The lambda used to implement `OnClickListener` has one parameter of type `View`, as in the `onClick` method. The mapping is illustrated in figure 5.10.

```
public interface OnClickListener {
    void onClick(View v);                 ━━━━━━▶  { view -> ... }
}
```

Figure 5.10   Parameters of the lambda correspond to method parameters.

This works because the `OnClickListener` interface has only one abstract method. Such interfaces are called *functional interfaces*, or *SAM interfaces*, where SAM stands for *single abstract method*. The Java API is full of functional interfaces like `Runnable` and `Callable`, as well as methods working with them. Kotlin allows you to use lambdas when calling Java methods that take functional interfaces as parameters, ensuring that your Kotlin code remains clean and idiomatic.

> **NOTE**   Unlike Java, Kotlin has proper function types. Because of that, Kotlin functions that need to take lambdas as parameters should use function types, not functional interface types, as the types of those parameters. Automatic conversion of lambdas to objects implementing Kotlin interfaces isn't supported. We'll discuss the use of function types in function declarations in section 8.1.

Let's look in detail at what happens when you pass a lambda to a method that expects an argument of a functional interface type.

5.4.1   Passing a lambda as a parameter to a Java method

You can pass a lambda to any Java method that expects a functional interface. For example, consider this method, which has a parameter of type `Runnable`:

```
/* Java */
void postponeComputation(int delay, Runnable computation);
```

In Kotlin, you can invoke it and pass a lambda as an argument. The compiler will automatically convert it into an instance of `Runnable`:

```
postponeComputation(1000) { println(42) }
```

Note that when we say "an instance of `Runnable`," what we mean is "an instance of an anonymous class implementing `Runnable`." The compiler will create that for you and will use the lambda as the body of the single abstract method—the run method, in this case.

You can achieve the same effect by creating an anonymous object that implements Runnable explicitly:

```
postponeComputation(1000, object : Runnable {        ◄───  Passes an object expression
    override fun run() {                                    as an implementation of a
        println(42)                                         functional interface
    }
})
```

But there's a difference. When you explicitly declare an object, a new instance is created on each invocation. With a lambda, the situation is different: if the lambda doesn't access any variables from the function where it's defined, the corresponding anonymous class instance is reused between calls:

```
postponeComputation(1000) { println(42) }     ◄───  One instance of Runnable is
                                                    created for the entire program.
```

Therefore, the equivalent implementation with an explicit object declaration is the following snippet, which stores the Runnable instance in a variable and uses it for every invocation:

```
                                                  ┌─  Compiled to a global variable;
                                                  │   only one instance in the program
val runnable = Runnable { println(42) }    ◄──────┘
fun handleComputation() {
    postponeComputation(1000, runnable)    ◄───  One object is used for every
}                                                handleComputation call.
```

If the lambda captures variables from the surrounding scope, it's no longer possible to reuse the same instance for every invocation. In that case, the compiler creates a new object for every call and stores the values of the captured variables in that object. For example, in the following function, every invocation uses a new Runnable instance, storing the id value as a field:

```
                                              ┌─  Captures the variable
                                              │   "id" in a lambda
fun handleComputation(id: String) {    ◄──────┘
    postponeComputation(1000) { println(id) }    ◄───  Creates a new instance of Runnable
}                                                       on each handleComputation call
```

Lambda implementation details

As of Kotlin 1.0, every lambda expression is compiled into an anonymous class, unless it's an inline lambda. Support for generating Java 8 bytecode is planned for later versions of Kotlin. Once implemented, it will allow the compiler to avoid generating a separate .class file for every lambda expression.

If a lambda captures variables, the anonymous class will have a field for each captured variable, and a new instance of that class will be created for every invocation.

(continued)

Otherwise, a single instance will be created. The name of the class is derived by adding a suffix from the name of the function in which the lambda is declared: `Handle-Computation$1`, for this example.

Here's what you'll see if you decompile the code of the previous lambda expression:

```
class HandleComputation$1(val id: String) : Runnable {
    override fun run() {
        println(id)
    }
}
fun handleComputation(id: String) {
    postponeComputation(1000, HandleComputation$1(id))
}
```

> Under the hood, instead of a lambda, an instance of a special class is created.

As you can see, the compiler generates a field and a constructor parameter for each captured variable.

Note that the discussion of creating an anonymous class and an instance of this class for a lambda is valid for Java methods expecting functional interfaces, but does not apply to working with collections using Kotlin extension methods. If you pass a lambda to the Kotlin function that's marked `inline`, no anonymous classes are created. And most of the library functions are marked `inline`. Details of how this works are discussed in section 8.2.

As you've seen, in most cases the conversion of a lambda to an instance of a functional interface happens automatically, without any effort on your part. But there are cases when you need to perform the conversion explicitly. Let's see how to do that.

5.4.2 SAM constructors: explicit conversion of lambdas to functional interfaces

A *SAM constructor* is a compiler-generated function that lets you perform an explicit conversion of a lambda into an instance of a functional interface. You can use it in contexts when the compiler doesn't apply the conversion automatically. For instance, if you have a method that returns an instance of a functional interface, you can't return a lambda directly; you need to wrap it into a SAM constructor. Here's a simple example.

Listing 5.14 Using a SAM constructor to return a value

```
fun createAllDoneRunnable(): Runnable {
    return Runnable { println("All done!") }
}

>>> createAllDoneRunnable().run()
All done!
```

The name of the SAM constructor is the same as the name of the underlying functional interface. The SAM constructor takes a single argument—a lambda that will be used as the body of the single abstract method in the functional interface—and returns an instance of the class implementing the interface.

In addition to returning values, SAM constructors are used when you need to store a functional interface instance generated from a lambda in a variable. Suppose you want to reuse one listener for several buttons, as in the following listing (in an Android application, this code can be a part of the `Activity.onCreate` method).

Listing 5.15   Using a SAM constructor to reuse a `listener` instance

```
val listener = OnClickListener { view ->
    val text = when (view.id) {              ◁──┐  Uses view.id to determine
        R.id.button1 -> "First button"          │  which button was clicked
        R.id.button2 -> "Second button"
        else -> "Unknown button"
    }
    toast(text)                      ◁──────┐  Shows the value of
}                                            │  "text" to the user
button1.setOnClickListener(listener)
button2.setOnClickListener(listener)
```

`listener` checks which button was the source of the click and behaves accordingly. You could define a listener by using an object declaration that implements `OnClick-Listener`, but SAM constructors give you a more concise option.

Lambdas and adding/removing listeners

Note that there's no `this` in a lambda as there is in an anonymous object: there's no way to refer to the anonymous class instance into which the lambda is converted. From the compiler's point of view, the lambda is a block of code, not an object, and you can't refer to it as an object. The `this` reference in a lambda refers to a surrounding class.

If your event listener needs to unsubscribe itself while handling an event, you can't use a lambda for that. Use an anonymous object to implement a listener, instead. In an anonymous object, the `this` keyword refers to the instance of that object, and you can pass it to the API that removes the listener.

Also, even though SAM conversion in method calls typically happens automatically, there are cases when the compiler can't choose the right overload when you pass a lambda as an argument to an overloaded method. In those cases, applying an explicit SAM constructor is a good way to resolve the compilation error.

To finish our discussion of lambda syntax and usage, let's look at lambdas with receivers and how they're used to define convenient library functions that look like built-in constructs.

5.5   *Lambdas with receivers: "with" and "apply"*

This section demonstrates the with and apply functions from the Kotlin standard library. These functions are convenient, and you'll find many uses for them even without understanding how they're declared. Later, in section 11.2.1, you'll see how you can declare similar functions for your own needs. The explanations in this section, however, help you become familiar with a unique feature of Kotlin's lambdas that isn't available with Java: the ability to call methods of a different object in the body of a lambda without any additional qualifiers. Such lambdas are called *lambdas with receivers*. Let's begin by looking at the with function, which uses a lambda with a receiver.

5.5.1   *The "with" function*

Many languages have special statements you can use to perform multiple operations on the same object without repeating its name. Kotlin also has this facility, but it's provided as a library function called with, not as a special language construct.

To see how it can be useful, consider the following example, which you'll then refactor using with.

Listing 5.16   Building the alphabet

```
fun alphabet(): String {
    val result = StringBuilder()
    for (letter in 'A'..'Z') {
        result.append(letter)
    }
    result.append("\nNow I know the alphabet!")
    return result.toString()
}
>>> println(alphabet())
ABCDEFGHIJKLMNOPQRSTUVWXYZ
Now I know the alphabet!
```

In this example, you call several different methods on the result instance and repeating the result name in each call. This isn't too bad, but what if the expression you were using was longer or repeated more often?

Here's how you can rewrite the code using with.

Listing 5.17   Using with to build the alphabet

```
fun alphabet(): String {
    val stringBuilder = StringBuilder()          Specifies the receiver value on
    return with(stringBuilder) {                 which you're calling the methods
        for (letter in 'A'..'Z') {
            this.append(letter)                  Calls a method on the receiver
        }                                        value though an explicit "this"
        append("\nNow I know the alphabet!")
        this.toString()                          Returns a value
    }                                            from the lambda
}
```

Calls a method, omitting "this"

The with structure looks like a special construct, but it's a function that takes two arguments: stringBuilder, in this case, and a lambda. The convention of putting the lambda outside of the parentheses works here, and the entire invocation looks like a built-in feature of the language. Alternatively, you could write this as with(stringBuilder, { ... }), but it's less readable.

The with function converts its first argument into a *receiver* of the lambda that's passed as a second argument. You can access this receiver via an explicit this reference. Alternatively, as usual for a this reference, you can omit it and access methods or properties of this value without any additional qualifiers.

In listing 5.17, this refers to stringBuilder, which is passed to with as the first argument. You can access methods on stringBuilder via explicit this references, as in this.append(letter); or directly, as in append("\nNow...").

Lambdas with receiver and extension functions

You may recall that you saw a similar concept with this referring to the function receiver. In the body of an extension function, this refers to the instance of the type the function is extending, and it can be omitted to give you direct access to the receiver's members.

Note that an extension function is, in a sense, a function with a receiver. The following analogy can be applied:

Regular function	Regular lambda
Extension function	Lambda with a receiver

A lambda is a way to define behavior similar to a regular function. A lambda with a receiver is a way to define behavior similar to an extension function.

Let's refactor the initial alphabet function even further and get rid of the extra stringBuilder variable.

Listing 5.18 Using with and an expression body to build the alphabet

```
fun alphabet() = with(StringBuilder()) {
    for (letter in 'A'..'Z') {
        append(letter)
    }
    append("\nNow I know the alphabet!")
    toString()
}
```

This function now only returns an expression, so it's rewritten using the expression-body syntax. You create a new instance of StringBuilder and pass it directly as an argument, and then you reference it without the explicit this in the lambda.

> ### Method-name conflicts
>
> What happens if the object you pass as a parameter to `with` has a method with the same name as the class in which you're using `with`? In this case, you can add an explicit label to the `this` reference to specify which method you need to call.
>
> Imagine that the `alphabet` function is a method of the class `OuterClass`. If you need to refer to the `toString` method defined in the outer class instead of the one in `StringBuilder`, you can do so using the following syntax:
>
> `this@OuterClass.toString()`

The value that `with` returns is the result of executing the lambda code. The result is the last expression in the lambda. But sometimes you want the call to return the receiver object, not the result of executing the lambda. That's where the `apply` library function can be of use.

5.5.2 The "apply" function

The `apply` function works almost exactly the same as `with`; the only difference is that `apply` always returns the object passed to it as an argument (in other words, the receiver object). Let's refactor the `alphabet` function again, this time using `apply`.

Listing 5.19 Using `apply` to build the alphabet

```
fun alphabet() = StringBuilder().apply {
    for (letter in 'A'..'Z') {
        append(letter)
    }
    append("\nNow I know the alphabet!")
}.toString()
```

The `apply` function is declared as an extension function. Its receiver becomes the receiver of the lambda passed as an argument. The result of executing `apply` is `StringBuilder`, so you call `toString` to convert it to `String` afterward.

One of many cases where this is useful is when you're creating an instance of an object and need to initialize some properties right away. In Java, this is usually accomplished through a separate `Builder` object; and in Kotlin, you can use `apply` on any object without any special support from the library where the object is defined.

To see how `apply` is used for such cases, let's look at an example that creates an Android `TextView` component with some custom attributes.

Listing 5.20 Using `apply` to initialize a `TextView`

```
fun createViewWithCustomAttributes(context: Context) =
    TextView(context).apply {
        text = "Sample Text"
        textSize = 20.0
```

```
        setPadding(10, 0, 0, 0)
    }
```

The `apply` function allows you to use the compact expression body style for the function. You create a new `TextView` instance and immediately pass it to `apply`. In the lambda passed to `apply`, the `TextView` instance becomes the receiver, so you can call methods and set properties on it. After the lambda is executed, `apply` returns that instance, which is already initialized; it becomes the result of the `createViewWith-CustomAttributes` function.

The `with` and `apply` functions are basic generic examples of using lambdas with receivers. More specific functions can also use the same pattern. For example, you can simplify the `alphabet` function even further by using the `buildString` standard library function, which will take care of creating a `StringBuilder` and calling `toString`. The argument of `buildString` is a lambda with a receiver, and the receiver is always a `StringBuilder`.

Listing 5.21 Using `buildString` to build the alphabet

```
fun alphabet() = buildString {
    for (letter in 'A'..'Z') {
        append(letter)
    }
    append("\nNow I know the alphabet!")
}
```

The `buildString` function is an elegant solution for the task of creating a `String` with the help of `StringBuilder`.

You'll see more interesting examples in chapter 11, when we begin discussing domain-specific languages. Lambdas with receivers are great tools for building DSLs; we'll show you how to use them for that purpose and how to define your own functions that call lambdas with receivers.

5.6 Summary

- Lambdas allow you to pass chunks of code as arguments to functions.
- Kotlin lets you pass lambdas to functions outside of parentheses and refer to a single lambda parameter as `it`.
- Code in a lambda can access and modify variables in the function containing the call to the lambda.
- You can create references to methods, constructors, and properties by prefixing the name of the function with `::`, and pass such references to functions instead of lambdas.
- Most common operations with collections can be performed without manually iterating over elements, using functions such as `filter`, `map`, `all`, `any`, and so on.

- Sequences allow you to combine multiple operations on a collection without creating collections to hold intermediate results.
- You can pass lambdas as arguments to methods that take a Java functional interface (an interface with a single abstract method, also known as a SAM interface) as a parameter.
- Lambdas with receivers are lambdas in which you can directly call methods on a special receiver object.
- The `with` standard library function allows you to call multiple methods on the same object without repeating the reference to the object. `apply` lets you construct and initialize any object using a builder-style API.

The Kotlin type system

By now, you've seen a large part of Kotlin's syntax in action. You've moved beyond creating Java-equivalent code in Kotlin and are ready to enjoy some of Kotlin's productivity features that can make your code more compact and readable.

Let's slow down a bit and take a closer look at one of the most important parts of Kotlin: its type system. Compared to Java, Kotlin's type system introduces several new features that are essential for improving the reliability of your code, such as support for *nullable types* and *read-only collections*. It also removes some of the features of the Java type system that have turned out to be unnecessary or problematic, such as first-class support for arrays. Let's look at the details.

6.1   Nullability

Nullability is a feature of the Kotlin type system that helps you avoid `NullPointerException` errors. As a user of a program, you've probably seen an error message similar to "An error has occurred: java.lang.NullPointerException," with no additional details. Another version is a message like "Unfortunately, the application X has stopped," which often also conceals a `NullPointerException` as a cause. Such errors can be troublesome for both users and developers.

The approach of modern languages, including Kotlin, is to convert these problems from runtime errors into compile-time errors. By supporting nullability as part of the type system, the compiler can detect many possible errors during compilation and reduce the possibility of having exceptions thrown at runtime.

In this section, we'll discuss nullable types in Kotlin: how Kotlin marks values that are allowed to be `null`, and the tools Kotlin provides to deal with such values. Moving beyond that, we'll cover the details of mixing Kotlin and Java code with respect to nullable types.

6.1.1   *Nullable types*

The first and probably most important difference between Kotlin's and Java's type systems is Kotlin's explicit support for *nullable types*. What does this mean? It's a way to indicate which variables or properties in your program are allowed to be `null`. If a variable can be `null`, calling a method on it isn't safe, because it can cause a `NullPointerException`. Kotlin disallows such calls and thereby prevents many possible exceptions. To see how this works in practice, let's look at the following Java function:

```
/* Java */
int strLen(String s) {
    return s.length();
}
```

Is this function safe? If the function is called with a `null` argument, it will throw a `NullPointerException`. Do you need to add a check for `null` to the function? It depends on the function's intended use.

Let's try to rewrite this function in Kotlin. The first question you must answer is, do you expect the function to be called with a `null` argument? We mean not only the `null` literal directly, as in `strLen(null)`, but also any variable or other expression that may have the value `null` at runtime.

If you don't expect it to happen, you declare this function in Kotlin as follows:

```
fun strLen(s: String) = s.length
```

Calling `strLen` with an argument that may be `null` isn't allowed and will be flagged as error at compile time:

```
>>> strLen(null)
ERROR: Null can not be a value of a non-null type String
```

The parameter is declared as type `String`, and in Kotlin this means it must always contain a `String` instance. The compiler enforces that, so you can't pass an argument containing `null`. This gives you the guarantee that the `strLen` function will never throw a `NullPointerException` at runtime.

If you want to allow the use of this function with all arguments, including those that can be `null`, you need to mark it explicitly by putting a question mark after the type name:

```
fun strLenSafe(s: String?) = ...
```

You can put a question mark after any type, to indicate that the variables of this type can store `null` references: `String?`, `Int?`, `MyCustom-Type?`, and so on (see figure 6.1).

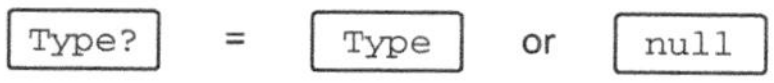

Type? = Type or null

Figure 6.1   A variable of a nullable type can store a `null` reference

To reiterate, a type without a question mark denotes that variables of this type can't store `null` references. This means all regular types are non-null by default, unless explicitly marked as nullable.

Once you have a value of a nullable type, the set of operations you can perform on it is restricted. For example, you can no longer call methods on it:

```
>>> fun strLenSafe(s: String?) = s.length()
ERROR: only safe (?.) or non-null asserted (!!.) calls are allowed
 on a nullable receiver of type kotlin.String?
```

You can't assign it to a variable of a non-null type:

```
>>> val x: String? = null
>>> var y: String = x
ERROR: Type mismatch: inferred type is String? but String was expected
```

You can't pass a value of a nullable type as an argument to a function having a non-null parameter:

```
>>> strLen(x)
ERROR: Type mismatch: inferred type is String? but String was expected
```

So what can you do with it? The most important thing is to compare it with `null`. And once you perform the comparison, the compiler remembers that and treats the value as being non-null in the scope where the check has been performed. For example, this code is perfectly valid.

Listing 6.1   Handling `null` values using `if` checks

```
fun strLenSafe(s: String?): Int =
    if (s != null) s.length else 0

>>> val x: String? = null
>>> println(strLenSafe(x))
0
>>> println(strLenSafe("abc"))
3
```

By adding the check for null, the code now compiles.

If using `if` checks was the only tool for tackling nullability, your code would become verbose fairly quickly. Fortunately, Kotlin provides a number of other tools to help deal with nullable values in a more concise manner. But before we look at those tools, let's spend time discussing the meaning of nullability and what variable types are.

6.1.2   *The meaning of types*

Let's think about the most general questions: what are types, and why do variables have them? The Wikipedia article on types (http://en.wikipedia.org/wiki/Data_type) gives a pretty good answer to what a type is: "A type is a classification … that determines the possible values for that type, and the operations that can be done on values of that type."

Let's try to apply this definition to some of the Java types, starting with the `double` type. As you know, a `double` is a 64-bit floating-point number. You can perform standard mathematical operations on these values. All of those functions are equally applicable to all values of type `double`. Therefore, if you have a variable of type `double`, then you can be certain that any operation on its value that's allowed by the compiler will execute successfully.

Now let's contrast this with a variable of type `String`. In Java, such a variable can hold one of two kinds of values: an instance of the class `String` or `null`. Those kinds of values are completely unlike each other: even Java's own `instanceof` operator will tell you that `null` isn't a `String`. The operations that can be done on the value of the variable are also completely different: an actual `String` instance allows you to call any methods on the string, whereas a `null` value allows only a limited set of operations.

This means Java's type system isn't doing a good job in this case. Even though the variable has a declared type—`String`—you don't know what you can do with values of this variable unless you perform additional checks. Often, you skip those checks because you know from the general flow of data in your program that a value can't be `null` at a certain point. Sometimes you're wrong, and your program then crashes with a `NullPointerException`.

Other ways to cope with NullPointerException errors

Java has some tools to help solve the problem of `NullPointerException`. For example, some people use annotations (such as `@Nullable` and `@NotNull`) to express the nullability of values. There are tools (for example, IntelliJ IDEA's built-in code inspections) that can use these annotations to detect places where a `NullPointerException` can be thrown. But such tools aren't part of the standard Java compilation process, so it's hard to ensure that they're applied consistently. It's also difficult to annotate the entire codebase, including the libraries used by the project, so that all possible error locations can be detected. Our own experience at JetBrains shows that even widespread use of nullability annotations in Java doesn't completely solve the problem of NPEs.

Another path to solving this problem is to never use `null` values in code and to use a special wrapper type, such as the `Optional` type introduced in Java 8, to represent values that may or may not be defined. This approach has several downsides: the code gets more verbose, the extra wrapper instances affect performance at runtime, and it's not used consistently across the entire ecosystem. Even if you do use `Optional` everywhere in your own code, you'll still need to deal with `null` values returned from methods of the JDK, the Android framework, and other third-party libraries.

Nullable types in Kotlin provide a comprehensive solution to this problem. Distinguishing nullable and non-`null` types provides a clear understanding of what operations are allowed on the value and what operations can lead to exceptions at runtime and are therefore forbidden.

> **NOTE** Objects of nullable or non-`null` types at runtime are the same; a nullable type isn't a wrapper for a non-`null` type. All checks are performed at compilation time. That means there's no runtime overhead for working with nullable types in Kotlin.

Now let's see how to work with nullable types in Kotlin and why dealing with them is by no means annoying. We'll start with the special operator for safely accessing a nullable value.

6.1.3 *Safe call operator: "?."*

One of the most useful tools in Kotlin's arsenal is the *safe-call* operator: `?.`, which allows you to combine a `null` check and a method call into a single operation. For example, the expression `s?.toUpperCase()` is equivalent to the following, more cumbersome one: `if (s != null) s.toUpperCase() else null`.

In other words, if the value on which you're trying to call the method isn't `null`, the method call is executed normally. If it's `null`, the call is skipped, and `null` is used as the value instead. Figure 6.2 illustrates.

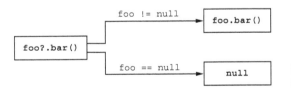

Figure 6.2 **The safe-call operator calls methods only on non-`null` values.**

Note that the result type of such an invocation is nullable. Although `String.toUpperCase` returns a value of type `String`, the result type of an expression `s?.toUpperCase()` when `s` is nullable will be `String?`:

```
fun printAllCaps(s: String?) {
    val allCaps: String? = s?.toUpperCase()        ◁— allCaps may
    println(allCaps)                                   be null.
}
```

```
>>> printAllCaps("abc")
ABC
>>> printAllCaps(null)
null
```

Safe calls can be used for accessing properties as well, not just for method calls. The following example shows a simple Kotlin class with a nullable property and demonstrates the use of a safe-call operator for accessing that property.

Listing 6.2   Using safe calls to deal with nullable properties

```
class Employee(val name: String, val manager: Employee?)

fun managerName(employee: Employee): String? = employee.manager?.name

>>> val ceo = Employee("Da Boss", null)
>>> val developer = Employee("Bob Smith", ceo)
>>> println(managerName(developer))
Da Boss
>>> println(managerName(ceo))
null
```

If you have an object graph in which multiple properties have nullable types, it's often convenient to use multiple safe calls in the same expression. Say you store information about a person, their company, and the address of the company using different classes. Both the company and its address may be omitted. With the ?. operator, you can access the country property for a Person in one line, without any additional checks.

Listing 6.3   Chaining multiple safe-call operators

```
class Address(val streetAddress: String, val zipCode: Int,
              val city: String, val country: String)

class Company(val name: String, val address: Address?)

class Person(val name: String, val company: Company?)

fun Person.countryName(): String {
    val country = this.company?.address?.country     ◁─┐  Several safe-call
    return if (country != null) country else "Unknown"  │  operators can be in a chain.
}
>>> val person = Person("Dmitry", null)
>>> println(person.countryName())
Unknown
```

Sequences of calls with null checks are a common sight in Java code, and you've now seen how Kotlin makes them more concise. But listing 6.3 contains unnecessary repetition: you're comparing a value to null and returning either that value or something else if it's null. Let's see if Kotlin can help get rid of that repetition.

6.1.4 *Elvis operator: "?:"*

Kotlin has a handy operator to provide default values instead of `null`. It's called the *Elvis operator* (or the *null-coalescing operator,* if you prefer more serious-sounding names for things). It looks like this: `?:` (you can visualize it being Elvis if you turn your head sideways). Here's how it's used:

```
fun foo(s: String?) {
    val t: String = s ?: ""      ◁── If "s" is null, the result
}                                     is an empty string.
```

The operator takes two values, and its result is the first value if it isn't `null` or the second value if the first one is `null`. Figure 6.3 shows how it works.

Figure 6.3 The Elvis operator substitutes a specified value for `null`.

The Elvis operator is often used together with the safe-call operator to substitute a value other than `null` when the object on which the method is called is `null`. Here's how you can use this pattern to simplify listing 6.1.

Listing 6.4 Using the Elvis operator to deal with `null` values

```
fun strLenSafe(s: String?): Int = s?.length ?: 0

>>> println(strLenSafe("abc"))
3
>>> println(strLenSafe(null))
0
```

The `countryName` function from listing 6.3 also fits on one line now.

```
fun Person.countryName() =
    company?.address?.country ?: "Unknown"
```

What makes the Elvis operator particularly handy in Kotlin is that operations such as `return` and `throw` work as expressions and therefore can be used on the operator's right side. In that case, if the value on the left side is `null`, the function will immediately return a value or throw an exception. This is helpful for checking preconditions in a function.

Let's see how you can use this operator to implement a function to print a shipping label with the person's company address. The following listing repeats the declarations of all the classes—in Kotlin, they're so concise that it's not a problem.

> **Listing 6.5   Using `throw` together with Elvis operator**

```
class Address(val streetAddress: String, val zipCode: Int,
              val city: String, val country: String)

class Company(val name: String, val address: Address?)

class Person(val name: String, val company: Company?)

fun printShippingLabel(person: Person) {
    val address = person.company?.address
      ?: throw IllegalArgumentException("No address")     ◁── Throws an exception
    with (address) {                              ◁──┐          if the address is absent
        println(streetAddress)             "address" is
        println("$zipCode $city, $country")    non-null.
    }
}

>>> val address = Address("Elsestr. 47", 80687, "Munich", "Germany")
>>> val jetbrains = Company("JetBrains", address)
>>> val person = Person("Dmitry", jetbrains)

>>> printShippingLabel(person)
Elsestr. 47
80687 Munich, Germany

>>> printShippingLabel(Person("Alexey", null))
java.lang.IllegalArgumentException: No address
```

The function `printShippingLabel` prints a label if everything is correct. If there's no address, it doesn't just throw a `NullPointerException` with a line number, but instead reports a meaningful error. If an address is present, the label consists of the street address, the ZIP code, the city, and the country. Note how the `with` function, which you saw in the previous chapter, is used to avoid repeating `address` four times in a row.

Now that you've seen the Kotlin way to perform "if not-null" checks, let's talk about the Kotlin safe version of `instanceof` checks: the *safe-cast operator* that often appears together with safe calls and Elvis operators.

6.1.5   *Safe casts: "as?"*

In chapter 2, you saw the regular Kotlin operator for type casts: the `as` operator. Just like a regular Java type cast, `as` throws a `ClassCastException` if the value doesn't have the type you're trying to cast it to. Of course, you can combine it with an `is` check to ensure that it does have the proper type. But as a safe and concise language, doesn't Kotlin provide a better solution? Indeed it does.

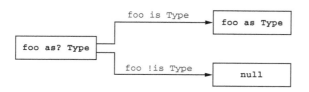

Figure 6.4 **The safe-cast operator tries to cast a value to the given type and returns `null` if the type differs.**

The `as?` operator tries to cast a value to the specified type and returns `null` if the value doesn't have the proper type. Figure 6.4 illustrates this.

One common pattern of using a safe cast is combining it with the Elvis operator. For example, this comes in handy for implementing the `equals` method.

> Listing 6.6 **Using a safe cast to implement** `equals`

```
class Person(val firstName: String, val lastName: String) {
    override fun equals(o: Any?): Boolean {
        val otherPerson = o as? Person ?: return false

        return otherPerson.firstName == firstName &&
               otherPerson.lastName == lastName
    }

    override fun hashCode(): Int =
        firstName.hashCode() * 37 + lastName.hashCode()
}

>>> val p1 = Person("Dmitry", "Jemerov")
>>> val p2 = Person("Dmitry", "Jemerov")
>>> println(p1 == p2)
true
>>> println(p1.equals(42))
false
```

Checks the type and returns false if no match

After the safe cast, the variable otherPerson is smart-cast to the Person type.

The == operator calls the "equals" method.

With this pattern, you can easily check whether the parameter has a proper type, cast it, and return `false` if the type isn't right—all in the same expression. Of course, smart casts also apply in this context: after you've checked the type and rejected `null` values, the compiler knows that the type of the `otherPerson` variable's value is `Person` and lets you use it accordingly.

The safe-call, safe-cast, and Elvis operators are useful and appear often in Kotlin code. But sometimes you don't need Kotlin's support in handling `null`s; you just need to tell the compiler that the value is in fact not `null`. Let's see how you can achieve that.

6.1.6 *Not-null assertions: "!!"*

The *not-null assertion* is the simplest and bluntest tool Kotlin gives you for dealing with a value of a nullable type. It's represented by a double exclamation mark and converts

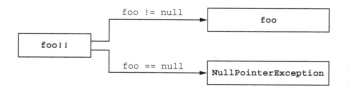

Figure 6.5 By using a not-null assertion, you can explicitly throw an exception if the value is null.

any value to a non-null type. For null values, an exception is thrown. The logic is illustrated in figure 6.5.

Here's a trivial example of a function that uses the assertion to convert a nullable argument to a non-null one.

Listing 6.7 Using a not-null assertion

```
fun ignoreNulls(s: String?) {
    val sNotNull: String = s!!                    The exception
    println(sNotNull.length)                      points to this line.
}

>>> ignoreNulls(null)
Exception in thread "main" kotlin.KotlinNullPointerException
    at <...>.ignoreNulls(07_NotnullAssertions.kt:2)
```

What happens if s is null in this function? Kotlin doesn't have much choice: it will throw an exception (a special kind of NullPointerException) at runtime. But note that the place where the exception is thrown is the assertion itself, not a subsequent line where you're trying to use the value. Essentially, you're telling the compiler, "I know the value isn't null, and I'm ready for an exception if it turns out I'm wrong."

> **NOTE** You may notice that the double exclamation mark looks a bit rude: it's almost like you're yelling at the compiler. This is intentional. The designers of Kotlin are trying to nudge you toward a better solution that doesn't involve making assertions that can't be verified by the compiler.

But there are situations when not-null assertions are the appropriate solution for a problem. When you check for null in one function and use the value in another function, the compiler can't recognize that the use is safe. If you're certain the check is always performed in another function, you may not want to duplicate it before using the value; then you can use a not-null assertion instead.

This happens in practice with action classes, which appear in many UI frameworks such as Swing. In an action class, there are separate methods for updating the state of an action (to enable or disable it) and for executing it. The checks performed in the update method ensure that the execute method won't be called if the conditions aren't met, but there's no way for the compiler to recognize that.

Let's look at an example of a Swing action that uses a not-null assertion in this situation. The `CopyRowAction` action is supposed to copy the value of the selected row in a list to the clipboard. We've omitted all the unnecessary details, keeping only the code responsible for checking whether any row was selected (meaning therefore the action can be performed) and obtaining the value for the selected row. The Action API implies that `actionPerformed` is called only when `isEnabled` is `true`.

Listing 6.8   Using a not-null assertion in a Swing action

```
class CopyRowAction(val list: JList<String>) : AbstractAction() {
    override fun isEnabled(): Boolean =
        list.selectedValue != null

    override fun actionPerformed(e: ActionEvent) {      ◁──┐ actionPerformed is
        val value = list.selectedValue!!                     called only if isEnabled
        // copy value to clipboard                           returns "true".
    }
}
```

Note that if you don't want to use `!!` in this case, you can write `val value = list.selectedValue ?: return` to obtain a value of a non-null type. If you use that pattern, a nullable value of `list.selectedValue` will cause an early return from the function, so `value` will always be non-null. Although the not-null check using the Elvis operator is redundant here, it may be a good protection against `isEnabled` becoming more complicated later.

There's one more caveat to keep in mind: when you use `!!` and it results in an exception, the stack trace identifies the line number in which the exception was thrown but not a specific expression. To make it clear exactly which value was `null`, it's best to avoid using multiple `!!` assertions on the same line:

```
person.company!!.address!!.country              ◁──┐ Don't write code like this!
```

If you get an exception in this line, you won't be able to tell whether it was `company` or `address` that held a `null` value.

So far, we've discussed mostly how to *access* the values of nullable types. But what should you do if you need to pass a nullable value as an argument to a function that expects a non-null value? The compiler doesn't allow you to do that without a check, because doing so is unsafe. The Kotlin language doesn't have any special support for this case, but there's a standard library function that can help you: it's called `let`.

6.1.7   The "let" function

The `let` function makes it easier to deal with nullable expressions. Together with a safe-call operator, it allows you to evaluate an expression, check the result for `null`, and store the result in a variable, all in a single, concise expression.

One of its most common uses is handling a nullable argument that should be passed to a function that expects a non-null parameter. Let's say the function send-EmailTo takes one parameter of type String and sends an email to that address. This function is written in Kotlin and requires a non-null parameter:

```
fun sendEmailTo(email: String) { /*...*/ }
```

You can't pass a value of a nullable type to this function:

```
>>> val email: String? = ...
>>> sendEmailTo(email)
ERROR: Type mismatch: inferred type is String? but String was expected
```

You have to check explicitly whether this value isn't null:

```
if (email != null) sendEmailTo(email)
```

But you can go another way: use the let function, and call it via a safe call. All the let function does is turn the object on which it's called into a parameter of the lambda. If you combine it with the safe call syntax, it effectively converts an object of a nullable type on which you call let into a non-null type (see figure 6.6).

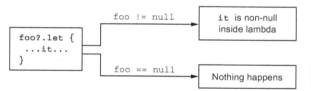

Figure 6.6 **Safe-calling "let" executes a lambda only if an expression isn't** null.

The let function will be called only if the email value is non-null, so you use the email as a non-null argument of the lambda:

```
email?.let { email -> sendEmailTo(email) }
```

After using the short syntax, the autogenerated name it, the result is much shorter: `email?.let { sendEmailTo(it) }`. Here's a more complete example that shows this pattern.

Listing 6.9 Using `let` **to call a function with a non-null parameter**

```
fun sendEmailTo(email: String) {
    println("Sending email to $email")
}

>>> var email: String? = "yole@example.com"
>>> email?.let { sendEmailTo(it) }
Sending email to yole@example.com
>>> email = null
>>> email?.let { sendEmailTo(it) }
```

Note that the `let` notation is especially convenient when you have to use the value of a longer expression if it's not `null`. You don't have to create a separate variable in this case. Compare this explicit `if` check

```
val person: Person? = getTheBestPersonInTheWorld()
if (person != null) sendEmailTo(person.email)
```

to the same code without an extra variable:

```
getTheBestPersonInTheWorld()?.let { sendEmailTo(it.email) }
```

This function returns `null`, so the code in the lambda will never be executed:

```
fun getTheBestPersonInTheWorld(): Person? = null
```

When you need to check multiple values for `null`, you can use nested `let` calls to handle them. But in most cases, such code ends up fairly verbose and hard to follow. It's generally easier to use a regular `if` expression to check all the values together.

One other common situation is properties that are effectively non-`null` but can't be initialized with a non-`null` value in the constructor. Let's see how Kotlin allows you to deal with that situation.

6.1.8 Late-initialized properties

Many frameworks initialize objects in dedicated methods called after the object instance has been created. For example, in Android, the activity initialization happens in the `onCreate` method. JUnit requires you to put initialization logic in methods annotated with `@Before`.

But you can't leave a non-`null` property without an initializer in the constructor and only initialize it in a special method. Kotlin normally requires you to initialize all properties in the constructor, and if a property has a non-`null` type, you have to provide a non-`null` initializer value. If you can't provide that value, you have to use a nullable type instead. If you do that, every access to the property requires either a `null` check or the `!!` operator.

Listing 6.10 Using non-`null` assertions to access a nullable property

```
class MyService {
    fun performAction(): String = "foo"
}

class MyTest {
    private var myService: MyService? = null        ◁─── Declares a property
                                                          of a nullable type to
                                                          initialize it with null
    @Before fun setUp() {
        myService = MyService()          ◁─── Provides a real initializer
    }                                          in the setUp method

    @Test fun testAction() {
        Assert.assertEquals("foo",
```

```
            myService!!.performAction())            ⟵┐ You have to take care of
    }                                                └ nullability: use !! or ?.
}
```

This looks ugly, especially if you access the property many times. To solve this, you can declare the `myService` property as *late-initialized*. This is done by applying the `lateinit` modifier.

Listing 6.11   Using a late-initialized property

```
class MyService {
    fun performAction(): String = "foo"
}

class MyTest {                                         ┐ Declares a property of a non-null
    private lateinit var myService: MyService   ⟵─────┘ type without an initializer

    @Before fun setUp() {
        myService = MyService()              ⟵┐ Initializes the property in the
    }                                         └ setUp method as before

    @Test fun testAction() {
        Assert.assertEquals("foo",
            myService.performAction())        ⟵┐ Accesses the property
    }                                         └ without extra null checks
}
```

Note that a late-initialized property is always a `var`, because you need to be able to change its value outside of the constructor, and `val` properties are compiled into final fields that must be initialized in the constructor. But you no longer need to initialize it in a constructor, even though the property has a non-null type. If you access the property before it's been initialized, you get an exception "lateinit property myService has not been initialized". It clearly identifies what has happened and is much easier to understand than a generic `NullPointerException`.

> **NOTE**   A common use case for `lateinit` properties is dependency injection. In that scenario, the values of `lateinit` properties are set externally by a dependency-injection framework. To ensure compatibility with a broad range of Java frameworks, Kotlin generates a field with the same visibility as the `lateinit` property. If the property is declared as `public`, the field will be `public` as well.

Now let's look at how you can extend Kotlin's set of tools for dealing with `null` values by defining extension functions for nullable types.

6.1.9   *Extensions for nullable types*

Defining extension functions for nullable types is one more powerful way to deal with `null` values. Rather than ensuring that a variable can't be `null` before a method call, you can allow the calls with `null` as a receiver, and deal with `null` in the function.

This is only possible for extension functions; regular member calls are dispatched through the object instance and therefore can never be performed when the instance is null.

As an example, consider the functions isEmpty and isBlank, defined as extensions of String in the Kotlin standard library. The first one checks whether the string is an empty string "", and the second one checks whether it's empty or if it consists solely of whitespace characters. You'll generally use these functions to check that the string is non-trivial in order to do something meaningful with it. You may think it would be useful to handle null in the same way as trivial empty or blank strings. And, indeed, you can do so: the functions isEmptyOrNull and isBlankOrNull can be called with a receiver of type String?.

Listing 6.12   Calling an extension function with a nullable receiver

```
fun verifyUserInput(input: String?) {
    if (input.isNullOrBlank()) {                    ◄──────  No safe call is needed.
        println("Please fill in the required fields")
    }
}

>>> verifyUserInput(" ")                    No exception happens when
Please fill in the required fields         you call isNullOrBlank with
>>> verifyUserInput(null)              ◄──  "null" as a receiver.
Please fill in the required fields
```

You can call an extension function that was declared for a nullable receiver without safe access (see figure 6.7). The function handles possible null values.

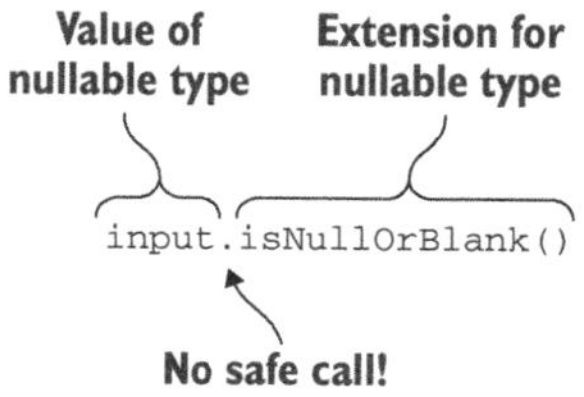

Value of nullable type   Extension for nullable type

input.isNullOrBlank()

No safe call!

Figure 6.7   Extensions for nullable types can be accessed without a safe call.

The function isNullOrBlank checks explicitly for null, returning true in this case, and then calls isBlank, which can be called on a non-null String only:

```
fun String?.isNullOrBlank(): Boolean =        ◄──┐ Extension for a
        this == null || this.isBlank()           │ nullable String
                                          ◄──┐ A smart cast is applied
                                             │ to the second "this".
```

When you declare an extension function for a nullable type (ending with ?), that means you can call this function on nullable values; and this in a function body can be null, so you have to check for that explicitly. In Java, this is always not-null, because it references the instance of a class you're in. In Kotlin, that's no longer the case: in an extension function for a nullable type, this can be null.

Note that the `let` function we discussed earlier can be called on a nullable receiver as well, but it doesn't check the value for `null`. If you invoke it on a nullable type without using the safe-call operator, the lambda argument will also be nullable:

```
>>> val person: Person? = ...                          No safe call, so "it"
>>> person.let { sendEmailTo(it) }                     has a nullable type.
ERROR: Type mismatch: inferred type is Person? but Person was expected
```

Therefore, if you want to check the arguments for being non-`null` with `let`, you have to use the safe-call operator `?.`, as you saw earlier: `person?.let { sendEmailTo(it) }`.

> **NOTE** When you define your own extension function, you need to consider whether you should define it as an extension for a nullable type. By default, define it as an extension for a non-null type. You can safely change it later (no code will be broken) if it turns out it's used mostly on nullable values, and the `null` value can be reasonably handled.

This section showed you something unexpected. If you dereference a variable without an extra check, as in `s.isNullOrBlank()`, it doesn't immediately mean the variable is non-`null`: the function can be an extension for a nullable type. Next, let's discuss another case that may surprise you: a type parameter can be nullable even without a question mark at the end.

6.1.10 *Nullability of type parameters*

By default, all type parameters of functions and classes in Kotlin are nullable. Any type, including a nullable type, can be substituted for a type parameter; in this case, declarations using the type parameter as a type are allowed to be `null`, even though the type parameter `T` doesn't end with a question mark. Consider the following example.

Listing 6.13 Dealing with a nullable type parameter

```
fun <T> printHashCode(t: T) {
    println(t?.hashCode())                             You have to use a safe call
}                                                      because "t" might be null.
>>> printHashCode(null)           "T" is inferred
null                              as "Any?".
```

In the `printHashCode` call, the inferred type for the type parameter `T` is a nullable type, `Any?`. Therefore, the parameter `t` is allowed to hold `null`, even without a question mark after `T`.

To make the type parameter non-null, you need to specify a non-null upper bound for it. That will reject a nullable value as an argument.

Listing 6.14   Declaring a non-null upper bound for a type parameter

```
fun <T: Any> printHashCode(t: T) {
    println(t.hashCode())
}
>>> printHashCode(null)
Error: Type parameter bound for `T` is not satisfied
>>> printHashCode(42)
42
```

◁─┐ **Now "T" can't be nullable.**

◁─┐ **This code doesn't compile: you can't pass null because a non-null value is expected.**

Chapter 9 will cover generics in Kotlin, and section 9.1.4 will cover this topic in more detail.

Note that type parameters are the only exception to the rule that a question mark at the end is required to mark a type as nullable, and types without a question mark are non-null. The next section shows another special case of nullability: types that come from the Java code.

6.1.11   Nullability and Java

The previous discussion covered the tools for working with `null`s in the Kotlin world. But Kotlin prides itself on its Java interoperability, and you know that Java doesn't support nullability in its type system. So what happens when you combine Kotlin and Java? Do you lose all safety, or do you have to check every value for `null`? Or is there a better solution? Let's find out.

First, as we mentioned, sometimes Java code contains information about nullability, expressed using annotations. When this information is present in the code, Kotlin uses it. Thus `@Nullable String` in Java is seen as `String?` by Kotlin, and `@NotNull String` is just `String` (see figure 6.8)

Kotlin recognizes many different flavors of nullability annotations, including those from the JSR-305 standard (in the `javax`

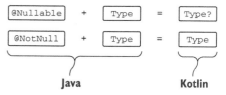

Figure 6.8   Annotated Java types are represented as nullable and non-null types in Kotlin, according to the annotations.

`.annotation` package), the Android ones (`android.support.annotation`), and those supported by JetBrains tools (`org.jetbrains.annotations`). The interesting question is what happens when the annotations aren't present. In that case, the Java type becomes a *platform type* in Kotlin.

PLATFORM TYPES

A platform type is essentially a type for which Kotlin doesn't have nullability information; you can work with it as either a nullable or a non-null type (see figure 6.9). This means, just as in Java, you have full responsibility for the operations you perform with that type. The compiler will allow all operations. It also won't highlight

Figure 6.9   Java types are represented in Kotlin as platform types, which you can use either as a nullable type or as a non-null type.

as redundant any `null`-safe operations on such values, which it normally does when you perform a `null`-safe operation on a value of a non-`null` type. If you know the value can be `null`, you can compare it with `null` before use. If you know it's not `null`, you can use it directly. Just as in Java, you'll get a `NullPointerException` at the usage site if you get this wrong.

Let's say the class `Person` is declared in Java.

Listing 6.15   A Java class without nullability annotations

```java
/* Java */
public class Person {
    private final String name;

    public Person(String name) {
        this.name = name;
    }

    public String getName() {
        return name;
    }
}
```

Can `getName` return `null` or not? The Kotlin compiler knows nothing about nullability of the `String` type in this case, so you have to deal with it yourself. If you're sure the name isn't `null`, you can dereference it in a usual way, as in Java, without additional checks. But be ready to get an exception in this case.

Listing 6.16   Accessing a Java class without `null` checks

```kotlin
fun yellAt(person: Person) {
    println(person.name.toUpperCase() + "!!!")         ◁──┐  The receiver person.name of
}                                                         │  the toUpperCase() call is null,
                                                          │  so an exception is thrown.
>>> yellAt(Person(null))
java.lang.IllegalArgumentException: Parameter specified as non-null
 is null: method toUpperCase, parameter $receiver
```

Note that instead of a plain `NullPointerException`, you get a more detailed error message that the method `toUpperCase` can't be called on a `null` receiver.

In fact, for public Kotlin functions, the compiler generates checks for every parameter (and a receiver as well) that has a non-`null` type, so that attempts to call such a function with incorrect arguments are immediately reported as exceptions. Note that the value-checking is performed right away when the function is called, not when the parameter is used. This ensures that incorrect calls are detected early and won't cause hard-to-understand exceptions if the `null` value is accessed after being passed around between multiple functions in different layers of the codebase.

Your other option is to interpret the return type of `getName()` as nullable and access it safely.

Listing 6.17 Accessing a Java class with `null` checks

```
fun yellAtSafe(person: Person) {
    println((person.name ?: "Anyone").toUpperCase() + "!!!")
}

>>> yellAtSafe(Person(null))
ANYONE!!!
```

In this example, `null` values are handled properly, and no runtime exception is thrown.

Be careful while working with Java APIs. Most of the libraries aren't annotated, so you may interpret all the types as non-null, but that can lead to errors. To avoid errors, you should check the documentation (and, if needed, the implementation) of the Java methods you're using to find out when they can return `null`, and add checks for those methods.

Why platform types?

Wouldn't it be safer for Kotlin to treat all values coming from Java as nullable? Such a design would be possible, but it would require a large number of redundant `null` checks for values that can never be `null`, because the Kotlin compiler wouldn't be able to see that information.

The situation would be especially bad with generics—for example, every `Array-List<String>` coming from Java would be an `ArrayList<String?>?` in Kotlin, and you'd need to check values for `null` on every access or use a cast, which would defeat the safety benefits. Writing such checks is extremely annoying, so the designers of Kotlin went with the pragmatic option and allowed the developers to take responsibility for correctly handling values coming from Java.

You can't declare a variable of a platform type in Kotlin; these types can only come from Java code. But you may see them in error messages and in the IDE:

```
>>> val i: Int = person.name
ERROR: Type mismatch: inferred type is String! but Int was expected
```

The `String!` notation is how the Kotlin compiler denotes platform types coming from Java code. You can't use this syntax in your own code, and usually this exclamation mark isn't connected with the source of a problem, so you can usually ignore it. It just emphasizes that the nullability of the type is unknown.

As we said already, you may interpret platform types any way you like—as nullable or as non-null—so both of the following declarations are valid:

```
>>> val s: String? = person.name          Java's property can
                                           be seen as nullable ...
>>> val s1: String = person.name     ← ... or non-null.
```

In this case, just as with the method calls, you need to make sure you get the nullability right. If you try to assign a `null` value coming from Java to a non-null Kotlin variable, you'll get an exception at the point of assignment.

We've discussed how Java types are seen from Kotlin. Let's now talk about some pitfalls of creating mixed Kotlin and Java hierarchies.

INHERITANCE

When overriding a Java method in Kotlin, you have a choice whether to declare the parameters and the return type as nullable or non-null. For example, let's look at a `StringProcessor` interface in Java.

> **Listing 6.18   A Java interface with a `String` parameter**

```
/* Java */
interface StringProcessor {
    void process(String value);
}
```

In Kotlin, both of the following implementations will be accepted by the compiler.

> **Listing 6.19   Implementing the Java interface with different parameter nullability**

```
class StringPrinter : StringProcessor {
    override fun process(value: String) {
        println(value)
    }
}

class NullableStringPrinter : StringProcessor {
    override fun process(value: String?) {
        if (value != null) {
            println(value)
        }
    }
}
```

Note that it's important to get nullability right when implementing methods from Java classes or interfaces. Because the implementation methods can be called from non-Kotlin code, the Kotlin compiler will generate non-null assertions for every parameter that you declare with a non-null type. If the Java code does pass a `null` value to the method, the assertion will trigger, and you'll get an exception, even if you never access the parameter value in your implementation.

Let's summarize our discussion of nullability. We've discussed nullable and non-null types and the means of working with them: operators for safe operations (safe call `?.`, Elvis operator `?:`, and safe cast `as?`), as well as the operator for unsafe dereference (the not-null assertion `!!`). You've seen how the library function `let` can help you accomplish concise non-null checks and how extensions for nullable types can help move a not-null check into a function. We've also discussed platform types that represent Java types in Kotlin.

Now that we've covered the topic of nullability, let's talk about how the primitive types are represented in Kotlin. This knowledge of nullability will be important for understanding how Kotlin handles Java's boxed types.

6.2   *Primitive and other basic types*

This section describes the basic types used in programs, such as `Int`, `Boolean`, and `Any`. Unlike Java, Kotlin doesn't differentiate primitive types and wrappers. You'll shortly learn why, and how it works under the hood. You'll see the correspondence between Kotlin types and such Java types as `Object` and `Void`, as well.

6.2.1   *Primitive types: Int, Boolean, and more*

As you know, Java makes a distinction between primitive types and reference types. A variable of a *primitive type* (such as `int`) holds its value directly. A variable of a *reference type* (such as `String`) holds a reference to the memory location containing the object.

Values of primitive types can be stored and passed around more efficiently, but you can't call methods on such values or store them in collections. Java provides special wrapper types (such as `java.lang.Integer`) that encapsulate primitive types in situations when an object is needed. Thus, to define a collection of integers, you can't say `Collection<int>`; you have to use `Collection<Integer>` instead.

Kotlin doesn't distinguish between primitive types and wrapper types. You always use the same type (for example, `Int`):

```
val i: Int = 1
val list: List<Int> = listOf(1, 2, 3)
```

That's convenient. What's more, you can call methods on values of a number type. For example, consider this snippet, which uses the `coerceIn` standard library function to restrict the value to the specified range:

```
fun showProgress(progress: Int) {
    val percent = progress.coerceIn(0, 100)
    println("We're ${percent}% done!")
}

>>> showProgress(146)
We're 100% done!
```

If primitive and reference types are the same, does that mean Kotlin represents all numbers as objects? Wouldn't that be terribly inefficient? Indeed it would, so Kotlin doesn't do that.

At runtime, the number types are represented in the most efficient way possible. In most cases—for variables, properties, parameters, and return types—Kotlin's `Int` type is compiled to the Java primitive type `int`. The only case in which this isn't possible is generic classes, such as collections. A primitive type used as a type argument of a generic class is compiled to the corresponding Java wrapper type. For example, if the `Int` type is used as a type argument of the collection, then the collection will store instances of `java.lang.Integer`, the corresponding wrapper type.

The full list of types that correspond to Java primitive types is:

- *Integer types*—Byte, Short, Int, Long
- *Floating-point number types*—Float, Double
- *Character type*—Char
- *Boolean type*—Boolean

A Kotlin type such as Int can be easily compiled under the hood to the corresponding Java primitive type, because the values of both types can't store the null reference. The other direction works in a similar way: When you use Java declarations from Kotlin, Java primitive types become non-null types (not platform types), because they can't hold null values. Now let's discuss the nullable versions of the same types.

6.2.2   *Nullable primitive types: Int?, Boolean?, and more*

Nullable types in Kotlin can't be represented by Java primitive types, because null can only be stored in a variable of a Java reference type. That means whenever you use a nullable version of a primitive type in Kotlin, it's compiled to the corresponding wrapper type.

To see the nullable types in use, let's go back to the opening example of the book and recall the Person class declared there. The class represents a person whose name is always known and whose age can be either known or unspecified. Let's add a function that checks whether one person is older than another.

Listing 6.20   Using nullable primitive types

```
data class Person(val name: String,
                  val age: Int? = null) {

    fun isOlderThan(other: Person): Boolean? {
        if (age == null || other.age == null)
            return null
        return age > other.age
    }
}

>>> println(Person("Sam", 35).isOlderThan(Person("Amy", 42)))
false
>>> println(Person("Sam", 35).isOlderThan(Person("Jane")))
null
```

Note how the regular nullability rules apply here. You can't just compare two values of type Int?, because one of them may be null. Instead, you have to check that both values aren't null. After that, the compiler allows you to work with them normally.

The value of the age property declared in the class Person is stored as a java.lang.Integer. But this detail only matters if you're working with the class from Java. To choose the right type in Kotlin, you only need to consider whether null is a possible value for the variable or property.

As mentioned earlier, generic classes are another case when wrapper types come into play. If you use a primitive type as a type argument of a class, Kotlin uses the boxed representation of the type. For example, this creates a list of boxed `Integer` values, even though you've never specified a nullable type or used a `null` value:

```
val listOfInts = listOf(1, 2, 3)
```

This happens because of the way generics are implemented on the Java virtual machine. The JVM doesn't support using a primitive type as a type argument, so a generic class (both in Java and in Kotlin) must always use a boxed representation of the type. As a consequence, if you need to efficiently store large collections of primitive types, you need to either use a third-party library (such as Trove4J, http://trove.starlight-systems.com) that provides support for such collections or store them in arrays. We'll discuss arrays in detail at the end of this chapter.

Now let's look at how you can convert values between different primitive types.

6.2.3   *Number conversions*

One important difference between Kotlin and Java is the way they handle numeric conversions. Kotlin doesn't automatically convert numbers from one type to the other, even when the other type is larger. For example, the following code won't compile in Kotlin:

```
val i = 1
val l: Long = i          ⟵———— Error: type mismatch
```

Instead, you need to apply the conversion explicitly:

```
val i = 1
val l: Long = i.toLong()
```

Conversion functions are defined for every primitive type (except `Boolean`): `toByte()`, `toShort()`, `toChar()` and so on. The functions support converting in both directions: extending a smaller type to a larger one, like `Int.toLong()`, and truncating a larger type to a smaller one, like `Long.toInt()`.

Kotlin makes the conversion explicit in order to avoid surprises, especially when comparing boxed values. The `equals` method for two boxed values checks the box type, not just the value stored in it. Thus, in Java, `new Integer(42).equals(new Long(42))` returns `false`. If Kotlin supported implicit conversions, you could write something like this:

```
val x = 1                  ⟵———— Int variable          ┐ List of Long
val list = listOf(1L, 2L, 3L)                  ⟵———┘ values
x in list                  ⟵——┐ False if Kotlin supported
                              │ implicit conversions
```

This would evaluate to `false`, contrary to everyone's expectations. Thus the line `x in list` from this example doesn't compile. Kotlin requires you to convert the types explicitly so that only values of the same type are compared:

```
>>> val x = 1
>>> println(x.toLong() in listOf(1L, 2L, 3L))
true
```

If you use different number types in your code at the same time, you have to convert variables explicitly to avoid unexpected behavior.

Primitive type literals

Kotlin supports the following ways to write number literals in source code, in addition to simple decimal numbers:

- Literals of type `Long` use the `L` suffix: `123L`.
- Literals of type `Double` use the standard representation of floating-point numbers: `0.12, 2.0, 1.2e10, 1.2e-10`.
- Literals of type `Float` use the `f` or `F` suffix: `123.4f, .456F, 1e3f`.
- Hexadecimal literals use the `0x` or `0X` prefix (such as `0xCAFEBABE` or `0xbcdL`).
- Binary literals use the `0b` or `0B` prefix (such as `0b000000101`).

Note that underscores in number literals are only supported starting with Kotlin 1.1.

For character literals, you use mostly the same syntax as in Java. You write the character in single quotes, and you can also use escape sequences if you need to. The following are examples of valid Kotlin character literals: `'1'`, `'\t'` (the tab character), `'\u0009'` (the tab character represented using a Unicode escape sequence).

Note that when you're writing a number literal, you usually don't need to use conversion functions. One possibility is to use the special syntax to mark the type of the constant explicitly, such as `42L` or `42.0f`. And even if you don't use it, the necessary conversion is applied automatically if you use a number literal to initialize a variable of a known type or pass it as an argument to a function. In addition, arithmetic operators are overloaded to accept all appropriate numeric types. For example, the following code works correctly without any explicit conversions:

```
fun foo(l: Long) = println(l)

>>> val b: Byte = 1                    ◁── Constant value gets
>>> val l = b + 1L                          the correct type
>>> foo(42)        ◁──                          ◁──  + works with Byte
42                      The compiler interprets        and Long arguments.
                        42 as a Long value.
```

Note that the behavior of Kotlin arithmetic operators with regard to number-range overflow is exactly the same in Java; Kotlin doesn't introduce any overhead for overflow checks.

Conversion from String

The Kotlin standard library provides a similar set of extension functions to convert a string into a primitive type (`toInt`, `toByte`, `toBoolean`, and so on):

```
>>> println("42".toInt())
42
```

> Each of these functions tries to parse the contents of the string as the corresponding type and throws a `NumberFormatException` if the parsing fails.

Before we move on to other types, there are three more special types we need to mention: `Any`, `Unit`, and `Nothing`.

6.2.4 *"Any" and "Any?": the root types*

Similar to how `Object` is the root of the class hierarchy in Java, the `Any` type is the supertype of all non-nullable types in Kotlin. But in Java, `Object` is a supertype of all reference types only, and primitive types aren't part of the hierarchy. That means you have to use wrapper types such as `java.lang.Integer` to represent a primitive type value when `Object` is required. In Kotlin, `Any` is a supertype of all types, including the primitive types such as `Int`.

Just as in Java, assigning a value of a primitive type to a variable of type `Any` performs automatic boxing:

```
val answer: Any = 42
```
⟵ **The value 42 is boxed, because Any is a reference type.**

Note that `Any` is a non-nullable type, so a variable of the type `Any` can't hold the value `null`. If you need a variable that can hold any possible value in Kotlin, including `null`, you must use the `Any?` type.

Under the hood, the `Any` type corresponds to `java.lang.Object`. The `Object` type used in parameters and return types of Java methods is seen as `Any` in Kotlin. (More specifically, it's viewed as a platform type, because its nullability is unknown.) When a Kotlin function uses `Any`, it's compiled to `Object` in the Java bytecode.

As you saw in chapter 4, all Kotlin classes have the following three methods: `toString`, `equals`, and `hashCode`. These methods are inherited from `Any`. Other methods defined on `java.lang.Object` (such as `wait` and `notify`) aren't available on `Any`, but you can call them if you manually cast the value to `java.lang.Object`.

6.2.5 *The Unit type: Kotlin's "void"*

The `Unit` type in Kotlin fulfills the same function as `void` in Java. It can be used as a return type of a function that has nothing interesting to return:

```
fun f(): Unit { ... }
```

Syntactically, it's the same as writing a function with a block body without a type declaration:

```
fun f() { ... }
```
⟵ **Explicit Unit declaration is omitted**

In most cases, you won't notice the difference between `void` and `Unit`. If your Kotlin function has the `Unit` return type and doesn't override a generic function, it's compiled to a good-old `void` function under the hood. If you override it from Java, the Java function just needs to return `void`.

What distinguishes Kotlin's Unit from Java's void, then? Unit is a full-fledged type, and, unlike void, it can be used as a type argument. Only one value of this type exists; it's also called Unit and is returned *implicitly*. This is useful when you override a function that returns a generic parameter and make it return a value of the Unit type:

```
interface Processor<T> {
    fun process(): T
}

class NoResultProcessor : Processor<Unit> {          Returns Unit, but you
    override fun process() {          ⟵─────────      omit the type specification
        // do stuff
    }                       ⟵──┐  You don't need an
}                              │  explicit return here.
```

The signature of the interface requires the process function to return a value; and, because the Unit type does have a value, it's no problem to return it from the method. But you don't need to write an explicit return statement in NoResult-Processor.process, because return Unit is added implicitly by the compiler.

Contrast this with Java, where neither of the possibilities for solving the problem of using "no value" as a type argument is as nice as the Kotlin solution. One option is to use separate interfaces (such as Callable and Runnable) to represent interfaces that don't and do return a value. The other is to use the special java.lang.Void type as the type parameter. If you use the second option, you still need to put in an explicit return null; to return the only possible value matching that type, because if the return type isn't void, you must always have an explicit return statement.

You may wonder why we chose a different name for Unit and didn't call it Void. The name Unit is used traditionally in functional languages to mean "only one instance," and that's exactly what distinguishes Kotlin's Unit from Java's void. We could have used the customary Void name, but Kotlin has a type called Nothing that performs an entirely different function. Having two types called Void and Nothing would be confusing because the meanings are so close. So what's this Nothing type about? Let's find out.

6.2.6   *The Nothing type: "This function never returns"*

For some functions in Kotlin, the concept of a "return value" doesn't make sense because they never complete successfully. For example, many testing libraries have a function called fail that fails the current test by throwing an exception with a specified message. A function that has an infinite loop in it will also never complete successfully.

When analyzing code that calls such a function, it's useful to know that the function will never terminate normally. To express that, Kotlin uses a special return type called Nothing:

```
fun fail(message: String): Nothing {
    throw IllegalStateException(message)
}
```

```
>>> fail("Error occurred")
java.lang.IllegalStateException: Error occurred
```

The Nothing type doesn't have any values, so it only makes sense to use it as a function return type or as a type argument for a type parameter that's used as a generic function return type. In all other cases, declaring a variable where you can't store any value doesn't make sense.

Note that functions returning Nothing can be used on the right side of the Elvis operator to perform precondition checking:

```
val address = company.address ?: fail("No address")
println(address.city)
```

This example shows why having Nothing in the type system is extremely useful. The compiler knows that a function with this return type never terminates normally and uses that information when analyzing the code calling the function. In the previous example, the compiler infers that the type of address is non-null, because the branch handling the case when it's null always throws an exception.

We've finished our discussion of the basic types in Kotlin: primitive types, Any, Unit, and Nothing. Now let's look at the collection types and how they differ from their Java counterparts.

6.3 Collections and arrays

You've already seen many examples of code that uses various collection APIs, and you know that Kotlin builds on the Java collections library and augments it with features added through extension functions. There's more to the story of the collection support in Kotlin and the correspondence between Java and Kotlin collections, and now is a good time to look at the details.

6.3.1 Nullability and collections

Earlier in this chapter, we discussed the concept of nullable types, but we only briefly touched on nullability of type arguments. But this is essential for a consistent type system: it's no less important to know whether a collection can hold null values than to know whether the value of a variable can be null. The good news is that Kotlin fully supports nullability for type arguments. Just as the type of a variable can have a ? character appended to indicate that the variable can hold null, a type used as a type argument can be marked in the same way. To see how this works, let's look at an example of a function that reads a list of lines from a file and tries to parse each line as a number.

Listing 6.21 Building a collection of nullable values

```
fun readNumbers(reader: BufferedReader): List<Int?> {
    val result = ArrayList<Int?>()                    ⟵┐ Creates a list of
    for (line in reader.lineSequence()) {             │ nullable Int values
        try {
            val number = line.toInt()
```

```
                    result.add(number)                        Adds an integer (a non-null
            }                                                 value) to the list
            catch(e: NumberFormatException) {
                    result.add(null)                          Adds null to the list, because
            }                                                 the current line can't be
        }                                                     parsed to an integer
        return result
}
```

`List<Int?>` is a list that can hold values of type `Int?`: in other words, `Int` or `null`. You add an integer to the `result` list if the line can be parsed, or `null` otherwise. Note that since Kotlin 1.1, you can shrink this example by using the function `String.toIntOrNull`, which returns `null` if the string value can't be parsed.

Note how the nullability of the type of the variable itself is distinct from the nullability of the type used as a type argument. The difference between a list of nullable `Int`s and a nullable list of `Int`s is illustrated in figure 6.10.

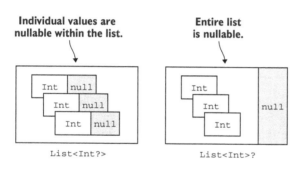

Figure 6.10   Be careful what you make nullable: the elements of the collection or the collection itself?

In the first case, the list itself is always not `null`, but each value in the list can be `null`. A variable of the second type may contain a `null` reference instead of a list instance, but the elements in the list are guaranteed to be non-`null`.

In another context, you may want to declare a variable that holds a nullable list of nullable numbers. The Kotlin way to write this is `List<Int?>?`, with two question marks. You need to apply `null` checks both when using the value of the variable and when using the value of every element in the list.

To see how you can work with a list of nullable values, let's write a function to add all the valid numbers together and count the invalid numbers separately.

Listing 6.22   Working with a collection of nullable values

```
fun addValidNumbers(numbers: List<Int?>) {
    var sumOfValidNumbers = 0
    var invalidNumbers = 0                        Reads a nullable
    for (number in numbers) {                     value from the list
```

```
        if (number != null) {                    ◄─┐  Checks the
            sumOfValidNumbers += number            │  value for null
        } else {
            invalidNumbers++
        }
    }
    println("Sum of valid numbers: $sumOfValidNumbers")
    println("Invalid numbers: $invalidNumbers")
}

>>> val reader = BufferedReader(StringReader("1\nabc\n42"))
>>> val numbers = readNumbers(reader)
>>> addValidNumbers(numbers)
Sum of valid numbers: 43
Invalid numbers: 1
```

There isn't much special going on here. When you access an element of the list, you get back a value of type `Int?`, and you need to check it for `null` before you can use it in arithmetical operations.

Taking a collection of nullable values and filtering out `null` is such a common operation that Kotlin provides a standard library function `filterNotNull` to perform it. Here's how you can use it to greatly simplify the previous example.

Listing 6.23 Using `filterNotNull` with a collection of nullable values

```
fun addValidNumbers(numbers: List<Int?>) {
    val validNumbers = numbers.filterNotNull()
    println("Sum of valid numbers: ${validNumbers.sum()}")
    println("Invalid numbers: ${numbers.size - validNumbers.size}")
}
```

Of course, the filtering also affects the type of the collection. The type of valid-Numbers is `List<Int>`, because the filtering ensures that the collection doesn't contain any `null` elements.

Now that you understand how Kotlin distinguishes between collections that hold nullable and non-`null` elements, let's look at another major distinction introduced by Kotlin: read-only versus mutable collections.

6.3.2 *Read-only and mutable collections*

An important trait that sets apart Kotlin's collection design from Java's is that it separates interfaces for accessing the data in a collection and for modifying the data. This distinction exists starting with the most basic interface for working with collections, `kotlin.collections.Collection`. Using this interface, you can iterate over the elements in a collection, obtain its size, check whether it contains a certain element, and perform other operations that read data from the collection. But this interface doesn't have any methods for adding or removing elements.

To modify the data in the collection, use the `kotlin.collections.Mutable-Collection` interface. It extends the regular `kotlin.collections.Collection` and

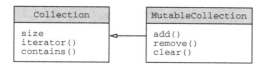

Figure 6.11 `MutableCollection` **extends** `Collection` **and adds methods to modify a collection's contents.**

provides methods for adding and removing the elements, clearing the collection, and so on. Figure 6.11 shows the key methods defined in the two interfaces.

As a general rule, you should use read-only interfaces everywhere in your code. Use the mutable variants only if the code will modify the collection.

Just like the separation between `val` and `var`, the separation between read-only and mutable interfaces for collections makes it much easier to understand what's happening with data in your program. If a function takes a parameter that is a `Collection` but not a `MutableCollection`, you know it's not going to modify the collection, but only read data from it. And if a function requires you to pass a `MutableCollection`, you can assume that it's going to modify the data. If you have a collection that's part of the internal state of your component, you may need to make a copy of that collection before passing it to such a function. (This pattern is usually called a *defensive copy*.)

For example, you can clearly see that the following `copyElements` function will modify the target collection but not the source collection.

Listing 6.24   Using read-only and mutable collection interfaces

```
fun <T> copyElements(source: Collection<T>,
                     target: MutableCollection<T>) {        Loops over all items
    for (item in source) {                                  in the source collection
        target.add(item)              Adds items to the mutable
    }                                 target collection
}

>>> val source: Collection<Int> = arrayListOf(3, 5, 7)
>>> val target: MutableCollection<Int> = arrayListOf(1)
>>> copyElements(source, target)
>>> println(target)
[1, 3, 5, 7]
```

You can't pass a variable of a read-only collection type as the `target` argument, even if its value is a mutable collection:

```
>>> val source: Collection<Int> = arrayListOf(3, 5, 7)
>>> val target: Collection<Int> = arrayListOf(1)          Error on the
>>> copyElements(source, target)                          "target" argument
Error: Type mismatch: inferred type is Collection<Int>
  but MutableCollection<Int> was expected
```

A key thing to keep in mind when working with collection interfaces is that *read-only collections aren't necessarily immutable.*[1] If you're working with a variable that has a

---

[1] Immutable collections are planned to be added to the Kotlin standard library later.

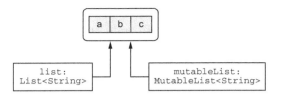

Figure 6.12   Two different references, one read-only and one mutable, pointing to the same collection object

read-only interface type, this can be just one of the many references to the same collection. Other references can have a mutable interface type, as illustrated in figure 6.12.

If you call the code holding the other reference to your collection or run it in parallel, you can still come across situations where the collection is modified by other code while you're working with it, which leads to `ConcurrentModification-Exception` errors and other problems. Therefore, it's essential to understand that *read-only collections aren't always thread-safe.* If you're working with data in a multi-threaded environment, you need to ensure that your code properly synchronizes access to the data or uses data structures that support concurrent access.

How does the separation between read-only and mutable collections work? Didn't we say earlier that Kotlin collections are the same as Java collections? Isn't there a contradiction? Let's see what really happens here.

6.3.3   *Kotlin collections and Java*

It's true that every Kotlin collection is an instance of the corresponding Java collection interface. No conversion is involved when moving between Kotlin and Java; there's no need for wrappers or copying data. But every Java collection interface has two *representations* in Kotlin: a read-only one and a mutable one, as you can see in figure 6.13.

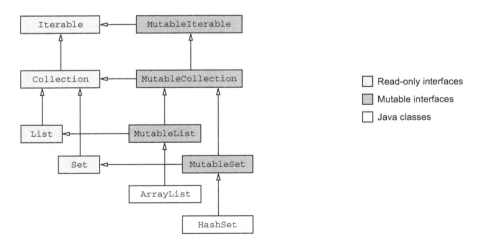

Figure 6.13   The hierarchy of the Kotlin collection interfaces. The Java classes `ArrayList` and `HashSet` extend Kotlin mutable interfaces.

All collection interfaces shown in figure 6.13 are declared in Kotlin. The basic structure of the Kotlin read-only and mutable interfaces is parallel to the structure of the Java collection interfaces in the `java.util` package. In addition, each mutable interface extends the corresponding read-only interface. Mutable interfaces correspond directly to the interfaces in the `java.util` package, whereas the read-only versions lack all the mutating methods.

Figure 6.13 also contains the Java classes `java.util.ArrayList` and `java.util.HashSet` to show how Java standard classes are treated in Kotlin. Kotlin sees them as if they inherited from the Kotlin's `MutableList` and `MutableSet` interfaces, respectively. Other implementations from the Java collection library (`LinkedList`, `SortedSet`, and so on) aren't presented here, but from the Kotlin perspective they have similar supertypes. This way, you get both compatibility and clear separation of mutable and read-only interfaces.

In addition to the collections, the `Map` class (which doesn't extend `Collection` or `Iterable`) is also represented in Kotlin as two distinct versions: `Map` and `MutableMap`. Table 6.1 shows the functions you can use to create collections of different types.

Table 6.1 Collection-creation functions

Collection type	Read-only	Mutable
List	`listOf`	`mutableListOf, arrayListOf`
Set	`setOf`	`mutableSetOf, hashSetOf, linkedSetOf, sortedSetOf`
Map	`mapOf`	`mutableMapOf, hashMapOf, linkedMapOf, sortedMapOf`

Note that `setOf()` and `mapOf()` return instances of classes from the Java standard library (at least in Kotlin 1.0), which are all mutable under the hood.[2] But you shouldn't rely on that: it's possible that a future version of Kotlin will use truly immutable implementation classes as return values of `setOf` and `mapOf`.

When you need to call a Java method and pass a collection as an argument, you can do so directly without any extra steps. For example, if you have a Java method that takes a `java.util.Collection` as a parameter, you can pass any `Collection` or `MutableCollection` value as an argument to that parameter.

This has important consequences with regard to mutability of collections. Because Java doesn't distinguish between read-only and mutable collections, Java code *can modify the collection* even if it's declared as a read-only `Collection` on the Kotlin side. The Kotlin compiler can't fully analyze what's being done to the collection in the Java code, and therefore there's no way for Kotlin to reject a call passing a read-only `Collection` to Java code that modifies it. For example, the following two snippets of code form a compilable cross-language Kotlin/Java program:

---

[2] Wrapping things into `Collection.unmodifiable` introduces indirection overhead, so it's not done.

```
/* Java */
// CollectionUtils.java
public class CollectionUtils {
    public static List<String> uppercaseAll(List<String> items) {
        for (int i = 0; i < items.size(); i++) {
            items.set(i, items.get(i).toUpperCase());
        }
        return items;
    }
}

// Kotlin
// collections.kt
fun printInUppercase(list: List<String>) {        ←────  Declares a read-only parameter
    println(CollectionUtils.uppercaseAll(list))    ←────  Calls a Java function that modifies the collection
    println(list.first())                          ←────  Shows that the collection has been modified
}

>>> val list = listOf("a", "b", "c")
>>> printInUppercase(list)
[A, B, C]
A
```

Therefore, if you're writing a Kotlin function that takes a collection and passes it to Java, *it's your responsibility to use the correct type for the parameter,* depending on whether the Java code you're calling will modify the collection.

Note that this caveat also applies to collections with non-null element types. If you pass such a collection to a Java method, the method can put a null value into it; there's no way for Kotlin to forbid that or even to detect that it has happened without compromising performance. Because of that, you need to take special precautions when you pass collections to Java code that can modify them, to make sure the Kotlin types correctly reflect all the possible modifications to the collection.

Now, let's take a closer look at how Kotlin deals with collections declared in Java code.

6.3.4 *Collections as platform types*

If you recall the discussion of nullability earlier in this chapter, you'll remember that types defined in Java code are seen as *platform types* in Kotlin. For platform types, Kotlin doesn't have the nullability information, so the compiler allows Kotlin code to treat them as either nullable or non-null. In the same way, variables of collection types declared in Java are also seen as platform types. A collection with a platform type is essentially a collection of unknown mutability—the Kotlin code can treat it as either read-only or mutable. Usually this doesn't matter, because, in effect, all the operations you may want to perform just work.

The difference becomes important when you're overriding or implementing a Java method that has a collection type in its signature. Here, as with platform types for nullability, you need to decide which Kotlin type you're going to use to represent a Java type coming from the method you're overriding or implementing.

You need to make multiple choices in this situation, all of which will be reflected in the resulting parameter type in Kotlin:

- Is the collection nullable?
- Are the elements in the collection nullable?
- Will your method modify the collection?

To see the difference, consider the following cases. In the first example, a Java interface represents an object that processes text in a file.

Listing 6.25   A Java interface with a collection parameter

```
/* Java */
interface FileContentProcessor {
    void processContents(File path,
        byte[] binaryContents,
        List<String> textContents);
}
```

A Kotlin implementation of this interface needs to make the following choices:

- The list will be nullable, because some files are binary and their contents can't be represented as text.
- The elements in the list will be non-`null`, because lines in a file are never `null`.
- The list will be read-only, because it represents the contents of a file, and those contents aren't going to be modified.

Here's how this implementation looks.

Listing 6.26   Kotlin implementation of `FileContentProcessor`

```
class FileIndexer : FileContentProcessor {
    override fun processContents(path: File,
        binaryContents: ByteArray?,
        textContents: List<String>?) {

        // ...
    }
}
```

Contrast this with another interface. Here the implementations of the interface parse some data from a text form into a list of objects, append those objects to the output list, and report errors detected when parsing by adding the messages to a separate list.

Listing 6.27   Another Java interface with a collection parameter

```
/* Java */
interface DataParser<T> {
    void parseData(String input,
        List<T> output,
        List<String> errors);
}
```

The choices in this case are different:

- `List<String>` will be non-null, because the callers always need to receive error messages.
- The elements in the list will be nullable, because not every item in the output list will have an associated error message.
- `List<String>` will be mutable, because the implementing code needs to add elements to it.

Here's how you can implement that interface in Kotlin.

> **Listing 6.28   Kotlin implementation of `DataParser`**

```
class PersonParser : DataParser<Person> {
    override fun parseData(input: String,
        output: MutableList<Person>,
        errors: MutableList<String?>) {

        // ...
    }
}
```

Note how the same Java type—`List<String>`—is represented by two different Kotlin types: a `List<String>?` (nullable list of strings) in one case and a `MutableList<String?>` (mutable list of nullable strings) in the other. To make these choices correctly, you must know the exact contract the Java interface or class needs to follow. This is usually easy to understand based on what your implementation needs to do.

Now that we've discussed collections, it's time to look at arrays. As we've mentioned before, you should prefer using collections to arrays by default. But because many Java APIs still use arrays, we'll cover how to work with them in Kotlin.

6.3.5   *Arrays of objects and primitive types*

The syntax of Kotlin arrays appears in every example, because an array is part of the standard signature of the Java `main` function. Here's a reminder of how it looks:

> **Listing 6.29   Using arrays**

```
fun main(args: Array<String>) {
    for (i in args.indices) {               ◁─── Uses the array.indices
        println("Argument $i is: ${args[i]}")      extension property to iterate
    }                                              over the range of indices
}                                          ◁─── Accesses elements by
                                                index with array[index]
```

An array in Kotlin is a class with a type parameter, and the element type is specified as the corresponding type argument.

To create an array in Kotlin, you have the following possibilities:

- The `arrayOf` function creates an array containing the elements specified as arguments to this function.
- The `arrayOfNulls` function creates an array of a given size containing `null` elements. Of course, it can only be used to create arrays where the element type is nullable.
- The `Array` constructor takes the size of the array and a lambda, and initializes each array element by calling the lambda. This is how you can initialize an array with a non-`null` element type without passing each element explicitly.

As a simple example, here's how you can use the `Array` function to create an array of strings from `"a"` to `"z"`.

Listing 6.30 Creating an array of characters

```
>>> val letters = Array<String>(26) { i -> ('a' + i).toString() }
>>> println(letters.joinToString(""))
abcdefghijklmnopqrstuvwxyz
```

The lambda takes the index of the array element and returns the value to be placed in the array at that index. Here you calculate the value by adding the index to the `'a'` character and converting the result to a string. The array element type is shown for clarity; you can omit it in real code because the compiler can infer it.

Having said that, one of the most common cases for creating an array in Kotlin code is when you need to call a Java method that takes an array, or a Kotlin function with a `vararg` parameter. In those situations, you often have the data already stored in a collection, and you just need to convert it into an array. You can do this using the `toTypedArray` method.

Listing 6.31 Passing a collection to a `vararg` method

```
>>> val strings = listOf("a", "b", "c")
>>> println("%s/%s/%s".format(*strings.toTypedArray()))
a/b/c
```
⟵ The spread operator (*) is used to pass an array when vararg parameter is expected.

As with other types, *type arguments of array types always become object types.* Therefore, if you declare something like an `Array<Int>`, it will become an array of boxed integers (its Java type will be `java.lang.Integer[]`). If you need to create an array of values of a primitive type without boxing, you must use one of the specialized classes for arrays of primitive types.

To represent arrays of primitive types, Kotlin provides a number of separate classes, one for each primitive type. For example, an array of values of type `Int` is called `IntArray`. For other types, Kotlin provides `ByteArray`, `CharArray`,

`BooleanArray`, and so on. All of these types are compiled to regular Java primitive type arrays, such as `int []`, `byte []`, `char []`, and so on. Therefore, values in such an array are stored without boxing, in the most efficient manner possible.

To create an array of a primitive type, you have the following options:

- The constructor of the type takes a `size` parameter and returns an array initialized with default values for the corresponding primitive type (usually zeros).
- The factory function (`intArrayOf` for `IntArray`, and so on for other array types) takes a variable number of values as arguments and creates an array holding those values.
- Another constructor takes a size and a lambda used to initialize each element.

Here's how the first two options work for creating an integer array holding five zeros:

```
val fiveZeros = IntArray(5)
val fiveZerosToo = intArrayOf(0, 0, 0, 0, 0)
```

Here's how you can use the constructor accepting a lambda:

```
>>> val squares = IntArray(5) { i -> (i+1) * (i+1) }
>>> println(squares.joinToString())
1, 4, 9, 16, 25
```

Alternatively, if you have an array or a collection holding boxed values of a primitive type, you can convert them to an array of that primitive type using the corresponding conversion function, such as `toIntArray`.

Next, let's look at some of the things you can do with arrays. In addition to the basic operations (getting the array's length and getting and setting elements), the Kotlin standard library supports the same set of extension functions for arrays as for collections. All the functions you saw in chapter 5 (`filter`, `map`, and so on) work for arrays as well, including the arrays of primitive types. (Note that the return values of these functions are lists, not arrays.)

Let's see how to rewrite listing 6.30 using the `forEachIndexed` function and a lambda. The lambda passed to that function is called for each element of the array and receives two arguments, the index of the element and the element itself.

Listing 6.32 Using `forEachIndexed` with an array

```
fun main(args: Array<String>) {
    args.forEachIndexed { index, element ->
        println("Argument $index is: $element")
    }
}
```

Now you know how to use arrays in your code. Working with them is as simple as working with collections in Kotlin.

6.4   *Summary*

- Kotlin's support of nullable types detects possible `NullPointerException` errors at compile time.

- Kotlin provides tools such as safe calls (`?.`), the Elvis operator (`?:`), not-null assertions (`!!`), and the `let` function for dealing with nullable types concisely.

- The `as?` operator provides an easy way to cast a value to a type and to handle the case when it has a different type.

- Types coming from Java are interpreted as platform types in Kotlin, allowing the developer to treat them as either nullable or non-null.

- Types representing basic numbers (such as `Int`) look and function like regular classes but are usually compiled to Java primitive types.

- Nullable primitive types (such as `Int?`) correspond to boxed primitive types in Java (such as `java.lang.Integer`).

- The `Any` type is a supertype of all other types and is analogous to Java's `Object`. `Unit` is an analogue of `void`.

- The `Nothing` type is used as a return type of functions that don't terminate normally.

- Kotlin uses the standard Java classes for collections and enhances them with a distinction between read-only and mutable collections.

- You need to carefully consider nullability and mutability of parameters when you extend Java classes or implement Java interfaces in Kotlin.

- Kotlin's `Array` class looks like a regular generic class, but it's compiled to a Java array.

- Arrays of primitive types are represented by special classes such as `IntArray`.

Part 2

Embracing Kotlin

By now, you should be very familiar with using Kotlin to access existing APIs. In this part of the book, you'll learn how to build your own APIs in Kotlin. It's important to remember that building APIs isn't restricted to library authors: every time you have two interacting classes in your program, one of them provides an API to the other.

In chapter 7, you'll learn about the principle of *conventions*, which are used in Kotlin to implement operator overloading and other abstraction techniques such as delegated properties. Chapter 8 takes a closer look at lambdas, and you'll see how you can declare your own functions that take lambdas as parameters. You'll become familiar with Kotlin's take on some more advanced Java concepts, such as generics (chapter 9) and annotations and reflection (chapter 10). Also in chapter 10, you'll study a fairly large real-world Kotlin project: JKid, a JSON serialization and deserialization library. And finally, in chapter 11, you'll reach one of Kotlin's crown jewels: its support for building domain-specific languages.

Operator overloading
and other conventions

As you know, Java has several language features tied to specific classes in the standard library. For example, objects that implement `java.lang.Iterable` can be used in `for` loops, and objects that implement `java.lang.AutoCloseable` can be used in try-with-resources statements.

Kotlin has a number of features that work in a similar way, where specific language constructs are implemented by calling functions that you define in your own code. But instead of being tied to specific types, in Kotlin those features are tied to functions with specific names. For example, if your class defines a special method named `plus`, then, by convention, you can use the + operator on instances of this class. Because of that, in Kotlin we refer to this technique as *conventions*. In this chapter, we'll look at different conventions supported by Kotlin and how they can be used.

Kotlin uses the principle of conventions, instead of relying on types as Java does, because this allows developers to adapt existing Java classes to the requirements of Kotlin language features. The set of interfaces implemented by a class is fixed, and Kotlin can't modify an existing class so that it would implement additional interfaces. On the other hand, defining new methods for a class is possible through the mechanism of extension functions. You can define any convention methods as extensions and thereby adapt any existing Java class without modifying its code.

As a running example in this chapter, we'll use a simple `Point` class, representing a point on a screen. Such classes are available in most UI frameworks, and you can easily adapt the definitions shown here to your environment:

```
data class Point(val x: Int, val y: Int)
```

Let's begin by defining some arithmetic operators on the `Point` class.

7.1   Overloading arithmetic operators

The most straightforward example of the use of conventions in Kotlin is arithmetic operators. In Java, the full set of arithmetic operations can be used only with primitive types, and additionally the + operator can be used with `String` values. But these operations could be convenient in other cases as well. For example, if you're working with numbers through the `BigInteger` class, it's more elegant to sum them using + than to call the `add` method explicitly. To add an element to a collection, you may want to use the += operator. Kotlin allows you to do that, and in this section we'll show you how it works.

7.1.1   Overloading binary arithmetic operations

The first operation you're going to support is adding two points together. This operation sums up the points' X and Y coordinates. Here's how you can implement it.

Listing 7.1   Defining the `plus` operator

```
data class Point(val x: Int, val y: Int) {
    operator fun plus(other: Point): Point {        ◁──  Defines an operator
        return Point(x + other.x, y + other.y)            function named "plus"
    }
}

>>> val p1 = Point(10, 20)
>>> val p2 = Point(30, 40)                         Calls the "plus"
>>> println(p1 + p2)                          ◁──  function using the + sign
Point(x=40, y=60)
```

Adds the coordinates and returns a new point

Note how you use the `operator` keyword to declare the `plus` function. All functions used to overload operators need to be marked with that keyword. This makes it explicit that you intend to use the function as an implementation of the corresponding convention and that you didn't define a function that accidentally had a matching name.

After you declare the `plus` function with the operator modifier, you can sum up your objects using just the +
sign. Under the hood, the `plus` function is called as
shown in figure 7.1.

**Figure 7.1   The + operator
is transformed into a `plus`
function call.**

As an alternative to declaring the operator as a member, you can define the operator as an extension function.

Listing 7.2   Defining an operator as an extension function

```
operator fun Point.plus(other: Point): Point {
    return Point(x + other.x, y + other.y)
}
```

The implementation is exactly the same. Future examples will use the extension function syntax because it's a common pattern to define convention extension functions
for external library classes, and the same syntax will work nicely for your own classes
as well.

Compared to some other languages, defining and using overloaded operators in
Kotlin is simpler, because you can't define your own operators. Kotlin has a limited set
of operators that you can overload, and each one corresponds to the name of the
function you need to define in your class. Table 7.1 lists all the binary operators you
can define and the corresponding function names.

Table 7.1   Overloadable binary arithmetic operators

Expression	Function name
a * b	times
a / b	div
a % b	mod
a + b	plus
a - b	minus

Operators for your own types always use the same precedence as the standard
numeric types. For example, if you write a + b * c, the multiplication will always be
executed before the addition, even if you've defined those operators yourself. The
operators *, /, and % have the same precedence, which is higher than the precedence
of the + and - operators.

Operator functions and Java

Kotlin operators are easy to call from Java: because every overloaded operator is defined as a function, you call them as regular functions using the full name. When you call Java from Kotlin, you can use the operator syntax for any methods with names matching the Kotlin conventions. Because Java doesn't define any syntax for marking operator functions, the requirement to use the `operator` modifier doesn't apply, and the matching name and number of parameters are the only constraints. If a Java class defines a method with the behavior you need but gives it a different name, you can define an extension function with the correct name that would delegate to the existing Java method.

When you define an operator, you don't need to use the same types for the two operands. For example, let's define an operator that will allow you to scale a point by a certain number. You can use it to translate points between different coordinate systems.

Listing 7.3   Defining an operator with different operand types

```
operator fun Point.times(scale: Double): Point {
    return Point((x * scale).toInt(), (y * scale).toInt())
}

>>> val p = Point(10, 20)
>>> println(p * 1.5)
Point(x=15, y=30)
```

Note that Kotlin operators don't automatically support *commutativity* (the ability to swap the left and right sides of an operator). If you want users to be able to write 1.5 * p in addition to p * 1.5, you need to define a separate operator for that: `operator fun Double.times(p: Point): Point`.

The return type of an operator function can also be different from either of the operand types. For example, you can define an operator to create a string by repeating a character a number of times.

Listing 7.4   Defining an operator with a different result type

```
operator fun Char.times(count: Int): String {
    return toString().repeat(count)
}

>>> println('a' * 3)
aaa
```

This operator takes a `Char` as the left operand and an `Int` as the right operand and has `String` as the result type. Such combinations of operand and result types are perfectly acceptable.

Note that you can overload `operator` functions like regular functions: you can define multiple methods with different parameter types for the same method name.

No special operators for bitwise operations

Kotlin doesn't define any bitwise operators for standard number types; consequently, it doesn't allow you to define them for your own types. Instead, it uses regular functions supporting the infix call syntax. You can define similar functions that work with your own types.

Here's the full list of functions provided by Kotlin for performing bitwise operations:

- `shl`—Signed shift left
- `shr`—Signed shift right
- `ushr`—Unsigned shift right
- `and`—Bitwise and
- `or`—Bitwise or
- `xor`—Bitwise xor
- `inv`—Bitwise inversion

The following example demonstrates the use of some of these functions:

```
>>> println(0x0F and 0xF0)
0
>>> println(0x0F or 0xF0)
255
>>> println(0x1 shl 4)
16
```

Now let's discuss the operators like += that merge two actions: assignment and the corresponding arithmetic operator.

7.1.2   *Overloading compound assignment operators*

Normally, when you define an operator such as `plus`, Kotlin supports not only the + operation but += as well. Operators such as +=, -=, and so on are called *compound assignment operators*. Here's an example:

```
>>> var point = Point(1, 2)
>>> point += Point(3, 4)
>>> println(point)
Point(x=4, y=6)
```

This is the same as writing `point = point + Point(3, 4)`. Of course, that works only if the variable is mutable.

In some cases, it makes sense to define the += operation that would modify an object referenced by the variable on which it's used, but not reassign the reference. One such case is adding an element to a mutable collection:

```
>>> val numbers = ArrayList<Int>()
>>> numbers += 42
>>> println(numbers[0])
42
```

If you define a function named `plusAssign` with the `Unit` return type, Kotlin will call it when the `+=` operator is used. Other binary arithmetic operators have similarly named counterparts: `minusAssign`, `timesAssign`, and so on.

The Kotlin standard library defines a function `plusAssign` on a mutable collection, and the previous example uses it:

```
operator fun <T> MutableCollection<T>.plusAssign(element: T) {
    this.add(element)
}
```

When you write `+=` in your code, theoretically both `plus` and `plusAssign` functions can be called (see figure 7.2). If this is the case, and both functions are defined and applicable, the compiler reports an error. One possibility to resolve it is replacing your use of the operator with a regular function call. Another is to replace a `var` with a

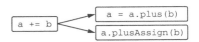

Figure 7.2   The += operator can be transformed into either the `plus` or the `plusAssign` function call.

`val`, so that the `plusAssign` operation becomes inapplicable. But in general, it's best to design new classes consistently: try not to add both `plus` and `plusAssign` operations at the same time. If your class is immutable, like `Point` in one of the earlier examples, you should provide only operations that return a new value (such as `plus`). If you design a mutable class, like a builder, provide only `plusAssign` and similar operations.

The Kotlin standard library supports both approaches for collections. The `+` and `-` operators always return a new collection. The `+=` and `-=` operators work on mutable collections by modifying them in place, and on read-only collections by returning a modified copy. (This means `+=` and `-=` can only be used with a read-only collection if the variable referencing it is declared as a `var`.) As operands of those operators, you can use either individual elements or other collections with a matching element type:

```
>>> val list = arrayListOf(1, 2)
>>> list += 3                              ⟵——— += changes "list".
>>> val newList = list + listOf(4, 5)      ⟵
>>> println(list)                              + returns a new list
[1, 2, 3]                                      containing all the elements.
>>> println(newList)
[1, 2, 3, 4, 5]
```

So far, we've discussed overloading of *binary* operators—operators that are applied to two values, such as `a + b`. In addition, Kotlin allows you to overload *unary* operators, which are applied to a single value, as in `-a`.

7.1.3   *Overloading unary operators*

The procedure for overloading a unary operator is the same as you saw previously: declare a function (member or extension) with a predefined name, and mark it with the modifier `operator`. Let's look at an example.

Listing 7.5 Defining a unary operator

```
operator fun Point.unaryMinus(): Point {
    return Point(-x, -y)
}

>>> val p = Point(10, 20)
>>> println(-p)
Point(x=-10, y=-20)
```

◁──── The unary minus function has no parameters.

Negates the coordinates of the point, and returns it

Functions used to overload unary operators don't take any arguments. As shown in figure 7.3, the unary plus operator works the same way. Table 7.2 lists all the unary operators you can overload.

Figure 7.3 The unary + operator is transformed into a `unaryPlus` function call.

Table 7.2 Overloadable unary arithmetic operators

Expression	Function name
+a	unaryPlus
-a	unaryMinus
!a	not
++a, a++	inc
--a, a--	dec

When you define the `inc` and `dec` functions to overload increment and decrement operators, the compiler automatically supports the same semantics for pre- and post-increment operators as for the regular number types. Consider the following example, which overloads the ++ operator for the `BigDecimal` class.

Listing 7.6 Defining an increment operator

```
operator fun BigDecimal.inc() = this + BigDecimal.ONE

>>> var bd = BigDecimal.ZERO
>>> println(bd++)
0
>>> println(++bd)
2
```

Increments after the first println statement executes

Increments before the second println statement executes

The postfix operation ++ first returns the current value of the `bd` variable and after that increases it, whereas the prefix operation works the other way round. The printed values are the same as you'd see if you used a variable of type `Int`, and you didn't need to do anything special to support this.

7.2   *Overloading comparison operators*

Just as with arithmetic operators, Kotlin lets you use comparison operators (==, !=, >, <, and so on) with any object, not just with primitive types. Instead of calling equals or compareTo, as in Java, you can use comparison operators directly, which is intuitive and concise. In this section, we'll look at the conventions used to support these operators.

7.2.1   *Equality operators: "equals"*

We touched on the topic of equality in section 4.3.1. You saw that using the == operator in Kotlin is translated into a call of the equals method. This is just one more application of the conventions principle we've been discussing.

Using the != operator is also translated into a call of equals, with the obvious difference that the result is inverted. Note that unlike all other operators, == and != can be used with nullable operands, because those operators check equality to null

Figure 7.4   An equality check == is transformed into an equals call and a null check.

under the hood. The comparison a == b checks whether a isn't null, and, if it's not, calls a.equals(b) (see figure 7.4). Otherwise the result is true only if both arguments are null references.

For the Point class, the implementation of equals is automatically generated by the compiler, because you've marked it as a data class (section 4.3.2 explained the details). But if you did implement it manually, here's what the code could look like.

Listing 7.7   Implementing the equals method

```
class Point(val x: Int, val y: Int) {
    override fun equals(obj: Any?): Boolean {
        if (obj === this) return true
        if (obj !is Point) return false
        return obj.x == x && obj.y == y
    }
}

>>> println(Point(10, 20) == Point(10, 20))
true
>>> println(Point(10, 20) != Point(5, 5))
true
>>> println(null == Point(1, 2))
false
```

Overrides the method defined in Any

Optimization: checks whether the parameter is the same object as "this"

Checks the parameter type

Uses a smart cast to Point to access the x and y properties

You use the *identity equals* operator (===) to check whether the parameter to equals is the same object as the one on which equals is called. The identity equals operator does exactly the same thing as the == operator in Java: it checks that both of its arguments reference the same object (or have the same value, if they have a primitive type). Using this operator is a common optimization when implementing `equals`. Note that the `===` operator can't be overloaded.

The `equals` function is marked as `override`, because, unlike other conventions, the method implementing it is defined in the `Any` class (equality comparison is supported for all objects in Kotlin). That also explains why you don't need to mark it as `operator`: the base method in `Any` is marked as such, and the `operator` modifier on a method applies also to all methods that implement or override it. Also note that `equals` can't be implemented as an extension, because the implementation inherited from the `Any` class would always take precedence over the extension.

This example shows that using the `!=` operator is also translated into a call of the `equals` method. The compiler automatically negates the return value, so you don't need to do anything for this to work correctly.

What about other comparison operators?

7.2.2 Ordering operators: compareTo

In Java, classes can implement the `Comparable` interface in order to be used in algorithms that compare values, such as finding a maximum or sorting. The `compareTo` method defined in that interface is used to determine whether one object is larger than another. But in Java, there's no shorthand syntax for calling this method. Only values of primitive types can be compared using `<` and `>`; all other types require you to write `element1.compareTo(element2)` explicitly.

Kotlin supports the same `Comparable` interface. But the `compareTo` method defined in that interface can be called by convention, and uses of comparison operators (`<`, `>`, `<=`, and `>=`) are translated into calls of `compareTo`, as shown in figure 7.5. The

Figure 7.5　Comparison of two objects is transformed into comparing the result of the `compareTo` call with zero.

return type of `compareTo` has to be `Int`. The expression `p1 < p2` is equivalent to `p1.compareTo(p2) < 0`. Other comparison operators work exactly the same way.

Because there's no obviously right way to compare points with one another, let's use the good-old `Person` class to show how the method can be implemented. The implementation will use address book ordering (compare by last name, and then, if the last name is the same, compare by first name).

Listing 7.8　Implementing the `compareTo` method

```
class Person(
        val firstName: String, val lastName: String
) : Comparable<Person> {
    override fun compareTo(other: Person): Int {
        return compareValuesBy(this, other,          ◁──┐ Evaluates the given callbacks
            Person::lastName, Person::firstName)          │ in order, and compares values
    }
}
```

```
>>> val p1 = Person("Alice", "Smith")
>>> val p2 = Person("Bob", "Johnson")
>>> println(p1 < p2)
false
```

In this case, you implement the Comparable interface so that the Person objects can be compared not only by Kotlin code but also by Java functions, such as the functions used to sort collections. Just as with equals, the operator modifier is applied to the function in the base interface, so you don't need to repeat the keyword when you override the function.

Note how you can use the compareValuesBy function from the Kotlin standard library to implement the compareTo method easily and concisely. This function receives a list of callbacks that calculate values to be compared. The function calls each callback in order for both objects and compares the return values. If the values are different, it returns the result of the comparison. If they're the same, it proceeds to the next callback or returns 0 if there are no more callbacks to call. The callbacks can be passed as lambdas or, as you do here, as property references.

Note, however, that a direct implementation comparing fields by hand would be faster, although it would contain more code. As always, you should prefer the concise version and worry about performance only if you know the implementation will be called frequently.

All Java classes that implement the Comparable interface can be compared in Kotlin using the concise operator syntax:

```
>>> println("abc" < "bac")
true
```

You don't need to add any extensions to make that work.

7.3 *Conventions used for collections and ranges*

Some of the most common operations for working with collections are getting and setting elements by index, as well as checking whether an element belongs to a collection. All of these operations are supported via operator syntax: To get or set an element by index, you use the syntax a[b] (called the *index operator*). The in operator can be used to check whether an element is in a collection or range and also to iterate over a collection. You can add those operations for your own classes that act as collections. Let's now look at the conventions used to support those operations.

7.3.1 *Accessing elements by index: "get" and "set"*

You know already that in Kotlin, you can access the elements in a map similarly to how you access arrays in Java—via square brackets:

```
val value = map[key]
```

You can use the same operator to change the value for a key in a mutable map:

```
mutableMap[key] = newValue
```

Now it's time to see how this works. In Kotlin, the index operator is one more convention. Reading an element using the index operator is translated into a call of the `get` operator method, and writing an element becomes a call to `set`. The methods are already defined for the `Map` and `MutableMap` interfaces. Let's see how to add similar methods to your own class.

You'll allow the use of square brackets to reference the coordinates of the point: `p[0]` to access the X coordinate and `p[1]` to access the Y coordinate. Here's how to implement and use it.

Listing 7.9 Implementing the `get` convention

```
operator fun Point.get(index: Int): Int {          ◁── Defines an operator
    return when(index) {                                function named "get"
        0 -> x            Gets the coordinate corresponding
        1 -> y            to the given index
        else ->
            throw IndexOutOfBoundsException("Invalid coordinate $index")
    }
}

>>> val p = Point(10, 20)
>>> println(p[1])
20
```

All you need to do is define a function named `get` and mark it as `operator`. Once you do that, expressions like `p[1]`, where `p` has type `Point`, will be translated into calls to the `get` method, as shown in figure 7.6.

Figure 7.6 Access via square brackets is transformed into a `get` function call.

Note that the parameter of `get` can be any type, not just `Int`. For example, when you use the indexing operator on a map, the parameter type is the key type of the map, which can be an arbitrary type. You can also define a `get` method with multiple parameters. For example, if you're implementing a class to represent a two-dimensional array or matrix, you can define a method such as `operator fun get(rowIndex: Int, colIndex: Int)` and call it as `matrix[row, col]`. You can define multiple overloaded `get` methods with different parameter types, if your collection can be accessed with different key types.

In a similar way, you can define a function that lets you change the value at a given index using the bracket syntax. The `Point` class is immutable, so it doesn't make sense to define such a method for `Point`. Let's define another class to represent a mutable point and use that as an example.

Listing 7.10 Implementing the `set` convention

```
data class MutablePoint(var x: Int, var y: Int)

operator fun MutablePoint.set(index: Int, value: Int) {    ◁── Defines an operator
    when(index) {                                               function named "set"
```

```
            0 -> x = value
            1 -> y = value
            else ->
                throw IndexOutOfBoundsException("Invalid coordinate $index")
        }
    }
}

>>> val p = MutablePoint(10, 20)
>>> p[1] = 42
>>> println(p)
MutablePoint(x=10, y=42)
```

This example is also simple: to allow the use of the index operator in assignments, you just need to define a function named set. The last parameter to set receives the value used on the right side of the assignment, and the other arguments are taken from the indices used inside the brackets, as you can see in figure 7.7.

Figure 7.7   Assignment through square brackets is transformed into a set function call.

7.3.2   *The "in" convention*

One other operator supported by collections is the in operator, which is used to check whether an object belongs to a collection. The corresponding function is called contains. Let's implement it so that you can use the in operator to check whether a point belongs to a rectangle.

Listing 7.11   Implementing the in convention

```
data class Rectangle(val upperLeft: Point, val lowerRight: Point)

operator fun Rectangle.contains(p: Point): Boolean {
    return p.x in upperLeft.x until lowerRight.x &&
           p.y in upperLeft.y until lowerRight.y
}

>>> val rect = Rectangle(Point(10, 20), Point(50, 50))
>>> println(Point(20, 30) in rect)
true
>>> println(Point(5, 5) in rect)
false
```

Uses the "until" function to build an open range

Builds a range, and checks that coordinate "x" belongs to this range

The object on the right side of in becomes the object on which the contains method is called, and the object on the left side becomes the argument passed to the method (see figure 7.8).

In the implementation of Rectangle .contains, you use the until standard library function to build an *open range* and then you use the in operator on a range to check that a point belongs to it.

Figure 7.8   The in operator is transformed into a contains function call.

An *open range* is a range that doesn't include its ending point. For example, if you build a regular (closed) range using `10..20`, this range includes all numbers from 10 to 20, including 20. An open range `10 until 20` includes numbers from 10 to 19 but doesn't include 20. A rectangle class is usually defined in such a way that its bottom and right coordinates aren't part of the rectangle, so the use of open ranges is appropriate here.

7.3.3 *The rangeTo convention*

To create a range, you use the `..` syntax: for instance, `1..10` enumerates all the numbers from 1 to 10. You met ranges in section 2.4.2, but now let's discuss the convention that helps create one. The `..` operator is a concise way to call the `rangeTo` function (see figure 7.9).

Figure 7.9 The `..` operator is transformed into a `rangeTo` function call.

The `rangeTo` function returns a range. You can define this operator for your own class. But if your class implements the `Comparable` interface, you don't need that: you can create a range of any comparable elements by means of the Kotlin standard library. The library defines the `rangeTo` function that can be called on any comparable element:

```
operator fun <T: Comparable<T>> T.rangeTo(that: T): ClosedRange<T>
```

This function returns a range that allows you to check whether different elements belong to it.

As an example, let's build a range of dates using the `LocalDate` class (defined in the Java 8 standard library).

Listing 7.12 Working with a range of dates

```
>>> val now = LocalDate.now()
>>> val vacation = now..now.plusDays(10)
>>> println(now.plusWeeks(1) in vacation)
true
```

Creates a 10-day range starting from now

Checks whether a specific date belongs to a range

The expression `now..now.plusDays(10)` is transformed into `now.rangeTo (now.plusDays(10))` by the compiler. The `rangeTo` function isn't a member of `LocalDate` but rather is an extension function on `Comparable`, as shown earlier.

The `rangeTo` operator has lower priority than arithmetic operators. But it's better to use parentheses for its arguments to avoid confusion:

```
>>> val n = 9
>>> println(0..(n + 1))
0..10
```

You can write 0..n + 1, but parentheses make it clearer.

Also note that the expression `0..n.forEach {}` won't compile, because you have to surround a range expression with parentheses to call a method on it:

```
>>> (0..n).forEach { print(it) }
0123456789
```
⊲─── Put a range in parentheses to call a method on it.

Now let's discuss how conventions allow you to iterate over a collection or a range.

7.3.4   *The "iterator" convention for the "for" loop*

As we discussed in chapter 2, `for` loops in Kotlin use the same `in` operator as range checks. But its meaning is different in this context: it's used to perform iteration. This means a statement such as `for (x in list) { ... }` will be translated into a call of `list.iterator()`, on which the `hasNext` and `next` methods are then repeatedly called, just like in Java.

Note that in Kotlin, it's also a convention, which means the `iterator` method can be defined as an extension. That explains why it's possible to iterate over a regular Java string: the standard library defines an extension function `iterator` on `Char-Sequence`, a superclass of `String`:

```
operator fun CharSequence.iterator(): CharIterator

>>> for (c in "abc") {}
```
⊲─── This library function makes it possible to iterate over a string.

You can define the `iterator` method for your own classes. For example, defining the following method makes it possible to iterate over dates.

Listing 7.13   Implementing a date range iterator

```
operator fun ClosedRange<LocalDate>.iterator(): Iterator<LocalDate> =
        object : Iterator<LocalDate> {
            var current = start

            override fun hasNext() =
                current <= endInclusive

            override fun next() = current.apply {
                current = plusDays(1)
            }
        }

>>> val newYear = LocalDate.ofYearDay(2017, 1)
>>> val daysOff = newYear.minusDays(1)..newYear
>>> for (dayOff in daysOff) { println(dayOff) }
2016-12-31
2017-01-01
```

This object implements an Iterator over LocalDate elements.

Note the compareTo convention used for dates.

Returns the current date as a result before changing it

Increments the current date by one day

Iterates over daysOff when the corresponding iterator function is available

Note how you define the `iterator` method on a custom range type: you use `Local-Date` as a type argument. The `rangeTo` library function, shown in the previous section, returns an instance of `ClosedRange`, and the `iterator` extension on `ClosedRange<LocalDate>` allows you to use an instance of the range in a `for` loop.

7.4   *Destructuring declarations and component functions*

When we discussed data classes in section 4.3.2, we mentioned that some of their features would be revealed later. Now that you're familiar with the principle of conventions, we can look at the final feature: *destructuring declarations*. This feature allows you to unpack a single composite value and use it to initialize several separate variables.

Here's how it works:

```
>>> val p = Point(10, 20)
>>> val (x, y) = p
>>> println(x)
10
>>> println(y)
20
```

Declares variables x and y, initialized with components of p

A destructuring declaration looks like a regular variable declaration, but it has multiple variables grouped in parentheses.

Under the hood, the destructuring declaration once again uses the principle of conventions. To initialize each variable in a destructuring declaration, a function named componentN is called, where N is the position of the variable in the declaration. In other words, the previous example would be transformed as shown in figure 7.10.

For a data class, the compiler generates a componentN function for every property declared in the primary constructor. The following example shows how you can declare these functions manually for a non-data class:

Figure 7.10   Destructuring declarations are transformed into componentN **function calls.**

```
class Point(val x: Int, val y: Int) {
    operator fun component1() = x
    operator fun component2() = y
}
```

One of the main use cases where destructuring declarations are helpful is returning multiple values from a function. If you need to do that, you can define a data class to hold the values you need to return and use it as the return type of the function. The destructuring-declaration syntax makes it easy to unpack and use the values after you call the function. To demonstrate, let's write a simple function to split a filename into a name and an extension.

Listing 7.14   Using a destructuring declaration to return multiple values

```
data class NameComponents(val name: String,
                          val extension: String)
fun splitFilename(fullName: String): NameComponents {
    val result = fullName.split('.', limit = 2)
    return NameComponents(result[0], result[1])
}
```

Declares a data class to hold the values

Returns an instance of the data class from the function

```
>>> val (name, ext) = splitFilename("example.kt")      ◁─┐ Uses the destructuring
>>> println(name)                                          declaration syntax to
example                                                    unpack the class
>>> println(ext)
kt
```

You can improve this example even further if you note that componentN functions are also defined on arrays and collections. This is useful when you're dealing with collections of a known size—and this is such a case, with split returning a list of two elements.

Listing 7.15   Using a destructuring declaration with a collection

```
data class NameComponents(
        val name: String,
        val extension: String)

fun splitFilename(fullName: String): NameComponents {
    val (name, extension) = fullName.split('.', limit = 2)
    return NameComponents(name, extension)
}
```

Of course, it's not possible to define an infinite number of such componentN functions so the syntax would work with an arbitrary number of items, but that wouldn't be useful, either. The standard library allows you to use this syntax to access the first five elements of a container.

A simpler way to return multiple values from a function is to use the Pair and Triple classes from the standard library. It's less expressive, because those classes don't make it clear what's contained in the returned object, but it requires less code because you don't need to define your own class.

7.4.1   Destructuring declarations and loops

Destructuring declarations work not only as top-level statements in functions but also in other places where you can declare variables—for example, in loops. One good use for that is enumerating entries in a map. Here's a small example using this syntax to print all entries in a given map.

Listing 7.16   Using a destructuring declaration to iterate over a map

```
fun printEntries(map: Map<String, String>) {
    for ((key, value) in map) {
        println("$key -> $value")      ◁─┐ Destructuring
    }                                      declaration in a loop
}

>>> val map = mapOf("Oracle" to "Java", "JetBrains" to "Kotlin")
>>> printEntries(map)
Oracle -> Java
JetBrains -> Kotlin
```

This simple example uses two Kotlin conventions: one to iterate over an object and another to destructure declarations. The Kotlin standard library contains an extension function `iterator` on a map that returns an iterator over map entries. Thus, unlike Java, you can iterate over a map directly. It also contains extensions functions `component1` and `component2` on `Map.Entry`, returning its key and value, respectively. In effect, the previous loop is translated to the equivalent of the following code:

```
for (entry in map.entries) {
    val key = entry.component1()
    val value = entry.component2()
    // ...
}
```

This example again illustrates the importance of extension functions for conventions.

7.5　*Reusing property accessor logic: delegated properties*

To conclude this chapter, let's look at one more feature that relies on conventions and is one of the most unique and powerful in Kotlin: *delegated properties*. This feature lets you easily implement properties that work in a more complex way than storing values in backing fields, without duplicating the logic in each accessor. For example, properties can store their values in database tables, in a browser session, in a map, and so on.

The foundation for this feature is *delegation*: a design pattern where an object, instead of performing a task, delegates that task to another helper object. The helper object is called a *delegate*. You saw this pattern earlier, in section 4.3.3, when we were discussing class delegation. Here this pattern is applied to a property, which can also delegate the logic of its accessors to a helper object. You can implement that by hand (you'll see examples in a moment) or use a better solution: take advantage of Kotlin's language support. We'll begin with a general explanation and then look at specific examples.

7.5.1　*Delegated properties: the basics*

The general syntax of a delegated property is this:

```
class Foo {
    var p: Type by Delegate()
}
```

The property p delegates the logic of its accessors to another object: in this case, a new instance of the `Delegate` class. The object is obtained by evaluating the expression following the `by` keyword, which can be anything that satisfies the rules of the convention for property delegates.

The compiler creates a hidden helper property, initialized with the instance of the delegate object, to which the initial property p delegates. For simplicity, let's call it `delegate`:

```
class Foo {
    private val delegate = Delegate()
```
　　　　　　　　　　　　　　　　　　　　　　　　　　　← **This helper property is generated by the compiler.**

```
        var p: Type
            set(value: Type) = delegate.setValue(..., value)
            get() = delegate.getValue(...)
    }
```

> Generated accessors of the "p" property call the getValue and setValue methods on "delegate".

By convention, the `Delegate` class must have `getValue` and `setValue` methods (the latter is required only for mutable properties). As usual, they can be members or extensions. To simplify the explanation, we omit their parameters; the exact signatures will be covered later in this chapter. In a simple form, the `Delegate` class might look like the following:

```
class Delegate {
    operator fun getValue(...) { ... }

    operator fun setValue(..., value: Type) { ... }
}

class Foo {
    var p: Type by Delegate()
}
```

> The getValue method contains the logic for implementing a getter.

> The setValue method contains the logic for implementing a setter.

> The "by" keyword associates a property with a delegate object.

```
>>> val foo = Foo()
>>> val oldValue = foo.p
>>> foo.p = newValue
```

> Accessing a property foo.p calls delegate.getValue(...) under the hood.

> Changing a property value calls delegate.setValue(..., newValue).

You use `foo.p` as a regular property, but under the hood the methods on the helper property of the `Delegate` type are called. To investigate how this mechanism is used in practice, we'll begin by looking at one example of the power of delegated properties: library support for lazy initialization. Afterward, we'll explore how you can define your own delegated properties and when this is useful.

7.5.2 *Using delegated properties: lazy initialization and "by lazy()"*

Lazy initialization is a common pattern that entails creating part of an object on demand, when it's accessed for the first time. This is helpful when the initialization process consumes significant resources and the data isn't always required when the object is used.

For example, consider a `Person` class that lets you access a list of the emails written by a person. The emails are stored in a database and take a long time to access. You want to load the emails on first access to the property and do so only once. Let's say you have the following function `loadEmails`, which retrieves the emails from the database:

```
class Email { /*...*/ }
fun loadEmails(person: Person): List<Email> {
    println("Load emails for ${person.name}")
    return listOf(/*...*/)
}
```

Here's how you can implement lazy loading using an additional _emails property that stores null before anything is loaded and the list of emails afterward.

Listing 7.17　Implementing lazy initialization using a backing property

```
class Person(val name: String) {
    private var _emails: List<Email>? = null                    "_emails" property that
                                                                stores the data and to
    val emails: List<Email>                                     which "emails" delegates
        get() {
            if (_emails == null) {
                _emails = loadEmails(this)
            }                                   Loads the data
            return _emails!!                    on access
        }                                                       If the data was loaded
}                                                               before, returns it
>>> val p = Person("Alice")
>>> p.emails
Load emails for Alice                                           Emails are loaded
>>> p.emails                                                    on first access.
```

Here you use the so-called *backing property* technique. You have one property, _emails, which stores the value, and another, emails, which provides read access to it. You need to use two properties because the properties have different types: _emails is nullable, whereas emails is non-null. This technique can be used fairly often, so it's worth getting familiar with it.

But the code is somewhat cumbersome: imagine how much longer it would become if you had several lazy properties. What's more, it doesn't always work correctly: the implementation isn't thread-safe. Surely Kotlin provides a better solution.

The code becomes much simpler with the use of a delegated property, which can encapsulate both the backing property used to store the value and the logic ensuring that the value is initialized only once. The delegate you can use here is returned by the lazy standard library function.

Listing 7.18　Implementing lazy initialization using a delegated property

```
class Person(val name: String) {
    val emails by lazy { loadEmails(this) }
}
```

The lazy function returns an object that has a method called getValue with the proper signature, so you can use it together with the by keyword to create a delegated property. The argument of lazy is a lambda that it calls to initialize the value. The lazy function is thread-safe by default; and if you need to, you can specify additional options to tell it which lock to use or to bypass the synchronization entirely if the class is never used in a multithreaded environment.

In the next section, we'll dive into details of how the mechanism of delegated properties works and discuss the conventions in play here.

7.5.3   *Implementing delegated properties*

To see how delegated properties are implemented, let's take another example: the task of notifying listeners when a property of an object changes. This is useful in many different cases: for example, when objects are presented in a UI and you want to automatically update the UI when the objects change. Java has a standard mechanism for such notifications: the `PropertyChangeSupport` and `PropertyChangeEvent` classes. Let's see how you can use them in Kotlin without using delegated properties first, and then refactor the code into a delegated property.

The `PropertyChangeSupport` class manages a list of listeners and dispatches `PropertyChangeEvent` events to them. To use it, you normally store an instance of this class as a field of the bean class and delegate property change processing to it.

To avoid adding this field to every class, you'll create a small helper class that will store a `PropertyChangeSupport` instance and keep track of the property change listeners. Later, your classes will extend this helper class to access `changeSupport`.

> **Listing 7.19   Helper class for using `PropertyChangeSupport`**

```
open class PropertyChangeAware {
    protected val changeSupport = PropertyChangeSupport(this)

    fun addPropertyChangeListener(listener: PropertyChangeListener) {
        changeSupport.addPropertyChangeListener(listener)
    }

    fun removePropertyChangeListener(listener: PropertyChangeListener) {
        changeSupport.removePropertyChangeListener(listener)
    }
}
```

Now let's write the `Person` class. You'll define a read-only property (the person's name, which typically doesn't change) and two writable properties: the age and the salary. The class will notify its listeners when either the age or the salary of the person is changed.

> **Listing 7.20   Manually implementing property change notifications**

```
class Person(
        val name: String, age: Int, salary: Int
) : PropertyChangeAware() {

    var age: Int = age
        set(newValue) {
            val oldValue = field          ◁——  The "field" identifier lets you access
            field = newValue                    the property backing field.
            changeSupport.firePropertyChange(  ◁——  Notifies listeners about
                    "age", oldValue, newValue)       the property change
        }
```

```
    var salary: Int = salary
        set(newValue) {
            val oldValue = field
            field = newValue
            changeSupport.firePropertyChange(
                    "salary", oldValue, newValue)
        }
}
```

```
>>> val p = Person("Dmitry", 34, 2000)                  │ Attaches a property
>>> p.addPropertyChangeListener(          ◁────┘ change listener
...        PropertyChangeListener { event ->
...            println("Property ${event.propertyName} changed " +
...                    "from ${event.oldValue} to ${event.newValue}")
...        }
... )
>>> p.age = 35
Property age changed from 34 to 35
>>> p.salary = 2100
Property salary changed from 2000 to 2100
```

Note how this code uses the `field` identifier to access the backing field of the `age` and `salary` properties, as we discussed in section 4.2.4.

There's quite a bit of repeated code in the setters. Let's try to extract a class that will store the value of the property and fire the necessary notification.

Listing 7.21 Implementing property change notifications with a helper class

```
class ObservableProperty(
    val propName: String, var propValue: Int,
    val changeSupport: PropertyChangeSupport
) {
    fun getValue(): Int = propValue
    fun setValue(newValue: Int) {
        val oldValue = propValue
        propValue = newValue
        changeSupport.firePropertyChange(propName, oldValue, newValue)
    }
}

class Person(
    val name: String, age: Int, salary: Int
) : PropertyChangeAware() {

    val _age = ObservableProperty("age", age, changeSupport)
    var age: Int
        get() = _age.getValue()
        set(value) { _age.setValue(value) }

    val _salary = ObservableProperty("salary", salary, changeSupport)
    var salary: Int
        get() = _salary.getValue()
        set(value) { _salary.setValue(value) }
}
```

Now you're close to understanding how delegated properties work in Kotlin. You've created a class that stores the value of the property and automatically fires property change notifications when it's modified. You removed the duplication in the logic, but instead quite a bit of boilerplate is required to create the ObservableProperty instance for each property and to delegate the getter and setter to it. Kotlin's delegated property feature lets you get rid of that boilerplate. But before you can do that, you need to change the signatures of the ObservableProperty methods to match those required by Kotlin conventions.

Listing 7.22   ObservableProperty as a property delegate

```
class ObservableProperty(
    var propValue: Int, val changeSupport: PropertyChangeSupport
) {
    operator fun getValue(p: Person, prop: KProperty<*>): Int = propValue

    operator fun setValue(p: Person, prop: KProperty<*>, newValue: Int) {
        val oldValue = propValue
        propValue = newValue
        changeSupport.firePropertyChange(prop.name, oldValue, newValue)
    }
}
```

Compared to the previous version, this code has the following changes:

- The getValue and setValue functions are now marked as operator, as required for all functions used through conventions.
- You add two parameters to those functions: one to receive the instance for which the property is get or set, and the second to represent the property itself. The property is represented as an object of type KProperty. We'll look at it in more detail in section 10.2; for now, all you need to know is that you can access the name of the property as KProperty.name.
- You remove the name property from the primary constructor because you can now access the property name through KProperty.

You can finally use the magic of Kotlin's delegated properties. See how much shorter the code becomes?

Listing 7.23   Using delegated properties for property change notifications

```
class Person(
    val name: String, age: Int, salary: Int
) : PropertyChangeAware() {

    var age: Int by ObservableProperty(age, changeSupport)
    var salary: Int by ObservableProperty(salary, changeSupport)
}
```

Through the by keyword, the Kotlin compiler does automatically what you did manually in the previous version of the code. Compare this code to the previous version of the Person class: the generated code when you use delegated properties is very similar. The object to the right of by is called the *delegate*. Kotlin automatically stores the delegate in a hidden property and calls getValue and setValue on the delegate when you access or modify the main property.

Instead of implementing the observable property logic by hand, you can use the Kotlin standard library. It turns out the standard library already contains a class similar to ObservableProperty. The standard library class isn't coupled to the Property-ChangeSupport class you're using here, so you need to pass it a lambda that tells it how to report the changes in the property value. Here's how you can do that.

> **Listing 7.24 Using** `Delegates.observable` **to implement property change notification**

```
class Person(
    val name: String, age: Int, salary: Int
) : PropertyChangeAware() {

    private val observer = {
        prop: KProperty<*>, oldValue: Int, newValue: Int ->
        changeSupport.firePropertyChange(prop.name, oldValue, newValue)
    }

    var age: Int by Delegates.observable(age, observer)
    var salary: Int by Delegates.observable(salary, observer)
}
```

The expression to the right of by doesn't have to be a new instance creation. It can also be a function call, another property, or any other expression, as long as the value of this expression is an object on which the compiler can call getValue and set-Value with the correct parameter types. As with other conventions, getValue and setValue can be either methods declared on the object itself or extension functions.

Note that we've only shown you how to work with delegated properties of type Int, to keep the examples simple. The delegated-properties mechanism is fully generic and works with any other type, too.

7.5.4 *Delegated-property translation rules*

Let's summarize the rules for how delegated properties work. Suppose you have a class with a delegated property:

```
class C {
    var prop: Type by MyDelegate()
}

val c = C()
```

The instance of `MyDelegate` will be stored in a hidden property, which we'll refer to as `<delegate>`. The compiler will also use an object of type `KProperty` to represent the property. We'll refer to this object as `<property>`.

The compiler generates the following code:

```
class Foo {
    private val <delegate> = MyDelegate()

    var c: Type
        get() = <delegate>.getValue(c, <property>)
        set(value: Type) = <delegate>.setValue(c, <property>, value)
}
```

Thus, inside every property accessor, the compiler generates calls to the corresponding `getValue` and `setValue` methods, as shown in figure 7.11.

Figure 7.11 When you access a property, the `getValue` **and** `setValue`
functions on `<delegate>` **are called.**

The mechanism is fairly simple, yet it enables many interesting scenarios. You can customize where the value of the property is stored (in a map, in a database table, or in the cookies of a user session) and also what happens when the property is accessed (to add validation, change notifications, and so on). All of this can be accomplished with compact code. Let's look at one more use for delegated properties in the standard library and then see how you can use them in your own frameworks.

7.5.5 *Storing property values in a map*

Another common pattern where delegated properties come into play is objects that have a dynamically defined set of attributes associated with them. Such objects are sometimes called *expando objects*. For example, consider a contact-management system that allows you to store arbitrary information about your contacts. Each person in the system has a few required properties (such as a name) that are handled in a special way, as well as any number of additional attributes that can be different for each person (youngest child's birthday, for example).

One way to implement such a system is to store all the attributes of a person in a map and provide properties for accessing the information that requires special handling. Here's an example.

Listing 7.25 Defining a property that stores its value in a map

```
class Person {
    private val _attributes = hashMapOf<String, String>()
```

```
    fun setAttribute(attrName: String, value: String) {
        _attributes[attrName] = value
    }

    val name: String
        get() = _attributes["name"]!!
}
```

◁── **Retrieves the attribute from the map manually**

```
>>> val p = Person()
>>> val data = mapOf("name" to "Dmitry", "company" to "JetBrains")
>>> for ((attrName, value) in data)
...     p.setAttribute(attrName, value)
>>> println(p.name)
Dmitry
```

Here you use a generic API to load the data into the object (in a real project, this could be JSON deserialization or something similar) and then a specific API to access the value of one property. Changing this to use a delegated property is trivial; you can put the map directly after the by keyword.

Listing 7.26 Using a delegated property which stores its value in a map

```
class Person {
    private val _attributes = hashMapOf<String, String>()

    fun setAttribute(attrName: String, value: String) {
        _attributes[attrName] = value
    }

    val name: String by _attributes
}
```

◁── **Uses the map as a delegated property**

This works because the standard library defines getValue and setValue extension functions on the standard Map and MutableMap interfaces. The name of the property is automatically used as the key to store the value in the map. As in listing 7.25, p.name hides the call of _attributes.getValue(p, prop), which in turn is implemented as _attributes[prop.name].

7.5.6 Delegated properties in frameworks

Changing the way the properties of an object are stored and modified is extremely useful for framework developers. In section 1.3.1, you saw an example of a database framework using delegated properties. This section shows a similar example and explains how it works.

Let's say your database contains the table Users with two columns: name of string type and age of integer type. You can define the classes Users and User in Kotlin. Then all the user entities stored in the database can be loaded and changed in Kotlin code via instances of the User class.

Listing 7.27   Accessing database columns using delegated properties

The object corresponds to a table in the database.

```
object Users : IdTable() {
    val name = varchar("name", length = 50).index()
    val age = integer("age")
}

class User(id: EntityID) : Entity(id) {
    var name: String by Users.name
    var age: Int by Users.age
}
```

Properties correspond to columns in this table.

Each instance of User corresponds to a specific entity in the table.

The value of "name" is the value stored in the database for that user.

The `Users` object describes a database table; it's declared as an object because it describes the table as a whole, so you only need one instance of it. Properties of the object represent columns of the table.

The `Entity` class, the superclass of `User`, contains a mapping of database columns to their values for the entity. The properties for the specific `User` have the values `name` and `age` specified in the database for this user.

Using the framework is especially convenient because accessing the property automatically retrieves the corresponding value from the mapping in the `Entity` class, and modifying it marks the object as dirty so that it can be saved to the database when needed. You can write `user.age += 1` in your Kotlin code, and the corresponding entity in the database will be automatically updated.

Now you know enough to understand how a framework with such an API can be implemented. Each of the entity attributes (`name`, `age`) is implemented as a delegated property, using the column object (`Users.name`, `Users.age`) as the delegate:

```
class User(id: EntityID) : Entity(id) {
    var name: String by Users.name
    var age: Int by Users.age
}
```

Users.name is a delegate for the "name" property.

Let's look at the explicitly specified types of columns:

```
object Users : IdTable() {
    val name: Column<String> = varchar("name", 50).index()
    val age: Column<Int> = integer("age")
}
```

For the `Column` class, the framework defines the `getValue` and `setValue` methods, satisfying the Kotlin convention for delegates:

```
operator fun <T> Column<T>.getValue(o: Entity, desc: KProperty<*>): T {
    // retrieve the value from the database
}
operator fun <T> Column<T>.setValue(o: Entity, desc: KProperty<*>, value: T) {
    // update the value in the database
}
```

You can use the `Column` property (`Users.name`) as a delegate for a delegated property (`name`). When you write `user.age += 1` in your code, the code will perform something similar to `user.ageDelegate.setValue(user.ageDelegate.get-Value() + 1)` (omitting the parameters for the property and object instances). The `getValue` and `setValue` methods take care of retrieving and updating the information in the database.

The full implementation of the classes in this example can be found in the source code for the Exposed framework (https://github.com/JetBrains/Exposed). We'll return to this framework in chapter 11, to explore the DSL design techniques used there.

7.6   *Summary*

- Kotlin allows you to overload some of the standard mathematical operations by defining functions with the corresponding names, but you can't define your own operators.
- Comparison operators are mapped to calls of `equals` and `compareTo` methods.
- By defining functions named `get`, `set`, and `contains`, you can support the `[]` and `in` operators to make your class similar to Kotlin collections.
- Creating ranges and iterating over collections and arrays also work through conventions.
- Destructuring declarations let you initialize multiple variables by unpacking a single object, which is handy for returning multiple values from a function. They work with data classes automatically, and you can support them for your own classes by defining functions named `componentN`.
- Delegated properties allow you to reuse logic controlling how property values are stored, initialized, accessed, and modified, which is a powerful tool for building frameworks.
- The `lazy` standard library function provides an easy way to implement lazily initialized properties.
- The `Delegates.observable` function lets you add an observer of property changes.
- Delegated properties can use any map as a property delegate, providing a flexible way to work with objects that have variable sets of attributes.

Higher-order functions: lambdas as parameters and return values

This chapter covers

- Function types
- Higher-order functions and their use for structuring code
- Inline functions
- Non-local returns and labels
- Anonymous functions

You were introduced to lambdas in chapter 5, where we explored the general concept and the standard library functions that use lambdas. Lambdas are a great tool for building abstractions, and of course their power isn't restricted to collections and other classes in the standard library. In this chapter, you'll learn how to create *higher-order functions*—your own functions that take lambdas as arguments or return them. You'll see how higher-order functions can help simplify your code, remove code duplication, and build nice abstractions. You'll also become acquainted with *inline functions*—a powerful Kotlin feature that removes the performance overhead associated with using lambdas and enables more flexible control flow within lambdas.

8.1 Declaring higher-order functions

The key new idea of this chapter is the concept of *higher-order functions*. By definition, a higher-order function is a function that takes another function as an argument or returns one. In Kotlin, functions can be represented as values using lambdas or function references. Therefore, a higher-order function is any function to which you can pass a lambda or a function reference as an argument, or a function which returns one, or both. For example, the `filter` standard-library function takes a predicate function as an argument and is therefore a higher-order function:

```
list.filter { x > 0 }
```

In chapter 5, you saw many other higher-order functions declared in the Kotlin standard library: `map`, `with`, and so on. Now you'll learn how you can declare such functions in your own code. To do this, you must first be introduced to *function types*.

8.1.1 Function types

In order to declare a function that takes a lambda as an argument, you need to know how to declare the type of the corresponding parameter. Before we get to this, let's look at a simpler case and store a lambda in a local variable. You already saw how you can do this without declaring the type, relying on Kotlin's type inference:

```
val sum = { x: Int, y: Int -> x + y }
val action = { println(42) }
```

In this case, the compiler infers that both the `sum` and `action` variables have function types. Now let's see what an explicit type declaration for these variables looks like:

```
val sum: (Int, Int) -> Int = { x, y -> x + y }    ◄─┐  Function that takes two Int
val action: () -> Unit = { println(42) }    ◄─┐      parameters and returns an Int value
                                              Function that takes no arguments
                                              and doesn't return a value
```

To declare a function type, you put the function parameter types in parentheses, followed by an arrow and the return type of the function (see figure 8.1).

As you remember, the `Unit` type is used to specify that a function returns no meaningful value. The `Unit` return type can be omitted when you declare a regular function, but a function type declaration always requires an explicit return type, so you can't omit `Unit` in this context.

Note how you can omit the types of the parameters x, y in the lambda expression { x, y -> x + y }. Because they're specified in the function type as part of the variable declaration, you don't need to repeat them in the lambda itself.

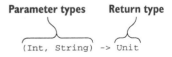

Figure 8.1 Function-type syntax in Kotlin

Just like with any other function, the return type of a function type can be marked as nullable:

```
var canReturnNull: (Int, Int) -> Int? = { null }
```

You can also define a nullable variable of a function type. To specify that the variable itself, rather than the return type of the function, is nullable, you need to enclose the entire function type definition in parentheses and put the question mark after the parentheses:

```
var funOrNull: ((Int, Int) -> Int)? = null
```

Note the subtle difference between this example and the previous one. If you omit the parentheses, you'll declare a function type with a nullable return type, and not a nullable variable of a function type.

Parameter names of function types

You can specify names for parameters of a function type:

```
fun performRequest(
        url: String,
        callback: (code: Int, content: String) -> Unit
) {
    /*...*/
}
```
The function type now has named parameters.

```
>>> val url = "http://kotl.in"
>>> performRequest(url) { code, content -> /*...*/ }
>>> performRequest(url) { code, page -> /*...*/ }
```
You can use the names provided in the API as lambda argument names ... ... or you can change them.

Parameter names don't affect type matching. When you declare a lambda, you don't have to use the same parameter names as the ones used in the function type declaration. But the names improve readability of the code and can be used in the IDE for code completion.

8.1.2   Calling functions passed as arguments

Now that you know how to declare a higher-order function, let's discuss how to implement one. The first example is as simple as possible and uses the same type declaration as the sum lambda you saw earlier. The function performs an arbitrary operation on two numbers, 2 and 3, and prints the result.

Listing 8.1   Defining a simple higher-order function

```
fun twoAndThree(operation: (Int, Int) -> Int) {
    val result = operation(2, 3)
    println("The result is $result")
}
```
Declares a parameter of a function type
Calls the parameter of a function type

```
>>> twoAndThree { a, b -> a + b }
The result is 5
>>> twoAndThree { a, b -> a * b }
The result is 6
```

The syntax for calling the function passed as an argument is the same as calling a regular function: you put the parentheses after the function name, and you put the parameters inside the parentheses.

As a more interesting example, let's reimplement one of the most commonly used standard library functions: the `filter` function. To keep things simple, you'll implement the `filter` function on `String`, but the generic version that works on a collection of any elements is similar. Its declaration is shown in figure 8.2.

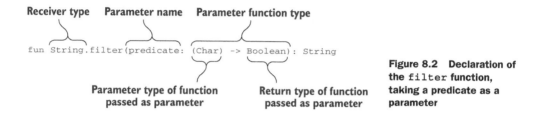

Figure 8.2 Declaration of the `filter` function, taking a predicate as a parameter

The `filter` function takes a predicate as a parameter. The type of `predicate` is a function that takes a character parameter and returns a `boolean` result. The result is `true` if the character passed to the predicate needs to be present in the resulting string, or `false` otherwise. Here's how the function can be implemented.

Listing 8.2 Implementing a simple version of the `filter` function

```
fun String.filter(predicate: (Char) -> Boolean): String {
    val sb = StringBuilder()
    for (index in 0 until length) {
        val element = get(index)
        if (predicate(element)) sb.append(element)      ⟵─── Calls the function passed
    }                                                        as the argument for the
    return sb.toString()                                     "predicate" parameter
}

>>> println("ab1c".filter { it in 'a'..'z' })      ⟵─── Passes a lambda as an
abc                                                     argument for "predicate"
```

The `filter` function implementation is straightforward. It checks whether each character satisfies the predicate and, on success, adds it to the `StringBuilder` containing the result.

INTELLIJ IDEA TIP IntelliJ IDEA supports smart stepping into lambda code in the debugger. If you step through the previous example, you'll see how execution moves between the body of the `filter` function and the lambda you pass through it, as the function processes each element in the input list.

8.1.3 Using function types from Java

Under the hood, function types are declared as regular interfaces: a variable of a function type is an implementation of a `FunctionN` interface. The Kotlin standard library defines a series of interfaces, corresponding to different numbers of function arguments: `Function0<R>` (this function takes no arguments), `Function1<P1, R>` (this function takes one argument), and so on. Each interface defines a single `invoke` method, and calling it will execute the function. A variable of a function type is an instance of a class implementing the corresponding `FunctionN` interface, with the `invoke` method containing the body of the lambda.

Kotlin functions that use function types can be called easily from Java. Java 8 lambdas are automatically converted to values of function types:

```
/* Kotlin declaration */
fun processTheAnswer(f: (Int) -> Int) {
    println(f(42))
}

/* Java */
>>> processTheAnswer(number -> number + 1);
43
```

In older Java versions, you can pass an instance of an anonymous class implementing the `invoke` method from the corresponding function interface:

```
/* Java */
>>> processTheAnswer(
...     new Function1<Integer, Integer>() {        ◁──┐ Uses the Kotlin function
...         @Override                                  │ type from Java code
...         public Integer invoke(Integer number) {    │ (prior to Java 8)
...             System.out.println(number);
...             return number + 1;
...         }
...     });
43
```

In Java, you can easily use extension functions from the Kotlin standard library that expect lambdas as arguments. Note, however, that they don't look as nice as in Kotlin—you have to pass a receiver object as a first argument explicitly:

```
/* Java */
>>> List<String> strings = new ArrayList();
>>> strings.add("42");
>>> CollectionsKt.forEach(strings, s -> {      ◁── You can use a function from the
...     System.out.println(s);                      Kotlin standard library in Java code.
...     return Unit.INSTANCE;            ◁──┐ You have to return a value
... });                                     │ of Unit type explicitly.
```

In Java, your function or lambda can return Unit. But because the Unit type has a value in Kotlin, you need to return it explicitly. You can't pass a lambda returning void as an argument of a function type that returns Unit, like (String) -> Unit in the previous example.

8.1.4 Default and null values for parameters with function types

When you declare a parameter of a function type, you can also specify its default value. To see where this can be useful, let's go back to the joinToString function that we discussed in chapter 3. Here's the implementation we ended up with.

Listing 8.3 joinToString **with hard-coded** toString **conversion**

```
fun <T> Collection<T>.joinToString(
        separator: String = ", ",
        prefix: String = "",
        postfix: String = ""
): String {
    val result = StringBuilder(prefix)

    for ((index, element) in this.withIndex()) {
        if (index > 0) result.append(separator)
        result.append(element)                        ⟵─┐ Converts the object to a
    }                                                    │ string using the default
                                                         │ toString method
    result.append(postfix)
    return result.toString()
}
```

This implementation is flexible, but it doesn't let you control one key aspect of the conversion: how individual values in the collection are converted to strings. The code uses StringBuilder.append(o: Any?), which always converts the object to a string using the toString method. This is good in a lot of cases, but not always. You now know that you can pass a lambda to specify how values are converted into strings. But requiring all callers to pass that lambda would be cumbersome, because most of them are OK with the default behavior. To solve this, you can define a parameter of a function type and specify a default value for it as a lambda.

Listing 8.4 Specifying a default value for a parameter of a function type

```
fun <T> Collection<T>.joinToString(
        separator: String = ", ",
        prefix: String = "",
        postfix: String = "",
        transform: (T) -> String = { it.toString() }   ⟵─┐ Declares a parameter of a
): String {                                               │ function type with a
    val result = StringBuilder(prefix)                    │ lambda as a default value

    for ((index, element) in this.withIndex()) {
        if (index > 0) result.append(separator)
```

```
        result.append(transform(element))
    }

    result.append(postfix)
    return result.toString()
}
```

◁── **Calls the function passed as an argument for the "transform" parameter**

```
>>> val letters = listOf("Alpha", "Beta")
>>> println(letters.joinToString())
Alpha, Beta
>>> println(letters.joinToString { it.toLowerCase() })
alpha, beta
>>> println(letters.joinToString(separator = "! ", postfix = "! ",
...            transform = { it.toUpperCase() }))
ALPHA! BETA!
```

◁── **Uses the default conversion function**

◁── **Passes a lambda as an argument**

◁── **Uses the named argument syntax for passing several arguments including a lambda**

Note that this function is generic: it has a type parameter T denoting the type of the element in a collection. The transform lambda will receive an argument of that type.

Declaring a default value of a function type requires no special syntax—you just put the value as a lambda after the = sign. The examples show different ways of calling the function: omitting the lambda entirely (so that the default toString() conversion is used), passing it outside of the parentheses, and passing it as a named argument.

An alternative approach is to declare a parameter of a nullable function type. Note that you can't call the function passed in such a parameter directly: Kotlin will refuse to compile such code, because it detects the possibility of null pointer exceptions in this case. One option is to check for null explicitly:

```
fun foo(callback: (() -> Unit)?) {
    // ...
    if (callback != null) {
        callback()
    }
}
```

A shorter version makes use of the fact that a function type is an implementation of an interface with an invoke method. As a regular method, invoke can be called through the safe-call syntax: callback?.invoke().

Here's how you can use this technique to rewrite the joinToString function.

Listing 8.5 Using a nullable parameter of a function type

```
fun <T> Collection<T>.joinToString(
        separator: String = ", ",
        prefix: String = "",
        postfix: String = "",
        transform: ((T) -> String)? = null
): String {
    val result = StringBuilder(prefix)
```

◁── **Declares a nullable parameter of a function type**

```
                 for ((index, element) in this.withIndex()) {
                     if (index > 0) result.append(separator)
                     val str = transform?.invoke(element)
                         ?: element.toString()
                     result.append(str)
                 }

                 result.append(postfix)
                 return result.toString()
             }
```

Uses the safe-call syntax to call the function → (points to `val str = transform?.invoke(element)`)

Uses the Elvis operator to handle the case when a callback wasn't specified ← (points to `?: element.toString()`)

Now you know how to write functions that take functions as arguments. Let's look next at the other kind of higher-order functions: functions that return other functions.

8.1.5 *Returning functions from functions*

The requirement to return a function from another function doesn't come up as often as passing functions to other functions, but it's still useful. For instance, imagine a piece of logic in a program that can vary depending on the state of the program or other conditions—for example, calculating the cost of shipping depending on the selected shipping method. You can define a function that chooses the appropriate logic variant and returns it as another function. Here's how this looks as code.

Listing 8.6 Defining a function that returns another function

```
enum class Delivery { STANDARD, EXPEDITED }

class Order(val itemCount: Int)

fun getShippingCostCalculator(
        delivery: Delivery): (Order) -> Double {
    if (delivery == Delivery.EXPEDITED) {
        return { order -> 6 + 2.1 * order.itemCount }
    }

    return { order -> 1.2 * order.itemCount }
}

>>> val calculator =
...     getShippingCostCalculator(Delivery.EXPEDITED)
>>> println("Shipping costs ${calculator(Order(3))}")
Shipping costs 12.3
```

Declares a function that returns a function ← (points to `delivery: Delivery): (Order) -> Double {`)

Returns lambdas from the function → (points to the two `return { order -> ... }` lines)

Stores the returned function in a variable ← (points to `val calculator = ...`)

Invokes the returned function ← (points to `println("Shipping costs ${calculator(Order(3))}")`)

To declare a function that returns another function, you specify a function type as its return type. In listing 8.6, `getShippingCostCalculator` returns a function that takes an `Order` and returns a `Double`. To return a function, you write a `return` expression followed by a lambda, a member reference, or another expression of a function type, such as a local variable.

Let's see another example where returning functions from functions is useful. Suppose you're working on a GUI contact-management application, and you need to determine which contacts should be displayed, based on the state of the UI. Let's say the UI allows you to type a string and then shows only contacts with names starting with that string; it also lets you hide contacts that don't have a phone number specified. You'll use the `ContactListFilters` class to store the state of the options.

```
class ContactListFilters {
    var prefix: String = ""
    var onlyWithPhoneNumber: Boolean = false
}
```

When a user types `D` to see the contacts whose first or last name starts with *D*, the `prefix` value is updated. We've omitted the code that makes the necessary changes. (A full UI application would be too much code for the book, so we show a simplified example.)

To decouple the contact-list display logic from the filtering UI, you can define a function that creates a predicate used to filter the contact list. This predicate checks the prefix and also checks that the phone number is present if required.

> **Listing 8.7   Using functions that return functions in UI code**

```
data class Person(
        val firstName: String,
        val lastName: String,
        val phoneNumber: String?
)

class ContactListFilters {
    var prefix: String = ""
    var onlyWithPhoneNumber: Boolean = false

    fun getPredicate(): (Person) -> Boolean {        ◄─── Declares a function
        val startsWithPrefix = { p: Person ->              that returns a function
            p.firstName.startsWith(prefix) || p.lastName.startsWith(prefix)
        }
        if (!onlyWithPhoneNumber) {
            return startsWithPrefix                  ◄─── Returns a variable
        }                                                 of a function type
        return { startsWithPrefix(it)
                    && it.phoneNumber != null }      ◄─── Returns a lambda
    }                                                      from this function
}

>>> val contacts = listOf(Person("Dmitry", "Jemerov", "123-4567"),
...                       Person("Svetlana", "Isakova", null))
>>> val contactListFilters = ContactListFilters()
>>> with (contactListFilters) {
>>>     prefix = "Dm"
>>>     onlyWithPhoneNumber = true
>>> }                                                ─── Passes the function
>>> println(contacts.filter(                             returned by getPredicate as
...     contactListFilters.getPredicate()))  ◄───        an argument to "filter"
[Person(firstName=Dmitry, lastName=Jemerov, phoneNumber=123-4567)]
```

The `getPredicate` method returns a function value that you pass to the `filter` function as an argument. Kotlin function types allow you to do this just as easily as for values of other types, such as strings.

Higher-order functions give you an extremely powerful tool for improving the structure of your code and removing duplication. Let's see how lambdas can help extract repeated logic from your code.

8.1.6   *Removing duplication through lambdas*

Function types and lambda expressions together constitute a great tool to create reusable code. Many kinds of code duplication that previously could be avoided only through cumbersome constructions can now be eliminated by using succinct lambda expressions.

Let's look at an example that analyzes visits to a website. The class `SiteVisit` stores the path of each visit, its duration, and the user's OS. Various OSs are represented with an enum.

Listing 8.8   Defining the site visit data

```
data class SiteVisit(
    val path: String,
    val duration: Double,
    val os: OS
)

enum class OS { WINDOWS, LINUX, MAC, IOS, ANDROID }

val log = listOf(
    SiteVisit("/", 34.0, OS.WINDOWS),
    SiteVisit("/", 22.0, OS.MAC),
    SiteVisit("/login", 12.0, OS.WINDOWS),
    SiteVisit("/signup", 8.0, OS.IOS),
    SiteVisit("/", 16.3, OS.ANDROID)
)
```

Imagine that you need to display the average duration of visits from Windows machines. You can perform the task using the `average` function.

Listing 8.9   Analyzing site visit data with hard-coded filters

```
val averageWindowsDuration = log
    .filter { it.os == OS.WINDOWS }
    .map(SiteVisit::duration)
    .average()

>>> println(averageWindowsDuration)
23.0
```

Now, suppose you need to calculate the same statistics for Mac users. To avoid duplication, you can extract the platform as a parameter.

Listing 8.10   Removing duplication with a regular function

```
fun List<SiteVisit>.averageDurationFor(os: OS) =                      ◀──────────┐
        filter { it.os == os }.map(SiteVisit::duration).average()
>>> println(log.averageDurationFor(OS.WINDOWS))                        Duplicated code
23.0                                                              extracted into the function
>>> println(log.averageDurationFor(OS.MAC))
22.0
```

Note how making this function an extension improves readability. You can even declare this function as a local extension function if it makes sense only in the local context.

But it's not powerful enough. Imagine that you're interested in the average duration of visits from the mobile platforms (currently you recognize two of them: iOS and Android).

Listing 8.11   Analyzing site visit data with a complex hard-coded filter

```
val averageMobileDuration = log
    .filter { it.os in setOf(OS.IOS, OS.ANDROID) }
    .map(SiteVisit::duration)
    .average()

>>> println(averageMobileDuration)
12.15
```

Now a simple parameter representing the platform doesn't do the job. It's also likely that you'll want to query the log with more complex conditions, such as "What's the average duration of visits to the signup page from iOS?" Lambdas can help. You can use function types to extract the required condition into a parameter.

Listing 8.12   Removing duplication with a higher-order function

```
fun List<SiteVisit>.averageDurationFor(predicate: (SiteVisit) -> Boolean) =
        filter(predicate).map(SiteVisit::duration).average()

>>> println(log.averageDurationFor {
...       it.os in setOf(OS.ANDROID, OS.IOS) })
12.15
>>> println(log.averageDurationFor {
...       it.os == OS.IOS && it.path == "/signup" })
8.0
```

Function types can help eliminate code duplication. If you're tempted to copy and paste a piece of the code, it's likely that the duplication can be avoided. With lambdas, you can extract not only the data that's repeated, but the behavior as well.

NOTE Some well-known design patterns can be simplified using function types and lambda expressions. Let's consider the Strategy pattern, for example. Without lambda expressions, it requires you to declare an interface with several implementations for each possible strategy. With function types in your language, you can use a general function type to describe the strategy, and pass different lambda expressions as different strategies.

We've discussed how to create higher-order functions. Next, let's look at their performance. Won't your code be slower if you begin using higher-order functions for everything, instead of writing good-old loops and conditions? The next section discusses why this isn't always the case and how the `inline` keyword helps.

8.2 *Inline functions: removing the overhead of lambdas*

You've probably noticed that the shorthand syntax for passing a lambda as an argument to a function in Kotlin looks similar to the syntax of regular statements such as `if` and `for`. You saw this in chapter 5, when we discussed the `with` and `apply` functions. But what about performance? Aren't we creating unpleasant surprises by defining functions that look exactly like Java statements but run much more slowly?

In chapter 5, we explained that lambdas are normally compiled to anonymous classes. But that means every time you use a lambda expression, an extra class is created; and if the lambda captures some variables, then a new object is created on every invocation. This introduces runtime overhead, causing an implementation that uses a lambda to be less efficient than a function that executes the same code directly.

Could it be possible to tell the compiler to generate code that's as efficient as a Java statement and yet lets you extract the repeated logic into a library function? Indeed, the Kotlin compiler allows you to do that. If you mark a function with the `inline` modifier, the compiler won't generate a function call when this function is used and instead will replace every call to the function with the actual code implementing the function. Let's explore how that works in detail and look at specific examples.

8.2.1 *How inlining works*

When you declare a function as `inline`, its body is inlined—in other words, it's substituted directly into places where the function is called instead of being invoked normally. Let's look at an example to understand the resulting code.

The function in listing 8.13 can be used to ensure that a shared resource isn't accessed concurrently by multiple threads. The function locks a `Lock` object, executes the given block of code, and then releases the lock.

> **Listing 8.13   Defining an inline function**

```
inline fun <T> synchronized(lock: Lock, action: () -> T): T {
    lock.lock()
    try {
        return action()
    }
    finally {
        lock.unlock()
    }
}
```

```
val l = Lock()
synchronized(l) {
    // ...
}
```

The syntax for calling this function looks exactly like using the synchronized state-ment in Java. The difference is that the Java synchronized statement can be used with any object, whereas this function requires you to pass a Lock instance. The defi-nition shown here is just an example; the Kotlin standard library defines a different version of synchronized that accepts any object as an argument.

But using explicit locks for synchronization provides for more reliable and main-tainable code. In section 8.2.5, we'll introduce the withLock function from the Kotlin standard library, which you should prefer for executing the given action under a lock.

Because you've declared the synchronized function as inline, the code gener-ated for every call to it is the same as for a synchronized statement in Java. Consider this example of using synchronized():

```
fun foo(l: Lock) {
    println("Before sync")
    synchronized(l) {
        println("Action")
    }
    println("After sync")
}
```

Figure 8.3 shows the equivalent code, which will be compiled to the same bytecode:

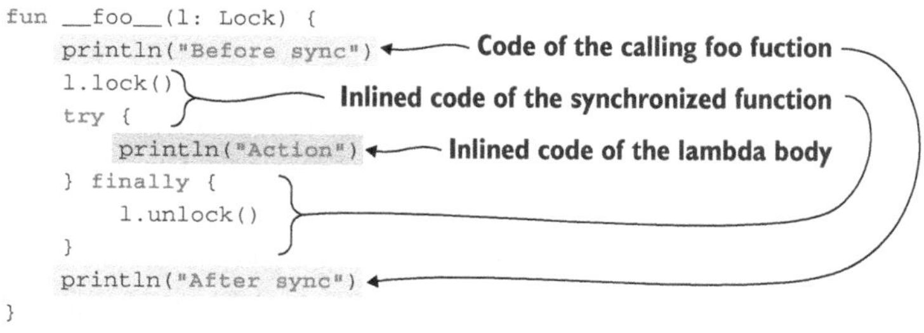

```
fun __foo__(l: Lock) {
    println("Before sync")  ◀──── Code of the calling foo fuction
    l.lock()
    try {                    ◀──── Inlined code of the synchronized function
        println("Action")    ◀──── Inlined code of the lambda body
    } finally {
        l.unlock()
    }
    println("After sync")  ◀────
}
```

Figure 8.3   The compiled version of the foo function

Note that the inlining is applied to the lambda expression as well as the implementa-tion of the synchronized function. The bytecode generated from the lambda becomes part of the definition of the calling function and isn't wrapped in an anony-mous class implementing a function interface.

Note that it's also possible to call an inline function and pass the parameter of a function type from a variable:

```
class LockOwner(val lock: Lock) {
    fun runUnderLock(body: () -> Unit) {
```

```
        synchronized(lock, body)
    }
}
```
← A variable of a function type is passed as an argument, not a lambda.

In this case, the lambda's code isn't available at the site where the inline function is called, and therefore it isn't inlined. Only the body of the synchronized function is inlined; the lambda is called as usual. The runUnderLock function will be compiled to bytecode similar to the following function:

```
class LockOwner(val lock: Lock) {
    fun __runUnderLock__(body: () -> Unit) {
        lock.lock()
        try {
            body()
        }
        finally {
            lock.unlock()
        }
    }
}
```
← This function is similar to the bytecode the real runUnderLock is compiled to.

← The body isn't inlined, because there's no lambda at the invocation.

If you have two uses of an inline function in different locations with different lambdas, then every call site will be inlined independently. The code of the inline function will be copied to both locations where you use it, with different lambdas substituted into it.

8.2.2 Restrictions on inline functions

Due to the way inlining is performed, not every function that uses lambdas can be inlined. When the function is inlined, the body of the lambda expression that's passed as an argument is substituted directly into the resulting code. That restricts the possible uses of the corresponding parameter in the function body. If this parameter is called, such code can be easily inlined. But if the parameter is stored somewhere for further use, the code of the lambda expression can't be inlined, because there must be an object that contains this code.

Generally, the parameter can be inlined if it's called directly or passed as an argument to another inline function. Otherwise, the compiler will prohibit the inlining of the parameter with an error message that says "Illegal usage of inline-parameter."

For example, various functions that work on sequences return instances of classes that represent the corresponding sequence operation and receive the lambda as a constructor parameter. Here's how the Sequence.map function is defined:

```
fun <T, R> Sequence<T>.map(transform: (T) -> R): Sequence<R> {
    return TransformingSequence(this, transform)
}
```

The map function doesn't call the function passed as the transform parameter directly. Instead, it passes this function to the constructor of a class that stores it in a property. To support that, the lambda passed as the transform argument needs to be compiled into the standard non-inline representation, as an anonymous class implementing a function interface.

If you have a function that expects two or more lambdas as arguments, you may choose to inline only some of them. This makes sense when one of the lambdas is expected to contain a lot of code or is used in a way that doesn't allow inlining. You can mark the parameters that accept such non-inlineable lambdas with the `noinline` modifier:

```
inline fun foo(inlined: () -> Unit, noinline notInlined: () -> Unit) {
    // ...
}
```

Note that the compiler fully supports inlining functions across modules, or functions defined in third-party libraries. You can also call most inline functions from Java; such calls will not be inlined, but will be compiled as regular function calls.

Later in the book, in section 9.2.4, you'll see another case where it makes sense to use `noinline` (with some constraints on Java interoperability, however).

8.2.3   *Inlining collection operations*

Let's consider the performance of Kotlin standard library functions that work on collections. Most of the collection functions in the standard library take lambda expressions as arguments. Would it be more efficient to implement these operations directly, instead of using the standard library functions?

For example, let's compare the ways you can filter a list of people, as shown in the next two listings.

Listing 8.14   Filtering a collection using a lambda

```
data class Person(val name: String, val age: Int)

val people = listOf(Person("Alice", 29), Person("Bob", 31))

>>> println(people.filter { it.age < 30 })
[Person(name=Alice, age=29)]
```

The previous code can be rewritten without lambda expressions, as shown next.

Listing 8.15   Filtering a collection manually

```
>>> val result = mutableListOf<Person>()
>>> for (person in people) {
>>>       if (person.age < 30) result.add(person)
>>> }
>>> println(result)
[Person(name=Alice, age=29)]
```

In Kotlin, the `filter` function is declared as inline. It means the bytecode of the `filter` function, together with the bytecode of the lambda passed to it, will be inlined where `filter` is called. As a result, the bytecode generated for the first version that uses `filter` is roughly the same as the bytecode generated for the second version. You can safely use idiomatic operations on collections, and Kotlin's support for inline functions ensures that you don't need to worry about performance.

Imagine now that you apply two operations, `filter` and `map`, in a chain.

```
>>> println(people.filter { it.age > 30 }
...                  .map(Person::name))
[Bob]
```

This example uses a lambda expression and a member reference. Once again, both `filter` and `map` are declared as `inline`, so their bodies are inlined, and no extra classes or objects are created. But the code creates an intermediate collection to store the result of filtering the list. The code generated from the `filter` function adds elements to that collection, and the code generated from `map` reads from it.

If the number of elements to process is large, and the overhead of an intermediate collection becomes a concern, you can use a sequence instead, by adding an `asSequence` call to the chain. But as you saw in the previous section, lambdas used to process a sequence aren't inlined. Each intermediate sequence is represented as an object storing a lambda in its field, and the terminal operation causes a chain of calls through each intermediate sequence to be performed. Therefore, even though operations on sequences are lazy, you shouldn't strive to insert an `asSequence` call into every chain of collection operations in your code. This helps only for large collections; smaller ones can be processed nicely with regular collection operations.

8.2.4 Deciding when to declare functions as inline

Now that you've learned about the benefits of the `inline` keyword, you might want to start using `inline` throughout your codebase, trying to make it run faster. As it turns out, this isn't a good idea. Using the `inline` keyword is likely to improve performance only with functions that take lambdas as arguments; all other cases require additional measuring and investigation.

For regular function calls, the JVM already provides powerful inlining support. It analyzes the execution of your code and inlines calls whenever doing so provides the most benefit. This happens automatically while translating bytecode to machine code. In bytecode, the implementation of each function is repeated only once and doesn't need to be copied to every place where the function is called, as with Kotlin's `inline` functions. What's more, the stacktrace is clearer if the function is called directly.

On the other hand, inlining functions with lambda arguments is beneficial. First, the overhead you avoid through inlining is more significant. You save not only on the call, but also on the creation of the extra class for each lambda and an object for the lambda instance. Second, the JVM currently isn't smart enough to always perform inlining through the call and the lambda. Finally, inlining lets you use features that are impossible to make work with regular lambdas, such as non-local returns, which we'll discuss later in this chapter.

But you should still pay attention to the code size when deciding whether to use the `inline` modifier. If the function you want to inline is large, copying its bytecode into every call site could be expensive in terms of bytecode size. In that case, you should try to extract the code not related to the lambda arguments into a separate non-inline function. You can verify for yourself that the `inline` functions in the Kotlin standard library are always small.

Next, let's see how higher-order functions can help you improve your code.

8.2.5   *Using inlined lambdas for resource management*

One common pattern where lambdas can remove duplicate code is resource management: acquiring a resource before an operation and releasing it afterward. *Resource* here can mean many different things: a file, a lock, a database transaction, and so on. The standard way to implement such a pattern is to use a `try/finally` statement in which the resource is acquired before the `try` block and released in the `finally` block.

Earlier in this section, you saw an example of how you can encapsulate the logic of the `try/finally` statement in a function and pass the code using the resource as a lambda to that function. The example showed the `synchronized` function, which has the same syntax as the `synchronized` statement in Java: it takes the lock object as an argument. The Kotlin standard library defines another function called `withLock`, which has a more idiomatic API for the same task: it's an extension function on the `Lock` interface. Here's how it can be used:

```
val l: Lock = ...
l.withLock {                                                    Executes the given
    // access the resource protected by this lock               action under the lock
}
```

Here's how the `withLock` function is defined in the Kotlin library:

```
fun <T> Lock.withLock(action: () -> T): T {                The idiom of working with locks is
    lock()                                                 extracted into a separate function.
    try {
        return action()
    } finally {
        unlock()
    }
}
```

Files are another common type of resource where this pattern is used. Java 7 has even introduced special syntax for this pattern: the try-with-resources statement. The following listing shows a Java method that uses this statement to read the first line from a file.

> **Listing 8.16   Using try-with-resources in Java**

```
/* Java */
static String readFirstLineFromFile(String path) throws IOException {
    try (BufferedReader br =
                new BufferedReader(new FileReader(path))) {
```

```
        return br.readLine();
    }
}
```

Kotlin doesn't have equivalent syntax, because the same task can be accomplished almost as seamlessly through a function with a parameter of a function type (that expects a lambda as an argument). The function is called `use` and is included in the Kotlin standard library. Here's how you can use this function to rewrite listing 8.16 in Kotlin.

Listing 8.17 Using the `use` function for resource management

```
fun readFirstLineFromFile(path: String): String {
    BufferedReader(FileReader(path)).use { br ->        ◁────┐   Creates the BufferedReader,
        return br.readLine()          ◁────┐                 │   calls the "use" function, and
    }                                       │                 │   passes a lambda to execute
}                             Returns the line                   the operation on the file
                              from the function
```

The `use` function is an extension function called on a closable resource; it receives a lambda as an argument. The function calls the lambda and ensures that the resource is closed, regardless of whether the lambda completes normally or throws an exception. Of course, the `use` function is inlined, so its use doesn't incur any performance overhead.

Note that in the body of the lambda, you use a non-local `return` to return a value from the `readFirstLineFromFile` function. Let's discuss the use of `return` expressions in lambdas in detail.

8.3 *Control flow in higher-order functions*

When you start using lambdas to replace imperative code constructs such as loops, you quickly run into the issue of `return` expressions. Putting a `return` statement in the middle of a loop is a no-brainer. But what if you convert the loop into the use of a function such as `filter`? How does `return` work in that case? Let's look at some examples.

8.3.1 *Return statements in lambdas: return from an enclosing function*

We'll compare two different ways of iterating over a collection. In the following listing, it's clear that if the person's name is Alice, you return from the function `look-ForAlice`.

Listing 8.18 Using `return` in a regular loop

```
data class Person(val name: String, val age: Int)

val people = listOf(Person("Alice", 29), Person("Bob", 31))

fun lookForAlice(people: List<Person>) {
    for (person in people) {
```

```
        if (person.name == "Alice") {
            println("Found!")
            return
        }
    }
    println("Alice is not found")
}
```

This line is printed if there's no Alice among "people".

```
>>> lookForAlice(people)
Found!
```

Is it safe to rewrite this code using `forEach` iteration? Will the `return` statement mean the same thing? Yes, it's safe to use the `forEach` function instead, as shown next.

> **Listing 8.19   Using `return` in a lambda passed to `forEach`**

```
fun lookForAlice(people: List<Person>) {
    people.forEach {
        if (it.name == "Alice") {
            println("Found!")
            return
        }
    }
    println("Alice is not found")
}
```

Returns from a function as in listing 8.18

If you use the `return` keyword in a lambda, it *returns from the function in which you called the lambda*, not just from the lambda itself. Such a `return` statement is called a *non-local return*, because it returns from a larger block than the block containing the return statement.

To understand the logic behind the rule, think about using a `return` keyword in a for loop or a `synchronized` block in a Java method. It's obvious that it returns from the function and not from the loop or block. Kotlin allows you to preserve the same behavior when you switch from language features to functions that take lambdas as arguments.

Note that the return from the outer function is possible *only if the function that takes the lambda as an argument is inlined.* In listing 8.19, the body of the `forEach` function is inlined together with the body of the lambda, so it's easy to compile the `return` expression so that it returns from the enclosing function. Using the `return` expression in lambdas passed to non-inline functions isn't allowed. A non-inline function can save the lambda passed to it in a variable and execute it later, when the function has already returned, so it's too late for the lambda to affect when the surrounding function returns.

8.3.2   *Returning from lambdas: return with a label*

You can write a *local* return from a lambda expression as well. A local return in a lambda is similar to a `break` expression in a for loop. It stops the execution of the lambda and continues execution of the code from which the lambda was invoked. To distinguish a local return from a non-local one, you use *labels*. You can label a lambda expression from which you want to return, and then refer to this label after the return keyword.

Labels the lambda expression

```
fun lookForAlice(people: List<Person>) {
    people.forEach label@{
        if (it.name == "Alice") return@label          return@label refers
    }                                                  to this label.
    println("Alice might be somewhere")               This line is
}                                                      always printed.

>>> lookForAlice(people)
Alice might be somewhere
```

To label a lambda expression, put the label name (which can be any identifier), followed by the @ character, before the opening curly brace of the lambda. To return from a lambda, put the @ character followed by the label name after the return keyword. This is illustrated in figure 8.4.

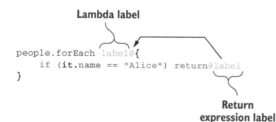

Figure 8.4   Returns from a lambda use the "@" character to mark a label.

Alternatively, the name of the function that takes this lambda as an argument can be used as a label.

```
fun lookForAlice(people: List<Person>) {
    people.forEach {
        if (it.name == "Alice") return@forEach        return@forEach returns from
    }                                                  the lambda expression.
    println("Alice might be somewhere")
}
```

Note that if you specify the label of the lambda expression explicitly, labeling using the function name doesn't work. A lambda expression can't have more than one label.

Labeled "this" expression

The same rules apply to the labels of `this` expressions. In chapter 5, we discussed lambdas with receivers—lambdas that contain an implicit context object that can be accessed via a `this` reference in a lambda (chapter 11 will explain how to write your own functions that expect lambdas with receivers as arguments). If you specify the label of a lambda with a receiver, you can access its implicit receiver using the corresponding labeled `this` expression:

```
>>> println(StringBuilder().apply sb@{
...     listOf(1, 2, 3).apply {
...         this@sb.append(this.toString())
...     }
... })
[1, 2, 3]
```

This lambda's implicit receiver is accessed by this@sb.

"this" refers to the closest implicit receiver in the scope.

All implicit receivers can be accessed, the outer ones via explicit labels.

As with labels for `return` expressions, you can specify the label of the lambda expression explicitly or use the function name instead.

The non-local return syntax is fairly verbose and becomes cumbersome if a lambda contains multiple return expressions. As a solution, you can use an alternate syntax to pass around blocks of code: *anonymous functions*.

8.3.3 Anonymous functions: local returns by default

An anonymous function is a different way to write a block of code passed to a function. Let's start with an example.

Listing 8.22   Using `return` in an anonymous function

```
fun lookForAlice(people: List<Person>) {
    people.forEach(fun (person) {
        if (person.name == "Alice") return
        println("${person.name} is not Alice")
    })
}

>>> lookForAlice(people)
Bob is not Alice
```

Uses an anonymous function instead of a lambda expression

"return" refers to the closest function: an anonymous function.

You can see that an anonymous function looks similar to a regular function, except that its name and parameter types are omitted. Here's another example.

Listing 8.23   Using an anonymous function with `filter`

```
people.filter(fun (person): Boolean {
    return person.age < 30
})
```

Anonymous functions follow the same rules as regular functions for specifying the return type. Anonymous functions with a block body, such as the one in listing 8.23, require the return type to be specified explicitly. If you use an expression body, you can omit the return type.

```
people.filter(fun (person) = person.age < 30)
```

Inside an anonymous function, a `return` expression without a label returns from the anonymous function, not from the enclosing one. The rule is simple: `return` *returns from the closest function declared using the* `fun` *keyword.* Lambda expressions don't use the `fun` keyword, so a `return` in a lambda returns from the outer function. Anonymous functions do use `fun`; therefore, in the previous example, the anonymous function is the closest matching function. Consequently, the `return` expression returns from the anonymous function, not from the enclosing one. The difference is illustrated in figure 8.5.

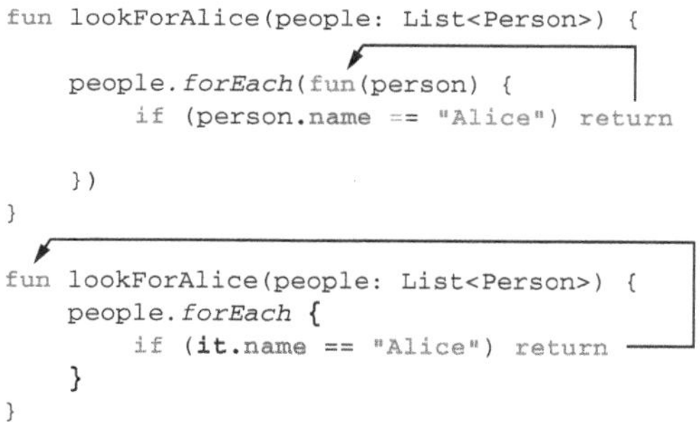

```
fun lookForAlice(people: List<Person>) {

    people.forEach(fun(person) {
        if (person.name == "Alice") return

    })
}

fun lookForAlice(people: List<Person>) {
    people.forEach {
        if (it.name == "Alice") return
    }
}
```

Figure 8.5   The return expression returns from the function declared using the `fun` keyword.

Note that despite the fact that an anonymous function looks similar to a regular function declaration, it's another syntactic form of a lambda expression. The discussion of how lambda expressions are implemented and how they're inlined for inline functions applies to anonymous functions as well.

8.4   *Summary*

- Function types allow you to declare a variable, parameter, or function return value that holds a reference to a function.
- Higher-order functions take other functions as arguments or return them. You can create such functions by using a function type as the type of a function parameter or return value.
- When an inline function is compiled, its bytecode along with the bytecode of a lambda passed to it is inserted directly into the code of the calling function,

which ensures that the call happens with no overhead compared to similar code written directly.

- Higher-order functions facilitate code reuse within the parts of a single component and let you build powerful generic libraries.

- Inline functions allow you to use *non-local returns*—return expressions placed in a lambda that return from the enclosing function.

- Anonymous functions provide an alternative syntax to lambda expressions with different rules for resolving the return expressions. You can use them if you need to write a block of code with multiple exit points.

Generics

This chapter covers

- Declaring generic functions and classes
- Type erasure and reified type parameters
- Declaration-site and use-site variance

You've already seen a few code examples that use generics in this book. The basic concepts of declaring and using generic classes and functions in Kotlin are similar to Java, so the earlier examples should have been clear without a detailed explanation. In this chapter, we'll return to some of the examples and look at them in more detail.

We'll then go deeper into the topic of generics and explore new concepts introduced in Kotlin, such as reified type parameters and declaration-site variance. These concepts may be novel to you, but don't worry; the chapter covers them thoroughly.

Reified type parameters allow you to refer at runtime to the specific types used as type arguments in an inline function call. (For normal classes or functions, this isn't possible, because type arguments are erased at runtime.)

Declaration-site variance lets you specify whether a generic type with a type argument is a subtype or a supertype of another generic type with the same base type and a different type argument. For example, it regulates whether it's possible to pass arguments of type List<Int> to functions expecting List<Any>. *Use-site variance* achieves the same goal for a specific use of a generic type and therefore accomplishes the same task as Java's wildcards.

9.1 *Generic type parameters*

Generics allow you to define types that have *type parameters*. When an instance of such a type is created, type parameters are substituted with specific types called *type arguments*. For example, if you have a variable of type List, it's useful to know what kind of things are stored in that list. The type parameter lets you specify exactly that—instead of "This variable holds a list," you can say something like "This variable holds a list of strings." Kotlin's syntax for saying "a list of strings" looks the same as in Java: List<String>. You can also declare multiple type parameters for a class. For example, the Map class has type parameters for the key type and the value type: class Map<K, V>. We can instantiate it with specific arguments: Map<String, Person>. So far, everything looks exactly as it does in Java.

Just as with types in general, type arguments can often be inferred by the Kotlin compiler:

```
val authors = listOf("Dmitry", "Svetlana")
```

Because the two values passed to the listOf function are both strings, the compiler infers that you're creating a List<String>. On the other hand, if you need to create an empty list, there's nothing from which to infer the type argument, so you need to specify it explicitly. In the case of creating a list, you have a choice between specifying the type as part of the variable declaration and specifying a type argument for the function that creates a list. The following example shows how this is done:

```
val readers: MutableList<String> = mutableListOf()

val readers = mutableListOf<String>()
```

These declarations are equivalent. Note that collection-creation functions are covered in section 6.3.

> **NOTE** Unlike Java, Kotlin always requires type arguments to be either specified explicitly or inferred by the compiler. Because generics were added to Java only in version 1.5, it had to maintain compatibility with code written for older versions, so it allows you to use a generic type without type arguments—a so-called *raw type*. For example, in Java, you can declare a variable of type List without specifying what kind of things it contains. Because Kotlin has had generics from the beginning, it doesn't support raw types, and the type arguments must always be defined.

9.1.1 *Generic functions and properties*

If you're going to write a function that works with a list, and you want it to work with any list (a generic one), not a list of elements of a specific type, you need to write a *generic function.* A generic function has type parameters of its own. These type parameters must be replaced with the specific type arguments on each function invocation.

Most of the library functions working with collections are generic. For example, let's look at the `slice` function declaration, shown in figure 9.1. This function returns a list containing only elements at indices in the specified range.

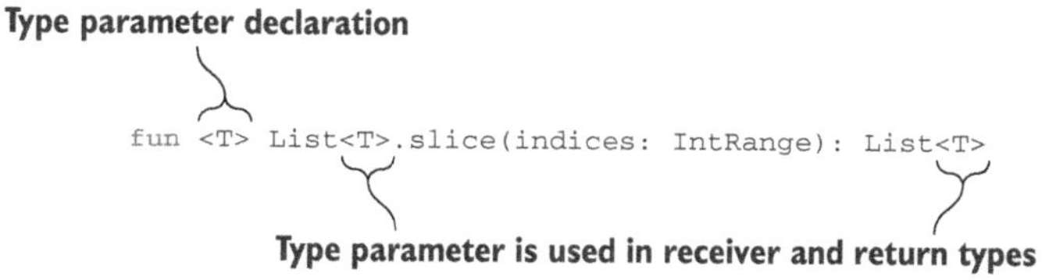

Type parameter declaration

```
fun <T> List<T>.slice(indices: IntRange): List<T>
```

Type parameter is used in receiver and return types

Figure 9.1   The generic function `slice` has the type parameter `T`.

The function's type parameter `T` is used in the receiver type and in the return type; both of them are `List<T>`. When you call such a function on a specific list, you can specify the type argument explicitly. But in almost all cases you don't need to, because the compiler infers it, as shown next.

Listing 9.1   Calling a generic function

```
>>> val letters = ('a'..'z').toList()
>>> println(letters.slice<Char>(0..2))
[a, b, c]
>>> println(letters.slice(10..13))
[k, l, m, n]
```

Specifies the type argument explicitly

The compiler infers that T is Char here.

The result type of both of these calls is `List<Char>`. The compiler substitutes the inferred type `Char` for `T` in the function return type `List<T>`.

In section 8.1, you saw the declaration of the `filter` function, which takes a parameter of the function type `(T) -> Boolean`. Let's see how you can apply it to the `readers` and `authors` variables from the previous examples.

Listing 9.2   Calling a generic higher-order function

```
val authors = listOf("Dmitry", "Svetlana")
val readers = mutableListOf<String>(/* ... */)

fun <T> List<T>.filter(predicate: (T) -> Boolean): List<T>

>>> readers.filter { it !in authors }
```

The type of the autogenerated lambda parameter `it` is `String` in this case. The compiler has to infer that: after all, in the declaration of the function, the lambda parameter has a generic type T (it's the type of the function parameter in (T) -> Boolean). The compiler understands that T is String, because it knows the function should be called on List<T>, and the actual type of its receiver, readers, is List<String>.

You can declare type parameters on methods of classes or interfaces, top-level functions, and extension functions. In the last case, the type parameter can be used in the types of the receiver and the parameters, as in listings 9.1 and 9.2: the type parameter T is part of the receiver type List<T>, and it's used in the parameter function type (T) -> Boolean as well.

You can also declare generic extension properties using the same syntax. For example, here's an extension property that returns the element before the last one in a list:

```
val <T> List<T>.penultimate: T                    ◁─── This generic extension property
    get() = this[size - 2]                               can be called on a list of any kind.

>>> println(listOf(1, 2, 3, 4).penultimate)       ◁─── The type parameter T is inferred
3                                                        to be Int in this invocation.
```

> ### You can't declare a generic non-extension property
>
> Regular (non-extension) properties can't have type parameters. It's not possible to store multiple values of different types in a property of a class, and therefore declaring a generic non-extension property doesn't make sense. If you try to do that, the compiler reports an error:
>
> ```
> >>> val <T> x: T = TODO()
> ERROR: type parameter of a property must be used in its receiver type
> ```

Now let's recap how you can declare generic classes.

9.1.2   *Declaring generic classes*

Just as in Java, you declare a Kotlin generic class or interface by putting angle brackets after the class name and the type parameters in the angle brackets. Once you do that, you can use the type parameters in the body of the class, just like any other types. Let's look at how the standard Java interface List can be declared in Kotlin. To simplify it, we've omitted the majority of the methods:

```
                                               The List interface defines
                                               a type parameter T.
interface List<T> {                       ◁───┘
    operator fun get(index: Int): T       ◁─── T can be used as a regular type
    // ...                                      in an interface or a class.
}
```

Later in this chapter, when we get to the topic of variance, you'll improve on this example and see how List is declared in the Kotlin standard library.

If your class extends a generic class (or implements a generic interface), you have to provide a type argument for the generic parameter of the base type. It can be either a specific type or another type parameter:

Note how
String is used
instead of T.

```
class StringList: List<String> {
    override fun get(index: Int): String = ... }

class ArrayList<T> : List<T> {
    override fun get(index: Int): T = ...
}
```

**This class implements List, providing
a specific type argument: String.**

**Now the generic type parameter T of
ArrayList is a type argument for List.**

The `StringList` class is declared to contain only `String` elements, so it uses `String` as the type argument of the base type. Any function from the subclass substitutes this proper type instead of T, so you have a signature `fun get(Int): String` in `StringList`, rather than `fun get(Int): T`.

The `ArrayList` class defines its own type parameter T and specifies that as a type argument of the superclass. Note that T in `ArrayList<T>` *is not the same* as in `List<T>`—it's a new type parameter, and it doesn't need to have the same name.

A class can even refer to itself as a type argument. Classes implementing the `Comparable` interface are the classical example of this pattern. Any comparable element must define how to compare it with objects of the same type:

```
interface Comparable<T> {
    fun compareTo(other: T): Int
}

class String : Comparable<String> {
    override fun compareTo(other: String): Int = /* ... */
}
```

The `String` class implements the generic `Comparable` interface, providing the type `String` for the type parameter T.

So far, generics look similar to those in Java. We'll talk about the differences later in the chapter, in sections 9.2 and 9.3. Now let's discuss another concept that works similar to Java: the one that allows you to write useful functions for working with comparable items.

9.1.3 *Type parameter constraints*

Type parameter constraints let you restrict the types that can be used as type arguments for a class or function. For example, consider a function that calculates the sum of elements in a list. It can be used on a `List<Int>` or a `List<Double>`, but not, for example, a `List<String>`. To express this, you can define a type parameter constraint that specifies that the type parameter of `sum` must be a number.

When you specify a type as an *upper bound* constraint for a type parameter of a generic type, the corresponding type arguments in specific instantiations of the generic type must be either the specified type or its subtypes. (For now, you can think of *subtype* as a synonym for *subclass*. Section 9.3.2 will highlight the difference.)

To specify a constraint, you put a colon after the type parameter name, followed by the type that's the upper bound for the type parameter; see figure 9.2. In Java, you use the keyword extends to express the same concept: `<T extends Number> T sum(List<T> list)`.

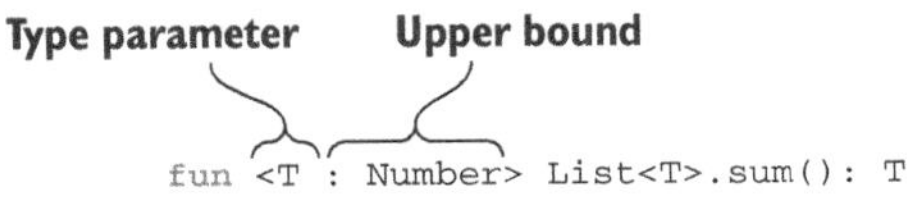

Type parameter   Upper bound

```
fun <T : Number> List<T>.sum(): T
```

Figure 9.2   Constraints are defined by specifying an upper bound after a type parameter.

This function invocation is allowed because the actual type argument (`Int` in the following example) extends `Number`:

```
>>> println(listOf(1, 2, 3).sum())
6
```

Once you've specified a bound for a type parameter `T`, you can use values of type `T` as values of its upper bound. For example, you can invoke methods defined in the class used as the bound:

```
fun <T : Number> oneHalf(value: T): Double {      ⟵  Specifies Number as the type
    return value.toDouble() / 2.0                      parameter upper bound
}                                                 ⟵  Invokes a method defined
                                                     in the Number class
>>> println(oneHalf(3))
1.5
```

Now let's write a generic function that finds the maximum of two items. Because it's only possible to find a maximum of items that can be compared to each other, you need to specify that in the signature of the function. Here's how you do that.

Listing 9.3   Declaring a function with a type parameter constraint

```
fun <T: Comparable<T>> max(first: T, second: T): T {   ⟵  The arguments of this
    return if (first > second) first else second           function must be
}                                                          comparable elements.

>>> println(max("kotlin", "java"))   ⟵  The strings are compared
kotlin                                   alphabetically.
```

When you try to call `max` on incomparable items, the code won't compile:

```
>>> println(max("kotlin", 42))
ERROR: Type parameter bound for T is not satisfied:
 inferred type Any is not a subtype of Comparable<Any>
```

The upper bound for `T` is a generic type `Comparable<T>`. As you saw earlier, the `String` class extends `Comparable<String>`, which makes `String` a valid type argument for the `max` function.

Remember, the short form `first > second` is compiled to `first.compareTo(second) > 0`, according to Kotlin operator conventions. This comparison is possible because the type of first, which is T, extends from Comparable<T>, and thus you can compare first to another element of type T.

In the rare case when you need to specify multiple constraints on a type parameter, you use a slightly different syntax. For example, the following listing is a generic way to ensure that the given CharSequence has a period at the end. It works with both the standard StringBuilder class and the java.nio.CharBuffer class.

> **Listing 9.4 Specifying multiple constraints for a type parameter**

```
fun <T> ensureTrailingPeriod(seq: T)
        where T : CharSequence, T : Appendable {        Calls an extension function defined
    if (!seq.endsWith('.')) {                            for the CharSequence interface
        seq.append('.')                        Calls the method from the
    }                                          Appendable interface
}
```

List of type parameter constraints

```
>>> val helloWorld = StringBuilder("Hello World")
>>> ensureTrailingPeriod(helloWorld)
>>> println(helloWorld)
Hello World.
```

In this case, you specify that the type used as a type argument must implement both the CharSequence and Appendable interfaces. This means both the operations accessing the data (endsWith) as well as the operation modifying it (append) can be used with values of that type.

Next, we'll discuss another case when type parameter constraints are common: when you want to declare a non-null type parameter.

9.1.4 *Making type parameters non-null*

If you declare a generic class or function, any type arguments, including nullable ones, can be substituted for its type parameters. In effect, a type parameter with no upper bound specified will have the upper bound of Any?. Consider the following example:

```
class Processor<T> {
    fun process(value: T) {
        value?.hashCode()          "value" is nullable, so you
    }                              have to use a safe call.
}
```

In the process function, the parameter value is nullable, even though T isn't marked with a question mark. This is the case because specific instantiations of the Processor class can use a nullable type for T:

```
val nullableStringProcessor = Processor<String?>()        String?, which is a nullable
nullableStringProcessor.process(null)                     type, is substituted for T.
```
This code compiles fine, having "null" as the "value" argument.

If you want to guarantee that a non-null type will always be substituted for a type parameter, you can achieve this by specifying a constraint. If you don't have any restrictions other than nullability, you can use Any as the upper bound, replacing the default Any?:

```
class Processor<T : Any> {                              Specifying a non-"null"
    fun process(value: T) {                             upper bound
        value.hashCode()          "value" of type T
    }                             is now non-"null".
}
```

The <T : Any> constraint ensures that the T type will always be a non-nullable type. The code Processor<String?> won't be accepted by the compiler, because the type argument String? isn't a subtype of Any (it's a subtype of Any?, which is a less specific type):

```
>>> val nullableStringProcessor = Processor<String?>()
Error: Type argument is not within its bounds: should be subtype of 'Any'
```

Note that you can make a type parameter non-null by specifying any non-null type as an upper bound, not only the type Any.

So far, we've covered the basics of generics—the topics that are most similar to Java. Now let's discuss another concept that may be somewhat familiar if you're a Java developer: how generics behave at runtime.

9.2   *Generics at runtime: erased and reified type parameters*

As you probably know, generics on the JVM are normally implemented through *type erasure*, meaning the type arguments of an instance of a generic class aren't preserved at runtime. In this section, we'll discuss the practical implications of type erasure for Kotlin, and how you can get around its limitations by declaring a function as inline. You can declare an inline function so that its type arguments aren't erased (or, in Kotlin terms, are reified). We'll discuss reified type parameters in detail and look at examples when they're useful.

9.2.1   *Generics at runtime: type checks and casts*

Just as in Java, Kotlin's generics are *erased* at runtime. This means an instance of a generic class doesn't carry information about the type arguments used to create that instance. For example, if you create a List<String> and put a bunch of strings into it, at runtime you'll only be able to see that it's a List. It's not possible to identify which type of elements the list was intended to contain. (Of course, you can get an element and check its type, but that won't give you any guarantees, because other elements may have different types.)

Consider what happens with these two lists when you run the code (shown in figure 9.3):

```
val list1: List<String> = listOf("a", "b")
val list2: List<Int> = listOf(1, 2, 3)
```

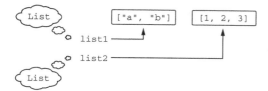

Figure 9.3　At runtime, you don't know whether `list1` and `list2` were declared as lists of strings or integers. Each of them is just `List`.

Even though the compiler sees two distinct types for the lists, at execution time they look exactly the same. Despite that, you can normally be sure that a `List<String>` contains only strings and a `List<Int>` contains only integers, because the compiler knows the type arguments and ensures that only elements of the correct type are stored in each list. (You can deceive the compiler through type casts or by using Java raw types to access the list, but you need to make a special effort to do that.)

Let's talk next about the constraints that go with erasing the type information. Because type arguments aren't stored, you can't check them—for example, you can't check whether a list is a list of strings rather than other objects. As a general rule, it's not possible to use types with type arguments in `is` checks. The following code won't compile:

```
>>> if (value is List<String>) { ... }
ERROR: Cannot check for instance of erased type
```

Even though it's perfectly possible to find out at runtime that value is a `List`, you can't tell whether it's a list of strings, persons, or something else: that information has been erased. Note that erasing generic type information has its benefits: the overall amount of memory used by your application is smaller, because less type information needs to be saved in memory.

As we stated earlier, Kotlin doesn't let you use a generic type without specifying type arguments. Thus you may wonder how to check that the value is a list, rather than a set or another object. You can do that by using the special *star projection* syntax:

```
if (value is List<*>) { ... }
```

Effectively, you need to include a `*` for every type parameter the type has. We'll discuss the star projection in detail (including why it's called a *projection*) later in the chapter; for now, you can think of it as a type with unknown arguments (or an analogue of Java's `List<?>`). In the previous example, you check whether a `value` is a `List`, and you don't get any information about its element type.

Note that you can still use normal generic types in `as` and `as?` casts. But the cast won't fail if the class has the correct base type and a wrong type argument, because the type argument isn't known at runtime when the cast is performed. Because of that, the compiler will emit an "unchecked cast" warning on such a cast. It's only a warning, so you can later use the value as having the necessary type, as shown next.

Listing 9.5 Using a type cast with a generic type

```
fun printSum(c: Collection<*>) {
    val intList = c as? List<Int>
            ?: throw IllegalArgumentException("List is expected")
    println(intList.sum())
}
>>> printSum(listOf(1, 2, 3))
6
```

> Warning here. Unchecked cast: List<*> to List<Int>

> Everything works as expected.

Everything compiles fine: the compiler only issues a warning, which means this code is legitimate. If you call the `printSum` function on a list of ints or a set, it works as expected: it prints a sum in the first case and throws an `IllegalArgument-Exception` in the second case. But if you pass in a value of a wrong type, you'll get a `ClassCastException` at runtime:

```
>>> printSum(setOf(1, 2, 3))
IllegalArgumentException: List is expected
>>> printSum(listOf("a", "b", "c"))
ClassCastException: String cannot be cast to Number
```

> Set isn't a list, so an exception is thrown.

> The cast succeeds, and another exception is thrown later.

Let's discuss the exception that's thrown if you call the `printSum` function on a list of strings. You don't get an `IllegalArgumentException`, because you can't check whether the argument is a `List<Int>`. Therefore the cast succeeds, and the function `sum` is called on such a list anyway. During its execution, an exception is thrown. This happens because the function tries to get `Number` values from the list and add them together. An attempt to use a `String` as a `Number` results in a `ClassCastException` at runtime.

Note that the Kotlin compiler is smart enough to allow `is` checks when the corresponding type information is already known at compile time.

Listing 9.6 Using a type check with a known type argument

```
fun printSum(c: Collection<Int>) {
    if (c is List<Int>) {
        println(c.sum())
    }
}
>>> printSum(listOf(1, 2, 3))
6
```

> This check is legitimate.

In listing 9.6, the check whether `c` has type `List<Int>` is possible because you know at compile time that this collection (no matter whether it's a list or another kind of collection) contains integer numbers.

Generally, the Kotlin compiler takes care of letting you know which checks are dangerous (forbidding `is` checks and emitting warnings for `as` casts) and which are possible. You just have to know the meaning of those warnings and understand which operations are safe.

As we already mentioned, Kotlin does have a special construct that allows you to use specific type arguments in the body of a function, but that's only possible for `inline` functions. Let's look at this feature.

9.2.2 *Declaring functions with reified type parameters*

As we discussed earlier, Kotlin generics are erased at runtime, which means if you have an instance of a generic class, you can't find out the type arguments used when the instance was created. The same holds for type arguments of a function. When you call a generic function, in its body you can't determine the type arguments it was invoked with:

```
>>> fun <T> isA(value: Any) = value is T
Error: Cannot check for instance of erased type: T
```

This is true in general, but there's one case where this limitation can be avoided: inline functions. Type parameters of inline functions can be reified, which means you can refer to actual type arguments at runtime.

We discussed `inline` functions in detail in section 8.2. As a reminder, if you mark a function with the `inline` keyword, the compiler will replace every call to the function with the actual code implementing the function. Making the function `inline` may improve performance if this function uses lambdas as arguments: the lambda code can be inlined as well, so no anonymous class will be created. This section shows another case when `inline` functions are helpful: their type arguments can be reified.

If you declare the previous `isA` function as `inline` and mark the type parameter as `reified`, you can check `value` to see whether it's an instance of T.

Listing 9.7 Declaring a function with a reified type parameter

```
inline fun <reified T> isA(value: Any) = value is T       ◁─── Now this code
                                                                 compiles.
>>> println(isA<String>("abc"))
true
>>> println(isA<String>(123))
false
```

Let's look at some less-trivial examples of the use of reified type parameters. One of the simplest examples where reified type parameters come into play is the `filterIs-Instance` standard library function. The function takes a collection, selects instances of the specified class, and returns only those instances. Here's how it can be used.

Listing 9.8 Using the `filterIsInstance` standard library function

```
>>> val items = listOf("one", 2, "three")
>>> println(items.filterIsInstance<String>())
[one, three]
```

You say that you're interested in strings only, by specifying `<String>` as a type argument for the function. The return type of the function will therefore be `List<String>`. In this case, *the type argument is known at runtime,* and `filterIsInstance` uses it to check which values in the list are instances of the class specified as the type argument.

Here's a simplified version of the declaration of `filterIsInstance` from the Kotlin standard library.

Listing 9.9   A simplified implementation of `filterIsInstance`

```
inline fun <reified T>
        Iterable<*>.filterIsInstance(): List<T> {
    val destination = mutableListOf<T>()
    for (element in this) {
        if (element is T) {
            destination.add(element)
        }
    }
    return destination
}
```

"reified" declares that this type parameter will not be erased at runtime.

You can check whether the element is an instance of the class specified as a type argument.

Why reification works for inline functions only

How does this work? Why are you allowed to write `element is T` in inline function but not in a regular class or function?

As we discussed in section 8.2, the compiler inserts the bytecode implementing the inline function into every place where it's called. Every time you call the function with a reified type parameter, the compiler knows the exact type used as the type argument in that particular call. Therefore, the compiler can generate the bytecode that references the specific class used as a type argument. In effect, for the `filterIsInstance<String>` call shown in listing 9.8, the generated code will be equivalent to the following:

```
for (element in this) {
    if (element is String) {
        destination.add(element)
    }
}
```

References a specific class.

Because the generated bytecode references a specific class, not a type parameter, it isn't affected by the type-argument erasure that happens at runtime.

Note that `inline` function with `reified` type parameters can't be called from Java code. Normal inline functions are accessible to Java as regular functions—they can be called but aren't inlined. Functions with reified type parameters require additional processing to substitute the type argument values into the bytecode, and therefore they must always be inlined. This makes it impossible to call them in a regular way, as the Java code does.

An inline function can have multiple reified type parameters, and it can have non-reified type parameters in addition to the reified ones. Note that the `filter-IsInstance` function is marked as `inline` even though it doesn't expect any lambdas as arguments. In section 8.2.4, we discussed that marking a function as inline only has performance benefits when the function has parameters of the function type and the corresponding arguments—lambdas—are inlined together with the function. But in this case, you aren't marking the function as `inline` for performance reasons; instead, you're doing it to enable the use of reified type parameters.

To ensure good performance, you still need to keep track of the size of the function marked as `inline`. If the function becomes large, it's better to extract the code that doesn't depend on the reified type parameters into separate non-inline functions.

9.2.3 *Replacing class references with reified type parameters*

One common use case for reified type parameters is building adapters for APIs that take parameters of type `java.lang.Class`. An example of such an API is `Service-Loader` from the JDK, which takes a `java.lang.Class` representing an interface or an abstract class and returns an instance of a service class implementing that interface. Let's look at how you can use reified type parameters to make those APIs simpler to call.

To load a service using the standard Java API of `ServiceLoader`, you use the following call:

```
val serviceImpl = ServiceLoader.load(Service::class.java)
```

The `::class.java` syntax shows how you can get a `java.lang.Class` corresponding to a Kotlin class. This is an exact equivalent of `Service.class` in Java. We'll cover this in much more detail in section 10.2, in our discussion of reflection.

Now let's rewrite this example using a function with a reified type parameter:

```
val serviceImpl = loadService<Service>()
```

Much shorter, isn't it? The class of the service to load is now specified as a type argument to the `loadService` function. Specifying a class as a type argument is easier to read because it's shorter than the `::class.java` syntax you need to use otherwise.

Next, let's see how this `loadService` function can be defined:

```
inline fun <reified T> loadService() {
    return ServiceLoader.load(T::class.java)
}
```

The type parameter is marked as "reified".

Accesses the class of the type parameter as T::class

You can use the same `::class.java` syntax on reified type parameters that you can use on regular classes. Using this syntax gives you the `java.lang.Class` corresponding to the class specified as the type parameter, which you can then use normally.

Simplifying the startActivity function on Android

If you're an Android developer, you may find another example to be more familiar: showing activities. Instead of passing the class of the activity as a `java.lang.Class`, you can also use a reified type parameter:

```
inline fun <reified T : Activity>            The type parameter is
        Context.startActivity() {            marked as "reified".
    val intent = Intent(this, T::class.java)      Accesses the class of the
    startActivity(intent)                         type parameter as T::class
}
                                      Invokes the method
startActivity<DetailActivity>()       to show an activity
```

9.2.4 *Restrictions on reified type parameters*

Even though reified type parameters are a handy tool, they have certain restrictions. Some are inherent to the concept, and others are determined by the current implementation and may be relaxed in future versions of Kotlin.

More specifically, here's how you can use a reified type parameter:

- In type checks and casts (`is`, `!is`, `as`, `as?`)
- To use the Kotlin reflection APIs, as we'll discuss in chapter 10 (`::class`)
- To get the corresponding `java.lang.Class` (`::class.java`)
- As a type argument to call other functions

You *can't* do the following:

- Create new instances of the class specified as a type parameter
- Call methods on the companion object of the type parameter class
- Use a non-reified type parameter as a type argument when calling a function with a reified type parameter
- Mark type parameters of classes, properties, or non-inline functions as `reified`

The last constraint leads to an interesting consequence: because reified type parameters can only be used in inline functions, using a reified type parameter means the function along with all the lambdas passed to it are inlined. If the lambdas can't be inlined because of the way the inline function uses them, or if you don't want them to be inlined for performance reasons, you can use the `noinline` modifier introduced in section 8.2.2 to mark them as non-inlineable.

Now that we've discussed how generics work as a language feature, let's take a more detailed look at the most common generic types that come up in every Kotlin program: collections and their subclasses. We'll use them as a starting point for exploring the concepts of subtyping and variance.

9.3 Variance: generics and subtyping

The concept of *variance* describes how types with the same base type and different type arguments relate to each other: for example, List<String> and List<Any>. First we'll discuss why this relation is important in general, and then we'll look at how it's expressed in Kotlin. Understanding variance is essential when you write your own generic classes or functions: it helps you create APIs that don't restrict users in inconvenient ways and don't break their type-safety expectations.

9.3.1 Why variance exists: passing an argument to a function

Imagine that you have a function that takes a List<Any> as an argument. Is it safe to pass a variable of type List<String> to this function? It's definitely safe to pass a string to a function expecting Any, because the String class extends Any. But when Any and String become type arguments of the List interface, it's not so clear any more.

For example, let's consider a function that prints the contents of the list.

```
fun printContents(list: List<Any>) {
    println(list.joinToString())
}

>>> printContents(listOf("abc", "bac"))
abc, bac
```

It looks like a list of strings works fine here. The function treats each element as Any, and because every string is Any, it's totally safe.

Now let's look at another function, which modifies the list (and therefore takes MutableList as a parameter):

```
fun addAnswer(list: MutableList<Any>) {
    list.add(42)
}
```

Can anything bad happen if you pass a list of strings to this function?

```
>>> val strings = mutableListOf("abc", "bac")          If this line
>>> addAnswer(strings)                                 compiled ...
>>> println(strings.maxBy { it.length })
ClassCastException: Integer cannot be cast to String   ... you'd get an
                                                       exception at runtime.
```

You declare a variable strings of type MutableList<String>. Then you try to pass it to the function. If the compiler accepted it, you'd be able to add an integer to a list of strings, which would then lead to a runtime exception when you tried to access the contents of the list as strings. Because of that, this call doesn't compile. This example shows that it's not safe to pass a MutableList<String> as an argument when a MutableList<Any> is expected; the Kotlin compiler correctly forbids that.

Now you can answer the question of whether it's safe to pass a list of strings to a function that expects a list of `Any` objects. It's not safe if the function adds or replaces elements in the list, because this creates the possibility of type inconsistencies. It's safe otherwise (we'll discuss why in more detail later in this section). In Kotlin, this can be easily controlled by choosing the right interface, depending on whether the list is mutable. If a function accepts a read-only list, you can pass a `List` with a more specific element type. If the list is mutable, you can't do that.

Later in this section, we'll generalize the same question for any generic class, not only `List`. You'll also see why two interfaces `List` and `MutableList` are different with regard to their type argument. But before that, we need to discuss the concepts of *type* and *subtype*.

9.3.2   *Classes, types, and subtypes*

As we discussed in section 6.1.2, the type of a variable specifies the possible values for this variable. We've sometimes used the terms *type* and *class* as equivalent, but they aren't, and now is the time to look at the difference.

In the simplest case, with a non-generic class, the name of the class can be used directly as a type. For example, if you write `var x: String`, you declare a variable that can hold instances of the `String` class. But note that the same class name can also be used to declare a nullable type: `var x: String?`. This means each Kotlin class can be used to construct at least two types.

The story becomes even more complicated with generic classes. To get a valid type, you have to substitute a specific type as a type argument for the class's type parameter. `List` isn't a type (it's a class), but all of the following substitutions are valid types: `List<Int>`, `List<String?>`, `List<List<String>>`, and so on. Each generic class produces a potentially infinite number of types.

In order for us to discuss the relation between types, you need to be familiar with the term *subtype*. A type B is a subtype of a type A if you can use the value of the type B whenever a value of the type A is required. For instance, `Int` is a subtype of `Number`, but `Int` isn't a subtype of `String`. This definition also indicates that a type is considered a subtype of itself. Figure 9.4 illustrates this.

The term *supertype* is the opposite of *subtype*. If A is a subtype of B, then B is a supertype of A.

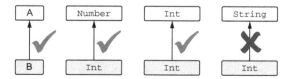

Figure 9.4   B is a subtype of A if you can use it when A is expected.

Why is it important whether one type is a subtype of the other? The compiler performs this check every time when you assign a value to a variable or pass an argument to a function. Consider the following example.

Listing 9.10 Checking whether a type is a subtype of another

```
fun test(i: Int) {
    val n: Number = i          ⟵  Compiles, because Int
                                   is a subtype of Number

    fun f(s: String) { /*...*/ }    Doesn't compile, because
    f(i)                       ⟵    Int isn't a subtype of String
}
```

Storing a value in a variable is allowed only when the value type is a subtype of the variable type; for instance, the type `Int` of the variable initializer `i` is a subtype of the variable type `Number`, so the declaration of `n` is valid. Passing an expression to a function is allowed only when the type of the expression is a subtype of the function parameter type. In the example the type `Int` of the argument `i` isn't a subtype of the function parameter `String`, so the invocation of the `f` function doesn't compile.

In simple cases, subtype means essentially the same thing as *subclass*. For example, the `Int` class is a subclass of `Number`, and therefore the `Int` type is a subtype of the `Number` type. If a class implements an interface, its type is a subtype of the interface type: `String` is a subtype of `CharSequence`.

Nullable types provide an example of when subtype isn't the same as subclass; see figure 9.5.

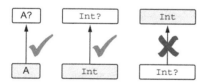

Figure 9.5   A non-null type A is a subtype of nullable A?, but not vice versa.

A non-null type is a subtype of its nullable version, but they both correspond to one class. You can always store the value of a non-null type in a variable of a nullable type, but not vice versa (`null` isn't an acceptable value for a variable of a non-null type):

```
val s: String  = "abc"         This assignment is legal because
val t: String? = s        ⟵    String is a subtype of String?.
```

The difference between subclasses and subtypes becomes especially important when we start talking about generic types. The question from the previous section of whether it's safe to pass a variable of type `List<String>` to a function expecting `List<Any>` now can be reformulated in terms of subtyping: is `List<String>` a subtype of `List<Any>`? You've seen why it's not safe to treat `MutableList<String>`

as a subtype of `MutableList<Any>`. Clearly, the reverse isn't true either: `Mutable-List<Any>` isn't a subtype of `MutableList<String>`.

A generic class—for instance, `MutableList`—is called *invariant* on the type parameter if, for any two different types A and B, `MutableList<A>` isn't a subtype or a supertype of `MutableList<B>`. In Java, all classes are invariant (even though specific uses of those classes can be marked as non-invariant, as you'll see soon).

In the previous section, you saw a class for which the subtyping rules are different: `List`. The `List` interface in Kotlin represents a read-only collection. If A is a subtype of B, then `List<A>` is a subtype of `List<B>`. Such classes or interfaces are called *covariant*. The next section discusses the concept of covariance in detail and explains when it's possible to declare a class or interface as covariant.

9.3.3 *Covariance: preserved subtyping relation*

A covariant class is a generic class (we'll use `Producer<T>` as an example) for which the following holds: `Producer<A>` is a subtype of `Producer<B>` if A is a subtype of B. We say that *the subtyping is preserved.* For example, `Producer<Cat>` is a subtype of `Producer<Animal>` because Cat is a subtype of Animal.

In Kotlin, to declare the class to be covariant on a certain type parameter, you put the `out` keyword before the name of the type parameter:

```
interface Producer<out T> {          ◁─┐ This class is declared
    fun produce(): T                     │ as covariant on T.
}
```

Marking a type parameter of a class as covariant makes it possible to pass values of that class as function arguments and return values when *the type arguments don't exactly match* the ones in the function definition. For example, imagine a function that takes care of feeding a group of animals, represented by the `Herd` class. The type parameter of the `Herd` class identifies the type of the animal in the herd.

Listing 9.11 Defining an invariant collection-like class

```
open class Animal {
    fun feed() { ... }
}

class Herd<T : Animal> {             ◁─┐ The type parameter isn't
    val size: Int get() = ...            │ declared as covariant.
    operator fun get(i: Int): T { ... }
}

fun feedAll(animals: Herd<Animal>) {
    for (i in 0 until animals.size) {
        animals[i].feed()
    }
}
```

Suppose that a user of your code has a herd of cats and needs to take care of them.

Listing 9.12   Using an invariant collection-like class

```
class Cat : Animal() {                        A Cat is
    fun cleanLitter() { ... }                 an Animal.
}

fun takeCareOfCats(cats: Herd<Cat>) {
    for (i in 0 until cats.size) {
        cats[i].cleanLitter()
        // feedAll(cats)                       Error: inferred type is Herd<Cat>,
    }                                          but Herd<Animal> was expected
}
```

Unfortunately, the cats will remain hungry: if you tried to pass the herd to the feed-All function, you'd get a type-mismatch error during compilation. Because you don't use any variance modifier on the T type parameter in the Herd class, the herd of cats isn't a subclass of the herd of animals. You could use an explicit cast to work around the problem, but that approach is verbose, error-prone, and almost never a correct way to deal with a type-mismatch problem.

Because the Herd class has an API similar to List and doesn't allow its clients to add or change the animals in the herd, you can make it covariant and change the calling code accordingly.

Listing 9.13   Using a covariant collection-like class

```
class Herd<out T : Animal> {                  The T parameter is
    ...                                       now covariant.
}

fun takeCareOfCats(cats: Herd<Cat>) {
    for (i in 0 until cats.size) {
        cats[i].cleanLitter()
    }                                   You don't
    feedAll(cats)                       need a cast.
}
```

You can't make any class covariant: it would be unsafe. Making the class covariant on a certain type parameter constrains the possible uses of this type parameter in the class. To guarantee type safety, it can be used only in so-called *out* positions, meaning the class can produce values of type T but not consume them.

Uses of a type parameter in declarations of class members can be divided into *in* and *out* positions. Let's consider a class that declares a type parameter T and contains a function that uses T. We say that if T is used as the return type of a function, it's in the out position. In this case, the function *produces* values of type T. If T is used as the type of a function parameter, it's in the in position. Such a function *consumes* values of type T. Figure 9.6 illustrates this.

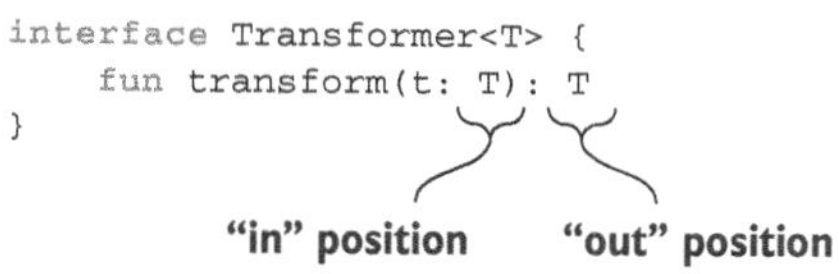

```
interface Transformer<T> {
    fun transform(t: T): T
}
                        "in"       "out"
                     position    position
```

Figure 9.6   The function parameter type is called in position, and the function return type is called out position.

The `out` keyword on a type parameter of the class requires that all methods using `T` have `T` only in `out` positions and not in `in` positions. This keyword constrains possible use of `T`, which guarantees safety of the corresponding subtype relation.

As an example, consider the `Herd` class. It uses the type parameter `T` in only one place: in the return value of the `get` method.

```
class Herd<out T : Animal> {
    val size: Int get() = ...
    operator fun get(i: Int): T { ... }          ┐ Uses T as the
}                                                ◄─┘ return type
```

This is an `out` position, which makes it safe to declare the class as covariant. Any code calling `get` on a `Herd<Animal>` will work perfectly if the method returns a `Cat`, because `Cat` is a subtype of `Animal`.

To reiterate, the `out` keyword on the type parameter `T` means two things:

- The subtyping is preserved (`Producer<Cat>` is a subtype of `Producer<Animal>`).
- `T` can be used only in `out` positions.

Now let's look at the `List<T>` interface. `List` is read-only in Kotlin, so it has a method `get` that returns an element of type `T` but doesn't define any methods that store a value of type `T` in the list. Therefore, it's also covariant.

```
interface List<out T> : Collection<T> {
    operator fun get(index: Int): T      ◄─┐  Read-only interface that defines
    // ...                                  │  only methods that return T
}                                          │  (so T is in the "out" position)
```

Note that a type parameter can be used not only as a parameter type or return type directly, but also as a type argument of another type. For example, the `List` interface contains a method `subList` that returns `List<T>`.

```
interface List<out T> : Collection<T> {
    fun subList(fromIndex: Int, toIndex: Int): List<T>   ◄─┐ Here T is in the "out"
    // ...                                                  │ position as well.
}
```

In this case, `T` in the function `subList` is used in the `out` position. We won't go deep into detail here; if you're interested in the exact algorithm that determines which position is `out` and which is `in`, you can find this information in the Kotlin language documentation.

Note that you can't declare `MutableList<T>` as covariant on its type parameter, because it contains methods that take values of type `T` as parameters and return such values (therefore, `T` appears in both `in` and `out` positions).

```
interface MutableList<T>                     ◄─┐  MutableList can't be declared
    : List<T>, MutableCollection<T> {          │  as covariant on T ...
    override fun add(element: T): Boolean   ◄─┐
}                                             │
                                             └─ ... because T is used
                                                in the "in" position.
```

The compiler enforces this restriction. It would report an error if the class was declared as covariant: `Type parameter T is declared as 'out' but occurs in 'in' position`.

Note that constructor parameters are in neither the `in` nor the `out` position. Even if a type parameter is declared as `out`, you can still use it in a constructor parameter declaration:

```
class Herd<out T: Animal>(vararg animals: T) { ... }
```

The variance protects the class instance from misuse if you're working with it as an instance of a more generic type: you just can't call the potentially dangerous methods. The constructor isn't a method that can be called later (after an instance creation), and therefore it can't be potentially dangerous.

If you use the `val` or `var` keyword with a constructor parameter, however, you also declare a getter and a setter (if the property is mutable). Therefore, the type parameter is used in the `out` position for a read-only property and in both `out` and `in` positions for a mutable property:

```
class Herd<T: Animal>(var leadAnimal: T, vararg animals: T) { ... }
```

In this case, `T` can't be marked as `out`, because the class contains a setter for the `leadAnimal` property that uses `T` in the `in` position.

Also note that the position rules cover only the externally visible (`public`, `protected`, and `internal`) API of a class. Parameters of private methods are in neither the `in` nor the `out` position. The variance rules protect a class from misuse by external clients and don't come into play in the implementation of the class itself:

```
class Herd<out T: Animal>(private var leadAnimal: T, vararg animals: T) { ... }
```

Now it's safe to make `Herd` covariant on `T`, because the `leadAnimal` property has been made private.

You may ask what happens with classes or interfaces where the type parameter is used only in an `in` position. In that case, the reverse relation holds. The next section presents the details.

9.3.4   *Contravariance: reversed subtyping relation*

The concept of *contravariance* can be thought of as a mirror to covariance: for a contravariant class, the subtyping relation is the opposite of the subtyping relations of classes used as its type arguments. Let's start with an example: the `Comparator` interface. This interface defines one method, `compare`, which compares two given objects:

```
interface Comparator<in T>  {
    fun compare(e1: T, e2: T): Int { ... }          ⟵┐ Uses T in
}                                                        "in" positions
```

You can see that the method of this interface only consumes values of type T. That means T is used only in in positions, and therefore its declaration can be preceded by the in keyword.

A comparator defined for values of a certain type can, of course, compare the values of any subtype of that type. For example, if you have a Comparator<Any>, you can use it to compare values of any specific type.

```
>>> val anyComparator = Comparator<Any> {
...       e1, e2 -> e1.hashCode() - e2.hashCode()
... }
>>> val strings: List<String> = ...
>>> strings.sortedWith(anyComparator)
```

> You can use the comparator for any objects to compare specific objects, such as strings.

The sortedWith function expects a Comparator<String> (a comparator that can compare strings), and it's safe to pass one that can compare more general types. If you need to perform comparisons on objects of a certain type, you can use a comparator that handles either that type or any of its supertypes. This means Comparator<Any> is a subtype of Comparator<String>, where Any is a supertype of String. The subtyping relation between comparators for two different types goes in the opposite direction of the subtyping relation between those types.

Now you're ready for the full definition of contravariance. A class that is *contravariant* on the type parameter is a generic class (let's consider Consumer<T> as an example) for which the following holds: Consumer<A> is a subtype of Consumer<B> if B is a subtype of A. The type arguments A and B changed places, so we say the subtyping is reversed. For example, Consumer<Animal> is a subtype of Consumer<Cat>.

Figure 9.7 shows the difference between the subtyping relation for classes that are covariant and contravariant on a type parameter. You can see that for the Producer class, the subtyping relation replicates the subtyping relation for its type arguments, whereas for the Consumer class, the relation is reversed.

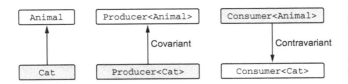

Figure 9.7 **For a covariant type** Producer<T>, **the subtyping is preserved, but for a contravariant type** Consumer<T>, **the subtyping is reversed.**

The in keyword means values of the corresponding type are *passed in* to methods of this class and consumed by those methods. Similar to the covariant case, constraining use of the type parameter leads to the specific subtyping relation. The in keyword on the type parameter T means the subtyping is reversed and T can be used only in in positions. Table 9.1 summarizes the differences between the possible variance choices.

Table 9.1 Covariant, contravariant, and invariant classes

Covariant	Contravariant	Invariant
`Producer<out T>`	`Consumer<in T>`	`MutableList<T>`
Subtyping for the class is preserved: `Producer<Cat>` is a subtype of `Producer<Animal>`.	Subtyping is reversed: `Consumer<Animal>` is a subtype of `Consumer<Cat>`.	No subtyping.
T only in `out` positions	T only in `in` positions	T in any position

A class or interface can be covariant on one type parameter and contravariant on another. The classic example is the `Function` interface. The following declaration shows a one-parameter `Function`:

```
interface Function1<in P, out R> {
    operator fun invoke(p: P): R
}
```

The Kotlin notation `(P) -> R` is another, more readable form to express `Function1<P, R>`. You can see that `P` (the parameter type) is used only in the `in` position and is marked with the `in` keyword, whereas `R` (the return type) is used only in the `out` position and is marked with the `out` keyword. That means the subtyping for the function type is reversed for its first type argument and preserved for the second. For example, if you have a higher-order function that tries to enumerate your cats, you can pass a lambda accepting any animals.

```
fun enumerateCats(f: (Cat) -> Number) { ... }
fun Animal.getIndex(): Int = ...

>>> enumerateCats(Animal::getIndex)
```

This code is legal in Kotlin. Animal is a supertype of Cat, and Int is a subtype of Number.

Figure 9.8 illustrates the subtyping relationships in the previous example.

Note that in all the examples so far, the variance of a class is specified directly in its declaration and applies to all places where the class is used. Java doesn't support that and instead uses wildcards to specify the variance for specific uses of a class. Let's look at the difference between the two approaches and see how you can use the second approach in Kotlin.

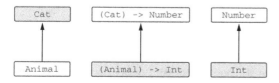

Figure 9.8 The function `(T) -> R` is contravariant on its argument and covariant on its return type.

9.3.5   *Use-site variance: specifying variance for type occurrences*

The ability to specify variance modifiers on class declarations is convenient because the modifiers apply to all places where the class is used. This is called *declaration-site variance*. If you're familiar with Java's wildcard types (? extends and ? super), you'll realize that Java handles variance differently. In Java, every time you use a type with a type parameter, you can also specify whether this type parameter can be replaced with its subtypes or supertypes. This is called *use-site variance*.

Declaration-site variance in Kotlin vs. Java wildcards

Declaration-site variance allows for more concise code, because you specify the variance modifiers once, and clients of your class don't have to think about them. In Java, to create APIs that behave according to users' expectations, the library writer has to use wildcards all the time: Function<? super T, ? extends R>. If you examine the source code of the Java 8 standard library, you'll find wildcards on every use of the Function interface. For example, here's how the Stream.map method is declared:

```
/* Java */
public interface Stream<T> {
    <R> Stream<R> map(Function<? super T, ? extends R> mapper);
}
```

Specifying the variance once on the declaration makes the code much more concise and elegant.

Kotlin supports use-site variance too, allowing you to specify the variance for a specific occurrence of a type parameter even when it can't be declared as covariant or contravariant in the class declaration. Let's see how that works.

You've seen that many interfaces, like MutableList, aren't covariant or contravariant in a general case, because they can both produce and consume values of types specified by their type parameters. But it's common for a variable of that type in a particular function to be used in only one of those roles: either as a producer or as a consumer. For example, consider this simple function.

Listing 9.14   A data copy function with invariant parameter types

```
fun <T> copyData(source: MutableList<T>,
                 destination: MutableList<T>) {
    for (item in source) {
        destination.add(item)
    }
}
```

This function copies elements from one collection to another. Even though both collections have an invariant type, the source collection is only used for reading, and the destination collection is only used for writing. In this situation, the element types of the collections don't need to match exactly. For example, it's perfectly valid to copy a collection of strings into a collection that can contain any objects.

To make this function work with lists of different types, you can introduce the second generic parameter.

Listing 9.15   A data copy function with two type parameters

```
fun <T: R, R> copyData(source: MutableList<T>,
                       destination: MutableList<R>) {
    for (item in source) {
        destination.add(item)
    }
}
>>> val ints = mutableListOf(1, 2, 3)
>>> val anyItems = mutableListOf<Any>()
>>> copyData(ints, anyItems)
>>> println(anyItems)
[1, 2, 3]
```

Source's element type should be a subtype of the destination's element type

You can call this function, because Int is a subtype of Any.

You declare two generic parameters representing the element types in the source and destination lists. To be able to copy elements from one list to the other, the source element type should be a subtype of elements in the `destination` list, like `Int` is a subtype of `Any` in listing 9.15.

But Kotlin provides a more elegant way to express this. When the implementation of a function only calls methods that have the type parameter in the `out` (or only in the `in`) position, you can take advantage of it and add variance modifiers to the particular usages of the type parameter in the function definition.

Listing 9.16   A data copy function with an out-projected type parameter

```
fun <T> copyData(source: MutableList<out T>,
                 destination: MutableList<T>) {
    for (item in source) {
        destination.add(item)
    }
}
```

You can add the "out" keyword to the type usage: no methods with T in the "in" position are used.

You can specify a variance modifier on any usage of a type parameter in a type declaration: for a parameter type (as in listing 9.16), local variable type, function return type, and so on. What happens here is called *type projection*: we say that `source` isn't a regular `MutableList`, but a *projected* (restricted) one. You can only call methods that return the generic type parameter or, strictly speaking, use it in the `out` position only. The compiler prohibits calling methods where this type parameter is used as an argument (in the `in` position):

```
>>> val list: MutableList<out Number> = ...
>>> list.add(42)
Error: Out-projected type 'MutableList<out Number>' prohibits
the use of 'fun add(element: E): Boolean'
```

Don't be surprised that you can't call some of the methods if you're using a projected type. If you need to call them, you need to use a regular type instead of a projection. This may require you to declare a second type parameter that depends on the one that was originally a projection, as in listing 9.15.

Of course, the right way to implement the function copyData would be to use List<T> as a type of the source argument, because we're only using the methods declared in List, not in MutableList, and the variance of the List type parameter is specified in its declaration. But this example is still important for illustrating the concept, especially keeping in mind that most classes don't have a separate covariant read interface and an invariant read/write interface, such as List and MutableList.

There is no sense to get an out projection of a type parameter that already has out variance, such as List<out T>. That would mean the same as List<T>, because List is declared as class List<out T>. The Kotlin compiler will warn that such a projection is redundant.

In a similar way, you can use the in modifier on a usage of a type parameter to indicate that in this particular location the corresponding value acts as a consumer, and the type parameter can be substituted with any of its supertypes. Here's how you can rewrite listing 9.16 using an in-projection.

Listing 9.17   A data copy function with an in-projected type parameter

```
fun <T> copyData(source: MutableList<T>,
                 destination: MutableList<in T>) {      ◁─┐  Allows the destination element
    for (item in source) {                                │  type to be a supertype of the
        destination.add(item)                             │  source element type
    }
}
```

NOTE Use-site variance declarations in Kotlin correspond directly to Java bounded wildcards. MutableList<out T> in Kotlin means the same as MutableList<? extends T> in Java. The in-projected MutableList<in T> corresponds to Java's MutableList<? super T>.

Use-site projections can help to widen the range of acceptable types. Now let's discuss the extreme case: when types with all possible type arguments become acceptable.

9.3.6   *Star projection: using * instead of a type argument*

While talking about type checks and casts earlier in this chapter, we mentioned the special *star-projection* syntax you can use to indicate that you have *no information about a generic argument*. For example, a list of elements of an unknown type is expressed using that syntax as List<*>. Let's explore the semantics of star projections in detail.

First, note that MutableList<*> isn't the same as MutableList<Any?> (it's important here that MutableList<T> is invariant on T). A MutableList<Any?> is a list that you know can contain elements of any type. On the other hand, a

`MutableList<*>` is a list that contains elements of a specific type, but you don't know what type it is. The list was created as a list of elements of a specific type, such as `String` (you can't create a new `ArrayList<*>`), and the code that created it expects that it will only contain elements of that type. Because you don't know what the type is, you can't put anything into the list, because any value you put there might violate the expectations of the calling code. But it's possible to get the elements from the list, because you know for sure that all values stored there will match the type `Any?`, which is the supertype of all Kotlin types:

```
>>> val list: MutableList<Any?> = mutableListOf('a', 1, "qwe")
>>> val chars = mutableListOf('a', 'b', 'c')
>>> val unknownElements: MutableList<*> =
...          if (Random().nextBoolean()) list else chars
>>> unknownElements.add(42)
Error: Out-projected type 'MutableList<*>' prohibits
the use of 'fun add(element: E): Boolean'
>>> println(unknownElements.first())
a
```

MutableList<*> isn't the same as **MutableList<Any?>**.

The compiler forbids you to call this method.

It's safe to get elements: first() returns an element of the Any? type.

Why does the compiler refers to `MutableList<*>` as an out-projected type? In this context, `MutableList<*>` is projected to (acts as) `MutableList<out Any?>`: when you know nothing about the type of the element, it's safe to get elements of `Any?` type, but it's not safe to put elements into the list. Speaking about Java wildcards, `MyType<*>` in Kotlin corresponds to Java's `MyType<?>`.

> **NOTE** For contravariant type parameters such as `Consumer<in T>`, a star projection is equivalent to `<in Nothing>`. In effect, you can't call any methods that have `T` in the signature on such a star projection. If the type parameter is contravariant, it acts only as a consumer, and, as we discussed earlier, you don't know exactly what it can consume. Therefore, you can't give it anything to consume. If you're interested in more details, see the Kotlin online documentation (http://mng.bz/3Ed7).

You can use the star-projection syntax when the information about type arguments isn't important: you don't use any methods that refer to the type parameter in the signature, or you only read the data and you don't care about its specific type. For instance, you can implement the `printFirst` function taking `List<*>` as a parameter:

```
fun printFirst(list: List<*>) {
    if (list.isNotEmpty()) {
        println(list.first())
    }
}
>>> printFirst(listOf("Svetlana", "Dmitry"))
Svetlana
```

Every list is a possible argument.

isNotEmpty() doesn't use the generic type parameter.

first() now returns Any?, but in this case that's enough.

As in the case with use-site variance, you have an alternative—to introduce a generic type parameter:

```
fun <T> printFirst(list: List<T>) {                    Again, every list is a
    if (list.isNotEmpty()) {                            possible argument.
        println(list.first())                  first() now returns
    }                                          a value of T.
}
```

The syntax with star projection is more concise, but it works only if you aren't interested in the exact value of the generic type parameter: you use only methods that produce values, and you don't care about the types of those values.

Now let's look at another example of using a type with a star projection and common traps you may fall into while using that approach. Let's say you need to validate user input, and you declare an interface `FieldValidator`. It contains its type parameter in the `in` position only, so it can be declared as contravariant. And, indeed, it's correct to use the validator that can validate any elements when a validator of strings is expected (that's what declaring it as contravariant lets you do). You also declare two validators that handle `String` and `Int` inputs.

Listing 9.18   Interfaces for input validation

```
                                                    Interface declared as
                                                    contravariant on T
interface FieldValidator<in T> {
    fun validate(input: T): Boolean            T is used only in the "in"
}                                              position (this method
                                               consumes a value of T).
object DefaultStringValidator : FieldValidator<String> {
    override fun validate(input: String) = input.isNotEmpty()
}

object DefaultIntValidator : FieldValidator<Int> {
    override fun validate(input: Int) = input >= 0
}
```

Now imagine that you want to store all validators in the same container and get the right validator according to the type of input. Your first attempt might use a map to store them. You need to store validators for any types, so you declare a map from `KClass` (which represents a Kotlin class—chapter 10 will cover `KClass` in detail) to `FieldValidator<*>` (which may refer to a validator of any type):

```
>>> val validators = mutableMapOf<KClass<*>, FieldValidator<*>>()
>>> validators[String::class] = DefaultStringValidator
>>> validators[Int::class] = DefaultIntValidator
```

Once you do that, you may have difficulties when trying to use the validators. You can't validate a string with a validator of the type `FieldValidator<*>`. It's unsafe, because the compiler doesn't know what kind of validator it is:

```
>>> validators[String::class]!!.validate("")
Error: Out-projected type 'FieldValidator<*>' prohibits
the use of 'fun validate(input: T): Boolean'
```
← The value stored in the map has the type FieldValidator<*>.

You saw this error earlier when you tried to put an element into `MutableList<*>`. In this case, this error means it's unsafe to give a value of a specific type to a validator for an unknown type. One of the ways to fix that is to cast a validator explicitly to the type you need. It's not safe and isn't recommended, but we show it here as a fast trick to make your code compile so that you can refactor it afterward.

Listing 9.19 Retrieving a validator using an explicit cast

```
>>> val stringValidator = validators[String::class]
                          as FieldValidator<String>
>>> println(stringValidator.validate(""))
false
```
← Warning: unchecked cast

The compiler emits a warning about the unchecked cast. Note, however, that this code will fail on validation only, not when you make the cast, because at runtime all the generic type information is erased.

Listing 9.20 Incorrectly retrieving a validator

You get an incorrect validator (may be by mistake), but this code compiles.

It's only a warning.

```
>>> val stringValidator = validators[Int::class]
                          as FieldValidator<String>
>>> stringValidator.validate("")
java.lang.ClassCastException:
  java.lang.String cannot be cast to java.lang.Number
  at DefaultIntValidator.validate
```
← The real error is hidden until you use the validator.

This incorrect code and listing 9.19 are similar in a sense that in both cases, only a warning is emitted. It becomes your responsibility to cast only values of the correct type.

This solution isn't type-safe and is error-prone. So, let's investigate what other options you have if you want to store validators for different types in one place.

The solution in listing 9.21 uses the same `validators` map but encapsulates all the access to it into two generic methods responsible for having only correct validators registered and returned. This code also emits a warning about the unchecked cast (the same one), but here the object `Validators` controls all access to the map, which guarantees that no one will change the map incorrectly.

Listing 9.21 Encapsulating access to the validator collection

```
object Validators {
    private val validators =
            mutableMapOf<KClass<*>, FieldValidator<*>>()
```
← Uses the same map as before, but now you can't access it outside

> Puts into the map only the correct key-value
> pairs, when a validator corresponds to a class

```
fun <T: Any> registerValidator(
        kClass: KClass<T>, fieldValidator: FieldValidator<T>) {
    validators[kClass] = fieldValidator                  ◄───────
}

@Suppress("UNCHECKED_CAST")                              ◄───────
operator fun <T: Any> get(kClass: KClass<T>): FieldValidator<T> =
    validators[kClass] as? FieldValidator<T>
            ?: throw IllegalArgumentException(     Suppresses the warning
                "No validator for ${kClass.simpleName}")  about the unchecked cast
}                                                          to FieldValidator<T>
```

```
>>> Validators.registerValidator(String::class, DefaultStringValidator)
>>> Validators.registerValidator(Int::class, DefaultIntValidator)

>>> println(Validators[String::class].validate("Kotlin"))
true
>>> println(Validators[Int::class].validate(42))
true
```

Now you have a type-safe API. All the unsafe logic is hidden in the body of the class; and by localizing it, you guarantee that it can't be used incorrectly. The compiler forbids you to use an incorrect validator, because the Validators object always gives you the correct validator implementation:

> Now the "get" method returns an
> instance of FieldValidator<String>.

```
>>> println(Validators[String::class].validate(42))        ◄───────
Error: The integer literal does not conform to the expected type String
```

This pattern can be easily extended to the storage of any custom generic classes. Localizing unsafe code in a separate place prevents misuse and makes uses of a container safe. Note that the pattern described here isn't specific to Kotlin; you can use the same approach in Java as well.

Java generics and variance are generally considered the trickiest part of the language. In Kotlin, we've tried hard to come up with a design that is easier to understand and easier to work with, while remaining interoperable with Java.

9.4 *Summary*

- Kotlin's generics are fairly similar to those in Java: you declare a generic function or class in the same way.
- As in Java, type arguments for generic types only exist at compile time.
- You can't use types with type arguments together with the is operator, because type arguments are erased at runtime.
- Type parameters of inline functions can be marked as reified, which allows you to use them at runtime to perform is checks and obtain java.lang.Class instances.

- Variance is a way to specify whether one of two generic types with the same base class and different type arguments is a subtype or a supertype of the other one if one of the type arguments is the subtype of the other one.
- You can declare a class as covariant on a type parameter if the parameter is used only in out positions.
- The opposite is true for contravariant cases: you can declare a class as contravariant on a type parameter if it's used only in in positions.
- The read-only interface List in Kotlin is declared as covariant, which means List<String> is a subtype of List<Any>.
- The function interface is declared as contravariant on its first type parameter and covariant on its second, which makes (Animal)->Int a subtype of (Cat)->Number.
- Kotlin lets you specify variance both for a generic class as a whole (*declaration-site variance*) and for a specific use of a generic type (*use-site variance*).
- The star-projection syntax can be used when the exact type arguments are unknown or unimportant.

Annotations and reflection

10

This chapter covers

- Applying and defining annotations
- Using reflection to introspect classes at runtime
- A real example of a Kotlin project

Up to this point, you've seen many features for working with classes and functions, but they all require you to specify the exact names of classes and functions you're using as part of the program source code. In order to call a function, you need to know the class in which it was defined, as well as its name and parameter types. *Annotations* and *reflection* give you the power to go beyond that and to write code that deals with arbitrary classes that aren't known in advance. You can use annotations to assign library-specific semantics to those classes; and reflection allows you to analyze the structure of the classes at runtime.

Applying annotations is straightforward. But writing your own annotations, and especially writing the code that handles them, is less trivial. The syntax for using annotations is exactly the same as in Java, whereas the syntax for declaring your own annotation classes is a bit different. The general structure of the reflection APIs is also similar to Java, but the details differ.

As a demonstration of the use of annotations and reflection, we're going to walk you through an implementation of a real-life project: a JSON serialization and deserialization library called JKid. The library uses reflection to access properties of arbitrary Kotlin objects at runtime and also to create objects based on data provided in JSON files. Annotations let you customize how specific classes and properties are serialized and deserialized by the library.

10.1 Declaring and applying annotations

Most modern Java frameworks use annotations extensively, so you've surely encountered them when working on Java applications. The core concept in Kotlin is the same. An annotation allows you to associate additional *metadata* with a declaration. The metadata can then be accessed by tools that work with source code, with compiled class files, or at runtime, depending on how the annotation is configured.

10.1.1 Applying annotations

You use annotations in Kotlin in the same way as in Java. To apply an annotation, you put its name, prefixed with the @ character, in the beginning of the declaration you're annotating. You can annotate different code elements, such as functions and classes.

For instance, if you're using the JUnit framework (http://junit.org/junit4/), you can mark a test method with the @Test annotation:

```
import org.junit.*

class MyTest {
    @Test fun testTrue() {
        Assert.assertTrue(true)
    }
}
```

⊲⎤ **The @Test annotation instructs
the JUnit framework to invoke
this method as a test.**

As a more interesting example, let's look at the @Deprecated annotation. Its meaning in Kotlin is the same as in Java, but Kotlin enhances it with the replaceWith parameter, which lets you provide a replacement pattern to support a smooth transition to a new version of the API. The following example shows how you can provide arguments for the annotation (a deprecation message and a replacement pattern):

```
@Deprecated("Use removeAt(index) instead.", ReplaceWith("removeAt(index)"))
fun remove(index: Int) { ... }
```

The arguments are passed in parentheses, just as in a regular function call. With this declaration, if someone uses the function remove, IntelliJ IDEA will not only show what function should be used instead (removeAt in this case) but also offer a quick fix to replace it automatically.

Annotations can have parameters of the following types only: primitive types, strings, enums, class references, other annotation classes, and arrays thereof. The syntax for specifying annotation arguments is slightly different from Java's:

- *To specify a class as an annotation argument,* put ::class after the class name: @MyAnnotation(MyClass::class).

- *To specify another annotation as an argument,* don't put the @ character before the annotation name. For instance, `ReplaceWith` in the previous example is an annotation, but you don't use @ when you specify it as an argument of the `Deprecated` annotation.
- *To specify an array as an argument,* use the `arrayOf` function: `@Request-Mapping(path = arrayOf("/foo", "/bar"))`. If the annotation class is declared in Java, the parameter named `value` is automatically converted to a vararg parameter if necessary, so the arguments can be provided without using the `arrayOf` function.

Annotation arguments need to be known at compile time, so you can't refer to arbitrary properties as arguments. To use a property as an annotation argument, you need to mark it with a `const` modifier, which tells the compiler that the property is a *compile-time constant.* Here's an example of JUnit's `@Test` annotation that specifies the timeout for the test, in milliseconds, using the `timeout` parameter:

```
const val TEST_TIMEOUT = 100L

@Test(timeout = TEST_TIMEOUT) fun testMethod() { ... }
```

As discussed in section 3.3.1, properties annotated with `const` need to be declared at the top level of a file or in an `object` and must be initialized with values of primitive types or `String`. If you try to use a regular property as an annotation argument, you'll get the error "Only 'const val' can be used in constant expressions."

10.1.2 *Annotation targets*

In many cases, a single declaration in the Kotlin source code corresponds to multiple Java declarations, and each of them can carry annotations. For example, a Kotlin property corresponds to a Java field, a getter, and possibly a setter and its parameter. A property declared in the primary constructor has one more corresponding element: the constructor parameter. Therefore, it may be necessary to specify which of these elements needs to be annotated.

You specify the element to be annotated with a *use-site target* declaration. The use-site target is placed between the @ sign and the annotation name and is separated from the name with a colon. The word `get` in figure 10.1 causes the annotation `@Rule` to be applied to the property getter.

Let's look at an example of using this annotation. In JUnit, you can specify a rule to be executed

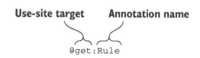

Figure 10.1 The syntax for specifying use-site targets

before each test method. For instance, the standard `TemporaryFolder` rule is used to create files and folders that are deleted when the test method finishes.

To specify a rule, in Java you declare a `public` field or method annotated with `@Rule`. But if you just annotate the property `folder` in your Kotlin test class with `@Rule`, you'll get a JUnit exception: "The @Rule 'folder' must be public." It happens because `@Rule` is applied to the field, which is private by default. To apply it to the getter, you need to write that explicitly, `@get:Rule`, as follows:

```
class HasTempFolder {
    @get:Rule
    val folder = TemporaryFolder()        The getter is annotated,
                                           not the property.
    @Test
    fun testUsingTempFolder() {
        val createdFile = folder.newFile("myfile.txt")
        val createdFolder = folder.newFolder("subfolder")
        // ...
    }
}
```

If you annotate a property with an annotation declared in Java, it's applied to the corresponding field by default. Kotlin also lets you declare annotations that can be directly applied to properties.

The full list of supported use-site targets is as follows:

- `property`—Java annotations can't be applied with this use-site target.
- `field`—Field generated for the property.
- `get`—Property getter.
- `set`—Property setter.
- `receiver`—Receiver parameter of an extension function or property.
- `param`—Constructor parameter.
- `setparam`—Property setter parameter.
- `delegate`—Field storing the delegate instance for a delegated property.
- `file`—Class containing top-level functions and properties declared in the file.

Any annotation with the `file` target needs to be placed at the top level of the file, before the `package` directive. One of the annotations commonly applied to files is `@JvmName`, which changes the name of the corresponding class. Section 3.2.3 showed you an example: `@file:JvmName("StringFunctions")`.

Note that unlike Java, Kotlin allows you to apply annotations to arbitrary expressions, not only to class and function declarations or types. The most common example is the `@Suppress` annotation, which you can use to suppress a specific compiler warning in the context of the annotated expression. Here's an example that annotates a local variable declaration to suppress an unchecked cast warning:

```
fun test(list: List<*>) {
    @Suppress("UNCHECKED_CAST")
    val strings = list as List<String>
    // ...
}
```

Note that IntelliJ IDEA will insert this annotation for you when you press Alt-Enter on a compiler warning and select Suppress from the intention options menu.

Controlling the Java API with annotations

Kotlin provides a variety of annotations to control how declarations written in Kotlin are compiled to Java bytecode and exposed to Java callers. Some of those annotations replace the corresponding keywords of the Java language: for example, the @Volatile and @Strictfp annotations serve as direct replacements for Java's volatile and strictfp keywords. Others are used to change how Kotlin's declarations are visible to Java callers:

- @JvmName changes the name of a Java method or field generated from a Kotlin declaration.
- @JvmStatic can be applied to methods of an object declaration or a companion object to expose them as static Java methods.
- @JvmOverloads, mentioned in section 3.2.2, instructs the Kotlin compiler to generate overloads for a function that has default parameter values.
- @JvmField can be applied to a property to expose that property as a public Java field with no getters or setters.

You can find more details on the use of those annotations in their documentation comments and in the Java interop section of the online documentation.

10.1.3 *Using annotations to customize JSON serialization*

One of the classic use cases for annotations is customizing object serialization. *Serialization* is a process of converting an object to a binary or text representation that can be then stored or sent over the network. The reverse process, *deserialization*, converts such a representation back to an object. One of the most common formats used for serialization is JSON. There are many widely used libraries for serializing Java objects to JSON, including Jackson (https://github.com/FasterXML/jackson) and GSON (https://github.com/google/gson). Just like any other Java library, they're fully compatible with Kotlin.

Over the course of this chapter, we'll discuss the implementation of a pure Kotlin library for this purpose, called JKid. It's small enough for you to read all of its source code easily, and we encourage you to do that while reading this chapter.

The JKid library source code and exercises

The full implementation is available as part of the book's source code, as well as online at https://manning.com/books/kotlin-in-action and http://github.com/yole/jkid. To study the library implementation and examples, open ch10/jkid/build.gradle as a Gradle project in your IDE. The examples can be found in the project under src/test/kotlin/examples. The library isn't as full-featured or flexible as GSON or Jackson, but it's performant enough for real use, and you're welcome to use it in your projects if it suits your needs.

The JKid project has a series of exercises you can work through after you finish reading the chapter to ensure that you understand the concepts. You can find a description of the exercises in the project's README.md file or read it at the project page on GitHub.

Let's start with the simplest example to test the library: serializing and deserializing an instance of the `Person` class. You pass the instance to the `serialize` function, and it returns a string containing its JSON representation:

```
data class Person(val name: String, val age: Int)

>>> val person = Person("Alice", 29)
>>> println(serialize(person))
{"age": 29, "name": "Alice"}
```

The JSON representation of an object consists of *key/value pairs*: pairs of property names and their values for the specific instance, such as `"age": 29`.

To get an object back from the JSON representation, you call the `deserialize` function:

```
>>> val json = """{"name": "Alice", "age": 29}"""
>>> println(deserialize<Person>(json))
Person(name=Alice, age=29)
```

When you create an instance from JSON data, you must specify the class explicitly as a type argument, because JSON doesn't store object types. In this case, you pass the `Person` class.

Figure 10.2 illustrates the equivalence between an object and its JSON representation. Note that the serialized class can contain not only values of primitive types or strings, as shown on the figure, but also collections and instances of other value object classes.

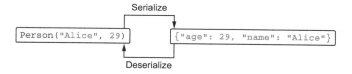

Figure 10.2 Serialization and deserialization of the `Person` instance

You can use annotations to customize the way objects are serialized and deserialized. When serializing an object to JSON, by default the library tries to serialize all the properties and uses the property names as keys. The annotations allow you to change the defaults. In this section, we'll discuss two annotations, `@JsonExclude` and `@Json-Name`, and you'll see their implementation later in the chapter:

- The `@JsonExclude` annotation is used to mark a property that should be excluded from serialization and deserialization.
- The `@JsonName` annotation lets you specify that the key in the key/value pair representing the property should be the given string, not the name of the property.

Consider this example:

```
data class Person(
    @JsonName("alias") val firstName: String,
    @JsonExclude val age: Int? = null
)
```

You annotate the property `firstName` to change the key used to represent it in JSON. You annotate the property `age` to exclude it from serialization and deserialization. Note that you must specify the default value of the property `age`. Otherwise, you wouldn't be able to create a new instance of `Person` during deserialization. Figure 10.3 shows how the representation of an instance of the `Person` class changes.

Figure 10.3   **Serialization and deserialization of the `Person` instance with annotations applied**

You've seen most of the features available in JKid: `serialize()`, `deserialize()`, `@JsonName`, and `@JsonExclude`. Now let's start our investigation of its implementation, starting with the annotation declarations.

10.1.4 *Declaring annotations*

In this section, you'll learn how to declare annotations, using the annotations from JKid as an example. The `@JsonExclude` annotation has the simplest form, because it doesn't have any parameters:

```
annotation class JsonExclude
```

The syntax looks like a regular class declaration, with the added `annotation` modifier before the `class` keyword. Because annotation classes are only used to define the structure of metadata associated with declarations and expressions, they can't contain any code. Therefore, the compiler prohibits specifying a body for an annotation class.

For annotations that have parameters, the parameters are declared in the primary constructor of the class:

```
annotation class JsonName(val name: String)
```

You use the regular primary constructor declaration syntax. The `val` keyword is mandatory for all parameters of an annotation class.

For comparison, here's how you'd declare the same annotation in Java:

```
/* Java */
public @interface JsonName {
    String value();
}
```

Note how the Java annotation has a method called `value`, whereas the Kotlin annotation has a `name` property. The `value` method is special in Java: when you apply an annotation, you need to provide explicit names for all attributes you're specifying except `value`. In Kotlin, on the other hand, applying an annotation is a regular constructor call. You can use the named-argument syntax to make the argument names explicit, or you can omit them: `@JsonName(name = "first_name")` means the same as `@JsonName("first_name")`, because `name` is the first parameter of the `JsonName` constructor. If you need to apply an annotation declared in Java to a Kotlin element, however, you're required to use the named-argument syntax for all arguments except `value`, which Kotlin also recognizes as special.

Next, let's discuss how to control annotation usage and how you can apply annotations to other annotations.

10.1.5 Meta-annotations: *controlling how an annotation is processed*

Just as in Java, a Kotlin annotation class can itself be annotated. The annotations that can be applied to annotation classes are called *meta-annotations*. The standard library defines several of them, and they control how the compiler processes annotations. Other frameworks use meta-annotations as well—for example, many dependency-injection libraries use meta-annotations to mark annotations used to identify different injectable objects of the same type.

Of the meta-annotations defined in the standard library, the most common is `@Target`. The declarations of `JsonExclude` and `JsonName` in JKid use it to specify the valid targets for those annotations. Here's how it's applied:

```
@Target(AnnotationTarget.PROPERTY)
annotation class JsonExclude
```

The `@Target` meta-annotation specifies the types of elements to which the annotation can be applied. If you don't use it, the annotation will be applicable to all declarations. That wouldn't make sense for JKid, because the library processes only property annotations.

The list of values of the `AnnotationTarget` enum gives the full range of possible targets for an annotation. It includes classes, files, functions, properties, property accessors, types, all expressions, and so on. You can declare multiple targets if you need to: `@Target(AnnotationTarget.CLASS, AnnotationTarget.METHOD)`.

To declare your own meta-annotation, use `ANNOTATION_CLASS` as its target:

```
@Target(AnnotationTarget.ANNOTATION_CLASS)
annotation class BindingAnnotation

@BindingAnnotation
annotation class MyBinding
```

Note that you can't use annotations with a `PROPERTY` target from Java code; to make such an annotation usable from Java, you can add the second target `AnnotationTarget.FIELD`. In this case, the annotation will be applied to properties in Kotlin and to fields in Java.

The @Retention annotation

In Java, you've probably seen another important meta-annotation, @Retention. You can use it to specify whether the annotation you declare will be stored in the .class file and whether it will be accessible at runtime through reflection. Java by default retains annotations in .class files but doesn't make them accessible at runtime. Most annotations do need to be present at runtime, so in Kotlin the default is different: annotations have RUNTIME retention. Therefore, the JKid annotations do not have an explicitly specified retention.

10.1.6 *Classes as annotation parameters*

You've seen how to define an annotation that holds static data as its arguments, but sometimes you need something different: the ability to refer to a *class* as declaration metadata. You can do so by declaring an annotation class that has a class reference as a parameter. In the JKid library, this comes up in the @DeserializeInterface annotation, which allows you to control the deserialization of properties that have an interface type. You can't create an instance of an interface directly, so you need to specify which class is used as the implementation created during deserialization.

Here's a simple example showing how this annotation is used:

```
interface Company {
    val name: String
}

data class CompanyImpl(override val name: String) : Company

data class Person(
    val name: String,
    @DeserializeInterface(CompanyImpl::class) val company: Company
)
```

Whenever JKid reads a nested company object for a Person instance, it creates and deserializes an instance of CompanyImpl and stores it in the company property. To specify this, you use CompanyImpl::class as an argument of the @Deserialize-Interface annotation. In general, to refer to a class, you use its name followed by the ::class keyword.

Now let's see how the annotation is declared. Its single argument is a class reference, as in @DeserializeInterface(CompanyImpl::class):

```
annotation class DeserializeInterface(val targetClass: KClass<out Any>)
```

The KClass type is Kotlin's counterpart to Java's java.lang.Class type. It's used to hold references to Kotlin classes; you'll see what it lets you do with those classes in the "Reflection" section later in this chapter.

The type parameter of KClass specifies which Kotlin classes can be referred to by this reference. For instance, CompanyImpl::class has a type KClass<Company-Impl>, which is a subtype of the annotation parameter type (see figure 10.4).

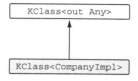

Figure 10.4   The type of the annotation argument
`CompanyImpl::class` (`KClass<CompanyImpl>`) **is a subtype of the annotation parameter type (`KClass<out Any>`).**

If you wrote `KClass<Any>` without the `out` modifier, you wouldn't be able to pass `CompanyImpl::class` as an argument: the only allowed argument would be `Any::class`. The `out` keyword specifies that you're allowed to refer to classes that extend `Any`, not just to `Any` itself. The next section shows one more annotation that takes a reference to generic class as a parameter.

10.1.7   *Generic classes as annotation parameters*

By default, JKid serializes properties of nonprimitive types as nested objects. But you can change this behavior and provide your own serialization logic for some values.

The `@CustomSerializer` annotation takes a reference to a custom serializer class as an argument. The serializer class should implement the `ValueSerializer` interface:

```
interface ValueSerializer<T> {
    fun toJsonValue(value: T): Any?
    fun fromJsonValue(jsonValue: Any?): T
}
```

Suppose you need to support serialization of dates, and you've created your own `DateSerializer` class for that, implementing the `ValueSerializer<Date>` interface. (This class is provided as an example in the JKid source code: http://mng.bz/73a7). Here's how you apply it to the `Person` class:

```
data class Person(
    val name: String,
    @CustomSerializer(DateSerializer::class) val birthDate: Date
)
```

Now let's see how the `@CustomSerializer` annotation is declared. The `Value-Serializer` class is generic and defines a type parameter, so you need to provide a type argument value whenever you refer to the type. Because you know nothing about the types of properties with which this annotation will be used, you can use a *star projection* (discussed in section 9.3.6) as the argument:

```
annotation class CustomSerializer(
    val serializerClass: KClass<out ValueSerializer<*>>
)
```

Figure 10.5 examines the type of the `serializerClass` parameter and explains its different parts. You need to ensure that the annotation can only refer to classes that implement the `ValueSerializer` interface. For instance, writing `@Custom-Serializer(Date::class)` should be prohibited, because `Date` doesn't implement the `ValueSerializer` interface.

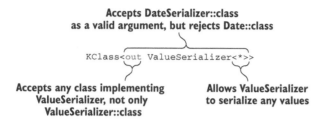

Accepts DateSerializer::class as a valid argument, but rejects Date::class

`KClass<out ValueSerializer<*>>`

Accepts any class implementing ValueSerializer, not only ValueSerializer::class

Allows ValueSerializer to serialize any values

Figure 10.5 The type of the `serializerClass` annotation parameter. Only class references to classes that extend `ValueSerializer` will be valid annotation arguments.

Tricky, isn't it? The good news is that you can apply the same pattern every time you need to use a class as an annotation argument. You can write `KClass<out Your-ClassName>`, and if `YourClassName` has its own type arguments, replace them with `*`.

You've now seen all the important aspects of declaring and applying annotations in Kotlin. The next step is to find out how to access the data stored in the annotations. For this, you need to use *reflection*.

10.2 *Reflection: introspecting Kotlin objects at runtime*

Reflection is, simply put, a way to access properties and methods of objects *dynamically* at runtime, without knowing in advance what those properties are. Normally, when you access a method or a property of an object, the source code of your program references a specific declaration, and the compiler *statically* resolves the reference and ensures that the declaration exists. But sometimes you need to write code that can work with objects of any type, or where the names of methods and properties to be accessed are only known at runtime. The JSON serialization library is a great example of such code: it needs to be able to serialize any object to JSON, so it can't reference specific classes and properties. This is where reflection comes into play.

When working with reflection in Kotlin, you deal with two different reflection APIs. The first is the standard Java reflection, defined in the `java.lang.reflect` package. Because Kotlin classes are compiled to regular Java bytecode, the Java reflection API supports them perfectly well. In particular, this means Java libraries that use the reflection API are fully compatible with Kotlin code.

The second is the Kotlin reflection API, defined in the `kotlin.reflect` package. It gives you access to concepts that don't exist in the Java world, such as properties and nullable types. But at this time it doesn't provide a comprehensive replacement for the Java reflection API, and, as you'll see later, there are cases where you need to fall back to Java reflection. An important note is that the Kotlin reflection API isn't restricted to Kotlin classes: you can use the same API to access classes written in any JVM language.

NOTE To reduce the runtime library size on platforms where it matters, such as Android, the Kotlin reflection API is packaged into a separate .jar file, kotlin-reflect.jar, which isn't added to the dependencies of new projects by default. If you're using the Kotlin reflection API, you need to make sure the library is added as a dependency. IntelliJ IDEA can detect the missing dependency and assist you with adding it. The Maven group/artifact ID for the library is org.jetbrains.kotlin:kotlin-reflect.

In this section, you'll see how JKid uses the reflection API. We'll walk you through the serialization part first, because it's more straightforward and easier for us to explain, and then proceed to JSON parsing and deserialization. But first let's take a close look at the contents of the reflection API.

10.2.1 *The Kotlin reflection API: KClass, KCallable, KFunction, and KProperty*

The main entry point of the Kotlin reflection API is KClass, which represents a class. KClass is the counterpart of java.lang.Class, and you can use it to enumerate and access all the declarations contained in the class, its superclasses, and so on. You get an instance of KClass by writing MyClass::class. To get the class of an object at runtime, first you obtain its Java class using the javaClass property, which is a direct equivalent to Java's java.lang.Object.getClass(). Then you access the .kotlin extension property to move from Java to Kotlin reflection API:

```
class Person(val name: String, val age: Int)

>>> val person = Person("Alice", 29)
>>> val kClass = person.javaClass.kotlin        ⟵—┐ Returns an instance
>>> println(kClass.simpleName)                        of KClass<Person>
Person
>>> kClass.memberProperties.forEach { println(it.name) }
age
name
```

This simple example prints the name of the class and the names of its properties and uses .memberProperties to collect all non-extension properties defined in the class, as well as in all of its superclasses.

If you browse the declaration of KClass, you'll see that it contains a bunch of useful methods for accessing the contents of the class:

```
interface KClass<T : Any> {
    val simpleName: String?
    val qualifiedName: String?
    val members: Collection<KCallable<*>>
    val constructors: Collection<KFunction<T>>
    val nestedClasses: Collection<KClass<*>>
    ...
}
```

Many other useful features of KClass, including memberProperties used in the previous example, are declared as extensions. You can see the full list of methods on

KClass (including extensions) in the standard library reference (http://mng.bz/em4i).

You may have noticed that the list of all members of a class is a collection of KCallable instances. KCallable is a superinterface for functions and properties. It declares the call method, which allows you to call the corresponding function or the getter of the property:

```
interface KCallable<out R> {
    fun call(vararg args: Any?): R
    ...
}
```

You provide the function arguments in a vararg list. The following code demonstrates how you can use call to call a function through reflection:

```
fun foo(x: Int) = println(x)
>>> val kFunction = ::foo
>>> kFunction.call(42)
42
```

You saw the ::foo syntax in section 5.1.5, and now you can see that the value of this expression is an instance of the KFunction class from the reflection API. To call the referenced function, you use the KCallable.call method. In this case, you need to provide a single argument, 42. If you try to call the function with an incorrect number of arguments, such as kFunction.call(), it will throw a runtime exception: "Illegal-ArgumentException: Callable expects 1 arguments, but 0 were provided."

In this case, however, you can use a more specific method to call the function. The type of the ::foo expression is KFunction1<Int, Unit>, which contains information about parameter and return types. The 1 denotes that this function takes one parameter. To call the function through this interface, you use the invoke method. It accepts a fixed number of arguments (1 in this case), and their types correspond to the type parameters of the KFunction1 interface. You can also call kFunction directly:[1]

```
import kotlin.reflect.KFunction2

fun sum(x: Int, y: Int) = x + y
>>> val kFunction: KFunction2<Int, Int, Int> = ::sum
>>> println(kFunction.invoke(1, 2) + kFunction(3, 4))
10
>>> kFunction(1)
ERROR: No value passed for parameter p2
```

Now you can't call the invoke method on kFunction with an incorrect number of arguments: it won't compile. Therefore, if you have a KFunction of a specific type, with known parameters and return type, it's preferable to use its invoke method. The

---

[1] Section 11.3 will explain the details of why it's possible to call kFunction without an explicit invoke.

`call` method is a generic approach that works for all types of functions but doesn't provide type safety.

> ## How and where are KFunctionN interfaces defined?
>
> Types such as `KFunction1` represent functions with different numbers of parameters. Each type extends `KFunction` and adds one additional member `invoke` with the appropriate number of parameters. For example, `KFunction2` declares `operator fun invoke(p1: P1, p2: P2): R`, where `P1` and `P2` represent the function parameter types and `R` represents the return type.
>
> These function types are *synthetic compiler-generated types*, and you won't find their declarations in the `kotlin.reflect` package. That means you can use an interface for a function with any number of parameters. The synthetic-types approach reduces the size of kotlin-runtime.jar and avoids artificial restrictions on the possible number of function-type parameters.

You can invoke the `call` method on a `KProperty` instance as well, and it will call the getter of the property. But the property interface gives you a better way to obtain the property value: the `get` method.

To access the `get` method, you need to use the correct interface for the property, depending on how it's declared. Top-level properties are represented by instances of the `KProperty0` interface, which has a no-argument `get` method:

```
var counter = 0
>>> val kProperty = ::counter
>>> kProperty.setter.call(21)          ⟵  Calls a setter through reflection,
>>> println(kProperty.get())                passing 21 as an argument
21                                      ⟵  Obtains a property
                                            value by calling "get"
```

A *member property* is represented by an instance of `KProperty1`, which has a one-argument `get` method. To access its value, you must provide the object instance for which you need the value. The following example stores a reference to the property in a `memberProperty` variable; then you call `memberProperty.get(person)` to obtain the value of this property for the specific `person` instance. So if a `memberProperty` refers to the age property of the `Person` class, `memberProperty.get(person)` is a way to dynamically get the value of `person.age`:

```
class Person(val name: String, val age: Int)

>>> val person = Person("Alice", 29)
>>> val memberProperty = Person::age
>>> println(memberProperty.get(person))
29
```

Note that `KProperty1` is a generic class. The `memberProperty` variable has the type `KProperty<Person, Int>`, where the first type parameter denotes the type of the receiver and the second type parameter stands for the property type. Thus you can call its get method only with a receiver of the right type; the call member-Property.get("Alice") won't compile.

Also note that you can only use reflection to access properties defined at the top level or in a class, but not local variables of a function. If you define a local variable x and try to get a reference to it using ::x, you'll get a compilation error saying that "References to variables aren't supported yet".

Figure 10.6 shows a hierarchy of interfaces that you can use to access source code elements at runtime. Because all declarations can be annotated, the interfaces that represent declaration at runtime, such as KClass, KFunction, and KParameter, all extend KAnnotatedElement. KClass is used to represent both classes and objects. KProperty can represent any property, whereas its subclass, KMutableProperty, represents a mutable property, which you declare with var. You can use the special interfaces Getter and Setter declared in Property and KMutableProperty to work with property accessors as functions—for example, if you need to retrieve their annotations. Both interfaces for accessors extend KFunction. For simplicity, we've omitted the specific interfaces for properties like KProperty0 in the figure.

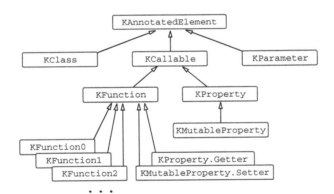

Figure 10.6   Hierarchy of interfaces in the Kotlin reflection API

Now that you're acquainted with the basics of the Kotlin reflection API, let's investigate how the JKid library is implemented.

10.2.2 *Implementing object serialization using reflection*

First, let's recall the declaration of the serialization function in JKid:

```
fun serialize(obj: Any): String
```

This function takes an object and returns its JSON representation as a string. It'll build up the resulting JSON in a StringBuilder instance. As it serializes object properties and their values, it'll append them to this StringBuilder object. To make the append calls more concise, let's put the implementation in an extension function to `String-Builder`. That way, you can conveniently call the append method without a qualifier:

```
private fun StringBuilder.serializeObject(x: Any) {
    append(...)
}
```

Converting a function parameter into an extension function receiver is a common pattern in Kotlin code, and we'll discuss it in detail in section 11.2.1. Note that `serializeObject` doesn't extend the `StringBuilder` API. It performs operations that make no sense outside of this particular context, so it's marked `private` to ensure that it can't be used elsewhere. It's declared as an extension to emphasize a particular object as primary for this code block and to make it easier to work with that object.

Consequently, the `serialize` function delegates all the work to `serialize-Object`:

```
fun serialize(obj: Any): String = buildString { serializeObject(obj) }
```

As you saw in section 5.5.2, `buildString` creates a `StringBuilder` and lets you fill it with content in a lambda. In this case, the content is provided by the call to `serializeObject(obj)`.

Now let's discuss the behavior of the serialization function. By default, it will serialize all properties of the object. Primitive types and strings will be serialized as JSON number, boolean, and string values, as appropriate. Collections will be serialized as JSON arrays. Properties of other types will be serialized as nested objects. As we discussed in the previous section, this behavior can be customized through annotations.

Let's look at the implementation of `serializeObject`, where you can observe the reflection API in a real scenario.

Listing 10.1   Serializing an object

```
private fun StringBuilder.serializeObject(obj: Any) {
    val kClass = obj.javaClass.kotlin              Gets the KClass for the object
    val properties = kClass.memberProperties        Gets all properties of the class

    properties.joinToStringBuilder(
        this, prefix = "{", postfix = "}") { prop ->
        serializeString(prop.name)                  Gets the property name
        append(": ")
        serializePropertyValue(prop.get(obj))       Gets the property value
    }
}
```

The implementation of this function should be clear: you serialize each property of the class, one after another. The resulting JSON will look like this: `{ prop1: value1, prop2: value2 }`. The `joinToStringBuilder` function ensures that properties are separated with commas. The `serializeString` function escapes special characters as required by the JSON format. The `serializePropertyValue` function checks whether a value is a primitive value, string, collection, or nested object, and serializes its content accordingly.

In the previous section, we discussed a way to obtain the value of the `KProperty` instance: the `get` method. In that case, you worked with the member reference `Person::age` of the type `KProperty1<Person, Int>`, which lets the compiler know the exact types of the receiver and the property value. In this example, however, the exact types are unknown, because you enumerate all the properties of an object's class. Therefore, the `prop` variable has the type `KProperty1<Any, *>`, and `prop.get(obj)` returns a value of `Any` type. You don't get any compile-time checks for the receiver type, but because you're passing the same object from which you obtained the list of properties, the receiver type will be correct. Next, let's see how the annotations that tune up serialization are implemented.

10.2.3 *Customizing serialization with annotations*

Earlier in this chapter, you saw the definitions of annotations that let you customize the process of JSON serialization. In particular, we discussed the `@JsonExclude`, `@JsonName`, and `@CustomSerializer` annotations. Now it's time to see how these annotations can be handled by the `serializeObject` function.

We'll start with `@JsonExclude`. This annotation allows you to exclude some properties from serialization. Let's investigate how you should change the implementation of the `serializeObject` function to support that.

Recall that to get all member properties of the class, you use the extension property `memberProperties` on the `KClass` instance. But now the task gets more complicated: properties annotated with `@JsonExclude` need to be filtered out. Let's see how this is done.

The `KAnnotatedElement` interface defines the property `annotations`, a collection of instances of all annotations (with runtime retention) applied to the element in the source code. Because `KProperty` extends `KAnnotatedElement`, you can access all annotations for a property by saying `property.annotations`.

But here the filtering doesn't use all annotations; it needs to find a specific one. The helper function `findAnnotation` does the job:

```
inline fun <reified T> KAnnotatedElement.findAnnotation(): T?
        = annotations.filterIsInstance<T>().firstOrNull()
```

The `findAnnotation` function returns an annotation of a type specified as an argument if such an annotation is present. It uses the pattern discussed in section 9.2.3 and makes the type parameter `reified` in order to pass the annotation class as the type argument.

Now you can use `findAnnotation` together with the `filter` standard library function to filter out the properties annotated with `@JsonExclude`:

```
val properties = kClass.memberProperties
        .filter { it.findAnnotation<JsonExclude>() == null }
```

The next annotation is `@JsonName`. As a reminder, we'll repeat its declaration and an example of its usage:

```
annotation class JsonName(val name: String)

data class Person(
    @JsonName("alias") val firstName: String,
    val age: Int
)
```

In this case, you're interested not only in its presence but also in its argument: the name that should be used for the annotated property in JSON. Fortunately, the `find-Annotation` function helps here:

```
val jsonNameAnn = prop.findAnnotation<JsonName>()       ◄─┐ Gets an instance of the
val propName = jsonNameAnn?.name ?: prop.name           ◄─┐ @JsonName annotation if it exists
                                                            Gets its "name" argument or
                                                            uses "prop.name" as a fallback
```

If a property isn't annotated with `@JsonName`, then `jsonNameAnn` is `null`, and you still use `prop.name` as the name for the property in JSON. If the property is annotated, you use the specified name instead.

Let's look at the serialization of an instance of the `Person` class declared earlier. During the serialization of the `firstName` property, `jsonNameAnn` contains the corresponding instance of the annotation class `JsonName`. Thus `jsonNameAnn?.name` returns the non-null value `"alias"`, which is used as a key in JSON. When the age property is serialized, the annotation isn't found, so the property name age is used as a key.

Let's combine the changes discussed so far and look at the resulting implementation of the serialization logic.

Listing 10.2 Serializing an object with property filtering

```
private fun StringBuilder.serializeObject(obj: Any) {
    obj.javaClass.kotlin.memberProperties
        .filter { it.findAnnotation<JsonExclude>() == null }
        .joinToStringBuilder(this, prefix = "{", postfix = "}") {
            serializeProperty(it, obj)
        }
}
```

Now the properties annotated with `@JsonExclude` are filtered out. We've also extracted the logic responsible for property serialization into a separate `serialize-Property` function.

Listing 10.3 Serializing a single property

```
private fun StringBuilder.serializeProperty(
        prop: KProperty1<Any, *>, obj: Any
) {
    val jsonNameAnn = prop.findAnnotation<JsonName>()
```

```
    val propName = jsonNameAnn?.name ?: prop.name
    serializeString(propName)
    append(": ")

    serializePropertyValue(prop.get(obj))
}
```

The property name is processed according to the @JsonName annotation discussed earlier.

Next, let's implement the remaining annotation, @CustomSerializer. The implementation is based on the function getSerializer, which returns the Value-Serializer instance registered via the @CustomSerializer annotation. For example, if you declare the Person class as shown next and call getSerializer() when serializing the birthDate property, it will return an instance of DateSerializer:

```
data class Person(
    val name: String,
    @CustomSerializer(DateSerializer::class) val birthDate: Date
)
```

Here's a reminder of how the @CustomSerializer annotation is declared, to help you better understand the implementation of getSerializer:

```
annotation class CustomSerializer(
    val serializerClass: KClass<out ValueSerializer<*>>
)
```

Here's how the getSerializer function is implemented.

Listing 10.4   Retrieving the value serializer for a property

```
fun KProperty<*>.getSerializer(): ValueSerializer<Any?>? {
    val customSerializerAnn = findAnnotation<CustomSerializer>() ?: return null
    val serializerClass = customSerializerAnn.serializerClass

    val valueSerializer = serializerClass.objectInstance
            ?: serializerClass.createInstance()
    @Suppress("UNCHECKED_CAST")
    return valueSerializer as ValueSerializer<Any?>
}
```

It's an extension function to KProperty, because the property is the primary object handled by the method. It calls the findAnnotation function to get an instance of the @CustomSerializer annotation if it exists. Its argument, serializerClass, specifies the class for which you need to obtain an instance.

The most interesting part here is the way you handle both classes and objects (Kotlin's singletons) as values of the @CustomSerializer annotation. They're both represented by the KClass class. The difference is that objects have a non-null value of the objectInstance property, which can be used to access the singleton instance created for the object. For example, DateSerializer is declared as an object, so its `objectInstance` property stores the singleton `DateSerializer` instance. You'll use that instance to serialize all objects, and `createInstance` won't be called.

If the `KClass` represents a regular class, you create a new instance by calling `createInstance`. This function is similar to `java.lang.Class.newInstance`.

Finally, you can use `getSerializer` in the implementation of `serialize-Property`. Here's the final version of the function.

Listing 10.5 Serializing a property, with custom serializer support

```
private fun StringBuilder.serializeProperty(
        prop: KProperty1<Any, *>, obj: Any
) {
    val name = prop.findAnnotation<JsonName>()?.name ?: prop.name
    serializeString(name)
    append(": ")

    val value = prop.get(obj)
    val jsonValue =
            prop.getSerializer()?.toJsonValue(value)      ◁─── Uses a custom serializer
            ?: value                                       ◁─── for the property if it exists
    serializePropertyValue(jsonValue)                           Otherwise uses the
}                                                               property value as before
```

`serializeProperty` uses the serializer to convert the property value to a JSON-compatible format by calling `toJsonValue`. If the property doesn't have a custom serializer, it uses the property value.

Now that you've seen the implementation of the JSON serialization part of the library, we'll move to parsing and deserialization. The deserialization part requires quite a bit more code, so we won't examine all of it, but we'll look at the structure of the implementation and explain how reflection is used to deserialize objects.

10.2.4 JSON parsing and object deserialization

Let's start with the second part of the story: implementing the deserialization logic. First, recall that the API, like that used for serialization, consists of a single function:

```
inline fun <reified T: Any> deserialize(json: String): T
```

Here's an example of its use:

```
data class Author(val name: String)
data class Book(val title: String, val author: Author)

>>> val json = """{"title": "Catch-22", "author": {"name": "J. Heller"}}"""
>>> val book = deserialize<Book>(json)
>>> println(book)
Book(title=Catch-22, author=Author(name=J. Heller))
```

You pass the type of object to be deserialized as a reified type parameter to the `deserialize` function and get back a new object instance.

Deserializing JSON is a more difficult task than serializing, because it involves parsing the JSON string input in addition to using reflection to access object internals. The JSON deserializer in JKid is implemented in a fairly conventional way and consists of three main stages: a lexical analyzer, usually referred to as a *lexer*; a syntax analyzer, or *parser*; and the deserialization component itself.

The lexical analysis splits an input string consisting of characters into a list of tokens. There are two kinds of tokens: *character tokens*, which represent characters with special meanings in the JSON syntax (comma, colon, braces, and brackets); and *value tokens*, which correspond to string, number, Boolean, and `null` constants. A left brace ({), a string value (`"Catch-22"`), and an integer value (`42`) are examples of different tokens.

The parser is generally responsible for converting a plain list of tokens into a structured representation. Its task in JKid is to understand the higher-level structure of JSON and to convert individual tokens into semantic elements supported in JSON: key-value pairs, objects, and arrays.

The `JsonObject` interface keeps track of the object or array currently being deserialized. The parser calls the corresponding methods when it discovers new properties of the current object (simple values, composite properties, or arrays).

Listing 10.6   JSON parser callback interface

```
interface JsonObject {
    fun setSimpleProperty(propertyName: String, value: Any?)

    fun createObject(propertyName: String): JsonObject

    fun createArray(propertyName: String): JsonObject
}
```

The `propertyName` parameter in these methods receives the JSON key. Thus, when the parser encounters an `author` property with an object as its value, the `create-Object("author")` method is called. Simple value properties are reported as calls to `setSimpleProperty`, with the actual token value passed as the `value` argument. The `JsonObject` implementations are responsible for creating new objects for properties and storing references to them in the outer object.

Figure 10.7 shows the input and output of each stage for lexical and syntactic analyses when deserializing a sample string. Once again, the lexical analysis divides an input string into a list of tokens; then the syntactic analysis (the parser) processes this list of tokens and invokes an appropriate method of `JsonObject` on every new meaningful element.

The deserializer then provides an implementation for `JsonObject` that gradually builds a new instance of the corresponding type. It needs to find the correspondence between class properties and JSON keys (`title`, `author`, and `name` in figure 10.7) and build nested object values (an instance of `Author`); only after that it can create a new instance of the required class (`Book`).

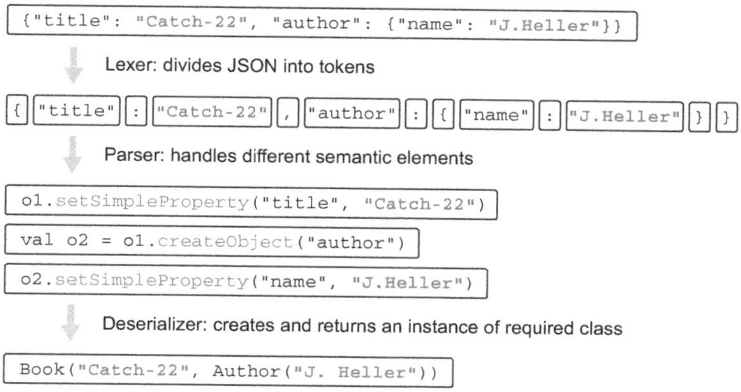

```
{"title": "Catch-22", "author": {"name": "J.Heller"}}
```
↓ Lexer: divides JSON into tokens
```
{ "title" : "Catch-22" , "author" : { "name" : "J.Heller" } }
```
↓ Parser: handles different semantic elements
```
o1.setSimpleProperty("title", "Catch-22")
val o2 = o1.createObject("author")
o2.setSimpleProperty("name", "J.Heller")
```
↓ Deserializer: creates and returns an instance of required class
```
Book("Catch-22", Author("J. Heller"))
```

Figure 10.7 JSON parsing: lexer, parser, and deserializer

The JKid library is intended to be used with data classes, and, as such, it passes all the name-value pairs loaded from the JSON file as parameters to the constructor of the class being deserialized. It doesn't support setting properties on object instances after they've been created. This means it needs to store the data somewhere while reading it from JSON and before it can construct the object.

The requirement to save the components before creating the object looks similar to the traditional Builder pattern, with the difference that builders are generally tailored to creating a specific kind of object, and the solution needs to be completely generic. To avoid being boring, we use the term *seed* for the implementation. In JSON, you need to build different types of composite structures: objects, collections, and maps. The classes `ObjectSeed`, `ObjectListSeed`, and `ValueListSeed` are responsible for building objects and lists of composite objects or simple values appropriately. The construction of maps is left as an exercise for you.

The basic `Seed` interface extends `JsonObject` and provides an additional `spawn` method to get the resulting instance after the building process is finished. It also declares the `createCompositeProperty` method that's used to create both nested objects and nested lists (they use the same underlying logic to create instances through seeds).

Listing 10.7 Interface for creating objects from JSON data

```
interface Seed: JsonObject {
    fun spawn(): Any?

    fun createCompositeProperty(
        propertyName: String,
        isList: Boolean
    ): JsonObject

    override fun createObject(propertyName: String) =
        createCompositeProperty(propertyName, false)
```

```
override fun createArray(propertyName: String) =
    createCompositeProperty(propertyName, true)

// ...
}
```

You may think of spawn as an analogue of build—a method that returns the result value. It returns the constructed object for ObjectSeed and the resulting list for ObjectListSeed or ValueListSeed. We won't discuss in detail how lists are deserialized. We'll focus our attention on creating objects, which is more complicated and serves to demonstrate the general idea.

But before that, let's study the main deserialize function that does all the work of deserializing a value.

Listing 10.8   The top-level deserialization function

```
fun <T: Any> deserialize(json: Reader, targetClass: KClass<T>): T {
    val seed = ObjectSeed(targetClass, ClassInfoCache())
    Parser(json, seed).parse()
    return seed.spawn()
}
```

To start the parsing, you create an ObjectSeed to store the properties of the object being deserialized, and then you invoke the parser and pass the input stream reader json to it. Once you reach the end of the input data, you call the spawn function to build the resulting object.

Now let's focus on the implementation of ObjectSeed, which stores the state of an object being constructed. ObjectSeed takes a reference to the resulting class and a classInfoCache object containing cached information about the properties of the class. This cached information will be used later to create instances of that class. ClassInfoCache and ClassInfo are helper classes that we'll discuss in the next section.

Listing 10.9   Deserializing an object

```
class ObjectSeed<out T: Any>(
        targetClass: KClass<T>,
        val classInfoCache: ClassInfoCache
) : Seed {

    private val classInfo: ClassInfo<T> =          ◁── Caches the information needed to
            classInfoCache[targetClass]                create an instance of targetClass

    private val valueArguments = mutableMapOf<KParameter, Any?>()
    private val seedArguments = mutableMapOf<KParameter, Seed>()

    private val arguments: Map<KParameter, Any?>    ◁── Builds a map from
        get() = valueArguments +                        constructor parameters
            seedArguments.mapValues { it.value.spawn() }    to their values
```

```
                    override fun setSimpleProperty(propertyName: String, value: Any?) {
                        val param = classInfo.getConstructorParameter(propertyName)
                        valueArguments[param] =
                                classInfo.deserializeConstructorArgument(param, value)
                    }

                    override fun createCompositeProperty(
                            propertyName: String, isList: Boolean
                    ): Seed {
                        val param = classInfo.getConstructorParameter(propertyName)
                        val deserializeAs =
                            classInfo.getDeserializeClass(propertyName)
                        val seed = createSeedForType(
                            deserializeAs ?: param.type.javaType, isList)
                        return seed.apply { seedArguments[param] = this }
                    }

                    override fun spawn(): T =
                            classInfo.createInstance(arguments)
                }
```

Records a value for the constructor parameter, if it's a simple value

Loads the value of the DeserializeInterface annotation for the property, if any

Creates an ObjectSeed or CollectionSeed according to the parameter type...

...and records it in the seedArguments map

Creates the resulting instance of targetClass, passing an arguments map

`ObjectSeed` builds a map from constructor parameters to their values. Two mutable maps are used for that: `valueArguments` for simple value properties and `seedArguments` for composite properties. While the result is being built, new arguments are added to the `valueArguments` map by calling `setSimpleProperty` and to the `seedArguments` map by calling `createCompositeProperty`. New composite seeds are added in an empty state and are then filled with data coming from the input stream. Finally, the `spawn` method builds all nested seeds recursively by calling `spawn` on each.

Note how calling `arguments` in the body of the `spawn` method launches the recursive building of composite (seed) arguments: the custom getter of `arguments` calls the `spawn` methods on each of the `seedArguments`. The `createSeedForType` function analyzes the type of the parameter and creates either `ObjectSeed`, `ObjectListSeed`, or `ValueListSeed`, depending on whether the parameter is some kind of collection. We'll leave the investigation of how it's implemented to you. Next, let's see how the `ClassInfo.createInstance` function creates an instance of `targetClass`.

10.2.5 Final deserialization step: callBy() and creating objects using reflection

The last part you need to understand is the `ClassInfo` class that builds the resulting instance and caches information about constructor parameters. It is used in `ObjectSeed`. But before we dive into the implementation details, let's look at the APIs that you use to create objects through reflection.

You've already seen the `KCallable.call` method, which calls a function or a constructor by taking a list of arguments. This method works great in many cases, but it has a restriction: it doesn't support default parameter values. In this case, if a user is trying to deserialize an object with a constructor that has default parameter values, you definitely don't want to require those arguments to be specified in the JSON. Therefore, you need to use another method, which does support default parameter values: KCallable.callBy.

```
interface KCallable<out R> {
    fun callBy(args: Map<KParameter, Any?>): R
    ...
}
```

The method takes a map of parameters to their corresponding values that will be passed as arguments. If a parameter is missing from the map, its default value will be used if possible. It's also nice that you don't have to put the parameters in the correct order; you can read the name-value pairs from JSON, find the parameter corresponding to each argument name, and put its value in the map.

One thing you do need to take care of is getting the types right. The type of the value in the args map needs to match the constructor parameter type; otherwise, you'll get an IllegalArgumentException. This is particularly important for numeric types: you need to know whether the parameter takes an Int, a Long, a Double, or another primitive type, and to convert the numeric value coming from JSON to the correct type. To do that, you use the KParameter.type property.

The type conversion works through the same ValueSerializer interface used for custom serialization. If a property doesn't have an @CustomSerializer annotation, you retrieve a standard implementation based on its type.

Listing 10.10   Getting a serializer based on value type

```
fun serializerForType(type: Type): ValueSerializer<out Any?>? =
        when(type) {
            Byte::class.java -> ByteSerializer
            Int::class.java -> IntSerializer
            Boolean::class.java -> BooleanSerializer
            // ...
            else -> null
        }
```

The corresponding ValueSerializer implementations perform the necessary type checking or conversion.

Listing 10.11   Serializer for Boolean values

```
object BooleanSerializer : ValueSerializer<Boolean> {
    override fun fromJsonValue(jsonValue: Any?): Boolean {
        if (jsonValue !is Boolean) throw JKidException("Boolean expected")
        return jsonValue
    }

    override fun toJsonValue(value: Boolean) = value
}
```

The callBy method gives you a way to invoke the primary constructor of an object, passing a map of parameters and corresponding values. The ValueSerializer mechanism ensures that the values in the map have the right types. Now let's see how you invoke the API.

The ClassInfoCache class is intended to reduce the overhead of reflection operations. Recall that the annotations used to control the serialization and deserialization process (@JsonName and @CustomSerializer) are applied to properties, rather than parameters. When you're deserializing an object, you're dealing with constructor parameters, not properties; and in order to retrieve the annotations, you need to find the corresponding property. Performing this search when reading every key-value pair would be exceedingly slow, so you do this once per class and cache the information. Here's the entire implementation of ClassInfoCache.

Listing 10.12 Storage of cached reflection data

```
class ClassInfoCache {
    private val cacheData = mutableMapOf<KClass<*>, ClassInfo<*>>()

    @Suppress("UNCHECKED_CAST")
    operator fun <T : Any> get(cls: KClass<T>): ClassInfo<T> =
            cacheData.getOrPut(cls) { ClassInfo(cls) } as ClassInfo<T>
}
```

You use the same pattern we discussed in section 9.3.6: you remove the type information when you store the values in the map, but the implementation of the get method guarantees that the returned ClassInfo<T> has the right type argument. Note the use of getOrPut: if the cacheData map already contains an entry for cls, you return that entry. Otherwise, you call the passed lambda, which calculates the value for the key, stores the value in the map, and returns it.

The ClassInfo class is responsible for creating a new instance of the target class and caching the necessary information. To simplify the code, we've omitted some functions and trivial initializers. Also, you may notice that instead of !!, the production code throws an exception with an informative message (which is a good pattern for your code as well).

Listing 10.13 Cache of constructor parameter and annotation data

```
class ClassInfo<T : Any>(cls: KClass<T>) {
    private val constructor = cls.primaryConstructor!!

    private val jsonNameToParamMap = hashMapOf<String, KParameter>()
    private val paramToSerializerMap =
        hashMapOf<KParameter, ValueSerializer<out Any?>>()
    private val jsonNameToDeserializeClassMap =
        hashMapOf<String, Class<out Any>?>()

    init {
        constructor.parameters.forEach { cacheDataForParameter(cls, it) }
    }
```

```
fun getConstructorParameter(propertyName: String): KParameter =
        jsonNameToParam[propertyName]!!

fun deserializeConstructorArgument(
        param: KParameter, value: Any?): Any? {
    val serializer = paramToSerializer[param]
    if (serializer != null) return serializer.fromJsonValue(value)

    validateArgumentType(param, value)
    return value
}

fun createInstance(arguments: Map<KParameter, Any?>): T {
    ensureAllParametersPresent(arguments)
    return constructor.callBy(arguments)
}

// ...
}
```

On initialization, this code locates the property corresponding to each constructor parameter and retrieves its annotations. It stores the data in three maps: jsonName-ToParam specifies the parameter corresponding to each key in the JSON file, param-ToSerializer stores the serializer for each parameter, and jsonNameTo DeserializeClass stores the class specified as the @DeserializeInterface argument, if any. ClassInfo can then provide a constructor parameter by the property name, and the calling code uses the parameter as a key for the parameter-to-argument map.

The cacheDataForParameter, validateArgumentType, and ensureAll-ParametersPresent functions are private functions in this class. Following is the implementation of ensureAllParametersPresent; you can browse the code of the others yourself.

Listing 10.14   Validating that required parameters are provided

```
private fun ensureAllParametersPresent(arguments: Map<KParameter, Any?>) {
    for (param in constructor.parameters) {
        if (arguments[param] == null &&
                !param.isOptional && !param.type.isMarkedNullable) {
            throw JKidException("Missing value for parameter ${param.name}")
        }
    }
}
```

This function checks that you provide all required values for parameters. Note how the reflection API helps you here. If a parameter has a default value, then param.isOptional is true and you can omit an argument for it; the default one will be used instead. If the parameter type is nullable (type.isMarkedNullable tells you that), null will be used as the default parameter value. For all other parameters, you must provide the corresponding arguments; otherwise, an exception will be thrown. The reflection cache ensures that the search for annotations that customize the deserialization process is performed only once, and not for every property you see in the JSON data.

This completes our discussion of the JKid library implementation. Over the course of this chapter, we've explored the implementation of a JSON serialization and deserialization library, implemented on top of the reflection APIs, and using annotations to customize its behavior. Of course, all the techniques and approaches demonstrated in this chapter can be used for your own frameworks as well.

10.3 *Summary*

- The syntax for applying annotations in Kotlin is almost the same as in Java.
- Kotlin lets you apply annotations to a broader range of targets than Java, including files and expressions.
- An annotation argument can be a primitive value, a string, an enum, a class reference, an instance of another annotation class, or an array thereof.
- Specifying the use-site target for an annotation, as in `@get:Rule`, allows you to choose how the annotation is applied if a single Kotlin declaration produces multiple bytecode elements.
- You declare an annotation class as a class with a primary constructor where all parameters are marked as `val` properties and without a body.
- Meta-annotations can be used to specify the target, retention mode, and other attributes of annotations.
- The reflection API lets you enumerate and access the methods and properties of an object dynamically at runtime. It has interfaces representing different kinds of declarations, such as classes (`KClass`), functions (`KFunction`), and so on.
- To obtain a `KClass` instance, you can use `ClassName::class` if the class is statically known and `obj.javaClass.kotlin` to get the class from an object instance.
- The `KFunction` and `KProperty` interfaces both extend `KCallable`, which provides the generic `call` method.
- The `KCallable.callBy` method can be used to invoke methods with default parameter values.
- `KFunction0`, `KFunction1`, and so on are functions with different numbers of parameters that can be called using the `invoke` method.
- `KProperty0` and `KProperty1` are properties with different numbers of receivers that support the `get` method for retrieving the value. `KMutableProperty0` and `KMutableProperty1` extend those interfaces to support changing property values through the `set` method.

DSL construction

This chapter covers
- Building domain-specific languages
- Using lambdas with receivers
- Applying the `invoke` convention
- Examples of existing Kotlin DSLs

In this chapter, we'll discuss how you can design expressive and idiomatic APIs for your Kotlin classes through the use of *domain-specific languages* (DSLs). We'll explore the differences between traditional and DSL-style APIs, and you'll see how DSL-style APIs can be applied to a wide variety of practical problems in areas as diverse as database access, HTML generation, testing, writing build scripts, defining Android UI layouts, and many others.

Kotlin DSL design relies on many language features, two of which we haven't yet fully explored. One of them you saw briefly in chapter 5: lambdas with receivers, which let you create a DSL structure by changing the name-resolution rules in code blocks. The other is new: the `invoke` convention, which enables more flexibility in combining lambdas and property assignments in DSL code. We'll study those features in detail in this chapter.

11.1 *From APIs to DSLs*

Before we dive into the discussion of DSLs, let's get a better understanding of the problem we're trying to solve. Ultimately, the goal is to achieve the best possible code readability and maintainability. To reach that goal, it's not enough to focus on individual classes. Most of the code in a class interacts with other classes, so we need to look at the interfaces through which these interactions happen—in other words, the APIs of the classes.

It's important to remember that the challenge of building good APIs isn't reserved to library authors; rather, it's something every developer has to do. Just as a library provides a programming interface for using it, every class in an application provides possibilities for other classes to interact with it. Ensuring that those interactions are easy to understand and can be expressed clearly is essential for keeping a project maintainable.

Over the course of this book, you've seen many examples of Kotlin features that allow you to build *clean APIs* for classes. What do we mean when we say an API is clean? Two things:

- It needs to be clear to readers what's going on in the code. This can be achieved with a good choice of names and concepts, which is important in any language.
- The code needs to look clean, with minimal ceremony and no unnecessary syntax. Achieving this is the main focus of this chapter. A clean API can even be indistinguishable from a built-in feature of a language.

Examples of Kotlin features that enable you to build clean APIs include extension functions, infix calls, lambda syntax shortcuts, and operator overloading. Table 11.1 shows how these features help reduce the amount of syntactic noise in the code.

Table 11.1 Kotlin support for clean syntax

Regular syntax	Clean syntax	Feature in use
`StringUtil.capitalize(s)`	`s.capitalize()`	Extension function
`1.to("one")`	`1 to "one"`	Infix call
`set.add(2)`	`set += 2`	Operator overloading
`map.get("key")`	`map["key"]`	Convention for the `get` method
`file.use({ f -> f.read() } )`	`file.use { it.read() }`	Lambda outside of parentheses

`sb.append("yes")`
`sb.append("no")`
	`with (sb) {`
	`    append("yes")`
	`    append("no")`
	`}`
		Lambda with a receiver

In this chapter, we'll take a step beyond clean APIs and look at Kotlin's support for constructing DSLs. Kotlin's DSLs build on the clean-syntax features and extend them with the ability to create *structure* out of multiple method calls. As a result, DSLs can be even more expressive and pleasant to work with than APIs constructed out of individual method calls.

Just like other features of the language, Kotlin DSLs are *fully statically typed*. This means all the advantages of static typing, such as compile-time error detection and better IDE support, remain in effect when you use DSL patterns for your APIs.

As a quick taste, here are a couple of examples that show what Kotlin DSLs can do. This expression goes back in time and returns the previous day (all right, just the previous date):

```
val yesterday = 1.days.ago
```

and this function generates an HTML table:

```
fun createSimpleTable() = createHTML().
    table {
        tr {
            td { +"cell" }
        }
    }
```

Over the course of the chapter, you'll learn how these examples are constructed. But before we begin a detailed discussion, let's look at what DSLs are.

11.1.1   *The concept of domain-specific languages*

The general idea of a DSL has existed for almost as long as the idea of a programming language. We make a distinction between a *general-purpose programming language*, with a set of capabilities complete enough to solve essentially any problem that can be solved with a computer; and a *domain-specific language*, which focuses on a specific task, or *domain*, and forgoes the functionality that's irrelevant for that domain.

The most common DSLs that you're no doubt familiar with are SQL and regular expressions. They're great for solving the specific tasks of manipulating databases and text strings, respectively, but you can't use them to develop an entire application. (At least, we hope you don't. The idea of an entire application built in the regular-expression language makes us shudder.)

Note how these languages can effectively accomplish their goal by reducing the set of functionality they offer. When you need to execute an SQL statement, you don't start by declaring a class or a function. Instead, the first keyword in every SQL statement indicates the type of operation you need to perform, and each type of operation has its own distinct syntax and set of keywords specific to the task at hand. With the regular-expression language, there's even less syntax: the program directly describes the text to be matched, using compact punctuation syntax to specify how the text can vary. Through such a compact syntax, a DSL can express a domain-specific operation much more concisely than an equivalent piece of code in a general-purpose language.

Another important point is that DSLs tend to be declarative, as opposed to general-purpose languages, most of which are imperative. Whereas an *imperative language* describes the exact sequence of steps required to perform an operation, a *declarative language* describes the desired result and leaves the execution details to the engine that interprets it. This often makes the execution more efficient, because the necessary optimizations are implemented only once in the execution engine; on the other hand, an imperative approach requires every implementation of the operation to be optimized independently.

As a counterweight to all of those benefits, DSLs of this type have one disadvantage: it can be difficult to combine them with a host application in a general-purpose language. They have their own syntax that can't be directly embedded into programs in a different language. Therefore, to invoke a program written in a DSL, you need to either store it in a separate file or embed it in a string literal. That makes it non-trivial to validate the correct interaction of the DSL with the host language at compile time, to debug the DSL program, and to provide IDE code assistance when writing it. Also, the separate syntax requires separate learning and often makes code harder to read.

To solve that issue while preserving most of the other benefits of DSLs, the concept of *internal DSLs* has recently gained popularity. Let's see what this is about.

11.1.2 *Internal DSLs*

As opposed to *external DSLs*, which have their own independent syntax, *internal DSLs* are part of programs written in a general-purpose language, using exactly the same syntax. In effect, an internal DSL isn't a fully separate language, but rather a particular way of using the main language while retaining the key advantages of DSLs with an independent syntax.

To compare the two approaches, let's see how the same task can be accomplished with an external and an internal DSL. Imagine that you have two database tables, `Customer` and `Country`, and each `Customer` entry has a reference to the country the customer lives in. The task is to query the database and find the country where the majority of customers live. The external DSL you're going to use is SQL; the internal one is provided by the Exposed framework (https://github.com/JetBrains/Exposed), which is a Kotlin framework for database access. Here's how you do this with SQL:

```
SELECT Country.name, COUNT(Customer.id)
    FROM Country
    JOIN Customer
      ON Country.id = Customer.country_id
GROUP BY Country.name
ORDER BY COUNT(Customer.id) DESC
    LIMIT 1
```

Writing the code in SQL directly may not be convenient: you have to provide a means for interaction between your main application language (Kotlin in this case) and the query language. Usually, the best you can do is put the SQL into a string literal and hope that your IDE will help you write and verify it.

As a comparison, here's the same query built with Kotlin and Exposed:

```
(Country join Customer)
    .slice(Country.name, Count(Customer.id))
    .selectAll()
    .groupBy(Country.name)
    .orderBy(Count(Customer.id), isAsc = false)
    .limit(1)
```

You can see the similarity between the two versions. In fact, executing the second version generates and runs exactly the same SQL query as the one written manually. But the second version is regular Kotlin code, and `selectAll`, `groupBy`, `orderBy`, and others are regular Kotlin methods. Moreover, you don't need to spend any effort on converting data from SQL query result sets to Kotlin objects—the query-execution results are delivered directly as native Kotlin objects. Thus we call this an internal DSL: the code intended to accomplish a specific task (building SQL queries) is implemented as a library in a general-purpose language (Kotlin).

11.1.3   *Structure of DSLs*

Generally speaking, there's no well-defined boundary between a DSL and a regular API; often the criterion is as subjective as "I know it's a DSL when I see it." DSLs often rely on language features that are broadly used in other contexts too, such as infix calls and operator overloading. But one trait comes up often in DSLs and usually doesn't exist in other APIs: *structure*, or *grammar*.

A typical library consists of many methods, and the client uses the library by calling the methods one by one. There's no inherent structure in the sequence of calls, and no context is maintained between one call and the next. Such an API is sometimes called a *command-query API*. As a contrast, the method calls in a DSL exist in a larger structure, defined by the *grammar* of the DSL. In a Kotlin DSL, structure is most commonly created through the nesting of lambdas or through chained method calls. You can clearly see this in the previous SQL example: executing a query requires a combination of method calls describing the different aspects of the required result set, and the combined query is much easier to read than a single method call taking all the arguments you're passing to the query.

This grammar is what allows us to call an internal DSL a *language*. In a natural language such as English, sentences are constructed out of words, and the rules of grammar govern how those words can be combined with one another. Similarly, in a DSL, a single operation can be composed out of multiple function calls, and the type checker ensures that the calls are combined in a meaningful way. In effect, the function names usually act as verbs (`groupBy`, `orderBy`), and their arguments fulfill the role of nouns (`Country.name`).

One benefit of the DSL structure is that it allows you to reuse the same context between multiple function calls, rather than repeat it in every call. This is illustrated by the following example, showing the Kotlin DSL for describing dependencies in Gradle build scripts (https://github.com/gradle/gradle-script-kotlin):

```
dependencies {
    compile("junit:junit:4.11")                    Structure through
    compile("com.google.inject:guice:4.1.0")       lambda nesting
}
```

In contrast, here's the same operation performed through a regular command-query API. Note that there's much more repetition in the code:

```
project.dependencies.add("compile", "junit:junit:4.11")
project.dependencies.add("compile", "com.google.inject:guice:4.1.0")
```

Chained method calls are another way to create structure in DSLs. For example, they're commonly used in test frameworks to split an assertion into multiple method calls. Such assertions can be much easier to read, especially if you can apply the infix call syntax. The following example comes from kotlintest (https://github.com/kotlintest/kotlintest), a third-party test framework for Kotlin that we'll discuss in more detail in section 11.4.1:

```
                                       Structure through
str should startWith("kot")            chained method calls
```

Note how the same example expressed through regular JUnit APIs is noisier and not as readable:

```
assertTrue(str.startsWith("kot"))
```

Now let's look at an example of an internal DSL in more detail.

11.1.4 *Building HTML with an internal DSL*

One of the teasers at the beginning of this chapter was a DSL for building HTML pages. In this section, we'll discuss it in more detail. The API used here comes from the kotlinx.html library (https://github.com/Kotlin/kotlinx.html). Here's a small snippet that creates a table with a single cell:

```
fun createSimpleTable() = createHTML().
    table {
        tr {
            td { +"cell" }
        }
    }
```

It's clear what HTML corresponds to the previous structure:

```
<table>
  <tr>
    <td>cell</td>
  </tr>
</table>
```

The createSimpleTable function returns a string containing this HTML fragment.

Why would you want to build this HTML with Kotlin code, rather than write it as text? First, the Kotlin version is type-safe: you can use the td tag only in tr; otherwise, this code won't compile. What's more important is that it's regular code, and you can use any language construct in it. That means you can generate table cells dynamically (for instance, corresponding to elements in a map) in the same place when you define a table:

```
fun createAnotherTable() = createHTML().table {
    val numbers = mapOf(1 to "one", 2 to "two")
    for ((num, string) in numbers) {
        tr {
            td { +"$num" }
            td { +string }
        }
    }
}
```

The generated HTML contains the desired data:

```
<table>
  <tr>
    <td>1</td>
    <td>one</td>
  </tr>
  <tr>
    <td>2</td>
    <td>two</td>
  </tr>
</table>
```

HTML is a canonical example of a markup language, which makes it perfect for illustrating the concept; but you can use the same approach for any languages with a similar structure, such as XML. Shortly we'll discuss how such code works in Kotlin.

Now that you know what a DSL is and why you might want to build one, let's see how Kotlin helps you do that. First we'll take a more in-depth look at *lambdas with receivers*: the key feature that helps establish the grammar of DSLs.

11.2 *Building structured APIs: lambdas with receivers in DSLs*

Lambdas with receivers are a powerful Kotlin feature that allows you to build APIs with a structure. As we already discussed, having structure is one of the key traits distinguishing DSLs from regular APIs. Let's examine this feature in detail and look at some DSLs that use it.

11.2.1 *Lambdas with receivers and extension function types*

You had a brief encounter with the idea of lambdas with receivers in section 5.5, where we introduced the buildString, with, and apply standard library functions. Now let's look at how they're implemented, using the buildString function as an example. This function allows you to construct a string from several pieces of content added to an intermediate `StringBuilder`.

To begin the discussion, let's define the `buildString` function so that it takes a regular lambda as an argument. You saw how to do this in chapter 8, so this should be familiar material.

Listing 11.1 Defining `buildString()` that takes a lambda as an argument

```
fun buildString(
        builderAction: (StringBuilder) -> Unit          ◁──┐ Declares a parameter
): String {                                                 │ of a function type
    val sb = StringBuilder()
    builderAction(sb)                        ◁──┐ Passes a StringBuilder as an
    return sb.toString()                        │ argument to the lambda
}

>>> val s = buildString {
...     it.append("Hello, ")          ◁──┐ Uses "it" to refer to the
...     it.append("World!")              │ StringBuilder instance
... }
>>> println(s)
Hello, World!
```

This code is easy to understand, but it looks less easy to use than we'd prefer. Note that you have to use `it` in the body of the lambda to refer to the `StringBuilder` instance (you could define your own parameter name instead of `it`, but it still has to be explicit). The main purpose of the lambda is to fill the `StringBuilder` with text, so you want to get rid of the repeated `it.` prefixes and invoke the `StringBuilder` methods directly, replacing `it.append` with `append`.

To do so, you need to convert the lambda into a *lambda with a receiver*. In effect, you can give one of the parameters of the lambda the special status of a *receiver*, letting you refer to its members directly without any qualifier. The following listing shows how you do that.

Listing 11.2 Redefining `buildString()` to take a lambda with a receiver

```
fun buildString(
        builderAction: StringBuilder.() -> Unit        ◁──┐ Declares a parameter of a
) : String {                                               │ function type with a receiver
    val sb = StringBuilder()
    sb.builderAction()               ◁──┐ Passes a StringBuilder as
    return sb.toString()                │ a receiver to the lambda
}

>>> val s = buildString {                          ┌─ The "this" keyword refers to
...     this.append("Hello, ")        ◁────────────┘  the StringBuilder instance.
...     append("World!")         ◁──┐ Alternatively, you can omit
... }                               │ "this" and refer to
>>> println(s)                        StringBuilder implicitly.
Hello, World!
```

Pay attention to the differences between listing 11.1 and listing 11.2. First, consider how the way you use `buildString` has improved. Now you pass a lambda with a receiver as an argument, so you can get rid of `it` in the body of the lambda. You replace the calls to `it.append()` with `append()`. The full form is `this.append()`, but as with regular members of a class, an explicit `this` is normally used only for disambiguation.

Next, let's discuss how the declaration of the `buildString` function has changed. You use an *extension function type* instead of a regular function type to declare the parameter type. When you declare an extension function type, you effectively pull one of the function type parameters out of the parentheses and put it in front, separated from the rest of the types with a dot. In listing 11.2, you replace `(StringBuilder) -> Unit` with `StringBuilder.() -> Unit`. This special type is called the *receiver type*, and the value of that type passed to the lambda becomes the *receiver object*. Figure 11.1 shows a more complex extension function type declaration.

Receiver type   **Parameter types**   **Return type**

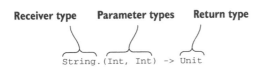

Figure 11.1   An extension function type with receiver type `String` and two parameters of type `Int`, returning `Unit`

Why an *extension* function type? The idea of accessing members of an external type without an explicit qualifier may remind you of extension functions, which allow you to define your own methods for classes defined elsewhere in the code. Both extension functions and lambdas with receivers have a *receiver object*, which has to be provided when the function is called and is available in its body. In effect, an extension function type describes a block of code that can be called as an extension function.

The way you invoke the variable also changes when you convert it from a regular function type to an extension function type. Instead of passing the object as an argument, you invoke the lambda variable as if it were an extension function. When you have a regular lambda, you pass a `StringBuilder` instance as an argument to it using the following syntax: `builderAction(sb)`. When you change it to a lambda with a receiver, the code becomes `sb.builderAction()`. To reiterate, `builderAction` here isn't a method declared on the `StringBuilder` class; it's a parameter of a function type that you call using the same syntax you use to call extension functions.

Figure 11.2 shows the correspondence between an argument and a parameter of the `buildString` function. It also illustrates the receiver on which the lambda body will be called.

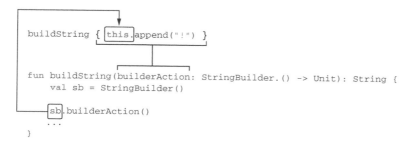

Figure 11.2 The argument of the `buildString` **function (lambda with a receiver) corresponds to the parameter of the extension function type (**`builderAction`**). The receiver (**`sb`**) becomes an implicit receiver (**`this`**) when the lambda body is invoked.**

You can also declare a variable of an extension function type, as shown in the following listing. Once you do that, you can either invoke it as an extension function or pass it as an argument to a function that expects a lambda with a receiver.

Listing 11.3 Storing a lambda with a receiver in a variable

```
val appendExcl : StringBuilder.() -> Unit =
        { this.append("!") }                          ◁──┐ appendExcl is a value of an
                                                          extension function type.

>>> val stringBuilder = StringBuilder("Hi")
>>> stringBuilder.appendExcl()
>>> println(stringBuilder)                    ◁──┐ You can call appendExcl
Hi!                                               as an extension function.

>>> println(buildString(appendExcl))          ◁──┐ You can also pass appendExcl
!                                                 as an argument.
```

Note that a lambda with a receiver looks exactly the same as a regular lambda in the source code. To see whether a lambda has a receiver, you need to look at the function to which the lambda is passed: its signature will tell you whether the lambda has a receiver and, if it does, what its type is. For example, you can look at the declaration of `buildString` or look up its documentation in your IDE, see that it takes a lambda of type `StringBuilder.() -> Unit`, and conclude from this that in the body of the lambda, you can invoke `StringBuilder` methods without a qualifier.

The implementation of `buildString` in the standard library is shorter than in listing 11.2. Instead of calling `builderAction` explicitly, it is passed as an argument to the `apply` function (which you saw in section 5.5). This allows you to collapse the function into a single line:

```
fun buildString(builderAction: StringBuilder.() -> Unit): String =
        StringBuilder().apply(builderAction).toString()
```

The `apply` function effectively takes the object on which it was called (in this case, a new `StringBuilder` instance) and uses it as an implicit receiver to call the function or lambda specified as argument (`builderAction` in the example). You've also seen another useful library function previously: `with`. Let's study their implementations:

```
inline fun <T> T.apply(block: T.() -> Unit): T {
    block()                              ⟵  Equivalent to this.block(); invokes
    return this                              the lambda with the receiver of
}                                            "apply" as the receiver object

inline fun <T, R> with(receiver: T, block: T.() -> R): R =
    receiver.block()                     ⟵  Returns the result of
                                             calling the lambda
```

Returns the receiver ⟶ *(annotation pointing to `return this`)*

Basically, all `apply` and `with` do is invoke the argument of an extension function type on the provided receiver. The `apply` function is declared as an extension to that receiver, whereas `with` takes it as a first argument. Also, `apply` returns the receiver itself, but `with` returns the result of calling the lambda.

If you don't care about the result, these functions are interchangeable:

```
>>> val map = mutableMapOf(1 to "one")
>>> map.apply { this[2] = "two"}
>>> with (map) { this[3] = "three" }
>>> println(map)
{1=one, 2=two, 3=three}
```

The `with` and `apply` functions are used frequently in Kotlin, and we hope you've already appreciated their conciseness in your own code.

We've reviewed lambdas with receivers and talked about extension function types. Now it's time to see how these concepts are used in the DSL context.

11.2.2 *Using lambdas with receivers in HTML builders*

A Kotlin DSL for HTML is usually called an *HTML builder,* and it represents a more general concept of *type-safe builders*. Initially, the concept of builders gained popularity in the Groovy community (www.groovy-lang.org/dsls.html#_builders). Builders provide a way to create an object hierarchy in a declarative way, which is convenient for generating XML or laying out UI components.

Kotlin uses the same idea, but in Kotlin builders are type-safe. That makes them more convenient to use, safe, and in a sense more attractive than Groovy's dynamic builders. Let's look in detail at how HTML builders work in Kotlin.

> **Listing 11.4 Producing a simple HTML table with a Kotlin HTML builder**

```
fun createSimpleTable() = createHTML().
    table {
        tr {
            td { +"cell" }
        }
    }
```

This is regular Kotlin code, not a special template language or anything like that: `table`, `tr`, and `td` are just functions. Each of them is a higher-order function, taking a lambda with a receiver as an argument.

The remarkable thing here is that those lambdas *change the name-resolution rules.* In the lambda passed to the `table` function, you can use the `tr` function to create the `<tr>` HTML tag. Outside of that lambda, the `tr` function would be unresolved. In the same way, the `td` function is only accessible in `tr`. (Note how the design of the API forces you to follow the grammar of the HTML language.)

The name-resolution context in each block is defined by the receiver type of each lambda. The lambda passed to `table` has a receiver of a special type `TABLE`, which defines the `tr` method. Similarly, the `tr` function expects an extension lambda to `TR`. The following listing is a greatly simplified view of the declarations of these classes and methods.

Listing 11.5 Declaring tag classes for the HTML builder

```
open class Tag

class TABLE : Tag {
    fun tr(init : TR.() -> Unit)          The tr function expects a lambda
}                                         with a receiver of type TR.
class TR : Tag {
    fun td(init : TD.() -> Unit)          The td function expects a lambda
}                                         with a receiver of type TD.
class TD : Tag
```

`TABLE`, `TR`, and `TD` are utility classes that shouldn't appear explicitly in the code, and that's why they're named in capital letters. They all extend the `Tag` superclass. Each class defines methods for creating tags allowed in it: the `TABLE` class defines the `tr` method, among others, whereas the `TR` class defines the `td` method.

Note the types of the `init` parameters of the `tr` and `td` functions: they're extension function types `TR.() -> Unit` and `TD.() -> Unit`. They determine the types of receivers in the argument lambdas: `TR` and `TD`, respectively.

To make it clearer what happens here, you can rewrite listing 11.4, making all receivers explicit. As a reminder, you can access the receiver of the lambda that's the argument of the `foo` function as `this@foo`.

Listing 11.6 Making receivers of HTML builder calls explicit

```
fun createSimpleTable() = createHTML().
    table {                               this@table has
        (this@table).tr {                 type TABLE.
            (this@tr).td {
                +"cell"                   The implicit receiver this@td
            }                             of type TD is available here.
        }
    }
}
```

this@tr has type TR.

If you tried to use regular lambdas instead of lambdas with receivers for builders, the syntax would become as unreadable as in this example: you'd have to use the `it` reference to invoke the tag-creation methods or assign a new parameter name for every lambda. Being able to make the receiver implicit and hide the `this` reference makes the syntax of builders nice and similar to the original HTML.

Note that if one lambda with a receiver is placed in the other one, as in listing 11.6, the receiver defined in the outer lambda remains available in the nested lambda. For instance, in the lambda that's the argument of the `td` function, all three receivers (`this@table`, `this@tr`, `this@td`) are available. But starting from Kotlin 1.1, you'll be able to use the `@DslMarker` annotation to constrain the availability of outer receivers in lambdas.

We've explained how the syntax of HTML builders is based on the concept of lambdas with receivers. Next, let's discuss how the desired HTML is generated.

Listing 11.6 uses functions defined in the kotlinx.html library. Now you'll implement a much simpler version of an HTML builder library: you'll extend the declarations of the `TABLE`, `TR`, and `TD` tags and add support for generating the resulting HTML. As the entry point for this simplified version, a top-level `table` function creates a fragment of HTML with `<table>` as a top tag.

Listing 11.7   Generating HTML to a string

```
fun createTable() =
    table {
        tr {
            td {
            }
        }
    }

>>> println(createTable())
<table><tr><td></td></tr></table>
```

The `table` function creates a new instance of the `TABLE` tag, initializes it (calls the function passed as the `init` parameter on it), and returns it:

```
fun table(init: TABLE.() -> Unit) = TABLE().apply(init)
```

In `createTable`, the lambda passed as an argument to the `table` function contains the invocation of the `tr` function. The call can be rewritten to make everything as explicit as possible: `table(init = { this.tr { … } })`. The `tr` function will be called on the created `TABLE` instance, as if you'd written `TABLE().tr { … }`.

In this toy example, `<table>` is a top-level tag, and other tags are nested into it. Each tag stores a list of references to its children. Therefore, the `tr` function should not only initialize the new instance of the `TR` tag but also add it to the list of children of the outer tag.

Listing 11.8   Defining a tag builder function

```
fun tr(init: TR.() -> Unit) {
    val tr = TR()
    tr.init()
    children.add(tr)
}
```

This logic of initializing a given tag and adding it to the children of the outer tag is common for all tags, so you can extract it as a `doInit` member of the `Tag` superclass. The `doInit` function is responsible for two things: storing the reference to the child tag and calling the lambda passed as an argument. The different tags then just call it: for instance, the `tr` function creates a new instance of the `TR` class and then passes it to the `doInit` function along with the `init` lambda argument: `doInit(TR(), init)`. The following listing is the full example that shows how the desired HTML is generated.

Listing 11.9   A full implementation of a simple HTML builder

```
open class Tag(val name: String) {
    private val children = mutableListOf<Tag>()        ←── Stores all nested tags

    protected fun <T : Tag> doInit(child: T, init: T.() -> Unit) {
        child.init()            ←── Initializes the child tag
        children.add(child)     ←── Stores a reference to the child tag
    }

    override fun toString() =
        "<$name>${children.joinToString("")}</$name>"   ←── Returns the resulting HTML as String
}

fun table(init: TABLE.() -> Unit) = TABLE().apply(init)

class TABLE : Tag("table") {
    fun tr(init: TR.() -> Unit) = doInit(TR(), init)      ←── Creates, initializes, and adds to the children of TABLE a new instance of the TR tag
}
class TR : Tag("tr") {
    fun td(init: TD.() -> Unit) = doInit(TD(), init)      ←── Adds a new instance of the TD tag to the children of TR
}
class TD : Tag("td")

fun createTable() =
    table {
        tr {
            td {
            }
        }
    }
>>> println(createTable())
<table><tr><td></td></tr></table>
```

Every tag stores a list of nested tags and renders itself accordingly: it renders its name and all the nested tags recursively. Text inside tags and tag attributes aren't supported here; for the full implementation, you can browse the aforementioned kotlinx.html library.

Note that tag-creation functions add the corresponding tag to the parent's list of children on their own. That lets you generate tags dynamically.

Listing 11.10   Generating tags dynamically with an HTML builder

```
fun createAnotherTable() = table {
    for (i in 1..2) {
        tr {
            td {
            }
        }
    }
}
>>> println(createAnotherTable())
<table><tr><td></td></tr><tr><td></td></tr></table>
```

> Each call to "tr" creates a new TR tag and adds it to the children of TABLE.

As you've seen, lambdas with receivers are a great tool for building DSLs. Because you can change the name-resolution context in a code block, they let you create *structure* in your API, which is one of the key traits that distinguishes DSLs from flat sequences of method calls. Now let's discuss the benefits of integrating this DSL into a statically typed programming language.

11.2.3   *Kotlin builders: enabling abstraction and reuse*

When you write regular code in a program, you have a lot of tools to avoid duplication and to make the code look nicer. Among other things, you can extract repetitive code into new functions and give them self-explanatory names. That may not be as easy or even possible with SQL or HTML. But using internal DSLs in Kotlin to accomplish the same tasks gives you a way to abstract repeated chunks of code into new functions and reuse them.

Let's look at an example from the Bootstrap library (http://getbootstrap.com), a popular HTML, CSS, and JS framework for developing responsive, mobile-first projects on the web. We'll consider a specific example: adding drop-down lists to an application. To add such a list directly to an HTML page, you can copy the necessary snippet and paste it in the required place, under the button or other element that shows the list. You only need to add the necessary references and their titles for the drop-down menu. The initial HTML code (a bit simplified to avoid too many style attributes) looks like this.

Listing 11.11   Building a drop-down menu in HTML using Bootstrap

```
<div class="dropdown">
  <button class="btn dropdown-toggle">
    Dropdown
```

```
      <span class="caret"></span>
    </button>
    <ul class="dropdown-menu">
      <li><a href="#">Action</a></li>
      <li><a href="#">Another action</a></li>
      <li role="separator" class="divider"></li>
      <li class="dropdown-header">Header</li>
      <li><a href="#">Separated link</a></li>
    </ul>
</div>
```

In Kotlin with kotlinx.html, you can use the functions div, button, ul, li, and so on to replicate the same structure.

Listing 11.12   Building a drop-down menu using a Kotlin HTML builder

```
fun buildDropdown() = createHTML().div(classes = "dropdown") {
    button(classes = "btn dropdown-toggle") {
        +"Dropdown"
        span(classes = "caret")
    }
    ul(classes = "dropdown-menu") {
        li { a("#") { +"Action" } }
        li { a("#") { +"Another action" } }
        li { role = "separator"; classes = setOf("divider") }
        li { classes = setOf("dropdown-header"); +"Header" }
        li { a("#") { +"Separated link" } }
    }
}
```

But you can do better. Because div, button, and so on are regular functions, you can extract the repetitive logic into separate functions, improving the readability of the code. The result may look as follows.

Listing 11.13   Building a drop-down menu with helper functions

```
fun dropdownExample() = createHTML().dropdown {
    dropdownButton { +"Dropdown" }
    dropdownMenu {
        item("#", "Action")
        item("#", "Another action")
        divider()
        dropdownHeader("Header")
        item("#", "Separated link")
    }
}
```

Now the unnecessary details are hidden, and the code looks much nicer. Let's discuss how this trick is implemented, starting with the item function. This function has two parameters: the reference and the name of the corresponding menu item. The function code should add a new list item: li { a(href) { +name } }. The only question that remains is, how can you call `li` in the body of the function? Should it be an extension? You can indeed make it an extension to the `UL` class, because the `li` function is itself an extension to `UL`. In listing 11.13, `item` is called on an implicit `this` of type `UL`:

```
fun UL.item(href: String, name: String) = li { a(href) { +name } }
```

After you define the `item` function, you can call it in any `UL` tag, and it will add an instance of a `LI` tag. Having extracted `item`, you can change the original version to the following without changing the generated HTML code.

Listing 11.14 Using the `item` function for drop-down menu construction

```
ul {
    classes = setOf("dropdown-menu")
    item("#", "Action")                                     ◁── You can use the "item"
    item("#", "Another action")                                  function instead of "li" here.
    li { role = "separator"; classes = setOf("divider") }
    li { classes = setOf("dropdown-header"); +"Header" }
    item("#", "Separated link")
}
```

The other extension functions defined on `UL` are added in a similar way, allowing you to replace the remaining `li` tags.

```
fun UL.divider() = li { role = "separator"; classes = setOf("divider") }

fun UL.dropdownHeader(text: String) =
    li { classes = setOf("dropdown-header"); +text }
```

Now let's see how the `dropdownMenu` function is implemented. It creates a `ul` tag with the specified `dropdown-menu` class and takes a lambda with a receiver as an argument that's used to fill the tag with content.

```
dropdownMenu {
    item("#", "Action")
    ...
}
```

You replace the `ul { ... }` block with the invocation of `dropdownMenu { ... }`, so the receiver in the lambda can stay the same. The `dropdownMenu` function can take an extension lambda to `UL` as an argument, which allows you to call functions such as `UL.item` as you did before. Here's how the function is declared:

```
fun DIV.dropdownMenu(block: UL.() -> Unit) = ul("dropdown-menu", block)
```

The `dropdownButton` function is implemented in a similar way. We omit it here, but you can find the full implementation in the samples for the kotlinx.html library.

Last, let's look at the `dropdown` function. This one is less trivial, because it can be called on any tag: the drop-down menu can be put anywhere in the code.

Listing 11.15   The top-level function for building a drop-down menu

```
fun StringBuilder.dropdown(
        block: DIV.() -> Unit
): String = div("dropdown", block)
```

This is a simplified version that you can use if you want to print your HTML to a string. The full implementation in kotlinx.html uses an abstract TagConsumer class as the receiver and thus supports different destinations for the resulting HTML.

This example illustrates how the means of abstraction and reuse can help improve your code and make it easier to understand. Now let's look at one more tool that can help you support more flexible structures in your DSLs: the invoke convention.

11.3   *More flexible block nesting with the "invoke" convention*

The invoke convention allows you to call objects of custom types as functions. You've already seen that objects of function types can be called as functions; with the invoke convention, you can define your own objects that support the same syntax.

Note that this isn't a feature for everyday use, because it can be used to write hard-to-understand code, such as 1(). But it's sometimes very useful in DSLs. We'll show you why, but first let's discuss the convention itself.

11.3.1   *The "invoke" convention: objects callable as functions*

In chapter 7, we discussed in detail Kotlin's concept of *conventions*: specially named functions that are called not through the regular method-call syntax but using different, more concise notations. As a reminder, one of the conventions we discussed was get, which allows you to access an object using the index operator. For a variable foo of type Foo, a call to foo[bar] is translated into foo.get(bar), provided the corresponding get function is defined as a member in the Foo class or as an extension function to Foo.

In effect, the invoke convention does the same thing, except that the brackets are replaced with parentheses. A class for which the invoke method with an operator modifier is defined can be called as a function. Here's an example of how this works.

Listing 11.16   Defining an `invoke` method in a class

```
class Greeter(val greeting: String) {
    operator fun invoke(name: String) {          ◁──┐  Defines the "invoke"
        println("$greeting, $name!")                 │  method on Greeter
    }
}

>>> val bavarianGreeter = Greeter("Servus")
>>> bavarianGreeter("Dmitry")                    ◁──┐  Calls the Greeter instance
Servus, Dmitry!                                      │  as a function
```

This code defines the `invoke` method in `Greeter`, which allows you to call instances of `Greeter` as if they were functions. Under the hood, the expression `bavarianGreeter("Dmitry")` is compiled to the method call `bavarianGreeter.invoke("Dmitry")`. There's no mystery here. It works like a regular convention: it provides a way to replace a verbose expression with a more concise, clearer one.

The `invoke` method isn't restricted to any specific signature. You can define it with any number of parameters and with any return type, or even define multiple overloads of `invoke` with different parameter types. When you call the instance of the class as a function, you can use all of those signatures for the call. Let's look at the practical situations where this convention is used, first in a regular programming context and then in a DSL.

11.3.2 The "invoke" convention and functional types

You may remember seeing `invoke` earlier in the book. In section 8.1.2 we discussed that you can call a variable of a nullable function type as `lambda?.invoke()`, using the safe-call syntax with the `invoke` method name.

Now that you know about the `invoke` convention, it should be clear that the way you normally invoke a lambda (by putting parentheses after it: `lambda()`) is nothing but an application of this convention. Lambdas, unless inlined, are compiled into classes that implement functional interfaces (`Function1` and so on), and those interfaces define the `invoke` method with the corresponding number of parameters:

```
interface Function2<in P1, in P2, out R> {
    operator fun invoke(p1: P1, p2: P2): R
}
```

This interface denotes a function that takes exactly two arguments.

When you invoke a lambda as a function, the operation is translated into a call of the `invoke` method, thanks to the convention. Why might that be useful to know? It gives you a way to split the code of a complex lambda into multiple methods while still allowing you to use it together with functions that take parameters of a function type. To do so, you can define a class that implements a function type interface. You can specify the base interface either as an explicit `FunctionN` type or, as shown in the following listing, using the shorthand syntax: `(P1, P2) -> R`. This example uses such a class to filter a list of issues by a complex condition.

Listing 11.17 Extending a function type and overriding `invoke()`

```
data class Issue(
    val id: String, val project: String, val type: String,
    val priority: String, val description: String
)

class ImportantIssuesPredicate(val project: String)
        : (Issue) -> Boolean {

    override fun invoke(issue: Issue): Boolean {
        return issue.project == project && issue.isImportant()
    }
```

Uses the function type as a base class

Implements the "invoke" method

```
    private fun Issue.isImportant(): Boolean {
        return type == "Bug" &&
                (priority == "Major" || priority == "Critical")
    }
}

>>> val i1 = Issue("IDEA-154446", "IDEA", "Bug", "Major",
...                 "Save settings failed")
>>> val i2 = Issue("KT-12183", "Kotlin", "Feature", "Normal",
... "Intention: convert several calls on the same receiver to with/apply")
>>> val predicate = ImportantIssuesPredicate("IDEA")
>>> for (issue in listOf(i1, i2).filter(predicate)) {        ◁──┐ Passes the predicate
...         println(issue.id)                                    │ to filter()
... }
IDEA-154446
```

Here the logic of the predicate is too complicated to put into a single lambda, so you split it into several methods to make the meaning of each check clear. Converting a lambda into a class that implements a function type interface and overriding the `invoke` method is one way to perform such a refactoring. The advantage of this approach is that the scope of methods you extract from the lambda body is as narrow as possible; they're only visible from the predicate class. This is valuable when there's a lot of logic both in the predicate class and in the surrounding code and it's worthwhile to separate the different concerns cleanly.

Now let's see how the `invoke` convention can help you create a more flexible structure for your DSLs.

11.3.3 The "invoke" convention in DSLs: declaring dependencies in Gradle

Let's go back to the example of the Gradle DSL for configuring the dependencies of a module. Here's the code we showed you earlier:

```
dependencies {
    compile("junit:junit:4.11")
}
```

You often want to be able to support both a nested block structure, as shown here, and a flat call structure in the same API. In other words, you want to allow both of the following:

```
dependencies.compile("junit:junit:4.11")

dependencies {
    compile("junit:junit:4.11")
}
```

With such a design, users of the DSL can use the nested block structure when there are multiple items to configure and the flat call structure to keep the code more concise when there's only one thing to configure.

The first case calls the `compile` method on the `dependencies` variable. You can express the second notation by defining the `invoke` method on `dependencies` so that it takes a lambda as an argument. The full syntax of this call is `dependencies` `.invoke({...})`.

The `dependencies` object is an instance of the `DependencyHandler` class, which defines both `compile` and `invoke` methods. The `invoke` method takes a lambda with a receiver as an argument, and the type of the receiver of this method is again `DependencyHandler`. What happens in the body of the lambda is already familiar: you have a `DependencyHandler` as a receiver and can call methods such as `compile` directly on it. The following minimal example shows how that part of `Dependency-Handler` is implemented.

Listing 11.18 Using `invoke` to support flexible DSL syntax

```
class DependencyHandler {
    fun compile(coordinate: String) {          ◄──┐ Defines a regular
        println("Added dependency on $coordinate")  │ command API
    }

    operator fun invoke(                       ┌── Defines "invoke" to
            body: DependencyHandler.() -> Unit) {  ◄──┘ support the DSL API
        body()                                 ◄──┐
    }                                             │ "this" becomes a receiver of
}                                                 │ the body function: this.body()
```

```
>>> val dependencies = DependencyHandler()

>>> dependencies.compile("org.jetbrains.kotlin:kotlin-stdlib:1.0.0")
Added dependency on org.jetbrains.kotlin:kotlin-stdlib:1.0.0

>>> dependencies {
...     compile("org.jetbrains.kotlin:kotlin-reflect:1.0.0")
>>> }
Added dependency on org.jetbrains.kotlin:kotlin-reflect:1.0.0
```

When you add the first dependency, you call the `compile` method directly. The second call is effectively translated to the following:

```
dependencies.invoke({
    this.compile("org.jetbrains.kotlin:kotlin-reflect:1.0.0")
})
```

In other words, you're invoking `dependencies` as a function and passing a lambda as an argument. The type of the lambda's parameter is a function type with a receiver, and the receiver type is the same `DependencyHandler` type. The `invoke` method calls the lambda. Because it's a method of the `DependencyHandler` class, an instance of that class is available as an implicit receiver, so you don't need to specify it explicitly when you call `body()`.

One fairly small piece of code, the redefined `invoke` method, has significantly increased the flexibility of the DSL API. This pattern is generic, and you can reuse it in your own DSLs with minimal modifications.

You're now familiar with two new features of Kotlin that can help you build DSLs: lambdas with receivers and the `invoke` convention. Let's look at how previously discussed Kotlin features come in play in the DSL context.

11.4 Kotlin DSLs in practice

By now, you're familiar with all the Kotlin features used when building DSLs. Some of them, such as extensions and infix calls, should be your old friends by now. Others, such as lambdas with receivers, were first discussed in detail in this chapter. Let's put all of this knowledge to use and investigate a series of practical DSL construction examples. We'll cover fairly diverse topics: testing, rich date literals, database queries, and Android UI construction.

11.4.1 Chaining infix calls: "should" in test frameworks

As we mentioned previously, clean syntax is one of the key traits of an internal DSL, and it can be achieved by reducing the amount of punctuation in the code. Most internal DSLs boil down to sequences of method calls, so any features that let you reduce syntactic noise in method calls find a lot of use there. In Kotlin, these features include the shorthand syntax for invoking lambdas, which we've discussed in detail, as well as *infix function calls*. We discussed infix calls in section 3.4.3; here we'll focus on their use in DSLs.

Let's look at an example that uses the DSL of kotlintest (https://github.com/kotlintest/kotlintest, the testing library inspired by Scalatest), which you saw earlier in this chapter.

Listing 11.19 Expressing an assertion with the kotlintest DSL

```
s should startWith("kot")
```

This call will fail with an assertion if the value of the s variable doesn't start with "kot". The code reads almost like English: "The s string should start with this constant." To accomplish this, you declare the `should` function with the `infix` modifier.

Listing 11.20 Implementing the should function

```
infix fun <T> T.should(matcher: Matcher<T>) = matcher.test(this)
```

The `should` function expects an instance of `Matcher`, a generic interface for performing assertions on values. `startWith` implements `Matcher` and checks whether a string starts with the given substring.

Listing 11.21 Defining a matcher for the kotlintest DSL

```
interface Matcher<T> {
    fun test(value: T)
}
```

```
class startWith(val prefix: String) : Matcher<String> {
    override fun test(value: String) {
        if (!value.startsWith(prefix))
            throw AssertionError("String $value does not start with $prefix")
    }
}
```

Note that in regular code, you'd capitalize the name of the `startWith` class, but DSLs often require you to deviate from standard naming conventions. Listing 11.21 shows that applying infix calls in the DSL context is simple and can reduce the amount of noise in your code. With a bit more cunning, you can reduce the noise even further. The kotlintest DSL supports that.

Listing 11.22 Chaining calls in the kotlintest DSL

```
"kotlin" should start with "kot"
```

At first glance, this doesn't look like Kotlin. To understand how it works, let's convert the infix calls to regular ones.

```
"kotlin".should(start).with("kot")
```

This shows that listing 11.22 was a sequence of two infix calls, and `start` was the argument of the first one. In fact, `start` refers to an object declaration, whereas `should` and `with` are functions called using the infix call notation.

The `should` function has a special overload that uses the `start` object as a parameter type and returns the intermediate wrapper on which you can then call the `with` method.

Listing 11.23 Defining the API to support chained infix calls

```
object start

infix fun String.should(x: start): StartWrapper = StartWrapper(this)

class StartWrapper(val value: String) {
    infix fun with(prefix: String) =
        if (!value.startsWith(prefix))
            throw AssertionError(
                "String does not start with $prefix: $value")
}
```

Note that, outside of the DSL context, using an `object` as a parameter type rarely makes sense, because it has only a single instance, and you can access that instance rather than pass it as an argument. Here, it does make sense: the `object` is used not to pass any data to the function, but as part of the grammar of the DSL. By passing `start` as an argument, you can choose the right overload of `should` and obtain a `StartWrapper` instance as the result. The `StartWrapper` class has the `with` member, taking as an argument the actual value that you need to perform the assertion.

The library supports other matchers as well, and they all read as English:

```
"kotlin" should end with "in"
"kotlin" should have substring "otl"
```

To support this, the should function has more overloads that take object instances like end and have and return EndWrapper and HaveWrapper instances, respectively.

This was a relatively tricky example of DSL construction, but the result is so nice that it's worth figuring out how this pattern works. The combination of infix calls and object instances lets you construct fairly complex grammars for your DSLs and use those DSLs with a clean syntax. And of course, the DSL remains fully statically typed. An incorrect combination of functions and objects won't compile.

11.4.2 *Defining extensions on primitive types: handling dates*

Now let's take a look at the remaining teaser from the beginning of this chapter:

```
val yesterday = 1.days.ago
val tomorrow = 1.days.fromNow
```

To implement this DSL using the Java 8 java.time API and Kotlin, you need just a few lines of code. Here's the relevant part of the implementation.

Listing 11.24 Defining a date manipulation DSL

```
val Int.days: Period
    get() = Period.ofDays(this)            ◁─┐ "this" refers to the value
                                             of the numeric constant.
val Period.ago: LocalDate
    get() = LocalDate.now() - this         ◁─┐ Invokes LocalDate.minus
                                             using operator syntax
val Period.fromNow: LocalDate
    get() = LocalDate.now() + this         ◁─┐ Invokes LocalDate.plus
                                             using operator syntax
>>> println(1.days.ago)
2016-08-16
>>> println(1.days.fromNow)
2016-08-18
```

Here, days is an extension property on the Int type. Kotlin has no restrictions on the types that can be used as receivers for extension functions: you can easily define extensions on primitive types and invoke them on constants. The days property returns a value of type Period, which is the JDK 8 type representing an interval between two dates.

To complete the sentence and support the ago word, you need to define another extension property, this time on the Period class. The type of that property is a LocalDate, representing a date. Note that the use of the - (minus) operator in the ago property implementation doesn't rely on any Kotlin-defined extensions. The LocalDate JDK class defines a method named minus with a single parameter that matches the Kotlin convention for the - operator, so Kotlin maps the operator to that method automatically. You can find the full implementation of the library, supporting all time units and not just days, in the kxdate library on GitHub (https://github.com/yole/kxdate).

Now that you understand how this simple DSL works, let's move on to something more challenging: the implementation of the database query DSL.

11.4.3 *Member extension functions: internal DSL for SQL*

You've seen the significant role played by extension functions in DSL design. In this section, we'll study a further trick that we've mentioned previously: declaring extension functions and extension properties in a class. Such a function or property is both a member of its containing class and an extension to some other type at the same time. We call such functions and properties *member extensions.*

Let's look at a couple of examples that use member extensions. They come from the internal DSL for SQL, the Exposed framework, mentioned earlier. Before we get to that, though, we need to discuss how Exposed allows you to define the database structure.

In order to work with SQL tables, the Exposed framework requires you to declare them as objects extending the `Table` class. Here's a declaration of a simple `Country` table with two columns.

Listing 11.25   Declaring a table in Exposed

```
object Country : Table() {
    val id = integer("id").autoIncrement().primaryKey()
    val name = varchar("name", 50)
}
```

This declaration corresponds to a table in the database. To create this table, you call the `SchemaUtils.create(Country)` method, and it generates the necessary SQL statement based on the declared table structure:

```
CREATE TABLE IF NOT EXISTS Country (
    id INT AUTO_INCREMENT NOT NULL,
    name VARCHAR(50) NOT NULL,
    CONSTRAINT pk_Country PRIMARY KEY (id)
)
```

As with generating HTML, you can see how declarations in the original Kotlin code become parts of the generated SQL statement.

If you examine the types of the properties in the `Country` object, you'll see that they have the `Column` type with the necessary type argument: `id` has the type `Column<Int>`, and `name` has the type `Column<String>`.

The `Table` class in the Exposed framework defines all types of columns that you can declare for your table, including the ones just used:

```
class Table {
    fun integer(name: String): Column<Int>
    fun varchar(name: String, length: Int): Column<String>
```

```
        // ...
}
```

The `integer` and `varchar` methods create new columns for storing integers and strings, respectively.

Now let's see how to specify properties for the columns. This is when member extensions come into play:

```
val id = integer("id").autoIncrement().primaryKey()
```

Methods like `autoIncrement` and `primaryKey` are used to specify the properties of each column. Each method can be called on `Column` and returns the instance it was called on, allowing you to chain the methods. Here are the simplified declarations of these functions:

```
class Table {
    fun <T> Column<T>.primaryKey(): Column<T>          ◁—┘ Sets this column as a
    fun Column<Int>.autoIncrement(): Column<Int>       ◁—┐ primary key in the table
    // ...                                                 Only integer values can
}                                                          be auto-incremented.
```

These functions are members of the `Table` class, which means you can't use them outside of the scope of this class. Now you know why it makes sense to declare methods as member extensions: you constrain their applicability scope. You can't specify the properties of a column outside the context of a table: the necessary methods won't resolve.

Another great feature of extension functions that you use here is the ability to restrict the receiver type. Although any column in a table can be its primary key, only numeric columns can be auto-incremented. You can express this in the API by declaring the `autoIncrement` method as an extension on `Column<Int>`. An attempt to mark a column of a different type as auto-incremented will fail to compile.

What's more, when you mark a column as `primaryKey`, this information is stored in the table containing the column. Having this function declared as a member of `Table` allows you to store the information in the table instance directly.

Member extensions are still members

Member extensions have a downside, as well: the lack of extensibility. They belong to the class, so you can't define new member extensions on the side.

For example, imagine that you wanted to add support for a new database to Exposed and that the database supported some new column attributes. To achieve this goal, you'd have to modify the definition of the `Table` class and add the member extension functions for new attributes there. You wouldn't be able to add the necessary declarations without touching the original class, as you can do with regular (nonmember) extensions, because the extensions wouldn't have access to the `Table` instance where they could store the definitions.

Let's look at another member extension function that can be found in a simple
SELECT query. Imagine that you've declared two tables, Customer and Country, and
each Customer entry stores a reference to the country the customer is from. The following code prints the names of all customers living in the USA.

```
val result = (Country join Customer)
    .select { Country.name eq "USA" }
result.forEach { println(it[Customer.name]) }
```

◁─── **Corresponds to this SQL code:**
WHERE Country.name = "USA"

The select method can be called on Table or on a join of two tables. Its argument is
a lambda that specifies the condition for selecting the necessary data.

Where does the eq method come from? We can say now that it's an infix function
taking "USA" as an argument, and you may correctly guess that it's another member
extension.

Here you again come across an extension function on Column that's also a member and thus can be used only in the appropriate context: for instance, when specifying the condition of the select method. The simplified declarations of the select
and eq methods are as follows:

```
fun Table.select(where: SqlExpressionBuilder.() -> Op<Boolean>) : Query

object SqlExpressionBuilder {
    infix fun<T> Column<T>.eq(t: T) : Op<Boolean>
    // ...
}
```

The SqlExpressionBuilder object defines many ways to express conditions: compare values, check for being not null, perform arithmetic operations, and so on.
You'll never refer to it explicitly in the code, but you'll regularly call its methods when
it's an implicit receiver. The select function takes a lambda with a receiver as an
argument, and the SqlExpressionBuilder object is an implicit receiver in this
lambda. That allows you to use in the body of the lambda all the possible extension
functions defined in this object, such as eq.

You've seen two types of extensions on columns: those that should be used to
declare a Table, and those used to compare the values in a condition. Without member extensions, you'd have to declare all of these functions as extensions or members
of Column, which would let you use them in any context. The approach with member
extensions gives you a way to control that.

NOTE In section 7.5.6, we looked at some code that worked with Exposed
while talking about using delegated properties in frameworks. Delegated
properties often come up in DSLs, and the Exposed framework illustrates that
well. We won't repeat the discussion of delegated properties here, because

we've covered them in detail. But if you're eager to create a DSL for your own needs or improve your API and make it cleaner, keep this feature in mind.

11.4.4 *Anko: creating Android UIs dynamically*

While talking about lambdas with receivers, we mentioned that they're great for laying out UI components. Let's look at how the Anko library (https://github.com/Kotlin/anko) can help you build a UI for Android applications.

First let's see how Anko wraps familiar Android APIs into a DSL-like structure. The following listing defines an alert dialog that shows a somewhat bothersome message and two options (to proceed further or to stop the operation).

Listing 11.27   Using Anko to show an Android alert dialog

```
fun Activity.showAreYouSureAlert(process: () -> Unit) {
    alert(title = "Are you sure?",
          message = "Are you really sure?") {
        positiveButton("Yes") { process() }
        negativeButton("No") { cancel() }
    }
}
```

Can you spot the three lambdas in this code? The first is the third argument of the `alert` function. The other two are passed as arguments to `positiveButton` and `negativeButton`. The receiver of the first (outer) lambda has the type `Alert-DialogBuilder`. The same pattern comes up again: the name of the `AlertDialog-Builder` class won't appear in the code directly, but you can access its members to add elements to the alert dialog. The declarations of the members used in listing 11.27 are as follows.

Listing 11.28   Declarations of the `alert` API

```
fun Context.alert(
        message: String,
        title: String,
        init: AlertDialogBuilder.() -> Unit
)

class AlertDialogBuilder {
    fun positiveButton(text: String, callback: DialogInterface.() -> Unit)
    fun negativeButton(text: String, callback: DialogInterface.() -> Unit)
    // ...
}
```

You add two buttons to the alert dialog. If the user clicks the Yes button, the `process` action will be called. If the user isn't sure, the operation will be canceled. The `cancel` method is a member of the `DialogInterface` interface, so it's called on an implicit receiver of this lambda.

Now let's look at a more complex example where the Anko DSL acts as a complete replacement for a layout definition in XML. The next listing declares a simple form with two editable fields: one for entering an email address and another for putting in a password. At the end, you add a button with a click handler.

Listing 11.29   Using Anko to define a simple activity

```
                            Declares an EditText view element,
                              and stores a reference to it
verticalLayout {
    val email = editText {                      ◄           An implicit receiver in this lambda
        hint = "Email"                      ◄               is a regular class from Android
    }                                                        API: android.widget.EditText.
    val password = editText {       A short way to call
        hint = "Password"       ◄   EditText.setHint("Password")
        transformationMethod =                  ◄       Calls
            PasswordTransformationMethod.getInstance()      EditText.setTransformationMethod(...)
    }
    button("Log In") {
        onClick {                               ◄
            logIn(email.text, password.text)    ◄       ...and defines what
        }                                                should be done when
    }                           References declared UI      the button is clicked.
}                               elements to access their data
```

Declares a new button...

Lambdas with receivers are a great tool, providing a concise way to declare structured UI elements. Declaring them in code (compared to XML files) lets you extract repetitive logic and reuse it, as you saw in section 11.2.3. You can separate UI and business logic into different components, but everything will still be Kotlin code.

11.5   Summary

- Internal DSLs are an API design pattern you can use to build more expressive APIs with structures composed of multiple method calls.
- Lambdas with receivers employ a nesting structure to redefine how methods are resolved in the lambda body.
- The type of a parameter taking a lambda with a receiver is an extension function type, and the calling function provides a receiver instance when invoking the lambda.
- The benefit of using Kotlin internal DSLs rather than external template or markup languages is the ability to reuse code and create abstractions.
- Using specially named objects as parameters of infix calls allows you to create DSLs that read exactly like English, with no extra punctuation.
- Defining extensions on primitive types lets you create a readable syntax for various kinds of literals, such as dates.
- Using the `invoke` convention, you can call arbitrary objects as if they were functions.

- The kotlinx.html library provides an internal DSL for building HTML pages, which can be easily extended to support various front-end development frameworks.
- The kotlintest library provides an internal DSL that supports readable assertions in unit tests.
- The Exposed library provides an internal DSL for working with databases.
- The Anko library provides various tools for Android development, including an internal DSL for defining UI layouts.

appendix A
Building Kotlin projects

This appendix explains how to build Kotlin code with Gradle, Maven, and Ant. It also covers how to build Kotlin Android applications.

A.1 *Building Kotlin code with Gradle*

The recommended system for building Kotlin projects is Gradle. Gradle is the standard build system for Android projects, and it also supports all other kinds of projects where Kotlin can be used. Gradle has a flexible project model and delivers great build performance thanks to its support for incremental builds, long-lived build processes (the Gradle daemon), and other advanced techniques.

The Gradle team is working on the support for writing Gradle build scripts in Kotlin, which will allow you to use the same language for writing your application and its build scripts. As of this writing, this work is still in progress; you can find more information about it at https://github.com/gradle/gradle-script-kotlin. In this book, we use Groovy syntax for Gradle build scripts.

The standard Gradle build script for building a Kotlin project looks like this:

```
buildscript {
    ext.kotlin_version = '1.0.6'          Specifies the version
                                          of Kotlin to use
    repositories {
        mavenCentral()
    }                                            Adds a build-script dependency
    dependencies {                               on the Kotlin Gradle plugin
        classpath "org.jetbrains.kotlin:" +
                "kotlin-gradle-plugin:$kotlin_version"
    }
}

apply plugin: 'java'          Applies the Kotlin
apply plugin: 'kotlin'        Gradle plugin

repositories {
```

```
      mavenCentral()
}
dependencies {
    compile "org.jetbrains.kotlin:kotlin-stdlib:$kotlin_version"
}
```

> **Adds the dependency on the Kotlin standard library**

The script looks for Kotlin source files in the following locations:

- src/main/java and src/main/kotlin for the production source files
- src/test/java and src/test/kotlin for the test source files

In most cases, the recommended approach is to store both Kotlin and Java source files in the same directory. Especially when you're introducing Kotlin into an existing project, using a single source directory reduces friction when converting Java files to Kotlin.

If you're using Kotlin reflection, you need to add one more dependency: the Kotlin reflection library. To do so, add the following in the dependencies section of your Gradle build script:

```
compile "org.jetbrains.kotlin:kotlin-reflect:$kotlin_version"
```

A.1.1   *Building Kotlin Android applications with Gradle*

Android applications use a different build process compared to regular Java applications, so you need to use a different Gradle plugin to build them. Instead of apply plugin: 'kotlin', add the following line to your build script:

```
apply plugin: 'kotlin-android'
```

The rest of the setup is the same as for non-Android applications.

If you prefer to store your Kotlin source code in Kotlin-specific directories such as src/main/kotlin, you need to register them so that Android Studio recognizes them as source roots. You can do this using the following snippet:

```
android {
    ...

    sourceSets {
        main.java.srcDirs += 'src/main/kotlin'
    }
}
```

A.1.2   *Building projects that use annotation processing*

Many Java frameworks, especially those used in Android development, rely on annotation processing to generate code at compile time. To use those frameworks with Kotlin, you need to enable Kotlin annotation processing in your build script. You can do this by adding the following line:

```
apply plugin: 'kotlin-kapt'
```

If you have an existing Java project that uses annotation processing and you're introducing Kotlin to it, you need to remove the existing configuration of the apt tool. The

Kotlin annotation processing tool handles both Java and Kotlin classes, and having two separate annotation processing tools would be redundant. To configure dependencies required for annotation processing, use the `kapt` dependency configuration:

```
dependencies {
    compile 'com.google.dagger:dagger:2.4'
    kapt 'com.google.dagger:dagger-compiler:2.4'
}
```

If you use annotation processors for your `androidTest` or `test` source, the respective `kapt` configurations are named `kaptAndroidTest` and `kaptTest`.

A.2 Building Kotlin projects with Maven

If you prefer to build your projects with Maven, Kotlin supports that as well. The easiest way to create a Kotlin Maven project is to use the `org.jetbrains.kotlin:kotlin-archetype-jvm` archetype. For existing Maven projects, you can easily add Kotlin support by choosing Tools > Kotlin > Configure Kotlin in Project in the Kotlin IntelliJ IDEA plugin.

To add Maven support to a Kotlin project manually, you need to perform the following steps:

1 Add dependency on the Kotlin standard library (group ID `org.jetbrains.kotlin`, artifact ID `kotlin-stdlib`).
2 Add the Kotlin Maven plugin (group ID `org.jetbrains.kotlin`, artifact ID `kotlin-maven-plugin`), and configure its execution in the `compile` and `test-compile` phases.
3 Configure source directories, if you prefer to keep your Kotlin code in a source root separate from Java source code.

For reasons of space, we're not showing full pom.xml examples here, but you can find them in the online documentation at https://kotlinlang.org/docs/reference/using-maven.html.

In a mixed Java/Kotlin project, you need to configure the Kotlin plugin so that it runs before the Java plugin. This is necessary because the Kotlin plugin can parse Java sources, whereas the Java plugin can only read .class files; so, the Kotlin files need to be compiled to .class before the Java plugin runs. You can find an example showing how this can be configured at http://mng.bz/73od.

A.3 Building Kotlin code with Ant

To build projects with Ant, Kotlin provides two different tasks: the `<kotlinc>` task compiles pure Kotlin modules, whereas `<withKotlin>` is an extension to the `<javac>` task for building mixed Kotlin/Java modules. Here's a minimal example of using `<kotlinc>`:

```
<project name="Ant Task Test" default="build">
    <typedef resource="org/jetbrains/kotlin/ant/antlib.xml"
            classpath="${kotlin.lib}/kotlin-ant.jar"/>
```
Defines the `<kotlinc>` task

```
        <target name="build">
            <kotlinc output="hello.jar">        ◁─┐  Builds a single source directory
                <src path="src"/>                    │  with <kotlinc>, and packs the
            </kotlinc>                               │  result into a jar file
        </target>
</project>
```

The `<kotlinc>` Ant task adds the standard library dependency automatically, so you don't need to add any extra arguments to configure it. It also supports packaging the compiled .class files into a jar file.

Here's an example of using a `<withKotlin>` task to build a mixed Java/Kotlin module:

```
<project name="Ant Task Test" default="build">
    <typedef resource="org/jetbrains/kotlin/ant/antlib.xml"
             classpath="${kotlin.lib}/kotlin-ant.jar"/>    ◁─┐  Defines the
                                                               │  <withKotlin> task
    <target name="build">
        <javac destdir="classes" srcdir="src">
            <withKotlin/>                        ◁─┐  Uses the <withKotlin>
        </javac>                                    │  task to enable mixed
        <jar destfile="hello.jar">                  │  Kotlin/Java compilation
            <fileset dir="classes"/>
        </jar>
    </target>
</project>
```

Packages the compiled classes into a jar file ┌─▷

Unlike the `<kotlinc>` task, `<withKotlin>` doesn't support automatic packaging of compiled classes, so this example uses a separate `<jar>` task to package them.

appendix B
Documenting Kotlin code

This appendix covers writing documentation comments for Kotlin code and generating API documentation for Kotlin modules.

B.1 Writing Kotlin documentation comments

The format used to write documentation comments for Kotlin declarations is similar to Java's Javadoc and is called KDoc. Just as in Javadoc, KDoc comments begin with /** and use tags starting with @ to document specific parts of a declaration. The key difference between Javadoc and KDoc is that the format used to write the comments themselves is Markdown (https://daringfireball.net/projects/markdown) rather than HTML. To make writing documentation comments easier, KDoc supports a number of additional conventions to refer to documentation elements such as function parameters.

Here's a simple example of a KDoc comment for a function.

Listing B.1 Using a KDoc comment

```
/**
 * Calculates the sum of two numbers, [a] and [b]
 */
fun sum(a: Int, b: Int) = a + b
```

To refer to declarations from a KDoc comment, you enclose their names in brackets. The example uses that syntax to refer to the parameters of the function being documented, but you can also use it to refer to other declarations. If the declaration you need to refer to is imported in the code containing the KDoc comment, you can use its name directly. Otherwise, you can use a fully qualified name. If you need to specify a custom label for a link, you use two pairs of brackets and put the label in the first pair and the declaration name in the second: [an example] [com.mycompany.SomethingTest.simple].

Here's a somewhat more complicated example, showing the use of tags in a comment.

Listing B.2 Using tags in a comment

```
/**
 * Performs a complicated operation.
 *
 * @param remote If true, executes operation remotely          ◄── Documents a parameter
 * @return The result of executing the operation
 * @throws IOException if remote connnection fails              ◄── Documents
 * @sample com.mycompany.SomethingTest.simple                        a possible exception
 */
fun somethingComplicated(remote: Boolean): ComplicatedResult { ... }
```

Documents the return value → (points to @return line)

Includes the text of the specified function as a sample in documentation text

The general syntax of using the tags is exactly the same as in Javadoc. In addition to the standard Javadoc tags, KDoc supports a number of additional tags for concepts that don't exist in Java, such as the `@receiver` tag for documenting the receiver of an extension function or property. You can find the full list of supported tags at http://kotlinlang.org/docs/reference/kotlin-doc.html.

The `@sample` tag can be used to include the text of the specified function into the documentation text, as an example of using the API being documented. The value of the tag is the fully qualified name of the method to be included.

Some Javadoc tags aren't supported in KDoc:

- `@deprecated` is replaced with the `@Deprecated` annotation.
- `@inheritdoc` isn't supported because in Kotlin, documentation comments are always automatically inherited by overriding declarations.
- `@code`, `@literal`, and `@link` are replaced with the corresponding Markdown formatting.

Note that the documentation style preferred by the Kotlin team is to document the parameters and the return value of a function directly in the text of a documentation comment, as shown in listing B.1. Using tags, as in listing B.2, is recommended only when a parameter or return value has complex semantics and needs to be clearly separated from the main documentation text.

B.2 *Generating API documentation*

The documentation-generation tool for Kotlin is called Dokka: https://github.com/kotlin/dokka. Just like Kotlin, Dokka fully supports cross-language Java/Kotlin projects. It can read Javadoc comments in Java code and KDoc comments in Kotlin code and generate documentation covering the entire API of a module, regardless of the language used to write each class in it. Dokka supports multiple output formats, including plain HTML, Javadoc-style HTML (using the Java syntax for all declarations and showing how the APIs can be accessed from Java), and Markdown.

You can run Dokka from the command line or as part of your Ant, Maven, or Gradle build script. The recommended way to run Dokka is to add it to the Gradle build script for your module. Here's the minimum required configuration of Dokka in a Gradle build script:

```
buildscript {
    ext.dokka_version = '0.9.13'                             Specifies the version
                                                             of Dokka to use
    repositories {
        jcenter()
    }
    dependencies {
        classpath "org.jetbrains.dokka:dokka-gradle-plugin:${dokka_version}"
    }
}


apply plugin: 'org.jetbrains.dokka'
```

With this configuration, you can run `./gradlew dokka` to generate documentation for your module in HTML format.

You can find information on specifying additional generation options in the Dokka documentation (https://github.com/Kotlin/dokka/blob/master/README.md). The documentation also shows how Dokka can be run as a standalone tool or integrated into Maven and Ant build scripts.

appendix C
The Kotlin ecosystem

Despite Kotlin's relatively young age, it already has a broad ecosystem of libraries, frameworks, and tools, most of which have been created by the external development community. In this appendix, we'll give you pointers to help you explore this ecosystem. Of course, a book isn't the perfect medium to describe a fast-growing collection of tools, so the first thing we'll do is point you to an online resource where you can find more up-to-date information: https://kotlin.link/

And to remind you again, Kotlin is fully compatible with the entire Java library ecosystem. When looking for the right library for your problem, you shouldn't need to restrict your search to libraries written in Kotlin—standard Java libraries work just as well. Now let's look at some libraries that are worth exploring. Some of the Java libraries offer Kotlin-specific extensions with more clean and idiomatic APIs, and you should strive to use such extensions whenever they are available.

C.1   Testing

In addition to the standard JUnit and TestNG, which work well with Kotlin, the following frameworks offer a more expressive DSL for writing tests in Kotlin:

- *KotlinTest* (https://github.com/kotlintest/kotlintest)—A flexible ScalaTest-inspired test framework, mentioned in chapter 11, that supports a number of different layouts for writing tests
- *Spek* (https://github.com/jetbrains/spek)—A BDD-style test framework for Kotlin, originally started by JetBrains and now maintained by the community

If you're fine with JUnit and are only interested in a more expressive DSL for assertions, check out *Hamkrest* (https://github.com/npryce/hamkrest). If you're using mocking in your tests, you should definitely look at *Mockito-Kotlin* (https://github.com/nhaarman/mockito-kotlin), which solves some of the issues of mocking Kotlin classes and provides a nicer DSL for mocking.

C.2   *Dependency injection*

Common Java dependency injection frameworks, such as Spring, Guice and Dagger, work well with Kotlin. If you're interested in a Kotlin-native solution, check out *Kodein* (https://github.com/SalomonBrys/Kodein), which provides a nice Kotlin DSL for configuring the dependencies and has a very efficient implementation.

C.3   *JSON serialization*

If you need a heavier-duty solution for JSON serialization than the JKid library described in chapter 10, you have a lot to choose from. If you prefer to use Jackson, *jackson-module-kotlin* (https://github.com/FasterXML/jackson-module-kotlin) provides deep Kotlin integration, including support for data classes. For GSON, *Kotson* (https://github.com/SalomonBrys/Kotson) provides a nice set of wrappers. And if you're after a lightweight, pure Kotlin solution, check out *Klaxon* (https://github.com/cbeust/klaxon).

C.4   *HTTP clients*

If you need to build a client for a REST API in Kotlin, look no further than Retrofit (http://square.github.io/retrofit). It's a Java library, also compatible with Android, and it works smoothly with Kotlin. For a lower-level solution, check out OkHttp (http://square.github.io/okhttp/), or Fuel, a pure Kotlin HTTP library (https://github.com/kittinunf/Fuel).

C.5   *Web applications*

If you're developing a server-side web application, the most mature options available today are Java frameworks such as Spring, Spark Java, and vert.x. Spring 5.0 will include Kotlin support and extensions out of the box. For using Kotlin with earlier versions of Spring, you can find additional information and helper functions in the Spring Kotlin project (https://github.com/sdeleuze/spring-kotlin). vert.x provides official support for Kotlin as well: https://github.com/vert-x3/vertx-lang-kotlin/

For pure Kotlin solutions, you can consider the following options:

- *Ktor* (https://github.com/Kotlin/ktor)—A JetBrains research project exploring how to build a modern, full-featured web application framework with an idiomatic API
- *Kara* (https://github.com/TinyMission/kara)—The original Kotlin web framework, used in production by JetBrains and other companies
- *Wasabi* (https://github.com/wasabifx/wasabi)—An HTTP framework built on top of Netty, with an expressive Kotlin API
- *Kovert* (https://github.com/kohesive/kovert)—A REST framework built on top of vert.x

For your HTML-generation needs, check out kotlinx.html (https://github.com/kotlin/kotlinx.html), which we discuss in chapter 11. Or, if you prefer a more traditional approach, use a Java template engine such as Thymeleaf (www.thymeleaf.org).

C.6   Database access

In addition to traditional Java options such as Hibernate, you have a number of Kotlin-specific choices for your database-access needs. We have the most experience with *Exposed* (https://github.com/jetbrains/Exposed), a SQL-generation framework discussed a few times in the book. A number of alternatives are listed at https://kotlin.link.

C.7   Utilities and data structures

One of the most popular new programming paradigms these days is *reactive programming*, and Kotlin is really well-suited for it. RxJava (https://github.com/ReactiveX/RxJava), the de-facto standard reactive programming library for the JVM, offers official Kotlin bindings at https://github.com/ReactiveX/RxKotlin.

The following libraries provide utilities and data structures that you may find useful in your projects:

- *funKTionale* (https://github.com/MarioAriasC/funKTionale)—Implements a broad range of functional programming primitives (such as partial function application)
- *Kovenant* (https://github.com/mplatvoet/kovenant)—An implementation of promises for Kotlin and Android

C.8   Desktop programming

If you're building desktop applications on the JVM these days, you're most likely using JavaFX. TornadoFX (https://github.com/edvin/tornadofx) provides a powerful set of Kotlin adapters for JavaFX, making it natural to use Kotlin for desktop development.

index